The Heart of War

On power, conflict and obligation in the twenty-first century

Gwyn Prins

London and New York

100333300

First published 2002
by Routledge
11 New Fetter Lane, London EC4P 4EE

Simultaneously published in the USA and Canada
by Routledge
29 West 35th Street, New York, NY 10001

Routledge is an imprint of the Taylor & Francis Group

Typeset in Times by Wearset Ltd, Boldon, Tyne and Wear
Printed and bound in Great Britain by TJ International Ltd,
Padstow, Cornwall

British Library Cataloguing in Publication Data
A catalogue record for this book is available from the British Library

Library of Congress Cataloging in Publication Data
A catalog record for this book has been requested

ISBN 0–415–36960–6 (hbk)
ISBN 0–415–36961–4 (pbk)

For Elizabeth and Susannah
and in memory of Gerard Evans

Know your enemy
Know yourself
And you will be safe
In a thousand battles

Sun Tzu

Contents

PART III
The nuclear issue in the new era **235**

Illustrations

Figures

Maps

Foreword

General Sir Mike Jackson
Commander-in-Chief
Land Command

It is salutary to remind ourselves that although the Cold War now seems a fading, even distant, memory, it is only a little over twelve years since the fall of the Berlin Wall. Events since then have vividly and convincingly demonstrated the changing context and utility of military power: from the putative titanic but almost unthinkable clash of a nuclear World War III; through the realities of the Gulf War of 1990/91, the Bosnian quagmire, the Kosovo conflict, various successful and unsuccessful peace support and intervention operations in Africa and Asia; to the enormity and tragedy of 11 September 2001, and the still developing consequences of that fateful day.

In these twelve turbulent years, the old stasis has disappeared. Previous certainties such as the inviolability of the sovereign state are challenged; new uncertainties surrounding the legality of intervention, and the priority to be accorded to human rights have emerged. Regional conflicts – both inter-state and intra-state – have burgeoned. The very meaning of the word 'war' is changing, it is less clear.

The military has an essential part to play in bringing order out of chaos; how best this can be done is the subject of much thought in military staff colleges and think-tanks. But conflict resolution is by no means the preserve of soldiers: the military is but a single dimension, and not necessarily the dominant one. There has to be a coordinated approach in all dimensions – political, diplomatic, legal, economic, humanitarian, reconstruction, as well as military.

I was fortunate enough to have Gwyn Prins as my mentor when I was a Defence Fellow at Cambridge in the last year of the Cold War. In this book he develops his themes of power, conflict and human rights, and projects them into the future; he also does not avoid uncomfortable thinking about nuclear weapons. His many and varied considerations are drawn together in a conclusion which provides guidance for the navigator of these somewhat unknown and turbulent future waters.

Preface

This book considers many past evils, out of whose long shadows it is our duty to ensure that something of good shall come. It seeks to engage a well-grounded, well-rounded understanding of contemporary global politics with practical thinking about how military power is, should be and can be used. The answers given in these chapters are all to questions that have been put to me in the course of my work since 1996, when I ceased to be a conventional university academic. I adopted instead what I have since discovered that the management studies expert, Charles Handy, has described as the coming future pattern of professional work: I became a 'portfolio' man.

In that year, I was approached separately by two individuals from two organisations who thereby changed the whole direction of my career. In 1995 I had been asked by the United Nations Association of the USA to conduct a study examining the potentials of the NATO model of politico-military operation for prospective future UN peace support operations. To that end, I enlisted the help of an old friend, Christopher Donnelly, the Special Advisor on Central and Eastern European Affairs to the Secretary-General of NATO, to arrange interviews for me. Chris was originally appointed as Sovietologist in Residence by the late Manfred Wörner, but his remit expanded and changed after the velvet revolutions: he is known and widely admired in professional circles as one of the unobtrusive heroes of the transformations in east–west relations. During that visit, we walked together through the joint Anglo-German First World War cemetery of St Symphorien, near Mons, which figures in the story of Chapter 3 below. Christopher invited me to join him as Senior Fellow in his Office to complement his expertise and thereby to broaden the scope of the views and advice which could be offered as the Alliance embarked upon the testing pathway of enlargement.

At about the same time, I was approached by Andrew Sleigh, Director of the Centre for Defence Analysis within what was then the newly-created Defence Evaluation and Research Agency of the UK Ministry of Defence. With the support of the Chief Executive, John Chisholm, Andrew was initiating a project, which sought to understand why it was that the existing methods of strategic analysis, inherited from the era of the Cold War, were evidently mismatched to the characteristics of the ensuing period. Such matters are of high practical importance not only because governments require indicators and warning of possible threats ahead, but also because the very long cycles of military R&D and systems procurement mean that there is a high premium upon defensible strategic assessment of trends and dynamics.

In his initial telephone call introducing himself, he intrigued me by his frank assertion that he and his colleagues within the Ministry of Defence analysis community did not know the answers to their questions, but did at least know that they did not know. From that contact has grown both the UK MoD's Strategic Assessment Method, which is now, in my opinion, the best structured and best tested methodology for strategic assessment in the new era available within North Atlantic Government circles and my own recruitment as the first Visiting Senior Fellow to the DERA.

Since my appointment to this privileged and absorbing role (latterly attached to the Defence Science and Technology Laboratory), I have, for the first time in my career, been exposed to the rigours of conducting research closely coupled to real decision-making cycles. My task has also been to help senior colleagues assess which areas and themes should best be pursued. In that capacity, I wrote a series of analyses of European and Euro-American affairs, developing the concept of the Diplomatic–Military Operation which is employed in the following pages, but is more fully displayed elsewhere. These studies have been collected and will shortly be published in a companion volume to this one.

I had the further good fortune to be asked to chair the 1999–2000 working group on asymmetric warfare and terrorism under a DERA contract to the Royal Institute of International Affairs. That experience has greatly informed my views on the nature of terrorism, given in Chapter 3. Third, as a consequence of my exposure to the range of problems and the types of work then being undertaken in the UK military Operational Analysis world, from participation in the Chief of the General Staff's Study Period for all the Brigadiers in the British Army, and with on-going advice and guidance from a clutch of Generals (notably Duncan, Irwin, Piggott and Richards) I was able to promote and to join in new directions of research.

In association with both scientific and military colleagues, principally Mrs Lorraine Dodd, Professor Jim Moffat and the Deputy Supreme Allied Commander, General Sir Rupert Smith, I have delineated and with them, begun to undertake fundamental research on a topic described in the pages which follow in Chapter 7, namely the nature of command in the new era. Throughout, I have enjoyed and profited from the support and wise counsel of two acute and distinguished military analysts, the Chief Analyst of dstl, Dr Roger Forder, and Peter Starkey, formerly of the Directorate of Scrutiny and Analysis in the Ministry and now Director of dstl Analysis.

The third element of my career portfolio was provided at first by the last couple of years of the two-decades-plus I spent at the University of Cambridge. I was enthusiastically encouraged to explore this new way of working by the then Vice-Chancellor, Professor Sir David Williams, by the Provost of King's, Patrick Bateson and by several close colleagues, in particular Dr Gerard Evans, Professor Sir Martin Rees and my former Heads of Department, Professor Anthony Giddens and Dr John Barber. But when, in 1997, another colleague of long-standing took over the Royal Institute of International Affairs and invited me to come to help him renovate and reorient Chatham House, the fit with the rising tempo and excitement of my work with Chris Donnelly and Andrew Sleigh was not to be resisted. Therefore, I also express my gratitude to Air Marshal Sir Timothy Garden and to the then Director of Studies at Chatham House, Dr George Joffé, for their imagination, comradeship and support. My move to Chatham House also became the impetus for that of another valued colleague, William Hopkinson. Bill had earlier spent a sabbatical with me as a Visiting Fellow in Cambridge, and now left the Ministry of Defence to join us, to our profit.

Latterly, I have migrated back into the university world, but in a professorial incarnation and to the special environment at the London School of Economics. In recent years, as is widely known, the LSE has become one of the most intellectually stimulating environments within which to explore the deeper dynamics of our age. The School has re-energised its original mission, to make ideas active in the world, which is strongly harmonious with the portfolio approach to work that I have found to be so conducive. I am indebted to many colleagues there. To Drs Howard Machin and

Alain Guyomarch for welcoming me into the European Institute; for creative discussions, to Professor Lord Wallace, first, and then to Professor John Gray as, successively, co-Chairmen with me of the London Seminar on Global Security, which we conducted in 1999 and 2000 (and to the MacArthur Foundation for funding it). John has also kindly read and criticised, to my benefit, work that I have thrust at him, and I value greatly our continuing discussions on the nature of political dynamics.

At the School I would also like to acknowledge particular debts to Anthony Giddens – again – this time in a new capacity as Director, where, in his genially polymathic way, he has sprinkled the magic dust of intellectual excitement as he did before, in Cambridge; to Professor David Held for continuing insight on issues of globalisation and to Professor Lord Desai and Professor Mary Kaldor for including me in their invaluable global perspectives seminar; to Professor Fred Halliday for his staunch encouragement of all my efforts over many years and to Gus Stewart of the Research & Development Division. Gus is one of the most creative university administrators with whom I have ever had the privilege to work and his efforts are instrumental in helping the School to respond as strongly, as flexibly and as successfully as it does to changing opportunities and agenda, most recently the Alliance Professorships jointly with Columbia. At the LSE, we owe a special debt to Professors John Dunn and Geoffrey Hawthorn for their single-minded and untiring work over more than a decade to ensure that the School could become the rewarding and sympathetic place that it now is.

I have developed my thinking on the subjects covered in the following pages in response to questions put principally in the non-university compartments of my professional life. But I have benefited from conversations with friends in all spheres. Some have been good enough to continue in fruitful and prolonged exchange, several over many years. I have debts in this respect to Professor Philip Allott, Dr Stephen Ashford, Vice-Admiral Sir Jeremy Blackham, Geoffrey Beare, Dr Jeffrey Boutwell, Victoria Elenowitz, Colonel Paul Fox, Professor Conor Gearty, Brigadier Christopher Holtom, Professor Bob Legvold, Professor Andy Mack, Johanna Moehring, Baroness Onora O'Neill, Professor John Polanyi, Michael Purvis, Professor Nicholas Rengger, Larry Smith, Professor Lionel Tiger, Patrick Wright and, in respect of the central subjects of this book, more than any other to General Sir Rupert Smith and, through him, to several of his staff at SHAPE, notably Colonel Gilbert Baldwin.

Professor Hylke Tromp has been one of my most valued friends and interlocutors. Almost as fiercely as my wife, he has driven me on in the writing, especially after, together, we edited the book arising from the Bloch Centenary Conference in St Petersburg. One period in our long collaboration stands out. During the later 1990s we sought to reanimate the Inter-University Centre in Dubrovnik – he as Director-General, I as Deputy Director General jointly with Professor Ivo Slaus of the Croatian Academy of Sciences. In the end we failed, defeated by rising Croatian nationalism. But the electricity of the courses on political violence which we ran, and the pupils that we taught there, in the sun, on the beach, with the help of other like-minded friends (Willem van Eekelen, Koen Koch, Luc Reychler, Jim Rosenau, Ivo Slaus, Bart Tromp, Nena Tromp-Vrkic, Immanuel Wallerstein, Haakon Wiberg, Jaap de Wilde) is one of the highlights of my learning experiences. It continues still in our joint efforts, now translocated to the University of St Petersburg.

In addition to individuals, I have incurred debts to several institutions, which by asking me to lecture on subjects or to discuss issues with them, have forced the crystallisation of my thinking. Among these are the CIA, which has included me in several immensely stimulating and informative exercises since 1996 as part of the work to develop the Strategic Assessment Method. A closed seminar at the Wye Plantation to consider the future of Euro-American relations, undertaken early in the new Bush Presidency, was especially fruitful for me. My association with the Maxwell School of Citizenship at the University of Syracuse began when Professor Sean O'Keefe invited me to assist with the framing of the new National Security Studies programme, which he directed; and my annual visits to that course have always served as an excellent intellectual stimulant. So, too, has been my even more regular involvement with the NATO Defense College in Rome, where the opportunity to meet a unique cross-section of senior military and diplomatic staff provides a splendid context in which to try out and refine ideas. The Director of the British Army Intelligence Corps, Brigadier Chris Holtom, has provided me with several invaluable fora within which, and people with whom, to explore ideas. He has been a strong supporter of the strategic assessment work, and the chance to participate in and to lecture at the Risk of Conflict study days which he introduced at the Defence Intelligence and Security Centre at Chicksands has been a great boon.

I have a special debt to Dr Jeffrey Boutwell, the Executive Director of the Pugwash Conferences on Science and World Affairs and to the current Secretary-General, George Rathjens. Since their inception, I have been a member of the Pugwash Working Group on Intervention and State Sovereignty and also that on the fundamental reconsideration of nuclear weapons. Chapter 5 owes much to what I have learned through my participation in the work of the former, as also to my engagement with the International Commission on Intervention and State Sovereignty. Dr Roger Williamson of Wilton Park – the Foreign Office conference centre – prodded me into a particularly helpful crystallisation of my thinking about intervention, for which I am grateful. On this topic, like all other people interested in it, I have a debt of gratitude to Dr Nicholas Wheeler. Chapter 8 was first written at George Rathjen's request to help launch the new Pugwash work on nuclear weapons in New Delhi in March 2001. The chance to work with Professor John Kenneth Galbraith and with the late McGeorge Bundy in the 1980s much influenced my thinking on these matters, as will be evident in that chapter.

My thinking about international institutions owes much to my association with the UN Association of the USA and in particular its brilliant and indispensable Director of Research, Dr Jeffrey Laurenti. The opportunity to work on the Carrington Report with Lord Carrington, Edward Luck and the Commissioners was a particular privilege and stimulus. Drs Ken Graham and Chris Williams gave generously of their time and advice at an early point in this work. Craig Fowlie, my editor at Routledge, was a briskly constructive critic. I owe him the title. In all these debts, the usual disclaimers apply.

Finally, because one keeps the deepest debts to last, I owe much thanks and gratitude to my former Research Assistant, Elizabeth Sellwood, now of the House of Commons Foreign Affairs Select Committee staff, who worked with me on aspects of most of these essays, and to my extraordinary and complementary personal assistants, Dee Noyes and Alison Suter. It is no exaggeration at all to say that without the constant support and help of Alison, Dee and Lizzie this book would not have been finished. Alison has carried the brunt of the task of typing and correcting my messy drafts, and of supporting me at the same time with helpful criticism and, on occasion, with research support as well.

My greatest debt of all, as ever during our long and eventful time together, is to my wife, Miriam. It was she who first put her foot down and told me that if I did not pull this book together in short order she would want to know the reason why! Without such tough love few of us would write, or maybe even survive. I know that I wouldn't. The book is dedicated to our daughters and, at the last minute, also and sadly, to the memory of my dear friend, fomer colleague and undergraduate tutor, Gerard Evans, who saw this book in manuscript, but not in print.

Great Eversden,
March 2002

Introduction

Hostis humani generis – an enemy of all mankind – is a concept that deserves the weight within the sonorous resonance of its Latin form, especially now, when its moment returns to be a leading actor on the political stage. It was prominent in the late eighteenth-century elaboration of the laws of nations. Emmer de Vattel explained that 'those who by the nature and habitual frequency of their crimes violate all public security ... may be eliminated wherever they are seized; for they attack and injure all nations by trampling under foot the very underpinning of their common security.'[1]

After lunch on 11 September 2001, when the bulk of this book was complete, I was writing a section of Chapter 5. It is the part which discusses the way in which two land-mark cases in two different jurisdictions – the Pinochet extradition in Britain and the Filartiga case in the USA – both made the same point, namely that torturers now joined pirates and slavers within the notorious category of *hostis humani generis*. This being accepted, the Lord Chief Justice had observed in the Pinochet case that in his opinion, the enlargement of the definition became *jus cogens* – an obligatory principle; so the case was justiciable and within it, the former Chilean dictator's extradition, valid.

Then the telephone rang in the little summer-house where I write. Ryan, the son of my assistant, Dee Noyes, had ear-ache that morning; so she had brought him back from school early and he was now watching the television. She had just come in from the kitchen to find him watching a news flash about a frightful plane crash in New York. I walked into my house and turned on the television just in time to witness live the death of the second plane flying into the second of the World Trade Center towers. The suicide pilot was to be seen carefully adjusting the angle and height of entry in the final seconds before the collision in order to hit the tower at exactly the right point to turn the floors above into a ram that would drive the building down (as I later learned from a consultant structural engineer who specialises in skyscrapers). Osama bin Laden told us in his video-taped reflections on the events that full collapse was more than he and his colleagues had anticipated.

'Know your enemy and know yourself; then you will be safe in a thousand battles' wrote the Chinese strategist Sun Tzu a millennium before in *The Art of War*. It is the guiding dictum of this book, and was never more vitally important to recall and follow than after 11 September 2001. During the next days, television screens were filled with babbling, loose, often wild, talk and little hard information. The constant in the coverage, however, was the mesmerising, traumatising repetition of the clip showing the moment of impact. Called to help colleagues at Independent Television News develop an active editorial engagement with the events and implications of that terrible and unexpected day, I spent the rest of that first week sitting in their newsroom. On the monitors, which gave a window on the American networks, one could see the image of the crash, hypnotically repeating, burning into the American consciousness as unwittingly, the TV stations assisted the perpetrators in one of their key objectives. For surely, as one sought to follow Sun Tzu's advice, it was not hard to deduce that the shattering of western cultural self-confidence by the shattering of the twin towers with a domestic airliner, turned by adamantine cruelty of imagination bound to inflexible will into a guided missile with 16,000 gallons of jet-fuel, was a prominent part of Osama bin Laden's intention? It was a deduction which he later confirmed.

We must also know ourselves as well as the perpetrators appear to have done. The stimulation of formless fears about any and all aspects of the complex, benign systems of daily life – airline travel, working in a skyscraper – was skilfully built into the theatrical design of this perfect terrorist act. Evidence of a suicide spike in the weeks following, and of large increases in prescription of Prozac, confirmed that 11 September did penetrate and ravage the moral community of many. A wave of clinical depression washed across America. A woman who, by merest luck, escaped with her life described how, nevertheless, she felt violated by the attack. One can see why the analogy to rape is called to mind. Architypically in New York, where there are more computers than in many a poor country, the individual can be fantastically wired, yet utterly deprived of multifaceted, complicated human relationships which form the moral community of the peasant. This special aspect of globalisation has engineered the circumstances which permit radical and self-conscious manipulation of identity (who shall I be today?) without constraint of time or space, as Anthony Giddens was one of the first to see and to explain.[2] An aspect of that is the enlargement of the reference frame of objects and groups for the individual.

So all the similar strangers in the towers are felt as kin. The towers are everyone's front room. A New York psychiatrist has calculated that in the region of 30,000 people experienced narrow escapes from death that day, to which must be added the mental sufferings of the families and co-workers of the nearly 3,000 victims. The studied, sadistic act of informing the hijacked passengers of their imminent deaths, instructing them to telephone their loved ones to say good-bye, further compounded the psychological trauma for the families and, by broadcast of this news and some of the messages, for the wider public which consumed such information with fascinated horror. It was without doubt the most devastating propaganda of the deed in modern times.[3]

In face of the enormity and novelty of 11 September 2001, it is hardly surprising that a common reflex reaction has been to ascribe to it as comprehensive and fundamental a status as a pivot point in history as the shockingness of the act itself seemed to deserve: a great action with a great consequence. But, as always in history, it is not automatically the case that this correlation holds.

Professor James Rosenau has proposed the essential question with which one should begin to interrogate any action that disorients or the meaning of which is unclear. 'Of what is this an instance?' is the question which starts the mind efficiently along the road of comparative contextualisation. In the case of 11 September 2001, Rosenau's question tells us at once (as will be further discussed in Chapter 3) that the event does not represent a new departure in the history of terrorism, but that the response to it, because of the psychological injury, in particular, that has been inflicted, may, indeed, be new. It is also an instance of that very category of event and social process, which is the primary subject of this book. This is a book about military power in the new era, and the nature and forms of political violence form a necessary part of that exploration.

In this work, I am seeking to touch the heart of war: to provide a necessary scope for understanding military power in contemporary global politics and to do so in terms which are accessible to a wide readership.

Therefore, none of the chapters presupposes deep prior know-ledge, only an interest in understanding the issues. However, it is hoped that among professionally interested constituencies, the work may be particularly of profit to those with military and political responsibilities.

The heart of war in the twenty-first century is formed from three interlocking sinews and its rhythm derives from their interacting tensions.

Power, as it is anatomised in these pages, both includes but exceeds raw physical force. Indeed, a central proposition about the main effort of military power in the modern age is that the leading edge of its effect is more often psychological than brutally or frontally kinetic. This proposition has radical implications for the manner in which military forces are shaped, equipped, trained and commanded in action. These changes (illuminated in the case study of strategic raiding) have the further effect of returning to relevance many aspects of Clausewitz's thinking about war that have been eclipsed during the era of mass industrial (historically new) wars. We have now returned to an era in which the characteristics of deployed military power are familiar to a medieval general, even if the means are modern. Modern wars are actually old wars in their nature.

The disjointed, almost ironic, juxtaposition of old and new characteristics and means of warfare is a product of the slippery phenomenon of 'globalisation'. It is a word that is now so pervasive and so easily invoked that it has largely lost any useful coherence. So, in Chapters 1 and 4 I am obliged to specify my meanings of this term.

In particular, I am impressed by the dialectic engagement of the simultaneous exploding and imploding forces that globalisation generates. On balance, I see a world of human societies where the centrifugal tendencies matter most for security. For the present purposes, the spawning of many fractured and frequently invented identities and histories has populated certain areas (the Balkans, the Caucasus, much of sub-Saharan Africa and parts of Central Asia) with angry and agitated potentials for conflict.

Conflict is the second of the great sinews in the heart of war. The case made here is one which insists upon the indispensability of maintaining historical memory. For the twentieth-century legacy which matters most in this respect is that of loss of constraint. The manner in which the Third Reich and Stalin's purges institutionalised 'democide' – death of citizens at the hands not of enemies but of their own governments – cracked the very matrix of the social contract inherited from the late eighteenth century. There are those who would argue that this fatal defect was always present in the French revolutionary project: Edmund Burke was certainly early in forming that view; so that when its children displayed their terrible claws, none should have been surprised. Whether or not, the fact is that this aspect of the twentieth century gave comfort to those who would sever the strands supporting civil society.

Uncivil war – old war in new guise – is the mark of the age. Wars of identity, frequently fought out among hardened opponents in failed or collapsing states. When there is so little common ground, the possibilities for 'conflict resolution' are small and diminishing.

Where the structural restraints upon civil violence are eroded or collapsed, the individual stands perilously exposed to risk of torture or death. In countervailing opposition to such gross abuse stands the surprising but enormously energetic rise and rise of the defence of human rights in a context of reconfigured state power. This is the third sinew tugging within the heart of modern war. It is the grandest expression of the centrapetal sense of the brotherhood of mankind which is among the most admirable of features in a world where the globalisation of information has made the empowered, television-watching rich acutely aware of the world beyond their safe shores – or shores presumed safe by most until 11 September shattered that sense of security.

Here is found a straightforward correlation. The more that the conditionality of sovereignty has been both seen and accepted, the more the sense of obligation and duty has been strengthened. For when the powerless and suffering have no rights which they may enforce, then their humanity appeals to the altruism (including the frequently selfish altruism) of the rich, powerful and free. A return to eighteenth-century ways of thinking and valuing relationships is helpful here. So Kant offers guidance in the area of obligation as Clausewitz does in that of power.

The structure of the book derives from these three connected concerns. It proceeds as a logical sequence starting with an exploration and definition of the nature of the new era. Part I seeks to engage all the necessary intellectual, technical, historical and cultural contexts to enable us to make useful judgements both about the relationships among them and of their amplitude. Events like those of 11 September 2001 raise in the plainest form the challenge of understanding which forces arise from long and which from short contexts and trends.

The working assumption employed is that of the greatest of modern French historians, Fernand Braudel. Embarking upon his huge two-volume history of the Mediterranean world in the reign of Philip II, he flung into the reader's face his opinion that contemporary historiography asked the essential question back to front.[4] What needed to be understood was not the impact of Philip II upon the Mediterranean world – Great Man causes change – but the effect of the Mediterranean world upon Philip II – a man of and in his time. So his masterpiece begins with an explanation of why mountains are not usually visible in the annals of civilisation because civilisations happen in *civis*'s – cities; and cities are usually found in the valleys and plains. These are also the places of feudal ties, mediated through relationships to rich agricultural land; whereas in the mountains, the shepherds may be poor, but they are free. And so he proceeds for 650 pages, describing first all aspects of the geological timescale, the climate history, the agricultural history. This he calls history of the Long Term (*la longue durée*). Then he turns to the relationship of humans to this natural world, but through a timescale set longer than the day-to-day consciousness of an individual. Scaled to the human lifetime, economic history (*l'histoire de la conjoncture*) has a faster rhythm than *la longue durée,* but still much slower than the rapid oscillations of event history (*l'histoire evénémentielle*).

Only 300 pages into Volume II does Braudel begin to describe and analyse 'events, politics, people'. This part of the work shows that the case for starting first with mountains is not to be equated with a scorn for detail. Quite the contrary, for he shows how a robust interpretation of Philip II's time must pivot around an understanding of the events of one day. This was 7 October 1571, a day famous for the Battle of Lepanto when Turkish supremacy was broken ('the most spectacular military event in the Mediterranean during the entire sixteenth century'.).

Braudel's assertion about Lepanto applies equally to many key events that will be described in the following pages. First, he states bluntly that it cannot be adequately understood in its own terms alone. ('Dazzling triumph of courage and maritime expertise that it was, it is hard to place it persuasively in a conventional historical perspective.') We only see its fuller meaning when we plumb the depths of *la conjoncture* and *la longue durée* ('beneath that sparkling film on the surface of history, we shall find that the ripples from Lepanto spread silently, unobtrusively, widely'.) So, Braudel concludes, 'part of its interest to us, as an historical event, is maybe that it is a glaring case of the very restrictions upon *l'histoire evénémentielle*'.

It is from this point of view that this book approaches the key events in its story: the Cuban Missile Crisis, the Able Archer crisis, the massacre in Srebrenica in summer 1995, the bombing of Pan Am 103 on 21 December 1988, the terrorist attacks of 11 September

2001. We need to be able to make sense of such events in Braudel's sense of the word. The book is planned and written as an invitation to do so.

The book opens by describing the nature of war as it was experienced during the previous century, identifying those characteristics of that experience which appear to shape the manner in which war lives on in our time. Chapter 2 argues the case against the common view that the Cold War, having ended peacefully, was a triumph that left no lasting injuries. Those injuries to bodies and to imaginations are described and analysed in Chapter 3. It employs a simple historians' methodology within which to conduct an examination and calibration of the relative risks in the two major forms of uncivil war in the world today – the gross abuse of human rights and the practice of unconditional terrorism.

Chapter 4 describes and discusses the manner in which all these matters have been theorised and reified within the academic disciplines of international relations and security studies. It shares the standpoint also occupied by Professor Barry Buzan and his colleagues of the Copenhagen school of security studies, which freely incorporates the analyst and his story as an hermeneutic part of the process to be explained. Chapter 4 ends with unvarnished advocacy of the utility of Immanuel Kant's political writings as a guide to understanding, made newly relevant for our times.

For among the themes which recur across these chapters is one which suggests that it is not only in the area of international law that we see issues which were alive in the late-eighteenth century returning to the central focus of our concern. The preoccupying debate of that period was about the ways in which individuals and groups might relate to each other. One firm answer was given after 1789, which really shut down most aspects of this debate as a central issue in politics until the 'long twentieth century' (as Eric Hobsbawm has mischievously but helpfully named it – 1789 to 1989 – ending with the implosion of the Soviet Union) was over.

The decade of the interregnum which followed the fall of Soviet communism contained strengthening indications of the return of a cosmopolitan agenda in active public politics. This expressed itself in particular through the challenge of humanitarian intervention and the rise and rise of human rights. Therefore, a second theme running through the first four chapters is more descriptive: an account of the problematic history of the rediscovery of human rights as a politically potent force.

Part II addresses the experiences in the practical implementation of the dominant themes of the new era, especially, but not exclusively, expressed through military power. A central concern of this section is to analyse the effects which new demands upon military forces have both in their use and, by extension, in their design, employment, self-images and philosophies. This task is approached first through a review of the experience of military intervention since the mid-1990s and then in an extended case study analysis of one such episode, placed in its proper historical context (operations in West Africa in 2000). The focus in this section is upon the political mission of humanitarian relief and the argument is that the most successful form of military contribution to the full cycle of activities necessary to achieve success in humanitarian intervention is that of strategic raiding. However, as is there pointed out, strategic raiding is likely also to be the shape of operation most likely to contribute to the full cycle of activities in the other principal mission of the near future, namely counter-terrorism.

The analysis has practical implications for those with responsibility for the design and deployment of armed forces and, therefore, the last chapter of Part II is presented in a deliberately different format to the rest, since it engages closely the single most sensitive and important aspect of military force that is affected by the demands of the new era, namely the exercise of command. Chapter 7 presents the requirements which the new era lays upon the exercise of the processes and structures of command when the military force is constantly tracking to and fro between diplomatic and military roles. It is derived from an internal but unclassified briefing paper written within the DERA and that format is preserved for the second half of the essay, for the convenience of military readers, to remind others of its origins and in passing to demonstrate the usefulness of such a format. Lawyers should not be granted a sole prerogative in the virtues of the numbered paragraph.

The final part and final chapter of the book return to the level of global political analysis in order to suggest that an under-explored aspect of our changed circumstances is the likelihood of the return of nuclear weapons to the stage. However, their return is happening in substantially different roles and contexts from those familiar during the Cold War. Accordingly, the ways of thinking about nuclear weapons developed during that period may no longer be fully adequate or even appropriate at all. This final chapter does not seek to argue for conclusions about what the answers are to the new questions about nuclear weapons. This would be premature, especially since the events of 11 September 2001 may or may not have impacts on the emerging new shape of strategic relationships and priorities. However, it is timely to restate the history of ideas and to expose the 'meta questions', which frame the nuclear issue. Among these, ironically, the humanitarian imperative has given new life and attractions to nuclear status; so the final chapter starts to elaborate the new range of ethical, legal, political and military arguments surrounding the nuclear question in 2001.

This sketch of themes and structures also suggests why the book has been given its particular format. Each chapter is written in such a way that it can be read alone without reference to any other. This responds to a sense, which I have gained from students both in universities and in the military profession over the last decade, that it is helpful if authors deliberately present material in this way. One consequence of it, which, it is to be hoped, other sorts of readers will not find overly irritating, is that there must therefore be a certain degree of repetition of points. In order to minimise this, I have also introduced occasional parentheses, which indicate cross-reference from one chapter to another. Readers can use these signposts if they wish.

But the book is also written simultaneously in the more traditional format as a developing chain of arguments, which can be read from beginning to end. The themes of historical continuity and change, of the recasting of social contract, of the re-emergence of a cosmopolitan agenda, of transformation in the purposes and consequent forms of armed force are interwoven and developed through the length of the book. Thus, for those readers wishing principally to gut the book, or to read only one or another chapter, given that not all subjects are of interest, it is hoped that not so much is assumed from previous argument as to make any single chapter opaque. For readers among my peers and colleagues, I trust that they will forgive the occasional recapitulations and reiterations that the sequence requires. Who knows, some might even find it helpful? It is a balancing act and runs the risk of pleasing none of the readers all of the time as one tries to please most of the readers most of the time!

Part I

Our intimate relationships with war

1   War, peace and the future of history

If you have no coal to dig, then what need is there for miners? If you have no pupils, what can teachers do? If you want to manufacture motor cars you must have the bits out of which to make them. And if you have no history, then historians become redundant also. Workers need a constant supply of raw material. But historians have always thought themselves a privileged group. After all, what is more predictable than a continuing supply of history?

In 1983, many people in Europe had a deep and public sense of doom. It was a period which is often now called the 'second Cold War'. Relations between the United States and the Soviet Union (which still existed at that time and whose disappearance as a state was in no western leader's mind) were acrimonious and bitter. A fierce arms race was in progress. Inventories of weapons, especially of nuclear weapons, expanded. There was a vigorous propaganda war over who was to blame. Many ordinary people felt that they were threatened with the extinction not only of themselves but of their children and of their futures; that a pall of nuclear threat hung across all of us. Huge demonstrations took place in West Germany – led by people such as Joschka Fischer, later the German Foreign Minister and Vice Chancellor – in the Netherlands where the IKV (Inter-Church Union) was a prominent force and in Britain where the second surge of CND (the Campaign for Nuclear Disarmament) was given political edge by the appearance of END (European Nuclear Disarmament), led by the social historian, the late E.P. Thompson.

On television, one banner stood out in the marching lines of the anti-nuclear protestors in London in 1983. A group of people who were clearly academics (tweeds, some gowns and mortarboards) carried the slogan on their banner, 'We demand a continuing supply of history'.

Those times are mercifully gone. Contemporary historians who have been able to start looking, through the American Freedom of Information Act, into what was actually happening in November 1983 now know that it was a much closer run thing than many had dreamed at the time. A film launched in 2001 in the States was called 'Thirteen Days'. It is a dramatisation of the Cuban missile crisis forty years ago, when President Kennedy and Premier Khruschev were eyeball-to-eyeball over the emplacement of Soviet missiles on the island of Cuba, just off the American coast. It is conventionally thought that this was the moment in the superpower confrontation of the Cold War when we were closest to nuclear war. Certainly we were close, but now we know that later we probably got even closer. We were probably most at risk just at the time of the European street demonstrations in November 1983 when the Soviets systematically misunderstood a NATO nuclear command exercise called Able Archer. The West did not know this; but because the Soviets had penetrated the communications of the West so effectively, they knew that all sorts of commands were being given to nuclear-missile-carrying submarines. They were not sure whether they were real or not, but assumed that they were real and reached the point where Soviet bombers carrying nuclear bombs were at the end of runways in East Germany with their engines running.[1]

This strangely surreal period is not the principal subject of this book, only the starting point; nor is its danger the reason for beginning with this rather sombre observation. It is that these episodes and fears populated informed imaginations, and thereby moulded the world view of people whose opinions influenced the general public mood, like these marching, protesting historians at that time. All history writing has an aim or a culminating point. You cannot write history unless you have a sense of what it is towards which your eye is directed. You may admit that to yourself, or you may pretend to some spurious objectivity, but you will have that point consciously or unconsciously in mind.[2] The questions that should have been asked of those people at that fraught moment almost twenty years ago were, 'Where is the Golden Age?', 'Are you optimistic about the future?', 'Are you pessimistic about the future?' We can guess the answer. The Golden Age, in so far as they would recognise the contemporary relevance of this medieval concept, was in the *past*. People were anxious. They were moving into a future about which they had apprehension.

That way of looking at the world stands in contrast to the Whig interpretation of history. The term describes the broad reaches and

strong currents flowing in the river navigated by the Victorian historians, Green or Maitland: people who wrote history *to a point*: teleo-
logical history. Why was it that the microbes emerged from the
primeval sludge in the Whig interpretation of history? Clearly, it was
so that eventually constitutional democracy and monarchy, with a
King and ultimately of course with a Queen Empress, could develop
through feudalism to the Tudor revolution in government, onwards
with the minor blip of a civil war to the Glorious Revolution of 1688,
thence to the culminating point of history, the perfection of the
British Victorian constitution. So, in 1898, at Queen Victoria's
diamond jubilee, the pinnacle was attained; a little old lady in a
bonnet steps down into a pinnace and sails out into Spithead
between the twin lines of the battleships of the Royal Navy, as far as
the eye can see. This was the whole purpose of the human adventure.

The Whig interpretation was not an aberration. It was animated
with the breath of the age. The behaviour of Victorians, in many
branches of endeavour, showed how they viewed the world in which
they lived through a common optic. Isambard Kingdom Brunel, the
engineer and designer of the Great Western Railway, did exactly all
of that. He surveyed the route. He designed the track, the locomo-
tives, the stations and the *bas reliefs* applied to their façades; bridges,
the bores, linings and classic portico entrances of Box Tunnel. In
short, he had an organic conception of what he was doing. From
Brunel's correspondence one discovers that he had a strongly moral
sense of his mission.[3] Indeed, both he and Stephenson, the other
most celebrated of the railway engineers, were known on occasion to
decline projects on the grounds (Stephenson was explicit in one case)
that the railway project proposed was not, in his view, to the benefit
of the people in the county through which the railway would go.
They made connections between cause and effect. These were men
who were enthused with the power of science. They were engineers
and took their practical knowledge to transform their world. They
overcame endless challenges. But the attitude of mind was not something that arose from being an engineer. It proceeds from something
much more pervasive and much deeper: the thought that the human
mind organised and rational, capable of reasoning, can subdue irrationality and can achieve progress.[4]

In other strands of life we find evidence of equivalently powerful
senses of the forward progression of the human project. Sir Henry
Maine, the legislator of India, wrote a famous book, published in
1861 (two years after Darwin's *Origin of Species* with which it is compared), entitled *Ancient Law*.[5] The argument of *Ancient Law* is

grandly simple. Human history, says Maine, may be reduced to the progression from *custom* to *contract*: I am prepared to give you a bag of maize, rather than this person, because you are my uncle's second cousin twice removed, whilst I have no relationship to her at all: that is a customary relationship, which means that I am going to favour people who are inside what anthropologists call my 'moral community' (moral not in the ethical sense but in the sense of regarding you as someone towards whom I have responsibility and, conversely, you to me; whereas she is on the outside, she is somebody else's responsibility). That is not a contractual relationship. In a contractual relationship, we depersonalise matters. It all comes down to 'do you have the money?': I have the goods. Do you have the money, cousin? No, she has the money. Fine, she gets the goods. This ability to objectify, argued Maine, was a very important indicator of progress in the human endeavour. It freed people to move away from the irrationality, the unpredictability of personality or emotionally based relationships, and the endlessness of such customary relationships which their nature entailed.

It was reflected in other schemes in which the Victorian age sought to apply the empire of reason to the explanation of the human condition. Here one can think of the application of Darwin's amazingly economical and elegant explanation of natural selection to the behaviour of societies in the work of Herbert Spencer. The common theme was that science conferred status. Friedrich Engels sought to capture the essence of his friend's lifetime work, as he stood beside the grave in Highgate Cemetery, when he compared Marx's 'laws' of human society to Darwin's uncovering of the organising laws of the natural world.[6]

But in contrast to our anxious, protesting historians and others of twenty years ago, what is the common feature here in the terms used above? These people are Victorians, for whom the Golden Age is in the *future*: it is coming, because there is everything to achieve. We can do more yet that we have yet done. We might even be able to abolish war.

The 'nineteenth-century peace movement', that inchoate amalgam of liberals, liberators and idealists, had confidence that, if only we could employ strictly the insights of reason, then the irrationality of war would be understood and its uselessness for the achievement of the objectives for which people went to war would be exposed. One man, more than any other, engaged in the task of trying to understand war in the last quarter of the nineteenth century. Until recently when his memory has been revived, he had become almost completely forgotten. He was an extraordinary man, a Polish–Jewish–Russian engineer and railway builder (he built the railway from Warsaw to St Petersburg) by the name of Jan (in Poland) or Ivan (in Russia) Bloch.

Bloch applied an engineer's insights to the study of war. He looked at it in all of its technical extravagance, because the means of war went through as dramatic an improvement in the late nineteenth century as most other technologies. In a series of enormous technical books, he argued that the destructiveness of war – prefigured in the horrendous destruction of the last battles of the American Civil War – was becoming rapidly such that rational people would foreswear such means of settling their disputes.

Bloch did not make this case by an appeal to rhetoric. He reported the results of experiments. In particular, he was impressed with the consequences of the combination of reduced weapon calibre (from the 11 mm Mauser 1871 standard to the 6 mm Mannlicher standard of the 1890s), with smokeless powder and increased bullet velocity and spin. The reduced size of bullets meant that the infantryman could carry more. Smokeless powder would not give away his position when he fired. Increased bullet velocity, from a rifle, improved flat-trajectory accuracy and range and hence lethality. Together, these made the soldier deadlier: between twenty and forty times more so, Bloch calculated. Nor did he hold with the argument of the German surgeons Reger and Beck that faster, smaller bullets were somehow more humane. (In an address to the Berlin Military Medical Society in 1885, Reger stated, 'I welcome the new bullet with great joy and believe that if it were generally adopted by international consent, all humanity would have cause to rejoice.') Musket balls at Waterloo inflicted huge, tearing wounds. Modern rifle bullets, especially 5.5 mm steel-cased composite bullets, Bloch discovered from firing experiments with animal and human corpses, were not less lethal because the entry hole was smaller, as some contemporaries suggested. On the contrary, if the bullet struck bone, then the bullet and bone fragments could tumble inside the body, producing further damage; and the energy of a high-velocity projectile produced massive trauma in the soft tissue of internal organs.[7] In this discovery, he helped to create a discipline of battlefield medicine. This sort of mathematics and practical experimentation laid the foundations for modern Operational Analysis, of which Bloch is really the forgotten grandfather.

He applied his studies to all other aspects of modern warfare. His expertise with railways alerted him to the vital role of heavy logistics.

Combine trains and artillery and Bloch predicted the possibilities of the saturation shelling of the Great War. Combine logistics, artillery and infantry and he predicted battles which could never be won on the battlefield: where the surviving soldiers would shelter behind ramparts of corpses, and in which the scale of injury would so overwhelm medical resources that the wounded would envy the dead. He reported the harrowing description of what the Bavarian Chief Military Physician, Porth, found on the battlefield of Worth, of which he wrote that for wounded soldiers to be cast alive onto such a rampart 'will be the best of fates, for a new bullet will shortly end all sufferings, while those wounded who are left lying in the trenches will suffer long'.[8] In this stomach-churning prose, the worse for its studiously neutral tone, Bloch was predicting with horrible accuracy the Canadian attack at Beaumont-Hamel on 1 July 1916 – the first day of the Battle of the Somme. From his experiments and his reasoning, Bloch concluded that war had become unthinkable to rational people.[9]

The fact that he wrote all this *before* the Great War is interesting; but the reason that knowing about him is important is that Bloch persuaded one person, in particular, of this proposition. He was Tsar Nicholas II, the last Tsar of the Russias, who in 1898 issued an imperial rescript, and, jointly with Queen Wilhelmina of the Netherlands, summoned all the heads of states to a conference in The Hague the following year in order to discuss how the differences between Europeans might be resolved without recourse to war. Bloch was the driving force behind the great Hague Peace Conference held at Paleis Het Loo.

What was war, as it threatened or faced that generation just over 100 years ago? By the late nineteenth century, even with the enormous improvements in efficiency of killing, which the application of science and engineering had brought, war and peace were still strictly distinguishable. It was possible to know the difference between a state of war and a state of peace. Wars were, by and large, still declared and wars were, above all, a condition that existed between states. The French philosopher, Jean Bodin, offered a useful and widely-used definition of what it meant to be a state, in terms explicitly linking war and state, in his *Six Livres de la République* of 1576. To be a state meant to control the monopoly of force, the monopoly of violence, to possess 'supreme power over citizens and subjects, unrestrained by law'. As is evident, that is still close to a commonsense view of what it is that distinguishes states from other agencies. We privatise many things these days, but not armies and navies.

In this notion of a distinction between states of war and states of peace, where war is an inter-state activity, civil war was obnoxiously aberrant. During the American Civil War, a famous exchange occurred between the Union General Sherman and the Confederate General Hood, who commanded the city of Atlanta, the capital of Georgia. Sherman is well-known in the popular view as a person who massively increased the indiscriminate destructiveness of war. War is hell, said Sherman, but nonetheless it was he who put Atlanta to the torch and then burnt the farms and homesteads of Georgia in his march to the sea. Before he did this, he sent a letter to General Hood in which he demanded that he evacuate Atlanta of its people so that the city might be burned. Hood replied with indignant protest, 'And now, Sir,' he added, 'permit me to say that the unprecedented measure you propose transcends, in studied and ingenious cruelty, all acts ever before brought to my attention in the dark history of war.' Sherman, who was a deeply religious man, wrote back. 'War is cruelty and you cannot refine it. Those who brought war into our country deserve all the curses and maledictions a nation can pour out.' In short, all responsibility (by which he meant all moral responsibility) for the acts of destruction which he and others undertook lay solely with those who brought this war which, in his view, meant the rebels, the Confederates: 'I know I had no hand in making this war.'[10]

So, what he argued in the middle of the nineteenth century was something with which we have become grimly familiar in the twentieth: the notion that war being hell, such a horrendous state, the moral obligation of those whose cause is just is to *maximise* the terror and the destructiveness of their violence, the quicker to break the will of those who unjustly began the war and thus the more quickly to end the horror. Sherman's doctrine has come back to visit us in telling ways.

Although he was fighting in the middle of the nineteenth century, in many ways the American Civil War was the first war of the twentieth because it was the first war where technology really made the difference: where the later campaigns moved into the unlimited war of the twentieth century. But in one respect there was an important difference. These nineteenth-century wars were wars with an obvious characteristic. They had limited objectives and they employed relatively limited means. The level of destructiveness that could be marshalled was much less than became subsequently possible. These wars were governed to some extent by a chivalric etiquette. The exchange of letters between Hood and Sherman falls awkwardly upon the modern ear. The thought that you invite the population to leave the city before you torch it might seem odd to many twentieth-century commanders. The USAAF wrote no such letters before fire-bombing Tokyo, nor the RAF when it incinerated Dresden. But Sherman and Hood fought in the middle of the nineteenth century, and the warning to evacuate belongs alongside another nineteenth-century initiative to manage war. The St Petersburg Convention of 1868 was the first of the attempts to regulate the conduct of war in that century. Regulations prohibited the use of expanding bullets ('dum-dum bullets', as they are called). The erroneous belief in the humane effect of high-velocity, small-calibre bullets spoke to the same theme. The Convention stated plainly that 'the only legitimate object which states should endeavour to accomplish during war is to weaken the *military forces* [emphasis added] of the enemy'.

What are we to make of this frank contradiction – Sherman *versus* St Petersburg – in attempts to apply St Augustine's doctrine of Just War? If you have *jus ad bellum* (justice in the reason why you go to war) then, in Sherman's interpretation – which was new – you have a moral obligation to *escalate indiscriminate violence*, the most quickly to end the war by whatever means. This is divergent from the previously held interpretation, which is reflected in the St Petersburg Convention. It holds that *jus in bello* (fighting wars cleanly, having a limit upon certain things that you might do, having a proportion between the destructiveness that you employ and the cause) was the balance to strike. From the time of Sherman's exchange with Hood onwards, the tension between how *jus ad bellum* and *jus in bello* should be interpreted, related and balanced has been at the centre of the debate about the use of political violence in modern societies.

This was then and now is now. As we observe the phenomenon of war today, we see something quite dramatically different: pervasive political violence. That term, rather than war, is used deliberately because this political violence is frequently, indeed often, out of the hands of states. Then we call it something else: 'asymmetric violence' or terror, an issue taken up in the third chapter. This is the condition of up to two-thirds of the human family. We live in a world that is more stringently divided than it has ever been before in human history. Along the same fault line of the five billion of the human family, we find one-third which is rich, two-thirds which is poor; one-third which is safe (because statistically in rich societies we are safer now from personal violence than we have ever been), two-thirds which lives in constant fear of violence. One-third informed (all of us who have Internet accounts, mobile phones, watch the TV, etc.), but two-thirds of the human family has not yet made a telephone call. In this divided world, how stands the state of war?

The military historian, Sir John Keegan, argued in a lecture, which he delivered in 1999 in St Petersburg at the conference to celebrate the memory of Jan Bloch, that the history of war can now, at last, be distilled to its essentials. It started, said Keegan, when those who 'have' used the means of violence that they had against the 'have-nots' in order to get what the 'have-nots' have got. That is imperialism: with guns and sails you go and take the gold or silver of Latin America, the products of colonies and bring them back home. That was then followed by a period when the 'have-nots' began to use political violence against the 'haves'. This is rebellion, this is anti-colonialism. That co-existed with an aberrant period when the 'haves' fratricidally engaged in a civil war, which occupied much of the first half of the twentieth century. European states, the old societies of Europe, went at each other's throats and on two occasions had to be rescued from their civil war by the intervention of outside bodies. In both cases, the intervention which was decisive was of the modern industrial societies that had not been swept into the war early on, the United States on both occasions and the Soviet Union, massively, on the second. But now where do we find war in the modern world? War, argues Keegan, has been largely excluded from the happy environment of the one-third which is rich. The prospect of major war, the sort of wars which bring utter destruction, has receded mercifully since the end of the nuclear threats of the Cold War. Where we see political violence, it is the 'have-nots' grovelling, rolling in the dust, fighting the other 'have-nots', because war today is overwhelmingly a phenomenon where the poor fight the poor with the weapons largely provided by the rich.[11]

How did this all come about? We must have crossed some sort of watershed. To discover where, when and how we should have in mind three key features of the twentieth century. The same knowledge will assist us as we seek to answer the challenge of Bloch's question posed again: about the shape of war that we might expect to see in the future.

The first feature is that the first half of the twentieth century in Europe was preoccupied not with what we conventionally call the First World War and the Second World War – these terms will fade. Instead, we will speak more accurately of the European civil war, which began with the summer crisis of July 1914 and continued, in hot phases and then in cold phases, until 1941, when it ended, not with victory for one side or other, but with its transformation into the

Second World War (the first was between the British and the French in the late eighteenth century). It began with Operation Barbarossa, the German invasion of Russia, in June, and with the Japanese bombing of Pearl Harbor, which brought the United States into the war in December. That World War then lasted until 1945.

What was the central feature of this European civil war to which we should attend? Surely, it was the Holocaust, the systematic killing of millions and millions of people, largely Jews but not exclusively – gypsies, Seventh Day Adventists, homosexuals – all those of whom the Third Reich did not approve? What is it about the Holocaust that is so debilitating for European high culture? The argument has never been put better than by the literary critic, George Steiner. The most important thing about the horrors of the Holocaust, he said, was that coming from the society of Goethe, of Beethoven, we were confronted with the challenge of wondering whether those who gassed Jews all day had somehow become barbaric, unable to return home and play string quartets in the evening. The answer is that plainly they had not, because they did. They saw their work as being that of people who exterminate rats. Such a piece of news, argued Steiner, pulls out any protection that we might have had from such information in the future. When you are told of the next atrocity, the defence 'people couldn't do things like that' is not available. All you can do, said Steiner, is sadly to enquire into the source of the information.[12]

This quality of the European civil war informs the second characteristic of war in the twentieth century. During the twentieth century, two hundred and four million people died premature deaths as a result of the actions of other people. Of those two hundred and four million people, only thirty-five million died in war. The other one hundred and seventy million were killed by their own governments. Professor Rudi Rummel has coined the term for this. He called it 'democide'. If you look at this gruesome two hundred and four million for the twentieth century, you discover that over 80 per cent of all the people killed unnaturally died at the hands of non-democratic, authoritarian, totalitarian and communist governments. Their war dead compose about 15 per cent. The democratic war dead are 2.2 per cent of the total and democidal action by democratic governments (because, sadly, there has been such) is about 1 per cent. The figures in more detail are, under totalitarian governments, one hundred and thirty-eight million victims of democide, fourteen million dead in war; communist governments, one hundred and ten million victims of democide, 9.7 million dead in war; authoritarian governments (military dictatorships in

South America, etc.), twenty-eight million victims of democide, fifteen million or so of war; and the democracies, two million victims of democide and 4.4 million dead in war.[13]

This points us directly towards the third key characteristic of the twentieth-century experience, which is that the period of killing is bracketed by the birth and death of the two communist states: Russia from 1917 to 1991 and China from 1948 to 1989, the events of Tienanmen Square. The Chinese communist government continues to this day, but a threshold was crossed after the events of the liberty demonstrations that were so brutally suppressed in that year.[14]

If we look at the twentieth century through these rather anguished spectacles, we might agree with Eric Hobsbawm that the twentieth century was a short century.[15] It did not end chronologically in 2000. It ended functionally in 1989. Therefore, we must now ask how that affects our view of history. This twentieth century – seen as a ghastly recital of figures of death – is a history that is comfortably interpreted by a cynical realism to be found in the work of the political historian, Martin Wight and his book on power politics,[16] or perhaps, more famously, Hans Morgenthau's celebrated exposition of the way in which history is best understood, as a sort of game of billiards, when the self-interested state agents, as they pursue their own self-interests with no regard to the interests of any other party, bang off each other on the billiard table of history.[17] The career of academic security studies is the subject of Chapter 4.

Yet those historians and analysts who held this view about how to interpret modern affairs, which prided itself on its street-wise ability not to be deceived by the false consciousness of soppy idealists, had the rug pulled from under them by the monumental failure of 1989 when no prediction of the sudden end of communism was made. No-one knew that communism would implode in the way that it did during that amazing autumn of 1989.

How would we interpret history after that? Several tried as we began to enter the 1990s. Francis Fukuyama was early on the scene with a book, which argued that the answer to the question was that we had now reached the end of history because all the most important questions were now resolved. Liberal capitalism and democracy had triumphed and all that remained to be done was a bit of fine-tuning at the edges.[18] A rather more apocalyptic view was taken by Samuel Huntington, who said that the great rupture between the ideologies of the Cold War would now be replaced by other tectonic plates in human affairs. We will now see civilisations clash with each other, and, in particular, he proposed the Islamic world as the next bogey man to replace the Soviet Union.[19] Professor Paul Kennedy, in rather more measured terms, and earlier, argued in a book, which renovated the central insight of Edward Gibbons's *Decline and Fall of the Roman Empire*, that all great empires eventually experience what he called 'imperial overstretch'. The United States would be as much the victim of this as any previous empire.[20]

All these large ideas exploded rather like Roman candles. For a moment they illuminated everything and all the journals and the chattering classes and the radio programmes were full of discussion. Then suddenly they guttered out because, in fact, we have just lived through what Professor Ken Booth of the University of Wales at Aberystwyth, one of the most thoughtful of modern political analysts, describes as an 'intellectual inter-regnum'.[21] The king is dead but who is the new king? We cannot say for certain, despite the traumatic terrorist attacks on America on 11 September 2001, although a principal purpose of this book is to help to seek answers. During this period, many constituencies have sought to draw lessons. Some, unlike academics, have not the liberty, indeed the luxury of powerlessness. Governments need to have a sense of what comes next. That is one of the things we ask them to do.

Therefore, it is especially interesting to read a report that was published just before Christmas 2000 by the US Central Intelligence Agency, which tried to grapple in a non-ideological way with what it is that is going on. It sought to describe cohering trends which these days are too easily called 'globalisation'. It described the way in which the world became suddenly united and discussed the manner in which this could be benign to the interests of the US or hostile to the interests of the US. But it also understood that the world is not dominated only by forces which join. There are also many forces which divide. It discussed extensively regionalism, fractious, dissipating forces of introspective nationalism, such as we have seen fighting each other in the Balkans. It talked about the new threats to everybody that come from the global transference of the disease regimes of one region to the totality. The global spread of AIDS, for example. All of these are seen as aspects of a future, which the United States has to confront. The CIA painted four word pictures – so-called 'scenarios' – at the end of its investigation: benign globalisation, perverse globalisation, introspective regionalisation and then what is called 'post-polar world', which is really chaos. It came to the conclusion, rather surprising perhaps for the CIA, that in none of these worlds in the not very distant future will the US's absolute power, which it has today, continue.[22]

Our concern in what follows is principally with the place of military power in this new *post inter-regnum* era. What key elements should be in mind as we try (as we must) to delineate this future, in the same spirit as the CIA report did, reducing our insights to discrete characteristics? Let us find categories which are not apocalyptic, which are not Whiggish. We won't talk about golden ages.

The first category is of forces in tension: dialectical forces. No more central and contentious an example of this category exists than that of the slippery phenomenon of 'globalisation'.

For much of the decade which followed the collapse of communism, the aspects of globalisation that were uppermost in the attention of commentators and analysts were those which had impressed Fukuyama. The Velvet Revolutions were interpreted widely as evidence of the embracing qualities of the global market, especially as projected through the penetrating and pervasive tentacles of the global electronic media. In an ordering of effects that gave off a whiff of Marxist priorities as between the all-powerful material base and the dependent intellectual and cultural superstructure, the political culture of democratic capitalism was presented, trailing along behind and essentially, harmoniously.

A notable example of this was to be seen in the manner in which the so-called 'Third Way' account of modern political culture gave priority to the transforming potentials of the globalised world economy. Whereas the collapse of Yugoslavia was the most powerful dampener of that sunny disposition, in general commentary some analysts were prescient in their view that this was always likely to be a systematically fragile interpretation. John Gray has been prominent in offering this opinion. *False Dawn*, as its name suggests, excoriated the widespread assumptions about the amiable congruence between *laissez-faire* ideology in its modern American form and the key agents of change in global economics. 'At present, global markets work to fracture societies and weaken states,' he wrote. Whereas societies with highly competent governments or vigorous civil society might resist, to a point, this fracturing force, most of humanity possesses none of that protection, and so 'the spread of new technologies throughout the world is not working to advance human freedom. Instead it has resulted in the emancipation of market forces from social and political control.' Gray saw the terrorist attacks of September 2001 as confirmation of these trends. A monochrome essay by Jeremy Black plotted all manner of potential sources of conflict for the twenty-first century, arising principally from a similar view of the fracturing and centrifugal effects of globalisation.[23]

A serious attempt has been made to confront these polarised interpretations with evidence from a standardised 'Globalization Index'. It was a joint effort of the business consultancy A.T. Kearney Inc., with *Foreign Policy* magazine and the Carnegie Endowment for International Peace, and it measured four categories for fifty countries containing four-fifths of the human population and accounting for 95 per cent of world economic output. The categories are goods and services (represented by the convergence of domestic and international prices, and international trade as a share of GNP); finance (inward and outward-directed foreign investment, portfolio capital flows and income payments and receipts as a share of GDP); personal contact (cross-border remittances as a share of GDP, minutes of international telephone calls and number of international travellers, *per capita*) and technology (percentage of population on-line to the Internet, number of Internet hosts and secure servers, *per capita*).

The first results computed by the index, published in 2001, yielded four strong judgements, and did not resolve the contending views. They showed that small countries are the most globalised (Singapore, the Netherlands, Sweden, Switzerland); that measured across its categories, globalisation was slowing, compared to the 1990s; that the most globalised countries tended to have more egalitarian income distribution, but that there was a 'gaping digital chasm' in access to IT between North America and Scandinavia and the rest of the world. West Europe was five times less 'wired' than these two areas, and poor countries were on the far side of the 'digital chasm', with most phone lines in capital cities. All these divides are widening not closing.[24]

The limitations of a nation-by-nation index, for the purpose of the other three categories to be mentioned, will be evident, and were admitted by its creators; but, nevertheless, an intelligent mix of statistics like these is a necessary step in making the concept of globalisation sufficiently precise to be analytically tractable. Within its own terms, these results offered support to the proponents in the evidence of a positive correlation with some measures of equality and of civil liberty, and to the critics, in the evidence of the centrifugal forces of the 'digital chasm'. Yet the dialectical forces of globalisation must themselves be viewed in the context of simpler, gross trends of wealth, resources and hope.

Globally, we live in a world that is dramatically – brutally – divided between the rich and the poor, and we may agree with Professor Black that there is every expectation of coming conflict in key areas: conflict over energy and fuel, conflict over the availability of food, very traditional things about which people have fought in the past. But equally, we must note that awareness of mutual vulnerability can stimulate cooperation. The process of the Nile Users Conference in maintaining agreements on abstraction from the river on which all depend is a case in point: equally, Israeli/Jordanian water agreements. These dialectical forces that were always there are still there. Other aspects are explored in the next chapters, for an understanding of them is essential in framing the context for the return of the nuclear issue in the final section of this book.

The second of the four elements, although also old, only recently returned to the centre of the political stage. These are *transcending forces*: things which leap over divides; which identify common features. The last time that these issues of how a social contract that was cosmopolitan could be constructed between individuals and the state were extensively discussed in European intellectual life was by Enlightenment thinkers in the years before, during and immediately after the French Revolution. The debate was fierce. Eighteen months after the storming of the Bastille, Edmund Burke wrote in impassioned and prescient warning that revolutions eat their children sooner or later. His *Reflections on the Revolution in France* prompted Tom Paine's *The Rights of Man* in defence of the revolution the following year, the most famous among several replies that Burke's essay elicited. Burke's last word on the subject came the year before his death in 1797 in his *Letters on a Regicide Peace*. It was an overriding interest of contemporary philosophers.[25] The unfinished debates of the 1780s, promoted by the French Revolution, with its special answer to the question (*liberté, égalité, fraternité*), have now resumed. This resumption occurred in two stages, the later (since 1995) dependent upon and drawing from the seminal moment, which came when the great European war ended, during the narrow window between the end of hostilities and the onset of the Cold War in 1948–9.

One of the innovative responses to the evil nature of the Third Reich was the institution of the concept of 'war crime' by the Nuremberg Tribunal. The perpetrators of the crimes of the Third Reich were put on trial *as individuals*. It was found and established in international law that there is no defence in saying 'I was only doing what I was told because my superior told me to do it'. Each person is responsible for their own moral actions. The Nuremberg judgement stated that 'crimes against international law are committed by men, not by abstract entities, and only by punishing individuals who commit such crimes can the provisions of international law be enforced'.[26] The Nuremberg process and principles went underground for a long time during the Cold War, but in recent times, and most notably during the interregnum of the 1990s since the end of communism, have suddenly and dramatically re-emerged. We find that especially in the wealthy and wired world of massively informed citizens there is a generosity about human rights, a generosity towards others in crisis, which is to be seen every time the TV screens are filled with the vision of, for example, those suffering in floods, famines or wars. There is a great well of individual generosity which pours out in donations and also in the way that their governments respond. The manner in which that response has occurred, and what it may portend, is the subject of Part II of this book.

Nor is it just the actions of individuals. Those actions can create law. We have also seen, in the aftermath of the ghastly genocide that took place in Central Africa in the middle of the 1990s, the establishment of an *ad hoc* tribunal at Arusha to try those responsible for genocide in Rwanda, just as was done with the Nazis at the end of the Second World War. In the continuing tribunal for Yugoslavia, those who perpetrated uncivil war are made to answer for their actions as individuals. Biljana Plavsic, the recent President of the Serb Republic, surrendered herself in order to answer the charges in The Hague. The act of surrendering means an acceptance that one is willing to submit oneself to the authority of this new and cosmopolitan concept of public responsibility.[27]

Then, in July 2001, came a turning point for the future of both the International Tribunal and the prospective International Criminal Court, when a divided Yugoslavian parliament voted to breach the country's constitution and to surrender former President Slobodan Milosevic to The Hague. As this is written, the nature of this turning point is quite obscure. On the one hand, the surrender could be seen as a boost to the fortunes of an international enterprise which has been in some eclipse; but, for other reasons, Milosevic's trial may not have a net positive effect for the regime of human rights. When refusing to plead or to recognise the court's authority to try him, Milosevic simply (and accurately) stated (in English), 'That's your problem.' The problem in his arraignment is that it was not plain that a fair trial, with international participation, could not have been held in Serbia, thereby avoiding the local difficulties about Montenegran outrage and the breach of the constitution.[28] The option was not fully explored; the extradition foreclosed it. Arguably, this will matter most for the future prospects of the ICC, and especially the chances of obtaining American participation. For the Milosevic extradition in those unclear circumstances may be seen by American sceptics as just the evidence which they feared of an international process being used to override or to truncate a national process; whereas the principle of the ICC states that it would only ever be employed in Nuremberg-type contexts where there was no other recourse. Time will indeed tell.

Yet the Nuremberg principles and precedent only applied to contexts where human rights were trampled during times of war. They were reactive by circumstance and by nature. It was the prime purpose of the second of the three great responses to the experience of fascism and its ultimate defeat to prevent such circumstances occurring. Creation of the United Nations was the common effort 'to save succeeding generations from the scourge of war'; but it was the least well-remembered of the three seminal acts which provided the instrument upon which the priority of human rights, as transcending general principles defining the contemporary social contract, is grounded.

Until Professor Glendon's history restored the historical integrity of the Universal Declaration to us, by recounting the narrative of its creation, it had become moth-eaten in the public memory as a consequence of selective pillaging and quotation from its clauses. Its origin lay in the darkest time of the war, just before the European civil war became global; for it was in F.D. Roosevelt's 1941 'Four Freedoms' speech – itself then enshrined first as the Allies' war aims in the Churchill/Roosevelt Atlantic Charter issued just before American entry into the Second World War and thereafter indelibly in American public consciousness by Norman Rockwell's celebrated paintings of each.

Freedom of Speech, Freedom of Religion, Freedom from Want and Freedom from Fear were principles which, as Professor Glendon observed, bonded the two post-Enlightenment traditions in the definition of rights. The continental one, indebted to Rousseau, gave its emphasis to equality, whereas the Anglo-American tradition stressed liberty. Freedom from Want emphasised 'the social dimension of personhood' – and it was formulation of social and economic rights that proved to be the most time-consuming subjects in the drafting. But, Glendon stressed, the successful accomplishment of that marriage not only helped secure the adhesion of the Soviet Union and other states that valued the rights of the state above those of the individual; it had been instrumental in keeping the concept of human rights engaged and relevant in the circumstances of a world now radically divided by poverty and need more than by evangelical ideology. This – as much as any other part of our debt to her single greatest act – we owe to Eleanor Roosevelt's maintenance of her late husband's vision within the drafting of the Universal Declaration.[29] The centrality of this American role – both philosophically and procedurally – made the expulsion of the US from the Human Rights Commission in 2001, on the vote of countries such as China and Cuba, both ironic and, in the worst eventuality, threatening to the future viability of the UN, in the way that the failure to resolve the Abyssinian crisis in 1936 proved eventually to be fatal to the League of Nations.

Britain was the unexpected site of a notable case in the late 1990s that pushed this transcendent trend forward. It came as the consequence of the desire of a previous dictator of Chile to visit his old friend, Mrs Thatcher, to go shopping in Harrods and to have some surgery. General Pinochet was arrested on a warrant from a Spanish magistrate and was then subjected to a long and, in legal terms, highly important extradition procedure (a procedure which, in the end the Home Secretary, Mr Straw, suspended on the grounds of Mr Pinochet's infirmity), but which lead to several hearings before the highest court in the land, the Law Lords. Mr Justice Steyn, in his judgement on the first occasion that the case went to the House of Lords, found that Pinochet was liable for extradition to stand trial for crimes committed upon the people of Chile during the period of his dictatorship. In his ruling, he made an interesting and important analogy which resonates across the years. He said, in effect, that he found that the plaintiff's case was not sound because were it to be sound then, by implication, Nuremberg would have been a mistrial.[30] A less well-known American case of 1980 had several common features and, it will be argued in Chapter 5, possibly as great importance as the Pinochet extradition, given that it occurred within the American jurisdiction.

Both the Filartiga and the Pinochet cases helped to establish something, which seemed deeply antipathetic to the post-French Revolutionary European order. They establish that sovereignty is conditional. Indeed, it has always been so in principle, although less so in practice until recently. Hence, inevitably, the decisive unit of concern moves from the group to the individual: from Rousseau's General Will to Kant's Categorical Imperative.

We have seen in many countries (although Britain is one that is prominent) a move during the interregnum for the activation and, where necessary, prior incorporation into national law, of statutes which oblige the observation of human rights. In October 2000, Britain placed the Human Rights Act on the Statute Book. It is going to have enormous implications for the way in which both legal and legislative procedures are conducted within the English jurisdiction. The rising tide of these cosmopolitan, transcending forces is the second element, and will return as a repeated point of reference and contention in subsequent chapters.

The third element is that we live in a world where actors are important still, but not alone. Notable individuals, and states, make history in the traditional sense, but there are now *factors*, which are as powerful as such *actors*. The issue is taken up in more detail in Chapter 4; but one category may serve as illustration here.

In November 2000, the Hadley Centre for Climate Prediction and Research, which is part of the UK Meteorological Office, published a report on the most recent run of $HadCM^3$, the most sophisticated computer model of the world's natural and climatic systems, of which it is custodian. It offered a series of predictions about the continuing progress of global warming and climate change. What was notable about this report was that, for the first time, it has been possible to include the effects of the release of carbon dioxide in the modelling of possible climate change (a positive feedback). It showed that, on the present state of knowledge, by the 2080s we may be facing the prospect of massive dieback in the Amazonian rainforests, a loss of perhaps 5 per cent of the productivity of the North American grain lands, the food insurance policy of much of the rest of the planet, a mean temperature rise of up to six degrees centigrade, sea level rise of up to one metre and a number of other worrying predictions. These data also underlie the starkly more urgent tone of the third report of the Intergovernmental Panel on Climate Change, published in July 2001.[31]

These are factors. They are not produced by the actions of any single human being or state. They are a consequence of the way in which we live our lives, but they enter directly onto the scope of those who have to decide collective actions on behalf of us all and, as such, they provide the clearest illustration of the difficulty which inherited – and especially democratic – political processes experience in dealing with threats that do not arise from a specific and identifiable enemy. The problem is that the timescale for the action of environmental factors tends to be long and that the essential characteristic of contemporary foreign policy (again, particularly in democracies) is to *discount the future*. But, secondly, the action of environmental factors on security is not merely pervasive, acting as an accelerant of other more traditional sources of conflict, most commonly; it is also often unexpected in its nature. The best example of that is the way in which the release of chlorofluorocarbons (CFCs) (from refrigerants and, until they were banned, from aerosol propellants, etc.) through the stratospheric ozone layer is directly implicated in increasing skin cancer for humans, cataracts for sheep and killing of the phytoplankton in the southern oceans, thus depleting the very foundation of the food chain. In the case of CFCs, because the source of manufacture could be precisely identified, it was possible to produce a working diplomatic instrument – the Montreal Protocol – which has begun to have a demonstrable effect on the emission of the most harmful CFCs to the atmosphere by humanity.

But when that model of international negotiation and agreement was exported to the far more generalised problem of human action contributing to global climate change, through the emission of so-called 'greenhouse gases', the result was nowhere near as satisfactory. The UN Conference on the Environment held in Rio in 1992 set in place a diplomatic process that came to be called the Kyoto Protocol (after the city where it was given shape). The objective was to obtain general inter-state agreement to the observation of rules of emission of key greenhouse gases, notably carbon dioxide. After Kyoto, negotiating sessions were held in Buenos Aires and, in 2000, at The Hague, the process fell apart.

Analysts have argued that there were three good reasons why this outcome was to be expected. First, that the model of negotiation was an adaptation of arms control, as conducted between the superpowers during the Cold War and this was not necessarily a transferable model. Second, Professor Richard Cooper argued that no agreement has been successfully negotiated where there has been fundamental disagreement about what the aims are that are being sought, or about the means that should be employed to achieve them: and in the climate negotiations of the 1990s neither of these was in agreement. Third, as Dr David Victor has shown, not only was there no agreement about ends or means, but within the terms of an emission-controlling regime there was belief that there was unfairness between the standards applied to different countries. Notably, this referred to the fact that Russia and Ukraine stood to gain huge amounts of money for doing nothing other than having experienced the collapse of their Soviet economies. Under a regime of so-called 'emissions trading', their 1990 benchmarks were set at pre-collapse levels; so their ecological virtuousness thereafter (and scope for selling emission 'entitlements') was more apparent than real. United

Germany has benefited similarly from unification with the formerly hugely polluting DDR.[32]

What is noteworthy is to see that diplomacy instinctively reached into the traditional security arena for a template for negotiation, flawed as it has turned out to be. It is hardly surprising and is politically an obvious choice, because if an issue – any issue – is 'securitised' then it is given immediate priority over other issues in normal politics. The attempt – and by and large the failure – to 'securitise' the environment is, therefore, a particularly relevant case for study if the role of factors is likely to increase in the global political agenda, as is being suggested here. Professor Buzan captured the conundrum most precisely.[33] The political benefit of 'securitising' an issue, he noted, is that it leapfrogs the queue to the top of the political issue list. But 'securitisation', Buzan argued, unavoidably brings two consequences: first, that it is necessary to invoke fear of the issue being 'securitised' and, second, that it is necessary to empower the state as the prime actor of response, given that in societies with efficiently functioning governments the state has a monopoly in the control of armed force. By preference, he suggested, one would wish to deal with issues in the realm of normal politics without having to pay those two costs; but precisely because of the frustrating lack of progress in the large negotiating arena of the Kyoto process, many analysts, persuaded of the special importance of the environment as a security threat, were prepared to make the claim for special priority. In the process, claims that there was already evidence of the environment as a direct cause of security problems were made, for which the evidence was not persuasive on closer examination. So, the wider political community felt that the entire case for taking environmental threats seriously might be set aside, whereas those who were passionately committed to the overriding importance of environmental issues felt increased alienation and frustration, to the point (in certain tiny minorities) of engaging in terroristic violent action to promote their point of view.[34]

Whilst there are these large-scale factors, which seem so far distant from us as individuals, the fourth and last element that will compose this future history is that each of us as individuals lives in *new risk environments*. Here is a paradox. As individuals, those of us who live in the rich world are much less likely to face the horrors of war in the traditional sense, the killing sense, through soldiers and through concentration camps, than was the case with our grandparental, or great-grand-parental generations. But we also live in what the German sociologist, Ulrich Beck, called a new risk society.

We live in a world with BSE, with AIDS, with pervasive pollution which may have effects on us somatically as individuals which we do not know and, crucially, cannot control. We live in these threat environments in an intensively information-rich way, because we know about these things in theory and in principle. We can know about them in that way, but live in constant vague fear of the particular, when the general strikes us or our loved ones.

A consequence of this circumstance is that it produces what is often called the 'empowered single actor'. It means that individuals actually have more ability to affect and shape their destinies if they live in the one-third of the rich world than has been the case, perhaps for ever before. We also see the proliferation of non-state actors, where individuals who are concerned about the environment, for example, pay their subscriptions to Greenpeace, which then becomes an active and potent political force. Or those who are concerned about other primary, single issues but who are not concerned about the wider spectrum of social behaviour, also devote all of their energies to single causes. The contrast between the pervasive fear of terrorism and the reality of its threat to any given individual is another case in point. It influences the balance of judgement about both the relative importance and the balance of effort to be devoted to this threat in societies which feel themselves at risk. It is a fragmentary, fragmenting view of what society might be.[35] A further type of evidence which supports the opinion that, in their perceived risk environments, individuals value political society less is the trend across the mature democracies for participation in elections to decline, for single-issue candidates and parties to thrive relative to established, broad-spectrum parties, and for such parties to gravitate towards a less ideologically defined, more functional, consumer-oriented common norm. The 2000 Presidential election in the US and the June 2001 British general election both illustrated most of these forms of political behaviour.

These four elements – dialectical and transcending forces, the role of factors and the new risk environment – are useful indicators which will help us as we try to understand this new terrain into which we move, a terrain from which neither war nor violence has been abolished. It may have been pushed out of our immediate environment – we are statistically much less likely to face again the sort of threat which, unbeknown, we all faced during the Able Archer incident of November 1983 – but we nonetheless find ourselves confronted by a series of choices.

The actions which will increase or decrease the risks to us all will depend tremendously upon the degree to which – and the manner in which – individuals are capable of mobilising their own sense of responsibility for those beyond themselves. Garrit Hardin first stated the Tragedy of the Commons: where each goat herder maximises his own short-term security by increasing his herd size regardless, the subsequent erosion from over-grazing not only destroys his neighbours' livelihoods, but also his own. Looking after yourself and looking after no-one else will be a self-defeating activity in this interconnected and interactive world. The Hadley Centre report on climate change made that plain. In short, an agenda of political obligation is coming to supersede one animated by a concern for rights alone.[36]

When Jan Bloch looked into the future one hundred years ago, he thought that, with the application of reason, we might expect the abolition of war and a realm of perfect peace. He did not really expect that to happen because Bloch made three predictions in his book of 1898. First, that war, if it came, would be exactly as it was when it did. It would be massive, it would be bloody, it would be indecisive. The battles of the First World War would never decide the political issues, because he predicted, second, that if people were foolish enough to engage this new destructive capability then the ending of their conflicts would be brought about not on the battlefield but by the social collapse of the competing societies.

> Nothing will be demonstrated by the next war if it is made, in spite of warnings, but the impossibility of making war except, of course, for the purposes of self-destruction . . . it is impossible for the modern State to carry on war under the modern conditions with any prospect of being able to carry that war to a conclusion by defeating its adversary by force of arms on the battlefield. No decisive war is possible.

So indeed it was proved as well, with the breaking of five empires (Ottoman, Russian, German, French and, ultimately, British). And he made a third prediction. He predicted *that he would not be believed*: 'No doubt the nations may endeavour to prove that I am wrong, but you will see what will happen.'[37]

Our responsibility is to remember that third warning and to ensure that for us and for our children it will not be the fire next time. In order to do this, the next necessary task is to take a closer look at the ways in which the Cold War experience shaped not only our world materially, but especially our ways of looking at the world, which is the subject of the next chapter.

2 Cold Wars

The phantom menace: Part I?

The Fellowship of the Ring endured many frightful horrors. Weak and vulnerable before the guile and the armed legions of the evil empire of Mordor, the gentle, unassuming yeoman Frodo and his servant Sam, frail but brave companions, struggled to Mount Doom in the very heart of the empire of the Dark Lord Sauron, to cast the Ring of Power into the fires of the volcano. Once this ring was destroyed, the power of the Dark Lord would be destroyed with it. And so it came about.

A desperate battle was being fought at the walls of Mordor. The outnumbered and exhausted armies of the West (yes, indeed, that is what the author of *The Lord of the Rings* called them) faced defeat and annihilation. But at the very moment when the lonely hero succeeded in destroying the ring, it was as if a cloud lifted. The armies of darkness fell into confusion, their soldiers attacking each other; their airforce – the hideous flying fiends, the Nazgul – fell out of the sky; the Towers of the Teeth crumbled and collapsed into dust, as did the Dark Tower itself, from which the spirit of the Dark Lord flew up in despair to fizzle out in the sky. From all the titanic stone and steel of the evil empire, all that remained was piles of rubble and dust.

It is not odd that thinking about the nature of the Cold War gravitates easily towards the realm of fantasy and science fiction. That being so, an awkward but important task is to distinguish between phantoms and substance in judging the implications for global security of the strange, almost surreal, Cold War, both then and now.

So much of the later Cold War – era of the Strategic Defense Initiative (colloquially and logically called 'Star Wars') – seemed to draw its direct inspiration from science fiction. But it is the manner of the ending of the Cold War, which most arrestingly recalls the climax of the grandfather of all fantasy tales, J.R.R. Tolkien's vast moral fable of the remorseless battle between good and evil. This is therefore the place to begin in offering a balance sheet ten years on.[1]

The early winter days when the Berlin Wall was breached and when incredulous crowds, intoxicated with the spirit of that momentous time, flooded through the breach, has become – rightly – iconic in modern European memory. Tolkein's imaginary Towers of the Teeth were visibly concrete by the Brandenburg Gate, and they literally cracked before people's eyes. These were events that invited commensurately excited and complete explanations: such decisive endings are not common.

Therefore, when the German author, Günther Grass, dared to question the wisdom of the rush to German reunification, which shortly followed, calumny was poured upon him. He related an experience when a young man accosted him in a railway station, accusing him of being a traitor to the Fatherland; someone whose sort should be wiped out. Grass – the German author who more than anyone else has been responsible for forcing a confrontation with the hijacking of the German language during the Nazi period – described the chill which fell upon him to hear the reiteration of old phrases from young lips. 'I do not care to be,' he commented, 'a member of a society whose well-being involves the likes of me being exterminated.' A decade later, there may be both a wider and more chastened audience for Grass's words of those high days. But, at that time, the crackling enthusiasm was understandable and laudable, even if the murky sentiments to which it gave rise were not. They fitted with the spirit of the times (and the frosty weather). For there was no shortage of grand declarations at the end of the Cold War, and not only at railway stations in North Germany.

The first grand declaration was that with these events history had come to an end, if history was understood to refer to the wrestling match between opposites. The combination of different shades of liberal democracy with the globalisation of free market economics was henceforth a given, a benchmark, the Greenwich meridian of future political navigation. There were no more great ideological debates to be had. Henceforth, the task of politics would be to fine tune the motor of history to run more smoothly, not choosing the direction in which the vehicle would go. It was a victory indeed: the Third World War had been fought and won, bloodlessly, but a victory nonetheless. (This image was first proposed by Barry Buzan, and remains most closely associated with him.)

The second grand declaration was of the implications of the ending of the Cold War for the future of major war. From the moment when industrialisation consummated its union with rampant nationalism, to spawn in the shipyards and factories of late nineteenth-century Europe the armadas and armies, which clashed in the European civil war that began in 1914, there had seemed to be no prospect of escape from under their shadow. In between wars ('peacetime'), they burdened the shoulders of those trying to remake civil society after the last war; in wartime, their appetites were omnivorous.

After 1945, the fighting armies of the mid-century were, in due turn, transformed into the standing armies of the Cold War. These armies stood to attention, but did not fight. When the reason and the physical ground of their confrontation were taken from them after 1990, they began to fade. In the Soviet case, the vast Red Army did not so much fade as implode. Once the federal state, whose command economy had permitted the so-called 'warranty' system under which the Red Army procured weapons, was fractured, neither the army nor its procurement structure could survive.[2]

A third grand declaration was more morally ambivalent. It was the inverse of Buzan's bloodlessly won war and is the one of concern here. It asks the question which the rest of this chapter seeks to answer. The Cold War had been the period of the Long Peace. What had maintained that peace was explained very differently. Some favoured the view that the benign terror of nuclear weapons was restraining pent-up aggression. Others argued that actually neither of the superpowers had either the desire or stomach for a fight. Yet others took a middle course, arguing that the full spectrum of military capacity in the gigantic frozen posture of the central front should be given credit for it: not just – or even mainly – nuclear weapons. But, whatever the reason, all agreed that war had been avoided to the point that both sides could now be stood down. An inter-system stand-off, etched in military inertia, was described, and morally less committed than the first view: an historical judgement from the same pragmatic stable as the policy of recognising spheres of influence and seeking *détente*. If one side of the ambivalence tilted towards the judgement that the waste of resources implied in huge standing military establishments was justified by the result which their deployment produced, the other tilted towards outrage at the lost opportunities implied in a monstrous and wasteful arms race. But war had not come back to Cold War Europe.

The issue of opportunity/cost choice, raised by the critics of the arms races, illuminates immediately the question in the title of this chapter. To what extent was this a phantom menace, as to so many it appeared to be, looking back upon the European experience of 1945 to 1990 when no war in Europe happened? There are five categories of substance.

First, the Cold War only looks like a phantom menace if one's gaze is confined to the northern hemisphere. The proxy wars, which the superpowers supported and sustained, which were fought in other places – Korea, Vietnam, Cambodia, Angola, Nicaragua and the like – were bloodily substantial. Not only were these wars real and greedy for lives, but they were somehow linked in a grisly chain.[3]

Within the 6,000 words of his long telegram of 1946, George Kennan captured the essence of the view that the Soviet Union was no normal state, with which one could conduct normal diplomacy. It was, by ideological bent and totalitarian frame, irrepressibly expansionist, and therefore could only be dealt with by a policy of robust containment.[4] That view of the Soviet Union not only validated the forging of the ring of steel, that was given substance in NATO and in the nuclear arsenals; it also fed into the cruder stereotypes of the domino theory of world communist expansion, held by such as Eisenhower's Secretary of State, John Foster Dulles. The world communist enterprise would permit no political vacuums: therefore, distasteful as might be the regime of Singman Rhee in South Korea, it had to be supported to prevent the communists winning the whole peninsula: if the French went down to defeat at Dien Bien Phu in 1953 to the armies of General Giap, America must step into the vacuum in Vietnam, else the Chinese arm of world communism would prevail there.

By the time that the US had run the course of its Vietnamese nemesis, John Caldwell, the CIA Station Chief in Luanda, who saw something of the complication that was on the ground in Africa and who therefore pleaded otherwise, told us that it was directly in contemplation of the concealed but *de facto* defeat of the Treaty of Paris that Henry Kissinger identified Angola as the next ground upon which to confront the Soviet Union and its allies (in this case Cuba). And so the chain of proxy wars gained more links. If the Soviets were foolish enough to invade Afghanistan, then the *mudjahadeen* Islamic Fundamentalists, and Osama bin Laden, became the natural allies of the West: my enemy's enemy is my friend. *Pari passu*, a raft of dubious and distasteful South American generals and their friends. 'Authoritarian' was not the same as 'totalitarian', explained Richard Nixon in *Six Crises* – a point repeated by Ambassador Jeanne Kirkpatrick, one of the toughest and most intellectually consistent of the cold warriors, as President Reagan's Ambassador to the United Nations.[5]

So, the Cold War was no phantom for its victims in the battlefields of the Third World; nor was it a bloodless war. These were fatally hot wars, engendered by a frozen parent. How much of a phantom was it in its home ground of the nuclear confrontation? The second category. The case looks more compelling, at first glance; for by the end nothing bad had happened to the West, it appeared.

For many in the West, if they cared to think about it, reliance upon making an apocalyptic nuclear threat was morally uncomfortable at the very least. The squaring of this circle gave rise to a quasi-theological literature, which, in the delicacy of its constitution, is to be compared with those school men of the Middle Ages who debated how many angels might dance on the head of a pin. Perhaps, it was suggested by Cardinal Basil Hume in a letter to *The Times* on 7 November 1983 (a week after one of our closest shaves with nuclear death, as is now known but was not then), moral purity could be preserved by an inward reservation, whereby one confirmed to oneself one's certain knowledge that the threat of nuclear use that was publicly articulated was one that would never be executed? Cardinal Hume conceded that 'to condemn all use and yet to accept deterrence places us in a seemingly contradictory position'.[6]

Such contortions stood in contrast (as we now know) to a more straightforward and, in some ways, brutally practical consideration of nuclear weapons in the Soviet Union. There, no distinction was made between them and any other form of weaponry. This was just bigger artillery – artillery which Stalin called the prince of arms. Therefore, the western theology of a 'nuclear deterrence' had no equivalence. Ironically, only in the post-Cold War period has post-communist Russia come to adopt ideas about the possession and threat of use of nuclear weapons, which ape those held by the West in the Cold War.

Yet in that convoluted argument a consoling final line frequently observed that, whereas it should be conceded that the effect of nuclear threat could be neither proven nor disproven, it was best understood through the analogy of an insurance policy. One paid one's premium against an event which one hoped would not occur. If that event did not occur then at least the payment had done no harm.

The phantom claim is disproven even here. The concrete effects of the Cold War were not only those so bloodily visible at other people's expense in the proxy wars; they were also in the real threats that lay in potential misunderstanding and possible use between the nuclear powers themselves. The case of this, which comes at once to mind, is of course the Cuban missile crisis of 1962. It was a confrontation of which the general public was acutely aware at the time, and that was part of the context of its successful resolution. Eyeball-to-eyeball, Kennedy and Khruschev stared it out and, in the end, the Russians blinked.

The carefully self-aware conduct of the crisis by Kennedy's celebrated and cerebral group of advisers in the ExComm is often offered as model for the successful management of negotiation under extreme threat and pressure. The most dangerous day of the missile crisis was Saturday 27 October 1962. The missile bases on Cuba were under construction around the clock; and on that day, a U-2 spy-plane was shot down by the Soviets over Cuba, killing the pilot, Major Anderson. The published transcripts of the ensuing discussion in the ExComm show how the group thought its way through the possible sequence of events that might lead to an escalation beyond control, should the US be obliged to attack Cuba. The Secretary of Defense, Robert McNamara, reasoned that a Soviet strike on US Jupiter missiles in Turkey was the most likely response to an attack on Cuba; and that, therefore, to defuse the missiles in Turkey – letting Khruschev know – reduced the chance of that military action.[7]

In the event, there was no attack on Cuba, and subsequent information has shown how doubly fortunate that was; for, whereas the ExComm had accurately guessed Khruschev's probable response – he would have sanctioned the attack on Turkey as the least that would satisfy his military commanders – the other working assumption of that fateful Saturday is now known to have been false. Speaking in June 2001, McNamara related how Admiral Dennison, in overall command of US forces, had requested the release of nuclear weapons to US forces because of information that the Soviets now had deployed nukes in the missile bases. The request was denied by ExComm because the CIA stated that the nuclear warheads were coming on a ship, but were not yet present. In fact, McNamara relates, this information was incorrect: there were scores of tactical nuclear weapons on Cuba on 27 October. Had the pre-emptive non-nuclear air-strikes being contemplated on that day actually occurred, the consequences could indeed have been nuclear. In the event, the Turkish missile gambit provided Khruschev with a golden bridge across which he could retreat without complete loss of face, thereby ending the crisis. Throughout, the signals that were sent by the movement of military forces were largely under political control, and only really became dangerous when they were no longer so. Thus the

US Navy began, on its own authority, to track and flush to the surface Soviet submarines in the Atlantic once the alert status had been raised to one in which such activities were deemed (by it) to be appropriate. This was done without the knowledge of the higher political authorities and created great fear and consternation when it became known to them. Here again, amazing good fortune attended us. When he visited Moscow in 2001 to attend the screening of *Thirteen Days*, McNamara reported that he met there the Soviet submarine brigade commander who had been in charge of the submarines that the US Navy was flushing to the surface. He told the former Secretary that there had been four submarines on station, and that each carried one atomic torpedo. Here again, McNamara suggested, we were closer to the edge than we thought, even at the time.[8] But, arguably, the moment of most material and mortal threat to survival during the Cold War is much less well known. It came much later, in November 1983, at the depth of the second Cold War.

Two procedures collided: on the western side, 'Able Archer' is the code name of a regularly repeated NATO command post exercise to rehearse nuclear release procedures. On the Soviet side, from 1981 to 1984, under Operation RYAN, initiated by its Chief, Yuri Andropov, the KGB had instructed operatives to keep special watch for signs of western mobilisation. It was top priority in 1982. Now promoted to General Secretary, Andropov's anxieties were further inflamed in 1983 by the escalating sequence of Reagan's Orlando speech about the Evil Empire on 8 March, his 'Star Wars' announcement on 23 March, and, on 1 September, the shooting down of the Korean airliner KAL-007 trespassing over a Soviet missile submarine bastion. RYAN was given further increased priority. The sick and failing Andropov took a morbidly apocalyptic view. In November 1983, US bases were already on heightened alert following the bombing of the Marines' barracks in Lebanon. Russian expectation (conveyed in documents leaked by Oleg Gordievsky) was that a preemptive nuclear attack would most likely be initiated under cover of a military exercise. 'Able Archer' took place from 2–11 November 1983 in a context of high Soviet anxiety about American intentions.

In response, major elements of Soviet forces in the Group of Soviet Forces (Germany) and elsewhere, including nuclear forces, went onto alert. On 14 November, the first of the Cruise and Pershing II missile deployments to Europe arrived in the UK. Robert Gates (later Director of the CIA) reports all this and a British intelligence assessment, reviewing information supplied by its source, Gordievsky, that 'Able Archer' gave rise to exceptional anxiety within the Warsaw Pact and that they were not crying wolf. Yet, at the time, US intelligence failed to grasp that fact. 'Able Archer' *plus* RYAN *plus* US ignorance of the former's effect on Soviet paranoia made 1983 the most dangerous year, in Mr Gates's opinion, which, it might be agreed, is an opinion worth taking seriously.[9] Nor does the case rest only upon the two close shaves. Whereas the political and psychological conditions that brewed up the Cuban missile and 'Able Archer' crises have dispersed, the physical legacy of the superpower nuclear arms race has not, and, in truth, cannot without huge investment. All nuclear weapons states, large and small, are saddled with a waste disposal problem, but none is as large and pregnant with danger as the legacy of the Soviet military nuclear programmes.

During the Cold War the overriding imperative of speed resulted in at least one massive radiation accident. It was in a radioactive waste storage facility at Kyshtym, killing scores of people and contaminating sixty-five km^2 of land.[10] However, the future focus of threat lies on, around and in the Kola Peninsula, the Kara, Barents and White seas of the Russian North-West.

The Kola Peninsula contains the greatest concentration of *latent* potential for catastrophic release of radioactivity on the planet. The courageous Yablokov 'White Book' audit of 1993, ordered by President Yeltsin, opened the issue for scrutiny. There are more operating and defunct reactors sited here than anywhere else (178 and above 140 [the Yablokov figure], respectively). The USSR built 287 nuclear submarines, containing over 500 reactors, between 1954 and 1996, of which a minimum of 183 and perhaps as many as 245 are now out of service. Of those, at least 120 still have fuelled reactors. The Northern Fleet has 142 subs and three battle-cruisers (300 plus reactors) in or out of service. Then there are ten ice-breakers and a container ship. The tally known now counts, in addition to the queue of superannuated nuclear submarines and other ships awaiting disposal, sixteen dumped reactors, including six with unrecovered fuel from nuclear accidents, such as overtook the icebreaker *Lenin*, an overflowing abundance of spent nuclear fuel (SNF) needing containment, of which 10 per cent is damaged (Yablokov counted 30,000 assemblies containing 2.3 million curies of radioactivity in 1993). Then there is the Kola power station.

Of its four VVER 440/230 and 440/213 type reactors, the older pair (440/230) are judged by the IAEA to have a 25 per cent likelihood of critical failure in the next twenty years. There is no containment. This is the power station which powers the pumps that cool the shut-down submarine reactors that await decommissioning and disposal. When the utility company cut the Navy off for non-payment of bills a few years ago, Marines with balaclavas and sub-machine guns appeared to help change its mind. A new Kola station is planned. In a comprehensive review of radioactive sources in the Kola/Barents area, the Swedish Defence Research Agency (FOA) prepared a risk ladder. The current Kola station comes top (in red letters), followed by a refuelling accident with current submarines, the masses of ill-contained or audited SNF and then the armada of dead submarines.

This situation is directly a product of the segmented, sequential myopia which has been a general characteristic of nuclear industries. They tend to think in straight lines, and then only about the bits that they like, rather than of full-life cycles, unless forced to do so. The Russians are shocking exponents of this approach. Only now, with the dead armada swelling, is the Rubin Design Bureau, whose gifted engineers helped to build the Soviet submarine fleet, including the ill-fated Oscar II class *Kursk* which crashed in 2000, being asked to undesign them. This work has been given to the Nuclear Special Purpose Submarine Department under Yevgeni Gorigledzhan.

In addition to dealing with fresh materials, much previous work has to be redone, because such short-term provision for storage of SNF as has been built has been much reduced by past accidents which only came to light in the Yablokov report. Two storage ponds in Building 5 at the Murmansk naval facility at Andreyeva Bay had to be abandoned in 1982 because poor construction had led to huge leakage: cracked concrete; failed welds. It was not helped by dropping fuel rods (120 in total) onto the pond floor. V. Bulygin was made a Hero of the Soviet Union for leading its retrieval. Today, Building 5 can only be approached in a goon suit. The storage pool and Dry Dock SD-10 constructed at Gremikha, failed too, for similar reasons. The Bellona Foundation has evidence that drunkenness in the work-force prevented repair. So SNF has been left in TK-11 and TK-12 type transit flasks; but they leaked. (New ones [TUK-18] are being made, but the design is criticised.) Or stored in the eleven Northern Fleet service tenders. Four (in Murmansk and Severodvinsk) give special cause for concern, being over twenty-five years old and filled to capacity. One, the *Lepse* in Murmansk harbour, is so contaminated that it is singled out by FOA as a prime risk, and is now to be tackled by a French consortium. But with nowhere better to put the stuff, all these old, badly-maintained barges are candidates for future acciden-tal releases. Replacements of the Type 2020 'Malina' class are slow in building for lack of funds. Much SNF stands, inadequately shielded,

on the quayside – 700 fuel assemblies in 110 defective TK-11 contain-
ers at Gremikha, for over thirty years, for example.

The block decommissioning of the Soviet fleet is producing
increasing volumes of fresh SNF, at least thirty cores-worth a year,
like the brooms activated by the sorcerer's apprentice. The government is committed to decommissioning 150 submarines by 2007. The
present least-bad option appears to be to leave the fuel in the shut-
down reactors, in the hulks. But left too long, the fuel channels in the
reactors may distort and defuelling becomes impossible, making it
necessary to dispose of fuelled reactors. Also, unmaintained, the submarine hulls corrode and some have sunk at their moorings, needing
then to be salvaged and propped up with pontoons. Minatom reports
thirty to be at imminent risk of sinking. Seventeen 'November' and
'Victor' class hulks at Gremikha are too dangerous to tow.[11]

Especially since, at the time of writing, there is little confidence
that a safe and comprehensive national or international programme
to stabilise and manage these materials can be agreed, the Soviet
military nuclear legacy remains a material, not an imaginary threat of
the first order to the security of the northern hemisphere. After 11
September 2001, its ability to provide unconditional terrorists with
radioactive material has leapt to public attention; and some of the
funding cuts in American assistance ordered by the incoming Bush
Administration have been reversed.

The third concrete effect, produced by the Cold War, that was
decidedly not a phantom, was the manner in which it froze and prolonged the inter-state conflicts of the early twentieth century, not so
much in the familiar terms of the ideological confrontation that was
so publicly visible during that time, but more through the manner in
which conflict was locked into the format of *inter-state* confrontations. The Soviet Union and its successor states have clung to the
inviolability of their state sovereignty. No better illustration of this
pernicious consequence of the Cold War could be found than President's Yeltsin's slurred public recollection that Russia possessed a
full arsenal of nuclear weapons at the time of strong external criticism of Russia's conduct in the bloody suppression of the irredentist
movements of Chechnya in the autumn of 1999. In paraphase of Dr
Johnson's observation about patriotism, angry assertion of the inviolability of state sovereignty is the last refuge of a scoundrel. Societies
with weak or collapsed state structures tend to correlate strongly
with those that assert their rights of sovereign independence most
insistently, which points towards the fourth concrete effect of the
Cold War.

This has been the obverse of the third: masked and, in substantial ways, obstructed recognition of new threats to security than those emerging from its own narrow confines; and – more positively – in recognising the proliferation of new agents of legitimate political power, which has been one of the most striking characteristics of the end of the twentieth century. The superpower confrontation had an embracing grandeur about itself, which tended to absorb and organise other agents within its own view of the world. Thus, for example, the early debate about the influence of multinational companies fell for twenty years into an academic equivalent of the proxy wars that disfigured so much of the poor world. By the same token, non-state actors concerned with human rights or environmental issues, for example, were also subjected to the same caustic assay to discover whether they were with us or against us: Greenpeace was an Anglo-Saxon conspiracy when protesting about French nuclear tests in the Pacific, a new leftist expression of anti-Americanism when protesting about logging or nuclear dumping in the American West, and a tentacle of American power when reaching out to raise awareness about the nightmare of nuclear dumping by the Soviet Union in the Russian North-West. The Cold War delayed a fundamental assessment of the nature of the legitimacy of such organisations by many years. That has had to wait upon the reawakening of cosmopolitan political thought.[12]

Susan Strange wrote out the charge sheet in her final and posthumously published essay. The Westphalia System – taken as a shorthand for the international system of states – would have been better named as 'Westfailure': it failed, she argued, on three counts. It failed in the elementary duty of care to citizens of the world, the democidal victims of their own pathological governments. It failed because of its inability to find a way to drive the twentieth-century world economy efficiently or safely, controlling only the brake and the accelerator and not the steering wheel; and, third, it failed in the terrain of interest to some of the most lively of the new political actors. The state system, she suggested, has failed in its duty of care towards the protection of the global natural environment.[13]

In this sense, we may judge the material consequence of the Cold War to have been actively dangerous in a further respect. On top of the actual threat, which materialised in the superpower nuclear confrontations of 1962 and 1983, and persisting latent threat in the nuclear materials themselves, the preoccupation with a militarised interpretation of the ideological dispute between the superpowers obscured both identification of and early action upon the insidious and proliferating range of new security threats, which crowded in at the turn of the century. This is where it is important to recall that Cold Wars – plural – are our concern in this chapter.

Arguably, one of the most paradoxical consequences of the Cold War has been its disturbing effect upon the lenses through which security is viewed and conceptualised. It is paradoxical because it has had effects that rank among both the most damaging and persisting, and among the most creative and encouraging, in reaction. In this sense, Cold War (substantial and singular) spins off a mental picture of itself which, hermeneutically, takes on an active form: the Cold War of the Mind, hence, Cold Wars (plural) in the title of this chapter.

To understand the significance of this, first, Strange's point is to be taken. The Cold War both froze and prolonged, in increasingly brittle form, a fly-blown fiction of the uncontested and pervasive primacy of state power. In practice, this forced prolongation pushed the dialectical effect. On one group it served to further normalise, structure and confirm a state-dominated framework of analysis, but, on another and much more amorphous and wider community, it had quite the opposite effect.

Among the most grievously wounded were scholars of international relations – and even more their pupils, who were defence-less to know better – who organised their analyses around an asserted principle of Realism (its short-hand form usually genuflect-ing towards the works of Morgenthau and Waltz, for top cover). Many still do. A conversation with this literature in its own terms is undertaken in Chapter 4. But observations about the wider impact of that enterprise, not in its own terms, are necessary also – and they find their place here.

It has been rightly observed that disputes among academics are more vituperative, viciously pursued and deeply-felt than most between professional colleagues, because so little is at stake. George Steiner is Cambridge's most influential scholar of literature in modern times. His rejection and denial of tenure by the lesser lights of the Faculty of English was a *cause célèbre* of the 1960s, although consistent with the earlier treatment of the world-famous F.R. Leavis and the later ejection of the leading scholar of mass media, Colin McCabe. Steiner famously observed, in a phrase that infuriated exponents of literary criticism, but which is equally as applicable to academic analysts of international affairs, 'When the literary critic looks over his shoulder he sees a eunuch's shadow.' IR was heavily thought-policed during the depths of the Cold War. So the impetus to innovation frequently had to come from outside the phalanx.

Hylke Tromp was in the forefront of those students of international affairs most associated with the peace movement who, in the 1980s, refused to accept the cruder Realist terms within which much analysis and most public debate was cast. Like E.P. Thompson in Britain, Tromp insisted upon both the responsibility of the scholar for the effects of his utterances on others and upon the deadly seriousness of finding intellectually firm and independent foundations for analysis. These foundations, he (and Thompson) believed, were to be frankly informed by worst case assumptions about the potential *use* of nuclear explosives: neither had much truck with the casuistry of nuclear deterrence theory. In one memorable essay, Tromp wrote of 'scientists in orbit' to describe those who fell for this seduction.

Thompson was the founder of the modern study of social history in Britain, with his masterpiece *The Making of the English Working Class* in 1968. He had already ejected himself from a conventional university career, resigning from the University of Warwick because of disagreement with the commercialisation of higher education. He entered battle with the security academics as a proud and total outsider. He answered the security challenge posed by the falling temperatures of the Cold War after 1979, by being almost wholly propelled out of his historical researches for a time. He waded into political activism – through speeches and some of the finest pamphleteering seen in politics since the eighteenth century – and became one of the founders and leaders, along with Mary Kaldor, Dan Smith and others, of END (European Nuclear Disarmament). In contrast, Tromp retained a strong (although not uncontentious) footing in university research and teaching as Director of the Polemological Institute at the University of Groningen in the Netherlands, while also having, at key times, a high and controversial profile in the media.[14]

The orbiting ideas to which Tromp took exception appear all the stranger in retrospect. The attempt to produce a systematic taxonomy of international affairs was odd in the first place. Here was an enterprise in historical analysis, which seemed to claim a higher degree of explanatory power than the ordinary, professionally competent historian might care to hazard from such observations: too much deduction and not enough solid evidence. Here was an enterprise in social observation and explanation, which seemed to claim a quasi-scientific status. Indeed, part of its claim was an ability to predict and to shape the behaviour of enemies.

To all of this, the vast and seemingly immovable contrasts of the

Cold War seemed to provide evidence and certainly gave intellectual comfort. There were many questionable aspects of the manner in which realist analysis was hitched to the wheels of the Cold War. The Cold War, by its militarised nature, invited confusion between tactical and strategic analysis. It is true that the specialised circumstances of combat permits the extraction of principles (such as Clausewitzian 'friction') which apply regardless of culture, time or technology, when battle occurs. They are among the subjects of Part II. But it is a cardinal error to believe that such principles translate out of their context. Realist values and methods predisposed users to be vulnerable, too easily, to tumbling into that confusion.

The fact that nuclear weapons were so closely interwoven with the rhetoric and the symbols of the Cold War confrontation, promoted that confrontation, naturally enough, to the very front line of concern. Survival was at stake, and, in such circumstances, it is dangerous to allow hope, ideals or even the tiniest unrealised aspiration to cloud the clear, hard eye, its vision purified by a monkish intellectual asceticism that was essential for safety. Soft-heartedness or any taint of idealism might be a material danger to security. Better stick in this shell-hole, chum, until you are sure that you see a better one, was Sir Lawrence Martin's advice in his BBC Reith Lectures in 1981.[15] The Cold War and response of realist analysis to it lived in a comfortable symbiosis. The Cold War confrontation invited a sort of intellectual totalitarianism, which drew in the precision of military principles by association. In that way it might self-righteously squash attempts at more nuanced or distanced analysis, as witness Grass's encounter with the angry young man on a railway station after the fall of the Berlin Wall (see page 27). Now a decade later, when circumstance requires a modified form of power-political analysis, it is especially important to remember and to be warned by this past symbiosis.

The obverse of this necessarily, but not too much, abbreviated account of what happened to the mainstream of academic analysis was catalysis of a different view and a different political process: an excellently clear dialectic. Revulsion at the fact and potential of nuclear weapons – the sense that no human difference of opinion could possibly warrant such grotesque disproportionality in the making of threats – was the stimulus for many in democratic societies. But, largely unknown to them, a quite different dynamic was produced by counteraction to the Soviet system among people living under its power. It was Lech Walesa who observed that the principal effect of political education by communists was to ensure that while their food baskets might be empty, people's souls were filled with the exact

opposite of what their communist masters desired. To the founders of
Solidarity in Poland and the dissident leaders who kept the flame of
opposition burning in the countries of the Warsaw Pact during the
darkest hours of the 1980s, all credit is due. And this is denied by
none. But, by the same token, the effect of the international effort in
sustaining them should be praised, along with the valiant, often heroic
mission of the Scarlet Pimpernel philosophers of the Jan Hus Foundation, who crossed the Iron Curtain to conduct seminars in sitting
rooms in Prague, at risk to themselves and their students in the Underground University. In this work, domestic western differences of social
and political philosophy were transcended for a deeper purpose, a
point that is generously and affectionately made by one of the leading
lights of the enterprise, the prominent Conservative philosopher,
Roger Scruton, in a tribute to the prime mover of the Jan Hus Foundation, the left-wing philosopher, Kathy Wilkes.[16]

Those who stimulated and helped guide the spontaneous uprisings
of popular protest during the high days of the end of communism in
Central Europe have frequently referred to the inspiration they drew
from the sight of the huge public demonstrations of protest against
the continuation of the nuclear-laced Cold War confrontation. To
grant such credit to those whom politicians and Realist analysts in
the West at the time dismissed as useful fools of Stalin is still hard for
many who did not march through European capital cities, but rather
condemned the irresponsibility of the demonstrators.

I have a small personal recollection from that time: a transatlantic
conference in Washington to consider the implications of the successful installation of the Cruise and Pershing missiles. After the discussion, there was a quick summing up from each conference participant.
Repeated assertions of the fact that the Alliance had held firm in the
face of Moscow's agents: the systems had been installed. A triumph.
QED. Then, from a German officer with elevated responsibilities to
give strategic advice, the thoughtful observation that 'whereas we
may indeed have won the hardware battle, we have probably lost the
software battle', by which he meant the argument.[17]

So harsh and unyielding was the intellectual corset of Cold War
thought that enough people of sufficiently diverse identity were
shocked by it into a fundamental reconsideration of every part of its
assertions. There were – of course – those fellow travellers of the
Soviet Union in the West who would always hold a forgiving view,
and who sought and were paid and encouraged to seek the subversion of the popular movements of protest in the West, to Soviet ends.
They are conspicuous in their failure. What took root in the anti-

nuclear protests of the 1980s not only provided both inspiration and role model for the patient crowds of Protestant protesters who knelt before the East German soldiers in the last days of the DDR to register their dissent and for the subsequent demonstrations under the auspices of *Neues Forum*. It also fuelled directly the next wave of cosmopolitan and democratic modes of political expression: the environmental and human rights movements of the 1990s were their next direct successors.

In each case, the trajectory of human rights and environmental issues was sinuous and not without irony. Their origins were described in the previous chapter. What happened next? Human rights entered the Cold War history and political system under false colours.

The Helsinki principles were promoted for a multitude of motivations, no doubt; but a desire to use the concept of human rights as a stick with which to beat the Soviet Union was clearly one of them. If the intention had been entirely meanly framed, with the hope that the stick could be retained in the hands of the western powers alone, that illusion was soon dispelled. Citizens' groups, that equally had had their genesis in recoil at the horror and destruction of the World War, were swift to capitalise upon the advancement of the human rights issue by the great powers. Non-governmental organisations in the West, such as OXFAM – set up from a Christian commitment to the promotion of social justice and equal welfare – and Amnesty International – to protect critics of the Portuguese dictatorship in 1961, by keeping their cases in the public eye – were pervasive vectors carrying the human rights message in two directions. They educated engaged western public opinion, thus cultivating axia of commitment, which were among those that combined at the anti-nuclear moment in 1980–3.

The nature of the loose and iridescent coalition, which combined in the so-called 'peace movement', is obscured by the use of such a term. 'Movement' implies structure; whereas coalescence of interests, which came to critical mass and exploded in the vast, spectacular political illumination that was the world-wide anti-nuclear demonstrations of those years, is better understood by an analogy to the functioning of its atomic opponent. The infant western human rights movement spread outwards and through many windows. Some, such as Helsinki Human Rights Watch, were focused explicitly on the communist world. Now that the voices from the other side have spoken, the encouragement and example which this gave to the founders of Solidarity in Poland, of Charter 77 in Czechoslovakia, has been acknowledged. Indeed, in the most positive way, the sub-governmental contacts fed upon and nourished each other, each supporting the other symbiotically in their mould-breaking tendencies.

For the global human rights movements, the massacres in Tienanmen Square delivered a shocking opening to a decade of rapid growth. This growth was boosted by the telecommunications revolution which coincided with and facilitated it. Whereas the pro-democracy students in Tienanmen Square had relied upon a blizzard of fax messages to the outside world, which breached the walls of authoritarian communist China, the ability of the rights activists to pierce the walls of state sovereignty was revolutionised by the explosive growth of the World Wide Web in the industrialised world. By its origins and nature, the Web is anarchic – or more properly – self-organising. As one of its creators observed, 'Censorship is just perceived by the Web as a system fault around which it has to route.' Thus, although its points of entry from the poor world are few, once introduced into the system the proliferating effect in the wired world can be huge.[18]

The Chiapas rebellion in Mexico appears to have the honour of being the first human rights popular protest to have been both organised and publicised on the Internet and, thus fixed in the floodlights of world attention, to have been brought to an outcome. Looking back from a position where former dictators stand close to trial in order to face accusations of breach of human rights, one may wonder whether those anti-communist western diplomats who may have first thought to wheel the cannon of human rights onto the Cold War battlefield expected the initiative to have carried so far and with such dramatic consequences.

The other branch in the Cold War dialectic had an equally unexpected and somewhat different history. The intense illumination of the anti-nuclear moment coincided with the now well-documented and steady rise in public concern about global environmental stresses in many of the richer countries. Heightened awareness of the environment has occurred in three waves, each responding to slightly different sorts of stimulus. Rachel Carson's book *Silent Spring* raised awareness in the 1950s through her description of the effects of DDT insecticide on people and animals. This presented the environment as principally a pollution issue. Coincident with the oil price shocks, *The Limits to Growth* report of 1972 was an early attempt to represent feed-back effects within rather precise assumptions about the exhaustion of non-renewable resources that were uppermost in public concern at that time, and which proved to be incorrect. It was the first attempt at the direct 'securitisation' of the environment, and, whilst it was largely discredited in the eyes of mainstream politicians, it was influential in raising consciousness for the second wave of environmental activism. The energies released in the early 1980s flowed into the rapid growth during the rest of that decade of organisations such as Greenpeace International and Friends of the Earth. The logic, which might lead those concerned about nuclear weapons to hold also more comprehensive anxieties for the health of the planet, is straightforward to see.

What was not so obvious, until the revolutions of 1989 occurred, was the degree to which protest about gross environmental pollution served a triggering function for wider popular engagement in the revolutions which overthrew communism. In Hungary, the Duna Circle of intellectuals opposed to the construction of the Gabcikovo–Nagymaros Dam was one such catalyst; in both Bohemia and Slovakia gross environmental pollution – crippling smogs from the burning of brown coal and massively leaky and unsafe industrial plant – offered a legitimate focus of protest that was exploited by some, such as the late Josef Vavroušek, leader of the Czechoslovakian Greens and later Minister of the Environment in the Federal Czechoslovakian government.[19]

The discovery of this environmental concern behind the Iron Curtain was initially encouraging to the western Greens. Perhaps unexpected alliances could be exploited? It was a false dawn. As soon as other avenues of political expression opened, it appears that direct protest on environmental issues waned.[20] That said, the wholesale reconstruction and modernisation of eastern European industry has had an ameliorative effect. The removal of lignite smoke from the air of East Berlin and Prague by the substitution of natural gas was an early priority of post-communist governments. As explained in the previous chapter, the attempt to give political priority to the environment by arguing that it posed direct threats to state security failed at the second attempt also. We are now in a 'third wave' where environmental factors are not ruled out as direct causes of security crises, although not expected to be common. More frequently, the 'third wave' sees environmental factors as accelerants upon, engaged in synergistic feed-back with, other more traditional drivers of conflict.[21] While rapid improvement in understanding the science of global climate change occurred over the decade, expressed in the reports of the UN Intergovernmental Panel on Climate Change, which preceded the Rio and The Hague conferences, the attempt to negotiate global controls on emissions failed also, for reasons explained above (pp. 22–3). But whatever happens next in global environmental politics (which is not our subject here), none of these reverses detract from the motivating role of the Cold Wars. The relationship between these moments and forces is illustrated in Figure 2.1.

Therefore, at century's turn, in some ways the strongly catalytic role that environmental issues were seen to have among those over-throwing regimes in eastern Europe, and indeed more widely, has waned, whereas the concern for human rights has continued to wax

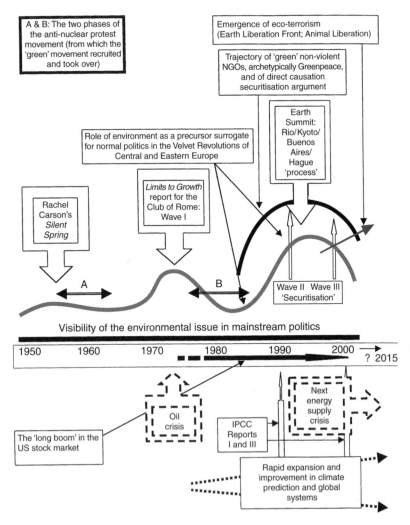

Figure 2.1 Environmental change and the re-structuring of international relations.

strongly. The emergence of both issues, in these proportions, may thus be seen as an unexpected but demonstrable consequence of the way in which the other Cold War – the Cold War of the mind – was presented and fought.

The final question in this chapter is to strike a balance of judgement about future prospects. The implication of what has just been suggested is that the mould of deeply, almost psychotically polarised presentation of opposites may have been broken. In the 1960s the psychoanalyst, Jerome Frank, was among the first to suggest that, given the apocalyptic nature of the nuclear threat, it was vital, for the maintenance of one's mental health, to possess an equally apocalyptic image of the enemy deserving of that dreadful fate. If this was the special cause, that cause is now removed. But there is another, more generalised line of argument, which suggests that, possibly regardless of cultures, people bond as groups and societies in adversity to others.

The evidence for this is copious. It includes the heroic: those who had the foresight, courage and moral fibre to create the European resistance movements to the Nazi occupation. It includes the benign: the evidence that conviviality blossomed among those who sought refuge in the London blitz by camping on the platforms in the deep tunnels of the London Underground. In each case, in material or abstract form, some Other provided the organising target against which collective identity could be constructed. The same phenomenon spreads into darker, violent and bloodstained channels. Jews or gypsies, blacks in Southern Africa, squatter farmers or rubber-tappers in the Brazilian rainforest – the list is endless.

The conquest of Peru in the 1530s shattered Inca society with the double devastation of smallpox and the sword. The manner in which the Spanish Conquistadors depersonalised and enslaved the Incas in the following decades only goes to confirm the notion that, while the Cold War paranoia may have been an extreme example, it was by no means unique; and it had an old parentage.[22]

The philosopher, Mary Midgley, wrote once, in sadly ironic vein, that humanity would only overcome the deep-set polarising aspect of how we perceive and organise our social relationship if the entire planet were seen and understood to be threatened from an extra-terrestrial cause.[23] Little green men from Mars were her candidate. There is, in fact, a whole genre of science fiction films which explores this theme. Some posit a coherent (and conveniently English-speaking) intelligence demanding something or other (the tiny galaxy hung around the cat's neck in the film *Men in Black*). Others fit more straightforwardly the Midgley thesis. Several posit rogue meteors, which can only be deflected by the combined (and therefore collaborative) use of the Cold War superpower nuclear arsenals to blast the object away. So, the theme is well-embedded in popular culture; and the evidence of the Cold Wars (both of them, and especially the War of the Mind) shows a dangerously comfortable fit with the human characteristic to bond in adversity to others.

Is the end of the Cold War, therefore, only the end of Part I, just as *Star Wars*, the movie, promises? Had the Austrians not lusted for war with Serbia; had the Germans not backed the Austrian demands; had the German Imperial General Staff possessed more realistic assessment of the technical competence of the Imperial Russian forces to mobilise than was actually the case; had (knowing the truth) the Russian generals not persuaded the last Tsar that his only option in response during the July crisis was full mobilisation or none; and finally had Archduke Ferdinand's chauffeur continued along the river bank in Sarajevo and turned at the next street corner, thus depriving Princep of his chance at a shot, perhaps the whole sixty years detour into communism might never have happened. After all, the Bolsheviks were never more than a minority. The Tsar and his family now rest with their ancestors in a side chapel in St Petersburg. Meanwhile, the ethnic time bombs, in the northern Caucasus and elsewhere, planted by Stalin after his steel-jawed terror sought to solve the nationalities problem by uprooting and mascerating communities, continue to explode, most recently in Chechnya.

So, might there be a Part II with Russia as the other player? It looks like one of the less likely prospects for the twenty-first century for reasons given seventy years ago. In August 1932 there was no American embassy in Moscow. The USA had not yet recognised the legitimacy of the USSR, and so the State Department peered into this diplomatic vacuum from a look-out in Riga, the capital of the still independent Latvia. George Kennan served as a young Russianist in the special section of the legation and, in that capacity, was asked to estimate the likely impact of the first Soviet Five-Year Plan on public opinion. In that seventy-year-old paper, he described the extreme happiness of Soviet young, 'as happy as human beings can be only when they are completely wrapped up in tasks which have no relation to their personal life'. Such mental force, whilst energised, would drive a massive political crusade; so his 1932 analysis was a foundation for his much more famous Long Telegram of 1946. But the other part of his prediction is the one which is pertinent now; for Kennan sensed the psychological and moral dangers attending such euphoria. He warned that should the millenarian Soviet project ever fail, 'from the most morally unified country in the world, Russia can overnight become the worst moral chaos'. Chapter and verse of the fulfilment of this prediction is to be found in the most important testament of the rise and fall of *perestroika* yet published. One of Gorbachev's closest confidants from February 1986 to the end was his chief foreign policy aide, Anatoly Chernyaev. His memoir documents closely the progressive disillusioning of his boss. Gorbachev started as an eager committed communist of enormous energy who sought to recapture the spirit of high moral purpose, which he believed to have been Lenin's and ended a tired, depressed and passive victim of the 1991 failed putsch, unable to change *homo sovieticus*, who Chernyaev described as 'the biggest, most difficult problem remaining for the fledgling democracy that Gorbachev created'.[24]

Humanity has abolished the Third World – that ugly label, which described the bin into which the poor were dropped, belonging neither to the First World of the rich and powerful in the West, nor the Second World of the communist bloc. However, the abolition has been achieved not by raising up the poor, but by the obliteration and impoverishment of the Second World. With the exception of the Baltic States, most of the rest of the former Soviet space has been tipped into poverty, ethnic strife, personal insecurity and declining life expectancy. Kennan's 1932 warning has been fulfilled: the misery and destructiveness are directed inwards.[25]

So far, we have seen the spluttering violence of religious fanaticism and several acts of terror, culminating on 11 September 2001 in New York and Washington. But these attacks despite, hitherto nothing has been seen which seeks to express systematically the new divide in fundamental terms of anger against privilege and excess. We have not yet seen global equivalents of attacks on the grain carts travelling to Paris in the early stages of the French Revolution, nor heard the political demands wrung out of the *crise de subsistence* in the alcohol-fired town meetings of the *Sans Culottes*.

It is argued, with some plausibility, that the pattern of wealth and poverty in a globalised world cannot be extrapolated from the gross contrast. Furthermore, that the more powerful force is the revolution of rising expectations that exists, and has been supplied with some success in Asia, both by the 'tiger' economies and by the Chinese communist choice to reverse Mr Gorbachev's order of procedure and to put political change last and economic transformation first. But the Cold War stands as a gaunt warning of the ease with which political thinking can slip into its old accustomed habits. Encouraging that may be thought to be one of the aims of the September 2001 perpetrators.

This chapter has argued that the Cold Wars were no phantoms, but that any Part II is unlikely to be cast with the same team of actors. What shapes strategic confrontation may take in the twenty-first century are considered in the next and final chapters. Here the case has been made that, in retrospect, we should pay most attention to the surprising range of positive as well as negative Cold War consequences. Lodged among the many material and intellectual injuries that the Cold Wars caused, lies the dialectic that blossomed in reaction as an unexpected bonus. After twenty years' hard slog by debt-relief campaigners, in 1999, the Jubilee 2000 alliance won the first significant relief of debt burdens upon the poorest nations, thereby firmly hitching human rights to the agenda of economic reform. The UN target of halving world poverty by 2015 looks less unattainable. The prospects for sustainable agriculture, fisheries and energy sources look brighter even if the route of direct 'securitisation' via formal politics was not the one best taken. They are all part of the post Cold War agenda. And how did they get there?

The vibrancy with which global concern for individual human rights and for global environmental security enter the twenty-first century, underpinning the mission to protect, is owed in part to the transformation of public politics and the re-emergence of cosmopolitan values in the 1980s. That, in its turn we must acknowledge to be directly and dialectically a product of the Cold Wars. Perhaps Lenin might have managed a smile?

But, even if this benefit is conceded, it is only a relative gain. It still sits in a balance with other, less progressive consequences of the era. Cold War habits of mind have persisted, specifically in two areas that affect directly how the objectives and roles of military power in the post-Cold War era have ranked and engaged. These were, respectively, the delayed response of the rich and militarily powerful to the appearance of pervasive insecurity – uncivil war – in much of the poor world, and the spectre of terrorism. The one was only galvanised when the genocide was no longer only African; the other has proved to be one of the toughest potential threats to security to analyse in a manner that is well-grounded in good empirical evidence. In part, this is because it has inherited the phantom's cloak, discarded by the former Soviet Union, and now because it is also overwhelmingly associated with the images of the shattered buildings in America after 11 September 2001.

Both of these aspects of 'uncivil war' are subjects to which we now turn.

3 The outside and inside of civil and uncivil war

On top of the ridge overlooking the valley of the River Ancre in Northern France stands a strange and lonely arch. The site of some of the fiercest fighting during the battle of the Somme in July to September 1916 is now the site of the largest British war memorial in the world. It commemorates the missing of the Somme: the 73,000 men whose bodies were never found. The memorial was designed by Sir Edwin Lutyens. It is stark. There are few carved wreaths, no helmets, no spears. The mathematics of the arches are such that each successive tier is a reduction of that below, reducing to nothing. The two flagpoles are slightly angled so that if their lines are extended, they intersect in the air, above the battlefield. Its eeriness was a source of comment at the time and has remained so. Some commentators have described it as being impossible to photograph; others, that into the vaults of its arches, from the four winds, march the spirits of the dead.[1]

Just at the moment when it was passing from living memory, the end of the twentieth century witnessed a strong resurgence of interest in the experiences of the Great War with which it was preoccupied at its beginning. Thiepval and the Somme have figured in some of the finest of recent British novels.[2] The memorial, as one may deduce that Lutyens intended, symbolises the great question-mark about war in the twentieth-century experience.

Half-way through that century, the historian R.G. Collingwood observed that 'the chief business of twentieth-century philosophy is to reckon with twentieth-century history'. What he meant by that was that in the nineteenth century something akin to the revolution in the natural sciences at the time of Galileo occurred, speeding up and broadening the range of history. Geoffrey Barraclough later took these same two – a qualitative difference and a structural change – as the defining characteristics of what he called 'contemporary' (as distinct from modern) history.[3] Collingwood had felt the deadly beat of these wings as he hurried to publish his first book in 1916, in case it should be his only one. As we saw in Chapter 1, Jan Bloch, in St Petersburg, had already got the measure of the creature twenty years before that.

The effect on Collingwood of surviving the Great War (and of studying archaeology) was to kill within him any willingness to be hobbled by lack of sources. Whereas he saw his nineteenth-century predecessors as passive 'scissors and paste men', his philosophy of history was activist:

> I had learnt by first-hand experience that history is not an affair of scissors and paste, but is much more like Bacon's notion of science. *The historian has to decide exactly what it is that he wants to know* [emphasis added]; and if there is no authority to tell him, as in fact (one learns in time) there never is, he has to find a piece of land, or something that has got the answer hidden in it, and get the answer out by fair means or foul.[4]

Knowing, as Collingwood could not, what was coming after 1939 in Part II of the century, we may reiterate his sentiment with added fervour. And we should take his advice. What do we want to know, exactly, about war in our times? What more than its own dark self did the Great War portend? Was it, as John Keegan has suggested, really the beginning of the end for war in Europe, as the 'gunpowder' nations turned in upon themselves, to begin the long European civil war 1914–1941? And most especially, what has been the consequence of what, with hindsight, we now know to have been one of the most reliable and disseminated products of the European wars – the loss of 'civility' in European warfare? What has been the consequence of this for all subsequent forms of political violence, and – a different question – for the ways in which we interpret the outward signs of actual and latent violence?

What do we need to know – what sources not conveniently to hand must we unearth – to answer these questions satisfactorily? Collingwood gives us some further advice to help answer his own question, advice which is simultaneously helpful and daunting. We should try to find pivotal moments, and then try our best to understand the forces that brought and mobilised them. Caesar returns to Rome, but crosses the Rubicon without disbanding his forces (Collingwood's example). Below, in our story and for our purposes, the pivotal moments will be the fall of Srebrenica in the summer of

1995 and the bombing of Pan Am flight 103 over Lockerbie on 21 December 1988. These were turning-points of a double sort: the trajectory of immediate history altered in consequence – the very meaning of 'crossing the Rubicon' in colloquial speech; and in slower time it became plain that the event altered the way that everyone thought about the world. The Lisbon earthquake of 1755 was another such event. Not only did it shatter a city, but it shook the minds of Voltaire, of Rousseau and of the young philosopher–lecturer Immanuel Kant. All of them reflected upon its meaning in the context of fierce debates at the time over the nature and role in human affairs of the medieval interventionist God. He was pushed off into the clouds; and not only by philosophers. The Marquis de Pombale, who was given responsibility for rebuilding Lisbon, put to death a Jesuit priest who preached repentance, blaming the victims for the disaster as a punishment, thereby driving people to despair. The geological earthquake materially triggered secondary shocks in the epistemological landscape; and that is no hyperbole. The attacks on America on 11 September 2001 may or may not be another such moment. It is too early to say, although the indications are that it is a secondary, not a primary pivot.

Such recognition begins to meet Collingwood's criterion of adequacy in historical explanation. All historical events, he wrote, have an 'outside' which is description of bodies and their movements, and an 'inside' which is represented 'in terms of thought'. A 'mere' event is mere because it consists only of description of the outside. What we need to understand are *actions*: 'the unity of the outside and the inside of an event.' If we aim for satisfactory standards of historical explanation then, Collingwood insisted, the historian 'must always remember that the event was an action, and that his main task is to think himself into this action, to discern the thought of its agent',[5] or, as I have added here, to seek to understand the effects of natural events (like earthquakes) upon the way that people then thought.

This advice and procedure is especially congenial at a time such as now, when the primary reference unit of ethical, legal and political concern in global politics is, increasingly, frequently the individual. Since our guide in the next chapter will be the same philosophy teacher whose outlook was shaken by the Lisbon earthquake, we may therefore feel its tremors again, across time. Thus equipped, let us begin our journey, during which we shall examine the outside and the inside first of the new form of war which the Great War represented and spawned, then of uncivil contemporary wars in the poor world, and finally the outside and inside of terrorism – the uncivil political violence, fear of which grips and fascinates the imagination of the safest people on the planet.

The new wars of the twentieth century

The traveller leaving the small Belgian town of Binche soon finds himself on a long, straight road that undulates up and down gentle hills in the direction of Mons. At the crest of a hill not far from Mons he reaches a crossroads. Today a yellow flashing warning light marks the spot; and flash it might because as the traveller passes across that intersection, unmarked, he passes the threshold into the European experience of war in the twentieth century.

On 20 August 1914, an advance party of German reconnaissance cavalry arrived, by train, at the station in Binche. They detrained and camped for the night and the next morning set off in the direction of Mons along that same road. They were spied by British observers on top of the mine dumps, who relayed the news to the British Expeditionary Force in Mons. A contingent of British reconnaissance bicyclists was sent out to investigate further. Meanwhile, the German cavalry, having reached a gentle slope in dead ground, moved from a walk to a trot and arrived across the brow of the hill sooner than the British bicyclists had expected. An exchange of fire took place and L/14196 Private Parr, of the Middlesex Regiment, became the first British soldier to lose his life in the First World War. He did so at about the place where now the yellow light flashes at the road intersection. Each party returned to report and the following day German forces began a two-pronged advance upon Mons.

The main thrust was towards the Mons–Condé canal, to the right. On 23 August at the Obourg cement works, during those first hours of the First World War, fierce fighting ensued. In the end, the Middlesex regiment could no longer hold its position and was forced to retreat. Lieutenant Maurice Dease kept his machine-gun section in action until he and all the gunners were dead, bar one. Private Sid Godley continued to fire until he ran out of ammunition. Dease and Godley were awarded the first Victoria Crosses for bravery of the war. In recognition of the courage with which the Middlesex regiment had defended the site, in the graveyard at St Symphorien, where British soldiers were buried by German hands, was also erected a granite column on which their German enemies inscribed a recognition of the courage of the 'Royal' Middlesex Regiment. The Middlesex regiment was not a royal regiment; but so bravely had the soldiers fought that their German adversaries assumed that it was or should have been.[6]

Such chivalrous – such civil – conduct continued to splutter in sporadic episodes; but it did not, could not, last long in the face of the brutalising juggernaut of war by gas, by shell and by machine-gun – an experience so terrible and so alien that, in the eyes of British war poets like Wilfred Owen, it took on a demonic life of its own, consuming lives and any fragile principles of humanity indiscriminately. In this respect, the arrival in Europe of Jan Bloch's predicted form of massed and simultaneously industrialised war was paradoxical in effect. Its dual nature awkwardly straddled old and new eras: the empty fields of northern France were suddenly filled with old world armies of men, of horses, even elephants, in previously unimaginable concentrations along with the logistics of the mass armies of the new. It was a grotesquely unequal contest, seen when Indian Army lancers bravely charged machine-guns, to predictable effect. The huge application of the new to the old made new war a commensurately potent solvent of that distinction between the war front and the home front which had been a strengthening feature of warfare in the nineteenth century. War then was most frequently expeditionary or, if fought in Europe (the Prussian campaigns against Austria and France), decided by geographically and chronologically discrete engagements.

The Great War started as a war of movement in August 1914, as just seen on the road from Binche – those cavalry, a small spinning cog in the intricate mechanism of the Schlieffen Plan. But it did not end on any single battlefield; rather with social unrest, threatening socialist revolution and the collapse of civilian morale in Germany in 1918.

That wild and wanton power of war, making itself its own end whatever may have been the initial impetus in political disagreement, has been the rising characteristic of war-making in Europe's long century of violence, returning us, after 1990, to that condition of pervasive and indiscriminate political violence seen during the seventeenth-century Wars of Religion, and earlier: for, at the other end from the gentlemanly tragedy of St Symphorien, we find Dame Anne Warburton's report on the employment of systematic rape in the wars of the former Yugoslavia. Copious and dreadful evidence exists of the manner in which the rape of Muslim women was used as one among the other available means to break the will and to annihilate the identity of Bosnian Muslims by Bosnian Serbs. Women of all ages were gathered together and subjected to continuous and random assault; certain women were taken aside and subjected to systematic rape with the explicit intention of making them pregnant so that, by carrying Serbian children, they would expiate the sin of being born Muslim, as their tormentors told them.

Such violation of body and mind led to suicides and to profound mental disturbance. It offers an unusually precise illustration of the manner in which uncivil behaviour has become the norm rather than the exception in civil wars. Mass rape was a feature of the Soviet occupation of Berlin in 1945, of the Bangladesh war of independence in 1971, of the Ugandan civil war of the mid-1980s and, massively, of the Rwandan genocide of the mid-1990s, also. It is, argues Martin van Creveld, a lasting consequence of the way in which the Nazi offensives of the Second World War (principal result of the First World War) flagrantly and deliberately added terrorising and killing civilians to war by soldiers against soldiers.[7] Just as the Cold War was to do later for the human rights, environmental and peace issues, a countervailing force arose also: the explicit *protection* of civilians under the expanded Geneva protocols.

The campaign of systematic rape in the former Yugoslavia is illuminating of the same fundamental proposition about the nature of war as the Geneva protocols. For war is recognised as being an exceptional activity. It is the licensed trespass to cross normally prohibited boundaries. To mark those boundaries, there is a need to 'exceptionalise' such acts: soldiers wear uniforms, are subject to discipline, they tread a narrow path between action and inaction in combat (a point well made in John Keegan's justly famous book, which explains, in harrowing but in some sense reassuring clarity, how so often commanders have experienced difficulty in motivating their troops to risk their lives and to take the lives of others, when all human instinct cries out that the sane thing to do is to flee).[8] There is a narrow path to be trodden between sanity and insanity also.

In May 1899, the participants in The Hague conference gathered under the shadow of the paradox that modern nineteenth-century ways of making war – the application of industrial process to killing that had first been seen on the later battlefields of the American Civil War – might make war simultaneously morally intolerable and politically useless. By the transformation of war in the twentieth century, we have been forced to enlarge our scope so that we consider not only uncivil behaviour in wars, but uncivil wars also as a product of their times.

Two uses of the word 'civil'

There are distinguishable ways in which the word 'civil' is employed. The first *recognises value in the enemy*. That value may be perhaps at the lowest level, only financial: it makes better sense to hold the unseated knight for ransom than to cut his throat. But, in the later nineteenth century, war widened its grasp upon a society that was itself facilitated by the powers of industry. In that sense, a centenary recollection of Bloch makes a wry point: for whereas railways made the Western Front possible, railway wealth had funded Jan Bloch's researches into war. In a similar manner, Andrew Carnegie's wealth went to support the establishment of the Court of Arbitration in The Hague. Yet these were not the first signs.

Simultaneously with the speeding tempo of industrialisation, there occurred formalisations, codifications of the fundamental humanity of enemies. It was as if, recognising the increasing strength of the military/technical momentum towards indiscriminate destruction, a countervailing tendency arose attempting to assert what had hitherto been implicitly assumed. There were two strands to this, mentioned in Chapter 1. To recapitulate, the first was a continuing reaction to the proliferating ingenuity of the means of destruction, of which the St Petersburg Convention of 1868 was the first attempt to outlaw inhumane weapons. It led to a succession of such arms control measures. The widespread use of poison gas in the First World War propelled initiatives to outlaw weapons of mass destruction. This led in 1997 to the effort to ban chemical weapons. There has been a continuing effort to extend this ambit, recently recurring in the World Court ruling of 1996 that the use of nuclear weapons, by virtue of their indiscriminate effects, fell under that prohibition. Similarly, attempts to proscribe the use of plastic shrapnel (used to make fragments in a victim's body invisible to X-ray) or blinding lasers have continued to make the St Petersburg point that clean and unclean ways of giving death to the legitimate enemy exist, whereas the Ottawa Convention campaign against land mines expressed the rising public demand that the means of waging war should not place non-combatants at risk in the way that, classically and most numerously in the world's arsenals, land mines do. The relative futility of these civil measures simply underlines the power of the forces they sought to stem.

The second strand in the countervailing tendency was first spun in the Tsar's Imperial Rescript of August 1898, in which the case for a new approach to conflict resolution was made.[9] It was soon followed by The Hague conference of 1899 and the Conventions of 1907 on the proper conduct of soldiers in war, with regard to civilians and non-combatants, and in the handling of prisoners of war. From this came a set of principles which, honoured in the breach, still have considerable power to shock international public opinion. It has been principally by these means that international opinion in the twentieth century has sought to outlaw 'uncivil' behaviour in wars. Now it becomes plain that a second meaning of the word 'civil' is more important.

'Civil' *distinguishes between war and crime.* It refers to two circumstances, which are quite different and only in part reconcilable, although both spring from the manner in which civil society is related to state power. By circumstance (in failed states) or, more rarely, by choice (in religious or survivalist communities, or football supporters' clubs) different, sub-state social forms come to replace the state as the dominant reference point for more people in the modern world. War slides into crime as the state is replaced as the dominant reference framework and source of legitimation of beliefs and of actions for such groups. Note, however, that in this usage crime does not automatically imply chaos, as when employed by the 'new barbarian' school of explanation to be encountered at greater length in the chapter on strategic raiding. What it means is that the sources of social and political legitimacy must be sought in less familiar places.

The first of these new senses was defined rapidly and strongly at the end of the Second World War, as a consequence of the behaviour of the Third Reich. It addresses the problem of *uncivil behaviour in wars by a rogue state*, whose leadership, supported by large parts of its population, subscribed to a doctrine obnoxious to civilised behaviour. Whether one bases judgement upon the contentious Hossbach Memorandum of the Wannzee Conference, upon Hitler's own writings about Jews, or upon the evidence of conduct in the war against the Jews (as Lucy Dawidowicz has named the entire period of genocidal action from 1932–1945), the fact was that this aspect in particular of the Third Reich faced the international community with a new problem.[10] The way that it was resolved was to establish the principle of individual responsibility and with it the concept of 'war crime'. By extension, Nuremberg gave prominence to a key question and a key concept that has framed the approach to uncivil war ever since; the question is that of who sets the norms. The Nuremberg answer, of course, was that it was the victors. Through instruments like the Helsinki process, that historically specific consequence became broadened and softened. The concept of 'human rights' led in 1948 not only to the Universal Declaration, but also to promulgation of the Genocide Convention, one of the most widely subscribed of all the international legal instruments of the post-Second World War period.

Until the early 1990s, it was generally thought that Europe would not see again such acts as led to Nuremberg, fifty years after the fiery collapse of the Third Reich and five years after the quiet collapse of the Soviet Union. The death of Yugoslavia proved that to be wrong. Within the evolution of that tangled conflict, a decisive development occurred. For, whereas the international motivation for intervention over Bosnia in 1991 was *raison d'état,* that in Kosovo in 1999 was fundamentally different. The motivation was expressed as a mandate for enforceable human rights, given priority over unqualified sovereignty. It stands beside that other notable example of the same trend at that time: the endeavour to extradite General Pinochet from Britain to Spain to answer for acts committed in Chile.

For better or worse (and largely not entirely for worse), this inheritance is the one deployed to face the second sense in which uncivil war is encountered. This is in the context of *civil war and intra-state violence.* In Israel, in the former Yugoslavia, in Rwanda, in the 'democratic' republic of Congo, Somalia, Angola, Sierra Leone and the surrounding parts of West Africa, a lengthening list of regions, either at the fault lines of international politics or so deeply ignored that only terrible atrocity awakens media – and thence international – interest, is scarred with what John Keane has called 'uncivil wars ... [which] ... ransack the legal monopoly of armed force long claimed by states. They put an end to the distinction between war and crime.'[11]

Intra-state violence in these inflamed and increasingly common contexts shares six features. First, they tend to occur in post-colonial territories or in regions where previously an imposed imperial solution enforced the legal monopoly of force; second, they are frequently, indeed usually, circumstances where differences are expressed in terms of ethnic differentiation. Mary Kaldor coins the useful term 'identity politics' as a defining characteristic. This second feature gives particular venom to the rest. Third, given that the language of conflict is ethnic, different groups deploy mutually-exclusive invented histories of themselves and their enemies; fourth, about these histories no argument is tolerated other than with bullets; for – the fifth characteristic – such riven communities are disfigured by a lust for simplification, a denial of complexity, a preference for (in John Keane's chillingly elegant phrase) 'a chosen ignorance'. All this gives peculiar impulsion to the sixth feature, which is that, in circumstances so defined and so described, the ends are easily seen by combatants to justify the means. Hence, the disturbing combination of cruelty and familiarity between persecutors and victims that was so prominent a feature of the wars during the death of Yugoslavia in the early 1990s and of the Rwandan genocide, occurring at the same time.[12]

Yet none of this is new or unfamiliar. During the later part of the eleventh century a series of closely related heresies spread across the Balkans, northern Italy and Languedoc in southern France. The Bogomils of Bulgaria, the Poor Men of Lyons, followers of Peter Waldo (the Waldensians) and the Cathars of the Languedoc, also known as Albigenians (after the city of Albi) or *bougres* – Bulgari – because of their affinity to the Bogomils, shared two tenets. One was an ascetic ideal – a belief that poverty and unworldliness were the mark and acme of a pure Christian faith (for Catharism was unambiguously a Christian heresy: hence the potency of its threat to Catholicism); the other a stark Manichaeanism which divided the world into the opposed kingdoms of light and dark, of Good and Evil. The Catholic church hierarchy was materially rebuked in its wealth and pomp by the antisacerdotalism of the former; orthodox monotheism by the latter. But the ranks of the Cathars swelled, especially after the First Crusade. In Languedoc the lesser nobility, as well as peasantry, were won over and under regional patronage the Cathars held a council in Toulouse in 1167, attended by representatives from Bulgaria, Bosnia and North Italy.

When Innocent III became Pope he resolved to extirpate the Cathar heresy. By then its presence touched all levels of society in Languedoc, such that Count Raymond VI of Toulouse was said to be of the persuasion. First Innocent sent St Dominic, an orthodox ascetic, to argue with the heretics in their own terms. When this failed, in 1204 the Pope sent Peter de Castelnau and Arnold Amalric, Abbot of Cîteaux as legates with a commission to suppress. They excommunicated Raymond and attempted to turn his orthodox vassals against him. In January 1208, de Castelnau was murdered. Innocent now renewed Raymond's excommunication, absolved his vassals of their oaths of fealty and declared a crusade not against the infidel Muslims to recover Jerusalem, but against the Christian heretic Cathars. It was preached in northern France, and in June 1209, a large force of land-hungry northern French barons, led by Simon de Montfort, assembled at Lyons to invade and despoil the richness of Languedoc. On 22 July the city of Beziers was stormed with indiscriminate and appalling violence – Catholics and Cathars alike were killed – which set the model for the manner in which de Montfort's barons harried Languedoc to death, hilltop fortress by hilltop fortress, over the next decade.

The Albigensian crusade was a campaign of ethnic cleansing – of 'identity politics' – which prefigured in detail the characteristics of contemporary uncivil war. Just like the Bosnian Serbs in the Bosnian war of the 1990s, the crusaders pursued a double goal, with the sanction of a higher authority and purpose: to take land and property and to extinguish, by genocide, the presence and the memory of a faith and its culture. Just as in the post-Cold War Balkans, the legitimacy of any given claim to statehood was contested unconditionally by its enemies, brooking no compromise. Just as with mafia and drug cartels, for example, during the death of Yugoslavia, the web of local grudges and rivalries among the minor nobility of Languedoc, became enmeshed in the larger contest, adding fuel and spite among neighbours within communities. And in both cases, those who set the process in motion (Slobodan Milosevic and Mira Markovic; Pope Innocent III) lost control of what they had started.[13]

For these reasons, it is more helpful to an understanding of modern uncivil wars to recognise these old affinities, and to see that 'new war' was, in fact, the twentieth-century exception. This point was made (rather more dogmatically than it is presented here) by Alain Minc in 1993 when he sketched those characteristics of trends as he saw them, which justified the suggestion that Europe might enter a new Middle Ages. Kaldor's account of the politics of uncivil wars, and her stress upon the centrality of contest over legitimacy rather than anything else (but not her taxonomy) also support this case.[14]

The outside and the inside of Srebrenica 1995

In all these circumstances since the end of the Cold War, the 'international community' – meaning, in so far as it exists, those flashes of self-conscious community of value and purpose expressed commonly and simultaneously in the streets, newspapers, parliaments or chancelleries of different countries – has felt increasingly obliged to intervene and do something. That is a laudable feature of the post-Nuremberg inheritance; but that same inheritance creates the problem which the international community has wrestled with since the end of the Soviet Union, namely that of applying institutions and mechanisms devised under and for the circumstances of dealing with uncivil behaviour in wars by rogue states, to circumstances of uncivil wars.

In the United Nations era, the first device for responding to pressures to intervene was 'peacekeeping'. Peacekeeping was the deployment of symbolic force based on the consent of all parties and in circumstances where all parties believed that they had more to lose by defying the international community, embodied in the blue-helmeted troops of the United Nations contingents, than they had to gain. Those troops, in turn, protected themselves by remaining entirely disengaged from the actual conflict; they were both impartial and neutral; they made no moral judgement as to the rights and wrongs of the combatant parties, but sought by their presence only to separate, to shame through observation of hostilities and atrocities and thereby to calm circumstances. Their own protection was their conspicuous vulnerability and, thus made explicit, moral authority.

That post-1945 device formed the leading concept with which the international community has entered almost all its interventions, recently and most notably so in the case of the former Yugoslavia. It was in that war that the turning-point occurred. It led to a sharper reorientation towards enforceable human rights.

The turning-point was in July 1995. The outside of the event was as follows. The place was the Muslim enclave of Srebrenica and the occasion was the forced evacuation of the enclave by the Dutch battalion of the United Nations Protection Force. The Dutch soldiers were forced to leave without equipment and powerless to protect the civilian inhabitants of the enclave from what followed. This was the planned and premeditated execution of around 6,000 Muslim men. All the elements of Auschwitz were suddenly again apparent in Europe: the forced separation of men from women; transport of the men to a killing ground; the victims ordered to undress before being killed in order to impede the identification of bodies at any future stage. A Dutch soldier being evacuated from Srebrenica in a bus reported seeing neat rows of shoes lined up beside the road in the area, of which, later that month, in the United Nations, American Ambassador Madeleine Albright waved spy satellite photographs showing the disturbed earth of mass graves. Subsequently, it transpired, through the investigations of *Der Spiegel*, that American spy satellites had earlier photographed lines of bodies after execution and awaiting burial. So, as Professor Tromp argued in his analysis of the Srebrenica episode, a conspicuous contrast between this and the Nazi final solution was the speed with which incontrovertible confirmation of the atrocity reached the public domain. In the case of the

German death camps, the public only became aware when Allied troops reached Belsen (although there is persuasive evidence that the Allied higher command knew the purpose of the camp much earlier). In the case of Srebrenica, it was a matter of days. This evidence combined with the memory of the position taken in Srebrenica during the first crisis in March 1993 when General Philippe Morillon had announced from the town post office to crowds of Muslim women and children: 'You are now under the protection of the UN forces ... I will never abandon you.' Yet abandoned they were. The evidence of Srebrenica led first to the passing of the United Nations Security Council Resolution 819 on Safe Areas and soon thereafter to the implementation of NATO airstrikes, including the use of cruise missiles to attack Bosnian Serb military installations around Banja Luka.

And the inside? The Srebrenica enclave became the focal point in the summer of 1995 because the strategies and ambitions of major players in the Bosnian crisis had come to pivot upon it. General Radko Mladic wanted the Bosnian civilians out, naturally, to incorporate the enclave into the Bosnian Serb republic. He also wanted to humiliate the international community in general and the Dutch in particular for interfering in the region. Revealingly, in an interview in March 1996, he was quoted as saying, 'There is no greater shame for us Serbs than to be bombed by some Dutchman. I have no idea whom Holland could bomb on its own. Not even Denmark, but they simply dared to bomb Serbs. Their miserable Van den Broek committed great atrocities and made a great contribution to the collapse of the former Yugoslavia.'[15]

The Bosnian Muslims equally strongly wished to keep civilians in the pocket, for only in this way could they keep the United Nations present and tied down, and only if the UN was present could the enclave be preserved, not in the expectation that it would be permanently held but as a chip to be bargained against land in a forthcoming settlement.

For its part, the international community wanted to take a principled stand. This was especially true in the Netherlands, where Dutch public opinion strongly supported a more robust line: and the Netherlands alone had offered the Secretary-General of the United Nations a promise of forces. In the event, Dutch deployment and its surrounding diplomacy were clumsily handled. Too many troops were sent, with poor logistics, without any agreement for a helicopter resupply corridor and incoherently armed – a mixture of 'peacekeeping' symbolism and a military mission to be sent into hostile territory.

This was not helped by the fact that the enclave was not demilitarised, so there was some force in the Bosnian Serb accusation that the United Nations was partial because it was acting as a military shield for Bosnian Muslim soldiers.

Second, Dutch diplomacy was inept, with opposition to withdrawal being maintained beyond the point at which military advice was that it was prudent and with veiled talk on the diplomatic circuit about the need to find a nation to replace the Netherlands in a *roulement* in Srebrenica. All this told the Bosnian Serbs that, put under pressure, the Dutch were likely to crack.

What finally precipitated the Dutch withdrawal was failure to secure air support in July 1995. As Honig and Both argue convincingly in their definitive account of the Srebrenica episode, Generals Janvier and Smith both sought to deploy an escalation package in support of DutchBat but were overruled by the United Nations representative, Mr Akashi, on the one hand and by the Dutch government on the other, which was fearful that military escalation would place the Dutch soldiers' lives at further risk.[16]

Axiomatic to the crisis of Srebrenica was the fact that no-one really believed that the Bosnian Serbs would press their defiance on the United Nations in the way in which Mladic did. After Srebrenica, American diplomacy in particular began to pay closer attention. The successful deployment of air power, the provision of the Rapid Reaction Force with heavy artillery to open the Mount Igman road into Sarajevo were overtures for the rough diplomatic handling which the region's combatants experienced at American hands at Dayton. After Dayton, with the change from UNPROFOR to IFOR, not only did the colour of the vehicles change from white to khaki, but the nature of communication with General Mladic changed also. One IFOR commander has described how, early during his turn, he met with the Bosnian Serb military authorities for a one-sided conversation in which he informed them that they would either comply with the Dayton terms or he would hit them with all the military force at his command.

After Bosnia, 'peace enforcement' became the rule rather than the exception. With the Bosnian fiasco, and even more so with the abrupt disintegration of the Middle East 'settlement' in 2000, we have probably seen the end of the curious career of 'conflict resolution' – presented as some sort of clever alternative between diplomacy and force. The problem, perhaps best exemplified by the so-called Oslo 'peace process' for the Middle East, is that it ascribes to the process of negotiation some special power which plainly it does not possess in the harsh world of *Realpolitik*. Concentrated force opened the road to Sarajevo which, in turn, led to the banging together of Balkan heads in Dayton by Richard Holbrooke and the Americans, which in turn led to the deployment of a khaki – not white painted – implementation force in the region. This is a developing trend (as Operation Alba showed, just down the coast in Albania). Strategic raiding is one trend in the future use of force.[17] It must be doubtful whether ever again NATO forces will be allowed to go symbolically clad or symbolically armed in harm's way.

The political leverage from late-twentieth-century force is switching away from the mid-century preoccupation (not to say obsession, in some quarters) with aspects of deterrence, back to a more straightforward, late nineteenth-century emphasis upon 'compellence'. 'The uses of force have changed in much of the world,' wrote Charles William Maynes. 'Throughout the Cold War, force was needed to deter the other side from doing bad things outside its borders. Today, force is needed to compel the other side to do good things inside its borders.'[18] What this means in practice is the focus of Part II of this book.

The uncivil violence of terror

Piled skulls of the victims of the Khmer Rouge on the killing fields of Cambodia; the blood-streaked walls of a church which became a charnal house during the Rwandan genocide; the accusatory stripes of disturbed earth in the aerial photographs of Srebrenica; Angolan amputee victims of land mines; Sierra Leonian amputee victims of guerrillas using terror as a weapon. Each of these descriptions conjures up a photograph whose image has come to stand for each of these uncivil wars. But these episodes come and go, in the newspaper headlines, radio and television news bulletins of the rich world; each new episode establishing a frail command of the attention of the media and then fading from view. In contrast, a different sort of uncivil war maintains an almost constant presence in public awareness. After 11 September 2001, the issue became an overwhelming presence in international political discussion. Few labels are as value laden as that of 'terrorism'.

The term is used constantly to describe a wide range of acts of violence, so wide, indeed, that the starting point of one of the most incisive analyses of terror opened by asking whether 'the words "terrorist" and "terrorism" have any coherent meaning today, twenty-three years after they first began to seep into our vocabulary, and if so what is that meaning?' (this book was published in 1991).[19] The label is used as a weapon in the battle for public sympathy in conflicts around the world because it produces such a powerful shudder in the public consciousness of the richest and (even after 11 September 2001) statistically the safest people on the planet. Succeed in making this label stick to your enemy and great advantage is obtained in the battle for public opinion. When stories of terror appear in the press many images can be used to draw the reader's attention. Masked gunmen are popular. But from the recent history of acts of terrorism, while the pictures of the crashing planes, the falling towers, the terrified watchers fleeing the rolling walls of dust and debris of 11 September 2001, now dominate, one other image is recurrent. It is of the broken half of the cockpit and nose of a Pan Am airliner, parts of the wreckage incongruously undamaged – portholes intact and part of the name of the aeroplane visible – lying on its side in a Scottish field.

On the night of 21 December 1988, in a fraction of a second at 31,000 feet over Scotland, Pan Am flight 103 was blown apart by a Semtex high-explosive bomb concealed in a cassette recorder in a suitcase stowed in the forward baggage hold. The central section of the wings and the fuselage fell onto Sherwood Crescent in Lockerbie where a crater thirty feet deep and 100 feet long was gouged. Three houses were pulverised and eleven more lives were taken, as well as the 270 victims who died on the aircraft. The ground operation at Lockerbie to recover their remains was one of the largest of its sort to be undertaken in Britain since the Second World War. People of many nationalities lost their lives; but there were many Europeans and North Americans among them. The largest single group consisted of students from the University of Syracuse returning from a period of study in Europe. Their memory is commemorated, both in a monument at the University and through the establishment of Remembrance Scholarships.

In opening a series of lectures to commemorate the tenth anniversary of the Lockerbie bombing, it was argued that, in order to obtain justice for the victims, on the one hand the legal process to discover and convict the perpetrators should be pursued, but on the other that part of finding justice lay in gaining an understanding of such acts – both the outside and the inside. Plato offered the helpful view that the elimination of injustice was not alone a case of repairing the protective web of rules which cocoon and thus protect a well-ordered society. In addition, he asserted that only to the degree in which citizens' minds are awake to what they could, should and might have in society (their right to life, liberty and the pursuit of happiness, for example) would they stir their will and efforts to preserve and to protect what they do have.[20]

The threat from terrorism makes it especially important to be clear about what it is that one is defending, particularly in a liberal and democratic society; for if there is overreaction, indiscriminate repression, the use of counter-terrorist tactics that are outside the law or the draconian suppression of free speech, then there is a risk not only of a loss of popular support and legitimacy in countering the terrorists, but that by forcing free and democratic societies into illiberal acts, the terrorists can damage their enemies not with their bombs but by such self-inflicted injuries.[21] The nature of that risk, in turn, makes it particularly important to assess clear-sightedly the nature and the scale of the threat which terrorism poses, so that the actions taken to counter it are both precisely applicable and proportionate. This is not easy when the targets are as manifestly powerless to defend themselves as passengers on a civil airliner and office workers in New York and Washington: the very quality which makes the target attractive to terrorists of a certain persuasion in the first place.

The bombing of Pan Am 103 was not the first attack of this sort. That occurred on 22 June 1985 when an Air India jumbo jet was destroyed by an explosion over the eastern Atlantic. There were no survivors and 329 people lost their lives. The atrocity opened a new phase of terrorist action, which will be further discussed below (p.69), in which sabotage bombing, by planting devices in luggage or by the use of unwitting mule passengers, or, in 2001, by suicide pilots, was undertaken or attempted. The objective was plainly different from hijacking, for there was no intention or ability to negotiate an outcome such as the release of prisoners. In the case of Lockerbie, no-one claimed responsibility for the act at the time or since. Aerial bombing was intended to kill and was likely to be comprehensively destructive; so the motive had to be different. It had to be revenge or warning or both, and in each case the recipients of those messages were likely to be a wider constituency than Israel, even if the stimulus might be Middle Eastern more often than not.

Lockerbie was followed on 19 September 1989 by the destruction of a French airliner (UTA flight 722) high over the Sahara, with the loss of 171 lives. The means of operation was very similar to the Lockerbie bombing and there is suspicion that the Semtex bomb might have come from the same manufacturer. Responsibility was disputed between two organisations, one Islamic fundamentalist and the other a Tchadian group opposed to French military activities in Africa. Since then, until the American suicide attacks, the prime focus of terrorist action had turned elsewhere. Certainly, the 1990s saw amplification of one of the characteristics of the aerial bombings of the late 1980s, namely the move away from negotiable acts towards acts of massive, absolute and socially-alienated destruction. Four episodes in particular stand out in popular memory. They mark the path to the culminating act of mass casualty terrorism in 2001.

The first was an attack by Sunni Islamic extremists in New York in 1993. Ramzi Ahmed Yousef and accomplices sought to kill as many people as possible by planting explosives in the basement of one of the two towers of the World Trade Center in Manhattan. It was a religiously-inspired attack against America for its role in the Middle Eastern conflict. Yousef obtained a fatwa from Sheik Omar-Abdel Rahman (himself now in prison in the United States) to sanctify their action. Rahman led Gamaya Islamiya, a fundamentalist organisation with links to Osama bin Laden's al-Qae'da, and also perpetrator of the massacre of tourists at Luxor. Had the 1993 attack succeeded in toppling one of the towers onto the other, many tens of thousands could have died. Equally, had the cyanide, which had been packed with the bomb, been released rather than vapourised by the explosion, fatalities could have resulted. But, unlike the attack of 11 September 2001, which struck the towers high up, with gigantic heat at the right places to cause them to implode, the towers did not fall and only six people lost their lives.

Two years later, on 20 March 1995, members of the Aum Shinrikyo cult (one of the world's richest, most sophisticated and strange religious sects, led by the charismatic and increasingly psychopathic Shoko Asahara) released Sarin gas on five underground trains simultaneously in the Tokyo subway system, injuring over 5,500 people, some very seriously, and killing twelve.

The following month, on 19 April 1995, Timothy McVeigh, a member of the Christian Patriots, a fundamentalist sect with links to the extremist militia movement with whom they shared a hatred of government and a desire to foment nationwide revolution, planted a huge bomb made of fertiliser and diesel fuel outside the Murrah federal office building in Oklahoma City, killing 168 people.

Two months later, the so-called 'Unabomber' promised to restrict his campaign of sending letter-bombs to persons associated with either universities or the airline industry if his 35,000 word diatribe against technology and modernity and the destruction of the environment were to be published in either the *New York Times* or the *Washington Post*. It was published in the *Washington Post* in September 1995, which stimulated information that subsequently led to the arrest of Theodor Kaczynski.

What all these attacks had in common was that the perpetrators held apocalyptic visions of the future, paranoically conspiratorial interpretations of the present, and deeply encapsulated, internally-consistent but socially entirely alienated belief systems. Three of them – the World Trade Center, subway and Murrah building attacks – like the aircraft bombings before them, sought to achieve the maximum number of deaths, randomly and indiscriminately inflicted upon innocent victims. In the case of two – the World Trade Center and subway attacks – the perpetrators sought to use weapons of mass destruction. Indeed, prior to the chemical attack on 15 March, the Aum cult had attempted to kill with a biological agent. Three briefcases filled with botulism prepared in their laboratories were planted at the Kasumigaseki station, one of the major subway intersections on the Tokyo system and the station used both by the national police agency and by thousands of senior officials working in Tokyo's bureaucratic centre. The attack only failed because a member of the sect, sent to deposit them, had decided at the last minute not to arm the devices.[22] Even though it failed in its fuller ambition, the effect of the World Trade Center attack was dramatic within the United States, whose population had hitherto considered itself safe from the attacks of international terrorism, which were actions that happened somewhere else.

Thus, by the mid-1990s, it began to appear as if international terrorism might be moving away from its modern origins in the Middle East conflict onto a much wider stage populated by a range of very different actors with different messages and motives, but all seeking to obtain access to biological, chemical, even nuclear weapons of mass destruction – Aum had an audacious programme in this field also – as well as to both highly sophisticated and extremely crude types of explosives.

Fear of a successful chemical attack is pervasive and insidious. The judge who presided over the trial of the bombers of the World Trade Center stated that had they succeeded in their intention to release the sodium cyanide in the bomb package it would have been sucked into the North Tower and killed everyone there. Another common anxiety was that with the collapse of the former Soviet Union there was the danger of the proliferation of nuclear materials, not only fissile materials that could be used to make a nuclear explosion but also radioactive products which could be spread by high explosive to create a zone of permanent radioactive contamination. Reviewing the entire spectrum of uncivil war by terrorism in 1998 after this sequence of episodes, one of the world's principal experts on the subject concluded that 'compelling new motives, notably those associated with religious terrorism, coupled with increased access to critical information and key components, notably involving weapons of mass destruction (WMD), leading to enhanced terrorist capabilities, could portend an even bloodier and more destructive era of violence ahead than any we have seen before'.[23]

In some ways, both the working assumptions and the published discussion of terrorism during the mid- to late-1990s moved in a parallel fashion to that about uncivil violence in the poor world, stimulated by publication of Kaplan's 1994 'Coming anarchy' article in the *Atlantic Monthly*, which gave impetus to the 'new barbarian' thesis of incoherent violence in the poor world that will be discussed in Part II. Both literatures appeared to be supplied with a distressing and proliferating catalogue of cases to support the arguments made. In American policy circles, in particular, the threat of a new terrorism was connected to two other perceived sources of threat: one older; the other its offspring. The role of certain states and leaders (prominently Colonel Gaddafi of Libya) in providing weapons, training and other forms of support to terrorist groups, was well-known and led directly to the American airforce attack on Tripoli in 1986 shortly after a nightclub was bombed in Berlin with, American sources categorically alleged, direct Libyan complicity. Despite denial, this precision attack by F-111 fighter-bombers based in England, which looked perilously like an attempt to conduct an assassination, has had a long tale of consequence, including the arrest, trial and conviction of one of the two Libyan airline employees accused of perpetrating the Lockerbie bombing.

The second type of threat took the concept of terror one step further by identifying 'rogue states' – North Korea is the favoured example – which were thought to be both capable of and likely to conduct acts of international terrorism without the use of intermediaries. This concern quickly merges into one of the threats which are said to justify the deployment of national missile defence against principally the threat of a ballistic missile being used by such a rogue state to deliver a weapon of mass destruction on the continental United States.

By the time that we reach this point in a ballooning argument about the scope of the new strategic environment, we have left any manageable discussion about the nature of terrorism well behind.

The collapse of the Oslo 'peace process', the recommencement of the Intifada and Israeli response to it in 2000 and growing recognition that the technical possibilities of biological attack may be both wider and easier to obtain than hitherto thought, have both served further to inflate an already large set of presumptions.[24] It stands in contrast to the actual record of terrorist attacks, in particular since the mid-1990s.

A review of data from the late 1960s to the 1990s shows a reduction in the frequency and intensity of international terrorism at the end of the Cold War. This pattern continued in the later 1990s. During that decade, eighty-seven Americans were killed by terrorists in a total of 1,372 attacks perpetrated against American targets overseas. In contrast, 571 died in 1,701 attacks during the 1980s.[25] In other words, the risk of death was six times greater, per incident, during the earlier period. Furthermore, of the 9,000 incidents recorded since 1968 in the Rand Chronology of International Terrorism, Hoffman notes that fewer than 100 contain evidence of any indication that terrorists plotted to attempt to use chemical, biological or radiological weapons or to steal or otherwise fabricate their own nuclear devices, much less to actually carry out such attacks. Indeed, he goes on to observe that, since the beginning of the twentieth century, little more than a dozen terrorist incidents have resulted in the deaths of more than 100 people at one time. Only if the criterion of numbers of death per incident is lowered to twenty-five does one begin to reach a substantial number of incidents. A Rand study on the likelihood of nuclear terrorism, cited by Hoffman, suggests 'That it is either very hard to kill large numbers of persons or very rarely tried'.[26]

The enormity, and the scale of casualties – around 3,000 – of the 11 September 2001 attacks in the US exceeded that of any previous single episode. The ultimate 'propaganda of the deed'. They demonstrated, with terrible efficiency, how suicide terrorists could turn airliners into massive guided missiles. The perpetrators did not try to use exotic means of attack. The toll of deaths from terrorism since 1968 was vastly increased in absolute number, at a single stroke: and it is amazing that the New York attacks did not kill many more. But even the new total remains modest relative to other causes of accidental death; and the events of that day do not change the trend of the 1990s.

If the risks are statistically small because the absolute number of victims is small, and therefore the likelihood of the risk to any individual person is far less than that from death through a road accident or choking on food, for example, how then does one explain the degree to which the issue of terrorism bulks so large in popular assessments of the risks people run? Part may be explained as filling the vacuum left by the collapse of the USSR. The cloak of the Other, of the perfect enemy, fell onto terrorists' shoulders. In the case of religious fundamentalists infused with a general hatred of the secular West, the cloak is welcomed. As one tries to deduce the objectives of the perpetrators of 11 September 2001, the desire to crystallise a 'clash of civilizations' stereotype of the Islamic world in western minds seems evident: for it might be thought to polarise further the Islamic world, and to strengthen the appeal of figures, such as Osama bin Laden, among the populations of states whose governments are opposed to the fundamentalists. That would assist another of their stated aims: the overthrow of regimes which they regard as treacherous to their version of Islam.

However, in the West, another aspect of terrorism – an aspect, the stimulation of which also we may deduce to have been central to the objectives of the 11 September 2001 terrorists – may explain the length of terrorism's shadow over western minds. As mentioned in the Introduction, this is the pervasive, formless fear created so expertly by the suicide pilots. These attacks used the complex systems of communications that Americans took for granted and turned the mundane experience of air travel into pure terror, both in the use of the 'planes as flying bombs' and in the mental anguish of the doomed passengers, told to telephone their loved ones before they died. In all this, the media, especially TV, was also hijacked to the terrorists' end. Their targets and their means of attack were perfectly chosen for their semiotic effect, among others. No-one will ever look at an ordinary domestic airliner in the same way again. That fear thus feeds a cultural self-doubt, which touches endless other threads of activity that, if cut, destroy the fabric of public confidence that underpins economic growth. If tipping the global economy into recession was also an aim of the 11 September 2001 terrorists, their timing in the economic cycle was well chosen, although, as this book goes to press, unsuccessful.

However, in order to place terrorism in an analytically productive comparative framework of uncivil violence, a task even more vital after 11 September 2001, we need to do more than to observe the trends, and to note the ghastly success of those attacks in striking the cultural and psychological equilibrium of their enemies.

In order to judge this form of uncivil violence against that to be found in the uncivil wars which pockmark the poor world, the first task is to return some precision to the words. That is what Professor

Gearty does. He provides the best working definition, which therefore we shall follow.

For many years, the working definition of terrorism has been that offered by Professor Paul Wilkinson. He states that 'political terrorism may be briefly defined as coercive intimidation. It is the systematic use of murder and destruction and the threat of murder and destruction in order to terrorise individuals, groups, communities or governments into conceding to the terrorists' political demands.'[27] Gearty proposes a narrower definition. He asserts, more systematically, that there are four essential elements, which must always be present: 'violence is unequivocally terrorist when it is politically motivated and carried out by sub-state groups; when its victims are chosen at random; and when the purpose behind the violence is to communicate a message to a wider audience.'[28]

The 2001 attacks fulfil the four elements precisely, but not all these phenomena being linked to it do. Gearty also adds another characteristic, which he calls 'the central paradox of terror. The methods terrorists use to get attention mean that the public learns of their aims but invariably rejects what they stand for.'[29] By employing Gearty's definition rigorously, it becomes possible to remove two large categories of evidence from discussion, which assists in obtaining a much clearer focus upon what remains.

First, we may dismiss the notion of 'state terrorism'. Terrorist acts are, by definition, committed by sub-state actors, not by states. But a state Terror is perfectly possible and was the regime in France in 1793 and 1794. Particularly after the passage of the Law of Suspects on 17 September 1793, a much wider group of victims than aristocrats could be identified. St Just explicitly associated action against enemies of the Revolution with the task of guarding the people's will; and that theme is an echo which some modern terrorists have sought to repeat. But, as Gearty pithily states it, 'The lesson of the French Revolution is that state terror can do more damage in a year than insurgents can do in a lifetime.'[30] He argues furthermore that the attempt to extend the label of terrorist to state actors was one of the single most damaging disservices done during the 1980s; for, by calling General Gaddafi or the Ayatollah Khomeini or President Assad a 'state terrorist' had the effect of harnessing the label into a subset of American foreign policy. We should be clear, he concludes, that the meaning of terrorism is 'indelibly linked to the idea of violent political subversion by substate groups'.[31]

The second category, which can be removed from consideration, is that of guerrillas (as well as states) who use terror aimed at specific groups or people as a tactic in their war. Assassination of individuals, whether the Prime Minister of India by a Tamil Tiger suicide bomber or a Palestinian bomb maker or strategist with an exploding mobile telephone or a precision attack from an army helicopter, does not fit within the working definition; for terrorist acts are, by definition, indiscriminate. That is what gives a pure terrorist act its powerful impact. Every reader of a newspaper or listener to a news bulletin thinks 'it could have been me'. This Gearty calls the trance of terror: we are all victims of a successful terrorist attack.[32]

Both Gearty and Hoffman are agreed that the Palestine Liberation Organisation is accurately described as a terrorist movement. But Hoffman points out that it is arguably unique in history. Not only was it the first truly international terrorist organisation, it was also one of the first terrorist groups actively to pursue the accumulation of capital as an organisational priority. By the mid-1980s it is estimated to have established an annual income of $600 million, of which $500 million was derived from investments – an astonishing fact, given that, when established in 1964, the PLO had no funds or infrastructure or real direction. Hoffman ascribes its trajectory to Arafat's election and continuation in power since 1968, as equally the emergence of more violent and extreme splinter groups dissatisfied with Arafat's line, particularly after his speech at the United Nations in November 1974, when the PLO made its first attempt to transcend its international terrorist image. But – and the point cannot be denied – Gearty underlines the centrality of the Middle Eastern conflict in the emergence of the modern preoccupation with the threat of terrorism in the rich world.

The development of political terror into a deliberate strategy took place in the Middle East. Its first heyday was during the years 1968 to 1974 and within that period of hijackings, gun attacks and bombings, conducted by Palestinians and increasingly by the Popular Front for the Liberation of Palestine, led by Dr George Habash, one episode more than any other signalled the arrival of international terrorism as a force in world opinion. This occurred on 10 September 1970. On the same day, members of the PFLP managed to hijack three jetliners, with a total of 475 hostages on board, bound for New York from Europe. One of the planes was flown to Cairo, where it was emptied and blown up; the other two were ordered to land at Dawson's Field, a deserted airstrip in Jordan, where they were joined by yet another plane, a BOAC VC-10 with over one hundred passengers and crew. After several days of negotiation, a deal was eventually made under which seven Palestinian detainees were released from prisons in

Switzerland, Britain and West Germany and all the hostages emerged alive. For the first time, the hijackers actively orchestrated the international press – even marking out the camera positions from which they would get the best view first of the emergence of the released hostages, then of the blowing-up of the planes.[33] But the PFLP's act of international theatre at Dawson's Field was too much for King Hussein of Jordan, who, on 17 September 1970, launched the Jordanian army in a ferocious crackdown on the PLO such that by the autumn of 1971 the Palestinians found themselves more isolated than ever, shunned by Arab states and actively hunted by both Israel and Jordan to whose land they had laid claim.

The response to the strategic defeat, which was the consequence of the PFLP's tactical success in conducting the airline hijackings, was the emergence of new militant strands of which the fiercest, Black September, took its name from the humiliations of September 1970. It perpetrated a number of gruesome attacks against Israelis overseas during 1972–3, culminating in the kidnapping and eventual death of Israeli athletes at the Olympic Games in Munich.[34] In contemporary public consciousness, it is the Palestinians who provide the model for ethno-nationalist terrorism (a claim which the Provisional IRA might dispute on grounds of seniority). But equally, an understanding of the motivations of these sorts of terrorist groups offers little help in decoding the inside of the actions perpetrated by other types of groups that are profoundly socially alienated and encapsulated within their own self-policed systems of belief, although the actions they undertake have common 'outside' features.

The watershed of the Lockerbie bombing

While the 2001 attacks will be the dominating image and memory of mass casualty terrorism, for purposes of understanding the phenomenon, not least that attack, it is the Lockerbie bombing that stands at a watershed. For, whereas lines leading back to the Middle East dispute may be seen in later incidents such as the bombing of the American embassies in East Africa in August 1998 and of the USS Cole in Aden Harbour in 2000, for which Osama bin Laden has been indicted, and now the culminating attacks of 2001, three common features of terrorists and their acts (which are not to be obscured by the recommencement of the Palestinian Intifada and the Israeli response to it) are increasingly evident.

The first is the move from conditional to unconditional acts. The PFLP hijackings of 1968 to 1970, and even the kidnapping of the

Israeli athletes by Black September at the Munich Olympics, were directed at a particular objective, like forcing the release of their comrades from jail in exchange for the lives of hostages, which either occurred (at Dawson's Field) or did not (at Munich). For this, it was necessary to reveal identity and to control carefully the escalation of the violence used: something which, Gearty observes, the Provisional IRA has always been careful to do. But if the motive is revenge or some form of declaration and warning or an apocalyptic statement about the nature of the world unrelated to any other party, then there is no negotiation to be had and no virtue in restraint. In this sense, Lockerbie displayed new tendencies even if its origins lay in revenge for past actions in the Middle East. It is the precursor of the suicide flights of 2001. But even here we are in the dark. The precise motivations behind Lockerbie are still obscure; for although the Scottish judges, sitting without a jury at Camp Zeist in the Netherlands as a Scottish jurisdiction under special dispensation, heard evidence upon which they found one of the two Libyan security officers, Abdel Baset al-Megrahi, guilty, the verdict has not ended the matter.

The judges placed particular weight on the evidence of a Maltese shopkeeper who identified al-Megrahi as the person who had bought the clothing which had surrounded the device that had exploded in the airliner. This, the judges said, together with evidence of the transmission of the baggage from Malta to London via Frankfurt, fitted together into a real and convincing pattern which caused them to find al-Megrahi guilty beyond reasonable doubt.[35] But both al-Megrahi and his co-accused, Lamin Khalifa Fhimah, who was acquitted, had exercised their right not to give evidence and, therefore, were never cross-examined; nor has anyone ever claimed responsibility for the attack. At a dramatic moment during the trial, Pierre Salinger, who had been Press Secretary to President John F. Kennedy, stated at the end of his testimony, when called by the prosecution, so that the court could be shown a recording of a filmed interview which he had conducted with the defendants in 1991, that in his opinion the two Libyans had nothing to do with the bombing and that he knew who the real culprits were. He was ordered out of the witness box by the presiding judge.[36] Others continue to adhere to other hypotheses. A persisting one is that the bombing was indeed in revenge for an American attack but not that of the US Air Force against Tripoli, rather the accidental shooting down of an Iranian airbus by the USS *Vincennes*.

The conviction depended crucially on the identification evidence of the Maltese shopkeeper, and on the pattern of circumstantial evidence. Megrahi has appealed against his conviction and so all that can be said in these circumstances is that the trial and conviction failed to provide a comprehensive answer to the question of what lay inside this action that many had hoped for. But the range of possibilities between the Libyan and Iranian hypotheses was quite constrained and potential motives could be logically deduced.

The same is broadly true of the terrorist attacks which are thought to have emanated from Osama bin Laden and his al-Qae'da ('the base') organisation and its closely linked allies, Egyptian Islamic Jihad (the assassins of President Sadat) and Gamaya Islamiya, led by Sheikh Omar Abdul Rahman, the perpetrators of the 1993 attack on the World Trade Center. Indeed, even before the gigantic police operation which followed the September 2001 attacks began to produce direct evidence linking the suicide hijackers to bin Laden and al-Qae'da, circumstantial evidence pointed towards bin Laden as the likely instigator. Both the choice of targets with a high degree of symbolism and the means of attack, using suicide killers, were reminiscent of the previous attacks attributed to this source. Significant too was the circumstantial evidence of the timing: an attack on 11 September comes in the first third of Black September – the month filled with many of the most traumatic anniversaries for the extremist and rejectionist wings involved in the Middle Eastern dispute.

The 10th is, of course, the anniversary of the multiple hijacking to Dawson's Field and thus the trigger to the events from which Black September (the organisation) emerged. The 13th is the anniversary of the (to rejectionists) infamous signing of the Oslo Peace Accord in 1994; the 16th conjures the memory of the massacres in the Lebanese refugee camps of Sabra and Chatila by Christian–Lebanese allies of the Israelis in 1982 – massacres which Ariel Sharon is alleged to have ordered; the 17th is the anniversary of the beginning of King Hussein's crackdown on the Palestinians in 1970, and the 28th is the anniversary of the walk on the Temple Mount taken by the same Sharon – by now leader of the Israeli Likud opposition – in 2000, which was followed by the undermining of the Oslo process, eventually the electoral defeat of the Barak government and Sharon's installation as Prime Minister and the commencement of the second Intifada.[37]

The web of practical, personal and religio-ideological linkages, which cover many of the Middle Eastern terrorist groups, is complex and detailed; but the broad outlines have been published. Bin Laden, son of a construction magnate originally from southern Yemen who made his fortune through renovation of the holy cities of Mecca and

Medina in Saudi Arabia, fell under the influence of Dr Abdullah Azzam while a student at Jeddah university. Azzam, a Palestinian of Jordanian origin, was an influential figure in the Muslim Brotherhood and is regarded as the historical leader of Hamas. After his move to Afghanistan, or Pakistan in the early 1980s, bin Laden assisted Azzam with the MaK (Maktab al Khidlatlil-mujahidin al-Arab), commonly known as the Afghan Bureau. This organisation assisted in the Afghan Jihad, recruiting Arab and Muslim youths from across the Arab world to fight the Soviet Union. Towards the end of the anti-Soviet Afghan campaign, bin Laden's relationship with Azzam deteriorated when the latter supported Ahmad Shah Massoud as leader of the Northern Alliance fighting the Taliban. It is alleged that bin Laden, who became close to the Taliban, was instrumental in arranging the assassination of Massoud in September 2001. There was a rapprochement with his mentor, Azzam, until he was assassinated in September 1989. Al-Qae'da benefited from the technical expertise and the financial networks which MaK had mobilised during the anti-Soviet campaign. Bin Laden's terror campaign against the US began as a consequence of the Gulf War, with the failure of the Saudi rulers to honour their pledge to cause foreign troops to be removed from Saudi Arabia after the liberation of Kuwait. Bin Laden therefore began a campaign against the Saudi royal house, claiming that they were false Muslims and that it was necessary to replace them with a true Islamic leadership. He was deported from Saudi Arabia in 1992 and his citizenship revoked in 1994.

The organisational structure of al-Qae'da appears to follow the classic form for successful terrorism demonstrated with great effect by the FLN during the war against the French in Algeria in the mid-1950s. This structure keeps the leadership insulated from the operatives and the operatives insulated from each other in cells so that the members of any one cell do not possess sufficient information to compromise anything beyond its own knowledge and operations. Bin Laden and his close associates, in the consultative council (Shura Majlis), including members of Egyptian Islamic Jihad and Gamaya Islamiya. Four executive military, religio-legal, media and finance committees make the strategic decisions which are then conveyed to the relevant operative cells via the military committee. The most complete recent account of al-Qae'da notes that, as a consequence of its structure and *modus operandi*, the operation 'has a high capacity for infiltrating any Muslim community irrespective of' size and geographic location'. This is because many operatives may act as 'sleepers' and because the network of banks and charities funnelling funds for the operations may draw from the charity of perfectly respectable and unsuspecting individuals. The fact that such a structure means that, in countering al-Qae'da, counterintelligence services are actually obliged to entertain the possibility that any Islamic or Muslim community may be wittingly or unwittingly involved, making it difficult to avoid the crystallisation of the 'clash of civilisations' stereotype, plays strongly into the hands of fundamentalists.[38]

The structure may be larger in number and in global reach; the sources of finance may be larger and more various; the imagination in designing terrorist attacks against the US may be greater but the fundamental nature of al-Qae'da and its purposes are recognisably located within that principal vortex of international terrorism, which had its origins in the Middle East in the late 1960s. It continues to draw on the problems of that region to sustain it. It is with that knowledge that, as with Lockerbie, it is possible with some confidence to set the outer parameters in the search for motive. And it is all these characteristics which caused the leading French expert on terrorism, Gérard Chaliand, to observe that 'The American response will not pour out over a wide-ranging conflict.' The attacks in the US are, in Chaliand's view, 'the final period of classical terrorism. I say classical,' he continued, 'because even if the attack is the most violent in its expression, the leap is a quantitative not a qualitative one.'[39]

This judgement is of high importance as one seeks to place the 2001 attacks in a defensible analytic context. They were the culminating unconditional terrorist attacks of which the Lockerbie bombing provides us with the original emblematic instance; and in all these regards the Middle Eastern road from Dawson's Field to the World Trade Center and the Pentagon, seen as best we may in terms of motivation and will on the inside, stand distinct from what we know of three other terrorist attacks of the mid-1990s which were of seminal importance in shaping the view of terrorism taken at that time by the US intelligence community. These cases were, respectively, the actions of the Aum Shinrikyo cult, of the American militias and of the so-called Unabomber. They too engaged in unconditional attacks, but exemplify the second characteristic, not to be found in the trail of unconditional terrorism with a Middle Eastern origin.

This is the prominence of what might best be called pastiche ideologies, whose contents are wildly various but which share the same characteristic with the beliefs of the Sierra Leonian RUF (to be discussed in Chapter 6), namely of strong encapsulation as an 'enclave' ideology. In their investigation of Aum, Kaplan and Marshall focused upon some of the highly talented young Japanese scientists, doctors and engineers who became members of the cult and who applied their skills in its state-of-the-art laboratories to produce chemical, biological and other exotic forms of killing. They included Seiichi Endo, with a doctorate in molecular biology, who was Aum's biological weapons chief; Masami Tsuchiya, a chemist who was in charge of synthesising nerve gases and other chemical agents, and the astro-physicist, Hideo Murai, who, as Aum's minister of science and technology, was one of Asahara's principal aides.

Unlike the austere attempt of bin Laden and the Islamic fundamentalists to recreate the religion of the medieval desert in the face of the future, Asahara's canny megalomania drew on every type of religious tradition. From the outset, Asahara preached a millenarian and apocalyptic message. He described himself as 'today's Christ', but also drew on the protocols of the Elders of Zion as a source of his anti-Semitism, and gave particular emphasis to the Hindu god of destruction and regeneration, Shiva, whose face dominated the entrance to the Satian-7 laboratory, where the Sarin nerve gas was manufactured. Nor did Aum confine itself to traditional religious sources. It drew heavily on science fiction. In an interview, the chief scientist, Murai, stated that Aum had used Isaac Asimov's classic science fiction *Foundation* series as a blueprint for the cult's long-term plans. Kaplan and Marshall spell out the remarkable similarities between the themes of Asimov's books and Asahara and his cult. The concoction had many of the qualities of cartoon film and computer game stories. Nor was that irrelevant; for the mixture proved to be effective in attracting precisely the withdrawn, obsessive loners who are addicted to such games: young, intelligent Japanese who were alienated from the pressurised goals of work and success in Japanese society; who were technically literate, highly knowledgeable young people lacking basic social skills, with little understanding of the world outside and strongly attracted by notions of apocalyptic redemption. At its peak, the Aum Shinrikyo cult had 10,000 members in Japan, an estimated 20,000 to 30,000 followers in Russia alone, and a further 10,000 to 20,000 converts around the world, with assets in the region of $1 billion.

The American white supremacists, of whom the Oklahoma bomber, Timothy McVeigh, was one, show a similar (if culturally narrower) amalgam of beliefs. Neither a purely anti-federalist nor extreme tax resistance movement, they couple religious hatred and racial intolerance within an ethos also heavily indebted to rabid anti-Semitism. Indeed, Hoffman suggested that the common thread running through most of the white supremacist movements that he had studied is the assertion that Jesus Christ was not a Jew but an Aryan; that white Anglo-Saxons and not Jews are the chosen people; that the US is the promised land and that Jews are to be viewed as impostors and children of Satan who must be exterminated.[40] McVeigh engineered the attack on the Murrah building in Oklahoma City to commemorate the second anniversary of the FBI's assault on the Branch Davidian's compound in Waco, Texas, in the course of which David Koresh, the deranged, charismatic leader, and over seventy other people died. The FBI assaults on Waco, and another at Ruby Ridge appear on most of the militia web sites, as confirmation of the federal government's plan to destroy liberty in America. McVeigh and those of his persuasion were vehemently opposed to gun control and subscribed to a range of fantastic conspiracy theories, many centring on the proposition that the United Nations was actively trying to form a one-world government and that the militias must train themselves in guerrilla warfare and survivalist techniques, in order to be able to resist armies of United Nations' soldiers that the US federal government intended to send against them.

Like Aum Shinrikyo, but unlike enclave millenarian movements of previous generations, the American white supremacist militias have made extensive use of the Internet to find and communicate with each other and with like-minded groups around the world, to advertise their beliefs and to seek recruits. A pilot study, which examined passively the Web site links, revealed, perhaps unsurprisingly, a world-wide network embracing, as well as the American white supremacists, similar groups in South Africa, Germany, Scandinavia and Russia, in particular. The concept of a 'leaderless resistance', advocated by Louis Beam, a computer security expert and head of the Aryan Nations, is intended to protect these groups from infiltration by use of a cell structure in cyberspace. However, the weakness of any group with a proselytising mission is that this priority always opens a window into the cell.[41] This is the third characteristic.

The solitary Unabomber, Theodore Kaczynski, formerly a mathematician at the University of California, conducted his letter-bomb campaign from a remote cabin in the Montana wilderness. His manifesto was a diatribe against technology and modernity and added a new twist to the common terrorist claim to be acting as a guardian of the will of the people. Kaczynski saw his campaign as being in some way a statement against humanity's destruction of the natural environment; and this theme is one which has recurred more recently in the justifications for their actions offered by the militant Animal Liberation Front in the UK and by the arsonists of the Earth Liberation Front, which has burned properties which, it claimed, were destroying the wilderness environment in Colorado. But the other feature of the Unabomber that deserves comment is that, by acting entirely alone, he showed the way in which a single individual bent on terrorism can obtain unprecedented publicity for his view. Of course, this third characteristic of the changed pattern of terrorism cuts both ways just like the second, for any terrorist who has a message to disseminate would find the temptation to do so irresistible, as Kaczynski did; and through the publicity which he thereby obtained the clues came to light which led to his discovery and arrest.

While it is possible that other lone individuals might possess the combination of beliefs, motives and skills which enabled Kaczynski to prosecute his seventeen-year terrorist campaign, arguably the role of the lone misfit with technical skills is more likely to be found in other forms of disruptive behaviour. In particular, profiling work that has been done on people engaging in computer hacking and in the writing of destructive computer viruses suggests that many of the personality traits that Kaplan and Marshall described for the recruits to the Aum Shinrikyo cult are equally applicable. However, attack by computer virus is not restricted to loners: there is evidence of terrorist groups engaging in virus attacks. In Japan, the computerised control systems of commuter trains have been paralysed in one incident. The so-called 'PLO virus' at the Hebrew University in Jerusalem may be another instance. The Italian Red Brigade included attacks on computer systems as a stated objective in its manifesto.[42]

The evidence which emerges from inside the actions of terrorism since Lockerbie is imperfect. But it shows sufficient common structural characteristics of encapsulated millenarian and apocalyptic beliefs to make one fearful that, as Hoffman predicted in 1998, much worse may yet be to come. This is particularly so if, at the same time, one takes account of the advances in technology, the spread of knowledge and evidence of the relatively greater ease of access to certain previously highly regulated substances, particularly since the disintegration of the USSR. Aum provided evidence of programmes in all three main types of weapons of mass destruction. When the police raided the Aum sect's laboratories they found huge quantities of Sarin. Aum had also produced and tested the VX nerve gas,

mustard gas and sodium cyanide. Within the biological agent programme, Dr Seiichi Endo had prepared botulism, anthrax and Q-
fever. The cult had shown an interest in turning the deadly Ebola
virus into a biological warfare agent. Asahara and followers had tra-
velled to Zaire on an 'African salvation tour' apparently in an effort
to obtain the virus.[43] The cult also sought a nuclear capability. It purchased a vast sheep station in western Australia where it hoped to
mine uranium and then stole, with ease, huge quantities of technical
data from Mitsubishi Heavy Industry's compound in Hiroshima in
order to build a laser isotope separator with which to obtain
weapons-grade uranium 235. Since the end of the Soviet Union, an
abiding fear of intelligence services has been that some of the large
quantities of weapons-grade fissile material, which the Soviet Union
produced, might fall into the hands of terrorist groups; and indeed in
2001 a substantial quantity of uranium 235 was intercepted being
offered for sale.

But at the turn of the millennium, much attention in the capability's analysis was directed at the threat of terrorism using one
biological agent in particular. One of the great successes of late-
twentieth-century public health has been the world-wide eradication
of smallpox. Therefore, populations which were once universally
vaccinated are now vulnerable to that disease. Furthermore, since
the eradication of the disease, world stockpiles of smallpox vaccine
have both shrunk and deteriorated from long storage. Plainly, the
theoretical threat of smallpox attack has increased if the virus can be
obtained from one of the two laboratories where it still exists.[44] The
combination of millenarian enclave ideologies with this range of capabilities might suggest that the decline in numbers and intensity of
terrorist attack recorded in the Rand and State Department databases for the later 1990s should not be expected to continue for
much longer. Would this be the correct inference to draw? The consensus among experts before 11 September was probably not. Should
that judgement now be revised?

The judgement does not imply complacency or the belief that the
present and potential future threat of terrorist violence should not be
countered. What it does suggest is that the nature of the response
must be shaped by an understanding of the inside and outside of terrorist acts and not just by a description of the proliferation of capabilities. Furthermore, that relationship between will and means
must also be assessed in light of performance.

Terrorism and combating it after 11 September 2001

All these issues were reviewed in the course of a major research project of the Norwegian Defence Research Establishment, entitled *Terrorism and asymmetric warfare: emerging security challenges after the Cold War*, which ran from spring 1999 to the summer of 2001 and engaged many of the most distinguished experts in the field, world-wide. The project synthesised its findings as a series of propositions. The first pair described the apparent tension between a declining trend and a massive high-impact incident. The first proposition is that

> the future ideological landscape will become less uniform and will change more rapidly than before ... no single ideology will be able to capture an entire generation like Marxism in its Maoist version was able to do. Instead we will continue to see the mushrooming of extremist ideas and 'power-ideologies' [called pastiche ideologies above, pp. 77–8] borrowing ideas and ideological substance from a wide variety of sources ... as a result we will probably witness a further decline of ideological socio-revolutionary terrorism.

Within that trend, the Norwegian study suggests that single-issue terrorism may rise in more dramatic forms and, in particular – their second proposition – that 'the number and strength of "counter cultures", in particular religious movements and cults, will continue to grow'. This suggests that 'religious terrorism will be a significant factor in future forms of terrorism. Religious terrorism tends to be more lethal, and we therefore may expect a rise in mass casualty terrorism.'

Noting that the global trend appears to be towards larger economic inequalities inside states as globalisation favours the highly skilled and educated, the individualisation of labour and weakening of trade unions, the study warns of a conjunction of these factors setting the stage for more ideological terrorism in the long run. But this is dependent partly on the rise of new radical socialist ideologies currently not in view and on the degree to which governments can maintain adequate legitimacy for policing functions in a context of decreasing governmental control over the economy. Presciently, the Norwegians 'predict a future shift in focus for terrorist groups away from states and symbols of the state towards businesses and transnational corporations'.

They expect an increase in transnational organised crime in the black part of the global economy and expect to see it engaged with terrorist organisations, particularly through the drugs-for-weapons trade and in people trafficking. Given the forms of terrorism which (correctly) they expected to see occur, the study stressed the importance for such terrorists of the propaganda of the deed. Given that acts of theatre ('attacks choreographed to effect maximum psychological effect on various audiences') are their objective, the means used would be the most reliable: hence the group thought that conventional rather than exotic means might be chosen and, in particular, it noted that to date there had been 'no serious cyber terrorist attacks reported, satisfying a meaningful definition of the term'.

Their overall conclusion was precisely confirmed in September 2001:

> there appears to be a trend towards more lethal forms of terrorism; ... we may also discern a gradual blurring of domestic and transnational terrorism. Terrorist organisations will become more transnational and may shift more quickly from one region to another. We may also expect a greater privatisation of terrorism with regard to target and sponsorship.

From this they suggest that against the gradual pattern of a declining trend 'we may expect that terrorism in rare cases will be what we may term a "low-probability high-consequence event" ... we do need to have a capability to handle short periods of very lethal forms of transnational terrorism.'[45]

In his February 2001 article and paper published in the Norwegian project, Hoffman revisited the expectations about the new forms of terrorism that were commonplace in the later 1990s and which led him to the bleak assessment, cited above, in his 1998 book. He restated those predictions and then observed that 'this new era of terrorism – supposedly more lethal and bloody than before – that the new terrorists were thought surely to wreak, has yet to materialise'.[46] Hard as it is to raise this question in the weeks immediately after the atrocities in the USA, it is vital to ask whether that act – predicted in source and form earlier that year in the Norwegian project – should force a further revision of Hoffman's view, back towards that expressed in 1998. On balance, probably not.

The point of Hoffman's 2001 view was not that mass casualty attacks might not be attempted, but that, in line with the general findings of the Norwegian study, he was sceptical about them being attempted or successfully achieved employing exotic means of killing. The September 2001 attacks do not disturb that position. The perpetrators carefully chose the most reliable form of attack – fully fuelled airliners. The failure of the cyanide element in the 1993 attack on the twin towers, as well as the lesson that the towers were least vulnerable in the basement, most vulnerable about two-thirds of the way up, seem to have been learned well.

Hoffman explained that shortly after the 1995 cluster of events, especially the Tokyo nerve gas attack and the Oklahoma City bomb, US policy swung to focus with greatly heightened priority upon the threat of terrorist attacks employing weapons of mass destruction. That assessment started with analysis of theoretical access to capabilities, placed those judgements in a worst case scenario threat assessment, and this approach, Hoffman asserted, has remained in place ever since: a fairly narrow high priority policy focus on 'lower-probability/higher-consequence threats, which in turn posit virtually limitless vulnerabilities, [that] does not reflect the realities of contemporary terrorist behaviour and operation'.[47] This broad judgement is supported in another substantial recent study of the threat of terrorism from WMDs.[48] What has happened in Hoffman's opinion is that perhaps because of the suddenness and strength of the swing to the new high priority threat assessment, the lessons of Aum Shinrikyo in particular have simply been misunderstood.

The description of the cult and its deadly ambitions given above is not complete. Indeed, there was more. In addition to the attempts to create WMDs, Aum also attempted to manufacture assault rifles, TNT, and is known to have purchased a surplus Russian Mi17 helicopter equipped with chemical spray dispersal devices. This, Hoffman observed, is part of the point: for Aum Shinrikyo is by no means a typical terrorist group with its huge assets, its highly-skilled scientific and engineering staff, its state-of-the-art laboratories and its thousands of devoted followers. Aum was unique. And yet with all these assets, Aum could not conduct even a single truly successful chemical or biological attack. This 'speaks volumes about the challenges facing any lesser-endowed terrorist organisation ... Aum's experience suggests – however counter-intuitively or contrary to popular belief – the immense technological difficulties faced by any non-state entity in attempting to weaponise and effectively disseminate chemical and biological weapons.'[49] The Tokyo attack has been the exception rather than the rule in terms of terrorist behaviour: for to date no similar or copycat act of terrorism, which was thought likely to occur, has materialised. Indeed, as already observed, fewer than 100 of the 9,000 incidents since 1969 show any indication of plotting to attempt to use WMDs, much less actually to carry out such attacks. In their study of globalisation and the future of terrorism, Lia and Hansen find that there are 'very few identifiable systemic factors promoting high fatality terrorism', which is a general judgement not in conflict with the specific observation that religious terrorism will be a significant factor in future forms of terrorism quoted above: a prediction of February that was appallingly fulfilled in September 2001. But there was, in Hoffman's February judgement, 'a thin line between prudence and panic',[50] and after September that point is reinforced, not weakened.

In order to avoid panic and to marshal appropriate resources both to guard against terrorist attacks and to break up terrorist structures and networks – the twin goals which the US set itself in the immediate aftermath of the attacks of 11 September, when Secretary of State, Colin Powell, described graphically how, once the perpetrators of those outrages had been brought to justice, the US intended to 'tear up network after network' – two other sources of insight, in addition to a knowledge of the inside and outside of the acts and actors, are valuable and best described diagrammatically.

Figure 3.1 shows how three principal actors can interact in two environments.

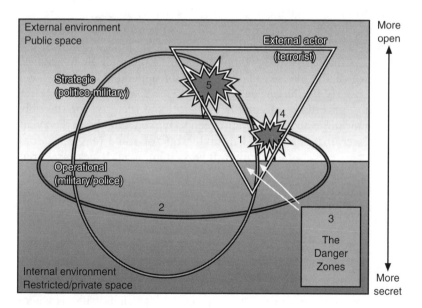

Figure 3.1 Scoping terrorists in social context.

The external environment, in the top half of the figure, signifies public space: civil environments of every type in which civil societies exist. In contrast, below the line is the internal environment which signifies worlds of private knowledge, usually reserved to the strategic and operational organs of state and usually known (one hopes) rather little to enemies. The triangle, representing the external actor – in this case the terrorist – exists principally in public space, but penetrates to some degree the internal environment. In contrast, the flat ellipse, representing the operational organs of the military and the police, exist equally in public and private space and has a broad presence in both: broad but shallow, relative to the orientation of the strategic politico-military organ. This has (again, one hopes) a deeper understanding of both the public and the private realms and those standpoints give – or should give – a higher vantage from which to survey both environments.

The strategic leadership of a terrorist organisation like al-Qae'da, for example, has an equivalent vantage point, but differently constructed, in that it seeks to operate principally in the public realm with carefully designed acts of terror tuned to maximise their disruptive psychological and cultural impact on each individual's inner sense of certainty and security. The knowledge which the terrorist obtains of the internal environment is principally important for operational reasons: but much of the necessary knowledge of complex systems in daily life, which need to be exploited for the purposes of the terrorist attack, is openly accessible in the public realm. In the case of 11 September, the complex timing of the multiple hijackings, upon which the success of the operation depended, was provided unconsciously by the airline timetable. This also gave the perpetrators the opportunity of complete operational security: for the only communications that they would need to make would be in the event of an aircraft being delayed in taking off for some reason. It does appear that possibly a fifth aircraft was an intended hijack target but was saved by being delayed on the ground.

The area numbered 1 is where the external actor, and the strategic and operational organs of state, are visible to each other: each knows that each is watching the other. This space is therefore relatively safe from attack. Number 2 labels that part of the private world where, together, the strategic and executive authorities can plan strategies to combat terrorism: the analogous area in the public realm is where there can be some confidence in active surveillance. Number 3 points to the two danger zones. The first, on the right-hand side, is where the terrorist gets 'inside the loop' of the operational organ of government without its knowledge and is able successfully to target it. If this penetration occurs, the result can be the deaths during 2002 of many Israeli civilians in numerous Palestinian suicide bombings of buses, bars, markets etc. The left-hand zone is the most dangerous of all. This is where the terrorist can successfully get 'inside the loop' of both the operational and the strategic organs of government without their prior knowledge. In that event, the result can be the attacks of 11 September 2001.

However, the diagram also indicates the two areas in which the terrorist organisation may be reciprocally vulnerable. Number 4 shows that space where, by police or military force, it is possible to take action against operative cells and to frustrate actual attacks. Number 5 shows the space in which, with strategic intelligence, it becomes possible to attack and neutralise the strategic functions – military, financial and media-related – of the terrorist organisation. Areas 4 and 5 are, therefore, areas of opportunity. The relationship between the shapes in Figure 3.1 is constantly changing, with the external actor constantly wishing to minimise its exposure and increase its opportunities to get 'inside the decision loop' in the internal environment. The strategic and operational organs of society wish to minimise the external actors' penetration of the internal environment (and hence the size of the danger zones) while at the same time maximising the scope for tactical or strategic strikes against the external actor.[51]

The struggle between the forces of terror and the forces of order occurs in four domains, which are represented in Figure 3.2.[52]

The first domain is that of time. What is in contention is time interpreted in two quite different ways. There is time as tempo: sometimes advantage will lie in deft coordination and a high speed of execution, as was the case with the suicide plane attacks of September 2001. Sometimes advantage will lie in maintaining a constant level of successful harrying of the terrorist in area 4 of Figure 3.1. Both fast and slow tempo affect stamina. The ability to outlast the opponent is one of the foundations of victory.

The second domain is that of space. Here again, there are two quite different types of space in contention. The first is the common sense view of space in the physical sense. The terrorist seeks to keep people out of buildings, out of the streets, out of aeroplanes and so do the forces of order with regard to the terrorist. There is also now an active struggle to occupy parts of cyberspace (which is really part of the next domain of operations).

Second, and of vital importance to democracies, there is moral

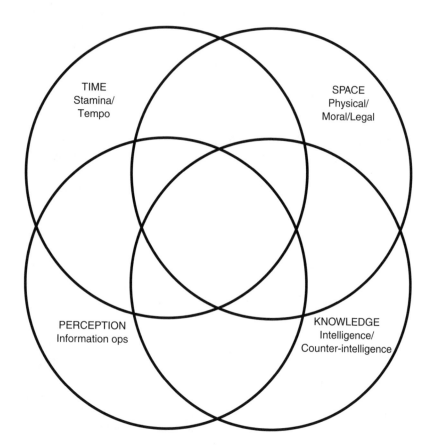

Figure 3.2 The four fields of contest.

and legal space. An objective of terrorists attacking democratic societies is always to try to provoke large, preferably indiscriminate, acts of revenge, which manifestly cannot be squared with the legal norms of society under attack. This was the first danger zone in the hours and days immediately after 11 September 2001 and it was successfully – brilliantly – avoided by the leaders of the West. On the one hand, the US made no military retaliation against anyone or anything and, on the other, the NATO Council on 12 September 2001, for the first time in the history of the Alliance, invoked Article 5 of the Washington Treaty ('The parties agree that an armed attack against one or more of them in Europe or North America should be considered an attack against them all...'). The following day the UN

General Assembly passed a resolution of condemnation and the Security Council unanimously approved Resolution 1368, which, as well as reiterating condemnation, expressed a preparedness to see all necessary means employed to bring the perpetrators to justice. These two actions – linked together through the second paragraph of Article 5 of the Washington Treaty, in which NATO undertook that 'any such armed attack and all measures taken as a result thereof shall immediately be reported to the Security Council' – provided an unprecedented and broad basis for legitimation of a wide spectrum of actions, including, but going far beyond, military actions in response to the atrocity.

Control of moral and legal space is one of the issues that is in contention in the third domain where the parties strive to control perception of the deed. This is the domain of information operations and media operations (distinct but linked activities) on behalf of the forces of order, and it is the domain in which the terrorist aims to achieve early dominance, first through the propagation of fear in the target population as described above and joy among supporters. When images of the latter are seen by the representatives of the former the results can be dramatic. Such was the case when western television audiences saw ululating women and chanting men welcoming the news of the attack on the World Trade Center in Palestinian territories of the West Bank of the Jordan. From a privileged seat in a newsroom, while assisting the ITN staff to interpret events during the days immediately after the attack, it was possible to see how swiftly and decisively those images transformed sympathies for the Palestinian cause among journalists and interviewed members of the public on television channels around the world.

One of the most important tactical objectives for an unconditional terrorist is to find ways in which to harness the broadcast media to the task of spreading despondency, fear and depression. That was the objective described by Murray Sayle when the PFLP positioned him and other members of the press for the best view at Dawson's Field in 1970. The tactic was brought to perfection when the two airliners in quick succession shattered the World Trade Center towers. The second, in particular, coming some minutes after the first was filmed throughout its approach to the tower. The footage was shown repeatedly throughout the following days and watched, in the most minute detail and with awful fascination, by enormous, suddenly inflated television audiences. This repetition of an attack that was originally seen as it happened on live television continued until the Chairman of ABC in the US ruled that it should only be repeated if necessary for the purposes of a particular television item. The degree to which this initial success by the perpetrators in controlling the domain of perception has produced lasting effects, particularly on children in coming years, is an issue now being raised by psychologists as this book goes to press.

The fourth domain of competition is the classic domain of spying, where each party seeks to obtain secret intelligence on the other, which can be used to harm the enemy. In the case of 11 September 2001, here again the perpetrators won decisive advantage. Either the relevant warning signals were not collected or were overlooked or were not brought together to make a pattern, which would have given some opportunity to try to frustrate the attack. In particular, the inappropriateness of a strong emphasis on electronic and signals intelligence, to the detriment of human intelligence, was evident. But organisations like al-Qae'da, particularly when using cells of suicide terrorists, are difficult, if not impossible, to penetrate with double agents, for obvious reasons. But the key counter-terrorist weapons are an effective early warning as a result of targeted surveillance and analysis by intelligence services: precisely the area of greatest failure by the Tokyo police in respect of the Aum cult, where copious evidence of its intentions and its behaviour was provided but discounted until it was almost too late. (In fact, the Sarin gas attack occurred where it did, with the intention of killing as many policemen as possible, in order to frustrate the investigation of the cult, which its members knew was then being actively pursued.) Terrorist organisations of all types, including unconditional ones, have an unavoidable area of vulnerability. Since most of the apocalyptic and millenarian ideologies encountered so far share some degree of motivation to state their beliefs, they thereby signal their presence and offer routes of entry behind their closed doors.

Where the four domains overlap one finds room for strategic manoeuvre. The objective of the terrorist is to pull the domains apart, thus minimising the overlap space; whereas the objective of the forces of order must be to dominate and bring together into alignment as much as possible the four domains, thereby enlarging the room for strategic manoeuvre (see Figure 3.3).

In the aftermath of the attacks of September 2001, it is hardly surprising that attention focuses almost entirely upon the threat of mass casualty terrorism. So at that moment it is important to restate the expectation from the Norwegian study, which is that the source of a future continuing stream of relatively small-scale incidents – but many of them – will come from other sources.

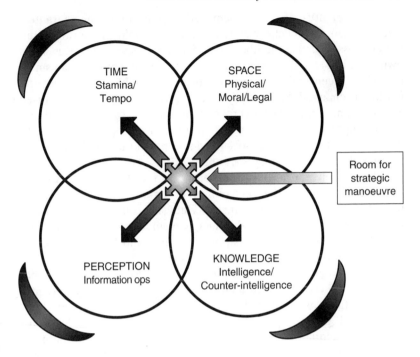

Figure 3.3 Compression increases the space for strategic manoeuvre.

The Norwegian study expects more single-issue terrorism (by socially-alienated environmentalists, for example) and anticipates a further decline in ideological socio-revolutionary terrorism, even if the language of this brand, that owes its origin to St Just and the Committee for Public Safety, continues to be adapted and used. Meanwhile, the form of terrorism most likely to produce casualties through a continuous stream of small-scale incidents rather than from mass action is the continuation of ethno-nationalist sub-groups. These include, with the erosion of their respective negotiated settlements, the rapid escalation of Palestinian terrorism and Israeli state terror in response, in the Middle East, and the creeping resumption of violence in Northern Ireland. These join the rising volume of terrorism in the post-Soviet space and most particularly the North Caucasus, as well as the other continuing post-colonial campaigns of the Basque separatists in Spain, the Tamil Tigers in Sri Lanka, militant Sikh and Kashmiri groups in the Indian sub-continent. The 'pseudo-colonials', writes Gearty, 'fight in pursuit of a total power, which even sovereignty – if it were achieved – could no longer guarantee. They are violent anachronisms in a changing political world.'[53] But, nonetheless, because the liberation ideology of some groups is, in its own way, as strongly encapsulated as the enclave millenarianism of the more recent religious groups, they are unable to see that the world has changed. Particularly where terrorist violence is socialised within a community over several generations, it is to be expected that any attempt by the major terrorist group to disengage will give rise to dissident fractions. This has occurred notably in the Middle East and in Ireland, two of the longest-running stories. The PLO's attempt to transform itself into a quasi-state entity as the 'Palestinian Authority', which involved the recognition of Israel as a *fait accompli*, recruited to the rejectionist wings of Hamas and Islamic Jihad. Likewise, the Provisional IRA's oblique engagement with the British and Irish governments, through its political wing, Sinn Fein, recruited to splinter groups of rejectionists (the Real IRA).

The Norwegian study judges that the well-established thesis that terrorism and civil violence tend to occur more frequently in democratising states or in countries undergoing rapid economic modernisation and growth, particularly where there are high levels of economic inequality, is well-substantiated in the case material. But, as Gearty was the first to note, such conflicts, while containing terrorists and terrorism, are not usefully and totally explained in those terms. They are known quantities and the anachronism in the political objectives of these conditional terrorists does not translate automatically into the reduction in the scale and intensity of terrorist actions that the databases all reveal for the later 1990s. The source of this, in the view of the Norwegian study group, is that the ending of the superpower competition meant that terrorism lost its power as a proxy war. That leads to the interesting thought that a world order with growing multilateral cooperation appears to correlate with a decline in international terrorism and thus, in turn, to the reverse hypothesis. Although it is early days, the signs of cooperation in a wide, if fragile, coalition against the perpetrators of the 11 September attacks might, if sustained, accelerate that effect. But should the shape of new strategic competitions lead again to hegemonic disputes, international terrorism might return. But that is, tentatively, not the present balance of judgement; which makes it all the more important that in responding to these threats of uncivil violence, which most preoccupy the minds of their citizens, democratic states do not fall into the trap of blanket overreaction.

The greatest danger probably does not lie in any single act of reaction or overreaction. It lies in the possibility that, as with the stone (or cough) which starts an avalanche, an appreciable danger exists of a cascade of risks, which might accelerate towards an unexpected – and probably unpredictable – precipice which, if passed, means that the future interaction of events – which may, and indeed most likely will, not be obviously interconnected – will be one where cause and effect becomes stochastic, uncontrollable.

The most helpful way of visualising this 'risk cascade' is with the help of a catastrophe cusp (see Figure 3.4). The figure shows how, at the danger surface, the urge to act under the influence of gross stereotyping may lead to the avalanche of uncontrollability. But equally the figure reveals that, if a positive risk cascade can be initi-

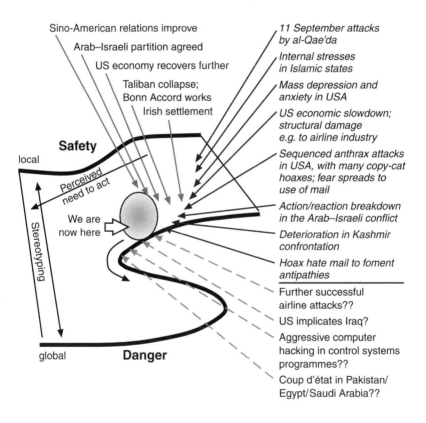

Figure 3.4 The risks of a 'risk cascade' illustrated on a catastrophe cusp.

ated, the opportunity is there to pull back up to the safety surface. At the time of going to press, it is not evident how we will proceed from the consequences of 11 September 2001. We are in a zone where the forces are in contention, with persuasive evidence of both safe and dangerous trends. Thus, the case for developing multilateral patterns of cooperation is underpinned by strong self-interest for the rich world. The further dangers of stereotyping are discussed in the next chapter.[54]

But equally, as this chapter has sought to argue, it is also vital, for the sake of the vastly more numerous actual and potential victims of uncivil war in the poor world, to ensure that, in their understandable fascination with the trance of terror, the rich and powerful do not so distort their priority and their actions that they diminish public awareness by distraction from the major tragedies of uncivil war in the world, which were described in the first part of this chapter, and the successful resolution of which will be an indispensable and indivisible part of defeating the terrorists.

4 A brief (and critical) encounter with academic security studies

Introduction

Huge and hugely unexpected trends and events burst into the land-scape of world politics. The ending of the East–West Cold War without a commensurate East–West hot war was the most promi-nent; it defined the framework of the years of the 'interregnum'. The preceding chapters have taken three principal facets of those times – the peculiar effects of Cold War thinking; uncivil war in the poor world and uncivil war, seen as terrorism, in the rich world – and examined them in relation to each other, and in turn. The purpose of this chapter is rather different. Its subject is the patterns of explana-tion which the academic study of security has offered. Four phases are described and its principal purpose follows from that: to propose some modification both to the substance and shape of academic security studies as they recover from a severe crisis of identity and confidence. The chapter suggests that, following the collapse of Clas-sical Realism, the neo-realist versus idealist tussle can be seen to have been miscast. A modified form of power-political analysis is now required: one which can grasp and use the continuing under-lying strengths of pragmatic realist description of an international system principally driven by the balance of power between states, while simultaneously accommodating the equally real presence of cosmopolitan values and of non-state actors, who believe in and promote them through campaigns for debt relief, for example, and structurally through the revived regime of human rights law and pro-cedure.

When Kant looked at the same question in the 1790s, he con-cluded that a reconciliation was not possible. However, following his advice that, since it is our moral duty to seek to 'terminate the disas-trous practice of war, we must simply act as if it [perpetual peace] could really come about ... Even if the fulfilment of this pacific intention were forever to remain a pious hope, we should still not be deceiving ourselves if we made it our maxim to work unceasingly towards it.'[1] We should therefore ask the question again in much changed circumstances. In the process, we should feel no embarrassment in getting help from wherever we can, which, this chapter suggests, is especially from Kant. To read his words for this purpose is, of course, to read them anachronistically, deliberately. That may offend historians of political thought who stress the importance of reading texts in context, so that their contemporary nuance is restored and understood by us, like an old master painting; but it should not do so for two reasons. First, the two purposes are simply different, but equally proper. Second, Kant in particular would surely approve because his quest also was for general principles that hold across different times and places.[2]

To do this, living, like Kant before us, in revolutionary times, we must first situate our present position within its own history. In our case, it is a history of ideas: the history of understanding the history of the Cold War and its ending.

That starting position is to be found in the received version of the discipline of security studies, a sub-set in the study of international relations (itself an uncomfortable derivative within the study of history[3]). It is a sub-set because it is less than the whole. This received version of security studies is defined by two self-limiting characteristics: by its general permeation with one (only) of the approaches to international relations, namely Classical Realism, and by its particular circumscription of interests, namely high politics – state politics – and military force, which secures the state.[4]

Security studies provided notably little help in understanding, let alone foretelling, the eruption of the largely bloodless Velvet Revolutions coming at the end of a bloody century, and the agenda of global issues is proving to be awkward. Why? Is this more to do with the nature of the issues or with the way that we examine them? To answer this question, the first task is to understand how we got to where we now are. Therefore, I offer an outline account of the stages through which the study of security has passed since the end of the World War. My main interest in doing this is to examine the scoping question about security studies: why it has the boundaries that it has.

We need to ask this first to see why the main preoccupations of security studies have offered so much less than might have been hoped for when the great transformations of the 1980s came upon us.

Second, it serves as a background to proposing different foundations for security studies.

This is, therefore, the story of an unfinished journey. So, in keeping with the theme of travel, the four stages in the operation of the internal combustion engine cycle provide us with the titles required to describe the four-stroke cycle in security studies: injection; compression; ignition; power.[5]

Injection

Shocks

From the first chapter onwards, the pivotal nature of the five years immediately after the end of the Second World War has been apparent in shaping the institutions and confrontations of the next sixty years. The late 1940s was also the previous formative moment before the present one in thinking about security. Four shocks and a specific view of knowledge served to shape the course which security studies took, and in which it has continued until now. The shocks came in two pairs, interactive and cumulative in effect, searching out and exposing the fault-lines in the existing views of security; and, as always, the view of knowledge current at the time gave intellectual legitimacy to the shape of the enterprise.

The evidence of the enormity of the Third Reich and its driving project, the Final Solution, had been known secretly in high circles for some time. It seeped out at last into public view at Nuremberg and thereafter in books like Lord Russell's *Scourge of the Swastika*, staining deeply and indelibly the cultural optimism of Enlightenment Europe.[6] A spreading realisation of what had been defeated, and hence of what it portended had it not been defeated, burned the conscience and sensibilities of scholars in the late 1940s.[7] Nor was it fully achieved: it took another human generation before the humiliation of occupation could begin to be openly confronted.

That first shock was amplified by another. Scholars, many of whom had been sympathetic to the project, recoiled in hindsight at the pitiful inadequacy of the inter-war structures of international conflict resolution, created in the League of Nations and flouted by the dictators. That, combined with the popular view of appeasement and with polemic writing, of which publication in 1946 of the second edition of E.H. Carr's *Twenty Years Crisis* was the most influential, conditioned the intellectual environment of the immediate post-war years to be caustic about alleged 'idealism' (utopianism, in Carr's book) in the interests of security. In Carr's astringent words, 'the inner meaning of the modern international crisis is the collapse of the whole structure of utopianism based on the concept of the harmony of interests ... the unpalatable fact [is] of a fundamental divergence of interest between nations desirous of maintaining the status quo and nations desirous to change it.'[8]

A.J.P. Taylor's *Origins of the Second World War*,[9] with its uncomfortable revision of who the appeasers were and why they were so much the norm and not the exception in the later 1930s, was still a decade away. Nor were the founders of Chatham House and the Council on Foreign Relations and promoters of the formal study of international politics through endowment of the Woodrow Wilson Chair at Aberystwyth – in 1919, the first of its kind – especially unusual or starry-eyed in seeing that something should be done to prevent recurrence of catastrophes like the Great War.

In addition to Carr's book, two further influential stimuli shaping post-war international security studies on each side of the Atlantic, respectively, were the publication in Britain, also in 1946, of Martin Wight's Chatham House 'Looking Forward' pamphlet, and in 1948 of Hans Morgenthau's *Politics among Nations* in the USA.[10] Both these works sought to isolate the underlying principles of the international 'system', and to promote accretion of deductive knowledge about it. They were free of the taint of too much optimism about human nature. All these characteristics resonated especially in the sub-set of international relations that was becoming security studies. Hence these works are especially noteworthy in its intellectual hinterland.

The Second World War – the Good War – had been framed and fought in the language of liberation. That might have been confirmation enough of the moral and intellectual imperative of Realism for scholars who had lived, and often fought, in the last World War. But, two further shocks were delivered in quick order.

The Japanese war ended with the mushroom clouds of Hiroshima and Nagasaki. The arrival of the atomic bomb in world politics was the first of a second pair of shocks. Its partner was the rapid transmutation of Stalin's Soviet Union from popular wartime ally to implacable ideological enemy. This was a process of image alteration recorded in Mass Observation and other early opinion polls. It was of such speed and conclusiveness during 1947–8 that it stimulated Jerome Frank and other clinical psychologists to apply the skills of their discipline to the explanation of public opinion in an age of mass media.[11] That view, of a Soviet opponent so ideologically driven that normal diplomacy was impossible, and only containment could produce security (argued by George Kennan both privately in The Long Telegram of 22 February 1946 and publicly as 'Mr X'), was an active force in the creation of an uncompromising cold peace.[12] Just as the atomic issue provided one of the shocks that shaped both the world order and our ways of viewing it then, the last section of this book suggests that the nuclear issue may be serving the same purpose – but in different ways – now.

Consequences

For security studies in the immediate post-war period, this second double shock prescribed a double agenda. One track explored the relationship of the atomic bomb to international relations. The other opened a complex and ultimately very large study of the military/technical dimensions of security. This included, but exceeded consideration of, the nuclear revolution in warfare. The work of Bernard Brodie opened this first track to thinking about the atomic bomb and deterrence.[13] Some of the thinking was unthinkable, truculently so in the case of Herman Kahn. However, the main thrust was towards the elaboration of a symmetrical argument, most clearly by F.H. Hinsley in *Power and the Pursuit of Peace* in 1963,[14] which elaborated Winston Churchill's famous, ironic aphorism that security was now the sturdy child of terror.

There was a comfortable affinity between a weighty account of the international system, moving, until 1945, through apparently inexorable cycles of war and peace, of the construction and failure of conflict avoidance institutions and the manner in which the threat of a Great Deterrent appeared to put an end to all this. A substrand of security studies built a bridge between deterrence theory and military technical considerations. This produced both nuclear histories, such as McGeorge Bundy's majestic review of the nuclear age,[15] and many studies of the way in which the immense technical impetus of nuclear weapons development pushed the arcane elaboration of nuclear deterrence away from the single Great Deterrent threat into, in Hinsley's view, the muddle-headed and dangerous elaboration of counter force. In a pithy essay, Howard observed that strategy was about a lot more than practical planning.[16]

With respect to the Soviet Union, the early importation of worst case assumptions gave a consistent tint to analysis of Soviet military preparations and plans. As Desmond Ball showed in his seminal study on politics and force levels, the combination of imperfect intelligence and vivid imagination under that assumption imparted fierce momentum to nuclear arsenals. Indeed, so strongly embedded had these maximal assumptions become that when, just before the arrival of *perestroika* proved important parts of their case, proponents of organically different interpretations of the dynamics of the Soviet military, such as Stephen Shenfield, Michael MccGwire and Christopher Donnelly at the Soviet Studies Research Centre, Sandhurst published, they encountered strong scepticism.[17] (A wider context to this account than this thumbnail sketch is given in the final section of the book.)

The response to this pair of double shocks was situated within the post-war expansion of universities, first in America, later in Britain and western Europe, and shaped for security studies itself by the idea and ambition of a social science. A 'discipline' could thus quickly be created and made routine. There were many hands to be set to work. In particular, the virtues of abstraction and the description of underlying repetitive structures were prominent features of a scholarly enterprise, whose dominant motif was 'Realism' – a shorthand usually interpreted as a harsh Bowdlerisation of Carr's seminal intervention.

The study of security has been a peculiarly regimented exercise when compared to other fields in the humanities (for in the humanities it lies, even if many practitioners would have it otherwise). What Robert Keohane calls 'Classical Realism' has been the single pivot around which most debates in security studies have turned for a generation.[18] It is defined by three main characteristics and two supporting qualities.

The first of the three main characteristics is of states as the prime and overwhelming actors in international affairs. The second is of assumed rationality in their conduct, accessible through deduction from actions (and, conversely, the ability to translate that rationality into action); and the third is of their prime and overwhelming pursuit of power, perceived and practised principally in diplomatic and military terms.

The two facilitating qualities, which have given Realism such vigour for so long, are, on the one hand, the assertive simplicity of these propositions and, on the other, the fact that, if the terms in which they are proposed are accepted, there is a natural closed logical loop.

These two characteristics help to explain the longevity and vigour with which the case for Realism (and latterly for 'neo-Realism') is maintained. Along with its self-image as a precise 'social science',

A brief encounter with security studies 101

which has an accumulating body of theory, and some predictive capacity, it also helps to explain the regimentation. Keohane points out an indication of this steadfastness in the face of evidence otherwise. He notices the persistent inconsistency between the preoccupation with the 'balance of power' as an explanatory device, to be found in the work of Martin Wight or Kenneth Waltz, and the third main characteristic mentioned above, namely the insistence that states seek maximum accumulation of power. These are evidently as incompatible one with the other as was America's lop-sided accumulation of gold during the First World War and the attempted restoration of the gold standard after it.[19]

But a more fundamental challenge has arisen. Progressively, the meaning and salience of each of the three main assumptions have been brought into question: first, power, then the state as prime actor, and most recently, presumptions of rationality. The Realist account has come under pressure. Once any of the three characteristics comes into question, the systemic form of explanation becomes hard to maintain because the wide scope to make assumptions about the behaviour of actors is sharply diminished. Put the other way around, in order to sustain confidence we need to know a lot more, substantively, about actors and their motives than usually we do and than was previously regarded as necessary.

Classical Realism is compressed by a need to explain new variables in world politics. The result of this compression was at one time thought by its critics in peace studies to be the elimination of Realism, and hence of the approach to security studies based upon it. But that would be both incorrect and unfortunate, for the approach unquestionably has had its successes in explaining aspects of world politics. Indeed, as the interregnum ends, those virtues become again more plainly apparent. However, while necessary, it is no longer a sufficient instrument even for that task, because high politics is no more immune to the forces of global transformation than other aspects of the contemporary world.[20] Hence the need for a modified approach, sketched at the end of the chapter.

Compression

The period during which Classical Realism was largely unchallenged in security studies coincided with the period of the post-Second World War long boom.[21] At the same time that President Nixon was untying the supports of the Bretton Woods system, by detaching the dollar from gold on 15 August 1971, Americans were coming to terms with defeat in South-east Asia. One group for whom Vietnam was a particular nemesis was the Realist practitioners, including members of the Kennedy circle, whose applied cynicism had failed to deliver victory. That experience had a long-lasting impact on their views as they grew older.[22] But it was the turn in the tide of the global economy that produced the first of three sources of compression.

Economic pressures

The optimism that wealth and wealth creation would cause to trickle down to the poor, which had underlain the main approach to the newly post-colonial world of the 1960s, was replaced in the 1970s with a more sombre mood. On the one hand, the Marxist and Marxist-derived school of 'underdevelopment' economists argued that the poverty of the so-called Third World was a pathological consequence of capitalist development; on the other, liberal economists and politicians took the view that something had to be done to help the poor in adversity. The Brandt Commission Report of 1983 exemplified the latter, set against a background conditioned by the former.[23] It marked a horizontal expansion of the scope of security, but not a frontal challenge to the three defining characteristics of Realism. Economic security was presented in the Brandt Report as part of the necessary condition for the maintenance of political security and the means to achieve it, by an ambitious scheme of global redistributed income tax between rich and poor, was proposed.

But, conceptually, the approach was no different from that implicit in the structure of the Charter of the United Nations, which, through its economic and social chapters and articles (Chapters IX and X, Articles 55–72), had recognised the same point. What differed was that in the 1970s there was a quickening sense of need to turn words into deeds. The mechanisms were state-centric: states would be the actors in an international system, which sought to animate the sleeping clauses of the UN Charter. It was not surprising, therefore, that, in addition to the Bretton Woods institutions (the World Bank and the International Monetary Fund), the United Nations specialist agencies (UNDP, UNICEF and UNHCR) were seen as the obvious links and conduits.

The development/economic facet of security (and an early signal of the environmental dimension to come) was crystallised by Richard Ullman in 1983 in *International Security*.[24] The economic security argument was grounded in a view that, as well as being active, violence could also be *structural*. This was soil shared with another sapling planted, like the concept of economic security, in the late 1940s, but only beginning to grow strongly in the 1970s: the idea of 'human rights'.

The received Classical Realist view of security became compressed from a second direction, as the temperature of the second Cold War rapidly fell after 1979. The coincidence of a sclerotic, gerontocratic Soviet leadership, the coming to power of muscular, confrontational conservatism with President Reagan, Mrs Thatcher and, to a lesser extent, Chancellor Kohl, and the fielding of three new technologies in nuclear delivery systems (faster, miniaturised, processing; satellite communication and navigation; and air-breathing, non-ballistic delivery vehicles) combined to form a considerable challenge to the received wisdom in security studies.

The transformation of war

This elicited several forms of response. The first was the arrival of a generation of security scholars whose roots were in a diversity of other disciplines, and whose earlier training owed little or nothing to Classical Realism, except in reaction to it. They found common ground with some of the less constrained scholars in security studies, notably, Ken Booth, Michael Clarke and Barrie Paskins, who were articulating views sharply less complacent than the official western norm.[25]

Responding, in particular, to moves towards explicit nuclear threats as a way of 'strengthening deterrence', these alternative security scholars produced volumes of criticism, arguing that, far from making the situation safer, the attempt to answer an ideological challenge in terms of nuclear missile hardware was thoroughly dangerous.[26] These views resonated with the western European protests against the deployment of intermediate-range nuclear systems in the early 1980s with which this book opened.[27] Theirs was essentially a 'levels of analysis' criticism, arguing that the militarising of security analysis meant that strategic questions were being treated in tactical technical terms. For churchmen, the conundrum of squaring nuclear deterrence with the criteria of Just War was a particular concern.

Whereas the peace movement activists and many of the alternative security scholars focused their attention principally upon nuclear weapons, a second and, in hindsight, analytically more influential approach was explored in work by Desmond Ball, Paul

Bracken and Bruce Blair.[28] They identified risk less in the claws, more in the nervous systems of the nuclear complexes of the super-powers. It was in their command and control systems that the greatest danger lay.

In particular, increasing sensitivity and increasing volumes of input data meant that the chance for misunderstanding increased; and with decreasing warning times and higher routine alert status the chance of accidental nuclear war was heightened. The Cuban missile crisis and the 'Able Archer' crisis have been noted as pivotal moments already in the preceding chapters; and they do, indeed, provide major punctuation of the era. But Desmond Ball argued in an arresting paper that the highest danger lay not in the risk of strategic systems being used first, but of smaller ('theater') nuclear weapons being used in a hitherto non-nuclear conflict, catalysing a general escalation through chaos. He documented the degree to which the penetration of western communications by the GRU and KGB signals intelligence agencies increased the opportunity for misunderstanding in crisis.[29]

Both these types of technically supported arguments about the inadequacy of nuclear deterrence derived from a deeper inadequacy. It was earliest signalled by W.B. Gallie. What made the problem of nuclear weapons so difficult to tackle, he argued, was a debilitating lack of historical sense in most security analysis.[30] To understand how to think about nuclear weapons, he shared with F.H. Hinsley a view of the importance of looking for long-term historical patterns, although disagreeing sharply with him about what conclusions we should draw. Hinsley saw the Great Deterrent putting full stop to the tragic cycle of failure in diplomatic instruments for the prevention of war before 1945. Gallie, in contrast, took the view that the problematic era of the nineteenth century, when the balance between impetus to war and to peace was not yet struck, was followed by a twentieth-century trajectory from total towards potential for genocidal warfare. This would only be halted if its darkest possibility was vividly and pre-emptively understood to be such. However, Gallie did not underestimate the difficulty of persuading people to do this, principally because it implied a challenge to central tenets of the modern, secular, scientific world-view and self-image.[31] And there the nuclear dragon has slept until reawakening, perhaps in quite different form, at the end of the interregnum (the subject of the final chapter).

The debate over the inadequacy of nuclear deterrence theory derived from Classical Realism was matched by a parallel crumbling of certainty within the steel-walled compartment in security studies where the dynamics of war are studied. This has been a progressive process, associated with the work of three scholars in particular.

In *The Face of Battle*, John Keegan insisted that the experience of soldiers and an attempt to understand their behaviour in battle was both neglected and fundamental. War studies could not be a weak derivative of Operational Analysis.[32] Martin van Creveld, beginning with his work on logistics in 1977, turned his fertile iconoclasm to the study of command and then to the transformed potentials for war. He produced a similar, but broader effect to that of Ball, Bracken and Blair in the nuclear field. He showed how the hidden, the over-looked, the under-estimated – in short all things prior to the deployment and engagement of guns and missiles on the front line – were actually the prime *foci* for analysis, if one sought to understand the changing dynamics in the relationship between war and security.[33] The third scholar of this triumvirate, Edward Luttwak, contributed in similar caustic vein through many works. Particularly in his 1987 book *On Strategy*, he added the most powerful recent restatement of the proposition that there is no linear correlation between increasing military power and effectiveness. There is a culminating point of efficiency beyond which the potential danger of a new capability is such that it quickly summons up counter measures to neutralise it.[34]

All three, Luttwak most self-consciously in his strategy book, sought to interrogate Clausewitz's propositions from the Napoleonic Wars in the late twentieth-century context. Some, such as his analysis of friction in warfare, were strongly reaffirmed, in particular by van Creveld's work. But the main drift of Keegan's 1998 Reith Lectures was that the changing relationship between agency, rationality and power in international affairs is such as to render Clausewitz's most celebrated dictum about war being the continuation of politics by other means obsolete as a guide to strategic insight.[35] His conclusion was not dissimilar to that reached by a different route by John Mueller who had earlier argued that major war in developed societies was obsolescent.[36]

Environmental pressures

Classical Realism in security studies has been compressed from a third direction also. The oil price shocks of the early 1970s galvanised thinking about the limits to economic growth that would be imposed by resource and environmental constraints. The systems dynamic modelling work of that name by the Club of Rome, presented as visually-arresting influence diagrams, was widely publicised and suggested that limits on availability of wasting assets essential for industrial society, notably oil and strategic minerals, would be a greater constraint than hitherto considered. The original 1972 study was hotly contentious, but widely influential.[37] In the West, it fuelled the growing environmentalist movement. An illicit copy, obtained by dissident Soviet analysts, stimulated them to build the first crude models on resource constraint at the Institute for Systems Studies in Moscow, which were influential in the thinking of those who advised and supported Mikhail Gorbachev in his drive to modernise and reform communism a decade later.[38]

In the West, the burgeoning field of environmental studies contained from the outset the proposition that this was a proper aspect of security studies. Since oil and strategic minerals had long had this status, that proposition was scarcely controversial. But when an attempt was made to 'securitise' the environment more extensively in the early 1990s, when extravagant predictions of Malthusian crises were also proposed as security issues, or extrapolations on the destruction of tropical rainforest (a particular concern of the 1970s curiously eclipsed in the 1980s and only returning to public prominence at the end of the century),[39] did the guardians of a narrower sense of security argue back. The guardians argued for the exclusion of a wider range of substantive environmental issues from two positions. The Classical Realists did so on the grounds that if it were to be conceded that loss of rainforest, or pollution or disease, is a security issue, 'defining the field in this way would destroy its intellectual coherence...' so that the term became diluted beyond useful meaning.[40] Security had to be contained conceptually within the box of state agency to be useful.[41] However, as described more fully already in Chapters 1 and 2, a second position reached the same conclusion from a premise that the fruitful understanding of environmental issues would be confused, indeed polluted, if it were 'militarised'. The benefit of 'securitising' the issue was less than the costs.[42]

In contrast to any of the above, others arguing for the inclusion of environmental issues in consideration of security concerns did so on different grounds. They argued that it was not any specific menu of material issues, but rather the shared characteristics of the threats, and in particular the singular appropriateness of worse-case assumptions (the core of military analysis of uncertainty) when dealing with phenomena whose potential downside risk was simultaneously uncertain and great, that made inclusion of the issues appropriate.[43]

What differed from the subject matter of traditional security studies was not the absence of threats, but the absence of *enemies*. These were threats without enemies; and threats are the defining criterion for inclusion.[44]

The case for this further horizontal extension, which solidified the third front compressing Classical Realism, was made prominent by Jessica Tuchman Mathews in a sequel, of the same title in *Foreign Affairs*, to Ullmann's article.[45] However, before 1989, the forces pressing in on each of these three fronts had not served to destabilise the Classical Realist paradigm in any fundamental way. That was only achieved by the collapse of Communism between 1988 and the August coup of 1991.

Ignition

Spring in winter

In February 1990, Jan Urban, the Chief of Staff of Vaclav Havel's Civic Forum, visited England for the first time since 1968 when, as a student, he had caught the last plane back to Prague in time to see Soviet tanks in the streets. This time, he came to lecture on the 'Velvet Revolution' of the previous November as seen from his cockpit in the Magic Lantern theatre in Prague, which had served as the coordinator of the events. It was an unseasonably early spring. 'You see,' he exclaimed, pointing to a tree in early leaf, 'we Czechoslovaks are so powerful: in 1968 we made winter in the middle of summer and now we make spring in the middle of winter!'[46]

As Chou en Lai observed of the French Revolution, when asked his opinion, it really was too early to tell. The years after the 'Velvet Revolutions' are only the blinking of an eye on his timescale. Yet some of the starker lessons for security studies are already plain. When the revolutions came, they caught the mainstream analysts quite by surprise. At a distance, it is evident that three vital characteristics were insufficiently appreciated by observers at the time. The first is the transformative power of ideas and, by extension, the transforming potential of idealism. The manner in which rationality was interpreted by Classical Realism obscured both the possibility that the political arrangements of Europe could change fundamentally and the thought that people in Eastern Europe believed that they might.

Second, its prescriptive self-assurance meant that the issues around which opposition clustered in the period leading to the breaching of the Berlin Wall tended to be regarded as marginal. The earliest *foci* of protest were environmental: protest about profound air pollution in the Black Triangle of northern Bohemia, southern Poland and the eastern part of the DDR; protest by the Duna Circle in Hungary against the grandiose scheme to build the Gabci-kovo–Nagymaros dam across the Danube.

While it is true that pollution and environmental issues were among the few categories of activity where any form of protest was possible and, once circumstance permitted, that political energy tended to move elsewhere, the issue area was not perceived as prime, even when it was pre-eminent. By the same token, Chernyaev stresses that the fundamental importance of the Chernobyl nuclear accident of 1986, for the manner in which *perestroika* was conceived, politically, by Gorbachev, was not fully grasped. In comparison, close attention continued to be paid to the intricate dances in and out of office among the *Nomenklatura*.[47]

Third, both in Eastern Europe and contemporaneously with the pro-democracy demonstrations in Tienanmien Square, there was the issue of information dissemination. Both broadcasting and 'narrow-casting' (the uses of faxes at that time and latterly of the Internet and e-mail also) can amplify the ability of critics both to form associations and to convey their messages. It was insufficiently appreciated. Then – and still now – it is in perplexing contention and insufficiently well-understood.[48]

Bonfire of the certainties

The direct effect of the 'Velvet Revolutions' upon security studies was profound. The old certainties were suddenly swept away by events in ways that the 1980s critics could never have achieved. New views proliferated. Prominent and colourful were early strong assertions that the fall of the Wall signalled the culmination of the Whig interpretation of history. Francis Fukuyama argued in his much-noticed article in 1989 that, suddenly, all the great debates had been resolved in favour of liberal capitalist democracy.[49] The future task was one of fine-tuning this global triumph of the winning formula.

Fukuyama's thesis certainly chimed with the political aspirations expressed in George Bush's 'New World Order'. But storm clouds quickly gathered over this sunny scene, in Somalia, in Bosnia and in many parts of sub-Saharan Africa. And so a second 'neo-Realist' response was to substitute the confrontations of the Cold War with an equally big and simple idea, namely that future clashes would be between discrete 'civilizational blocs', which is taken up in the next section. In the degree to which this new world bloc approach saw the action of actors being structurally prescribed, the view is harmonious with the central assumption of neo-Realism, as defined by Waltz and refined by Buzan.[50]

The great shock of 1989–91 was the degree to which individuals, armed with ideas and aspirations, proved able to challenge and break the iron grid of structure. How they did this is a question of inductive and cultural rather than deductive and logical study. This poses a problem for the discipline of security studies in the way that it has grown; for, as one of the most creative of those proposing new approaches to the study of global politics has observed, 'Culture is one of those terms that often prompts people (especially international relations scholars) to reach for their revolvers. It seems to represent everything that the good, positivistically-trained international relations specialists should hate.'[51] The sparks struck by the revolutionary events across Central Europe blew into the groves of academe, igniting a conflagration. Familiar shibboleths of international security studies burned on a bonfire of the certainties.[52] Each of the three key assumptions of Realism – of agency, of mode of thinking and of nature of power – has been brought into question; and so, in consequence, the neo-Realist belief that order could be returned to analysis by focus upon the shaping power of structure was also scorched. What phoenix, if any, might arise from these ashes?

The French Revolution in perspective

The year 1989 may not have been the end of history, but it was unquestionably the end of something and the beginning of something else. But what? By the manner in which it ended the twentieth-century's cycle of formal mass violence, bracketed by the life of the Soviet Union which came in like a lion and went out like a lamb, it signalled the end of the 'short twentieth century' – Eric Hobsbawm's phrase resonated widely.[53] It also signalled the end of a 'long twentieth century' of precisely two hundred years' duration, by the manner in which it forcefully restated a central question about what the individual gets from society, and vice versa, in a social contract.

It was the French Revolution rather than the Treaty of Westphalia which favoured and promoted a moral fusion between the higher interests of the individual and state. Its spirit infused the nineteenth-century march of nationalism and it provided foundations of legitimacy for the progressive intrusion of state action into the private sphere, promoted by the social legislation of Bismarck or Lloyd George and forced by the logistical requirements of the First World War. Max Weber made plain that this tighter coupling in the social contract was, in his view, both inevitable and desirable.[54]

The revolutions of 1989 have, at the least, exposed the degree to which the 1789–1989 settlement is unravelling. The challenge to security studies is from three directions. While Realist and neo-Realist practitioners protest that they never ever really held to the simple view of states as balls colliding and cannoning off each other in the anarchical space of the billiard table of international society,[55] the revolutions of 1989 established beyond dispute that ball-breaking, non-state and sub-state actors were active. Second, the horizontal expansion in the range of issues, now deemed relevant for security analysis, was irresistible. It gained practical impetus independent of itself. The flurry of interest in hitherto suspect social, economic and environmental approaches to security was in part a consequence of the redeployment of effort from the Soviet military coal face to others in the mines of academe. Third, new agents and new issues were linked through a newly named preoccupation: 'globalisation'. In the spirit of Fukuyama's first, exuberant reaction, the power of globalisation appeared so pervasive and irresistible that it seemed reasonable to substitute it for the previous paradigm of the balance of power. But reflection and events were swift to show that there was no single implied outcome from the operation of these combinations. They could cut both ways. Indeed, most of the warm feelings about globalisation may be misplaced, and its divisive power probably exceeds its potential for unification.[56]

Globalisation cuts both ways

Benjamin Barber has described the new Manichaeanism as a battle between the globalising forces of 'McWorld' (McDonald hamburgers from Kansas to Karachi, etc.) and the introspective forces of 'jihad' (taken to symbolise a sort of contrasting atavism).[57] When the new world order was swiftly disfigured with episodes of internecine violence in Chechnya and the former Yugoslavia, hitting western sensibilities and consciousness in a way that African and Asian genocide had not, it might have seemed a grim reaffirmation of the relevance of old-fashioned Classical Realism. For some security analysts it was. However, Keane and Ignatieff, in two eloquent interventions, argued that it was more fruitful to examine such episodes through an historical and cultural prism, to which we turn in a moment.[58]

The renovation of power politics depends upon an understanding that globalisation cuts both ways. A means of communication, which may unify and empower some, isolates and alienates others. In the age of the Internet, recollect that two-thirds of the human family has yet to make a telephone at all. When the first submarine telegraph cables linked Europe and North America instantaneously, technology created a world at once more unified in one part and relatively fragmented in another. So also today. Anthony Giddens puts it sombrely. To operate in a globalised world is to ride a juggernaut – or to be crushed by it. Even for the riders, for those who can use these new means to escape the tyranny of distance or time, a huge recasting of relationship between the public and private spheres of their lives is entailed.[59] Furthermore, the old Realist assumption about rationality stands awkwardly in the new world, for many of the new agents through which power is exercised are by their nature clearly unconscious *factors* and not actors at all as explained in Chapter 1. Both these points are combined and displayed for convenience in the table below.

Transformation in agency and in the means by which agents can exercise power over a much wider range of issues, argued Mathews in a further seminal essay in *Foreign Affairs*, constitutes a power shift.[60] The agents, objectives and processes of power being all questioned in this way, she suggests – and we may agree – that, for security studies to mesh evidence and explanation more efficiently, it would be prudent to make study of these interconnections a prime focus, and therefore one of the two legs upon which a renovation of security studies might stand.

A chosen ignorance

Travelling on a tram in Zagreb in 1997, I was jammed up against a Pakistani policeman who was part of the international monitoring force in eastern Slavonia. He expressed pessimism about his mission. 'But what else can one expect?' he asked. 'This is a conflict on a fault line between Muslims and the rest and, as Professor Huntington has explained, these are the battle lines of the future.'

Not since publication of George Kennan's 'Mr X' article has a single academic article had so wide and, as the anecdote suggests, pervasive an influence on perceptions on security as Samuel Huntington's 'clash of civilizations'.[61] The fact that he has had conspicu-

Table 4.1 On the knife-edge: agents of globalisation cut both ways

Agent	Globalising	Fragmenting
Agent as factor		
Technology (type 1): Motor car, jet plane and other military-derived technology.	Shrinking distance intra-nationally and then internationally.	Social emulsification, increased loneliness, social differentiation between those with and the majority without access; facilitating Hobbesian tendencies; facilitating terror and civil war.
Technology (type 2): Telecommunication: phone and fax.	Extending size and complexity of individual's moral community; breaching authoritarian rule.	Social emulsification, increased loneliness, social differentiation between those with and the majority without access; increased fear from surveillance; facilitating narrow and shifting patterns of relationships; auto-manipulative personalities.
Television.	Informing; facilitates simultaneous shared images.	Desensitising, homogenising, stimulus overload makes superficial, encouraging passivity and intellectual laziness; alienating, reason-destroying.
Technology (type 3): IT, computers; e-mail; Nintendo.	Facilitating new institutional agents; convenience; abolishing distance; cyberspace and information highways; can be used as political force multiplier by poor and weak against rich and conventionally strong.	Huge increase in surveillance potentials; trivialising communication; alienating, reason-destroying games; desensitising, homogenising; excessive powers of processing information triggers feedback crises, especially in global electronic financial markets; suppress ability to identify key indicators.

Table 4.1 continued.

Agent	Globalising	Fragmenting
Values: Human rights; property.	Enlarging the scope for extended responsibilities in current institutions; builds from familiarity; social property rights underpin community at all scales, local to global.	Human rights honoured in the breach: war crimes, especially in civil and undeclared wars; gun law. Exclusive property rights are archetypic fragmenters, but less pervasive than you might think.
Faith in science (science as salvation) and other fundamentalisms.	The main fibre in world-binding ideology.	Promotes exclusive religions; intolerance; stereotyping, especially when coupled to new technologies.
Effects: Global trade.	Anti-war prophylactic.	Stimulus to resource conflict over raw and scarce materials and, increasingly, over sink capacities.
Environmental stress and threat.	Galvanises awareness of shared vulnerability.	Galvanises self-protective denial and inaction.
Institutions (type 1): English language.	As universal functional control system; as key to individuals' liberation.	As key to globalising technologies and their fragmenting consequences; as reactor for introspective linguistic nationalism.
Agent as actor		
Institutions (type 2): Functional institutions; e.g. air traffic control; organised crime.	Policing and steering world systems; providing state and trade substitutes in grey zones.	'There is no such thing as society'; terror. Anti-social political ideologies of the culture of contentment; both are corrosive of structure and culture of welfare, strengthening stereotyping and racism.

continued

Table 4.1 continued.

Agent	Globalising	Fragmenting
Multi-national corporations; global electronic finance; insurance.	Defining the boundaries and rules of the world economy and actuating it within those limits.	Local powerlessness; regional protectionism leads to bloc confrontation; collapse of imperial ideologies; proliferation of unquantifiable risks.
Institutions (type 3): Non-governmental organisations.	Using new technologies to exert political leverage for new values ('power shift'); basis for cosmopolitan democracy.	Using new technologies to undermine local opposition to global political economy.

ously little support for his view of the Islamic world from among those with expert knowledge of it and equally little applause among historians for his view of discrete 'civilizations' that bump and grind like tectonic plates has been irrelevant to the continuing influence of this image in the policy and practitioner environments. The article and its arguments are now, for better or worse, active forces in shaping the way that international society is perceived. In consequence, they change the way in which a policeman in an international force in the Former Yugoslavia, and countless others, now acts, for ideas always have this hermeneutic effect.

The main tradition in security studies was also predicated upon there being a self-conscious sense of international society, admittedly of a thin, vestigial sort. Martin Wight saw it manifest 'in the inherent tendency of international politics to produce an even distribution of power' to preserve the independence of the member communities; and in the regular operations of international law.[62] This minimal consensus gave order amidst anarchy and, while continuously under attack during the twentieth century, has never been extinguished. Wight stoutly maintained that view: 'There is cooperation in international affairs as well as conflict.'[63] Hedley Bull pivoted his account of the sources of order in world politics around the assumption that all societies share what he called 'primary goals' (such as maintenance of a minimum security against violence), which thereby repel the return to some global state of nature whereby international anarchy reigns among states.[64]

Now, in the enthusiastic reception accorded the Huntington thesis, one perceives a willingness to believe that the fact of cultural diversity may imply the arrival of an age of global anarchy. That opinion was made explicit in another essay, which also achieved wide resonance and elicited widespread criticism among regional experts.[65] It seems to be a logical conclusion of the proliferation of actors and the diffusion of power among them.

It is beyond the present purposes to enter these disputes substantively (a critique of the 'new barbarism' thesis is provided through a case study in Chapter 6); but what is germane here is to notice the strength of the reaction. In an important sense it parallels the resurgent power of introspective, blood-thinking nationalism. That, John Keane sees, is locked in struggle. 'If the protagonists of civil society are engaged in a continuous struggle against the simplification of the world, then nationalism is a continuous struggle to undo complexity, a will not to know certain matters, a chosen ignorance – not the ignorance of innocence. It thereby has a tendency to crash into the world, crushing or throttling anything that crosses its path...'[66] His sentiment is applicable by extension to the simplifying tendency in security studies.

This simplifying tendency, the energetic search for new enemies, is an understandable reaction to the end of the Cold War world, illuminating in its nature, but unlikely to help us make any analytic progress. For this we need a renovated approach to the study of culture in global society, to match a re-examination of the relationship between power and agency, which is the other leg to stand on.

Power

Mismatches force the issue

At the same time that clanging stereotypes can become prominent and resonate as substitutes for hard thinking about or study of those so caricatured, there is another strange mismatch to be seen. The rise of the concept of 'human rights' has been one of the spectacular achievements of the late twentieth century and its consequences prescribe our concerns in the next section of this book.[67] From the Universal Declaration and the Nuremberg Principles through Helsinki to the *ad hoc* war crimes tribunals of Central Africa and the Former Yugoslavia to the July 1998 achievement at Rome of the principle of a permanent international criminal court, there has been a consistent story of ambition running ahead – often far ahead – of reluctant achievement. The wide divergence between the ambition for an ICC able to prosecute suspects, irrespective of the view of their state, and the far more restricted reality achieved under American pressure, is only the most recent illustration of the continuing relative weakness of a new conception of self-conscious global society to match the realities of living in a world of transforming relationships between agency and power. There may, in fact, be a reliable way to circumvent these obstacles, which is a subject of Chapter 5.[68]

The reason for this mismatch is not dishonourable to scholars. At the end of the century, circumstance permits us to give a firmer answer than Chou en Lai to the question about the French Revolution. It appeared for 200 years that it had given a permanent answer to late-eighteenth-century discussions about the nature of the social contract between the individual and superordinate power, which it abruptly interrupted. The French Revolution's answer was to fuse individual political and moral identity within a geopolitical hybrid, which we call the 'nation state'. We now know that this was only a provisional answer.

We are obliged, following Hedley Bull's lead, to state again the elementary or primary goals of society – of individuals in relation to *global* society, this time. So what principles and warnings should we bear in mind, as we prepare to resume thinking? And who can give us good advice, and do so in a manner which meshes with, and does not choose instead to ignore, the complexity of the new world?

What animates that complexity, and what must therefore lie at the very heart of the new security studies, is the central lesson of the Velvet Revolutions: that ideals broke structures. Before hammers, it was mental force that smashed the concrete of the Berlin Wall. In country after country, this was the common message of the leaders, when they reflected upon their recent achievement, in 1990; and that is the lesson which lasts.[69] A valuable advance has been secured by the spreading influence of the Copenhagen School of Critical International Relations. Professor Buzan and his colleagues have emphasised the primacy of socially constructed threats – what people perceive to be the case, whatever the 'hard facts' may be – in realistic political analysis.[70] A particular virtue of their conception is that it leaves both space and role for the continuing – indeed, again strengthening – actions of the state as one among many actors. Accommodating the paradoxical return of state power within the category of institutional agency is one of the unexpected but serious requirements that circumstance lays upon this reanimation of security analysis.

The task is more than descriptive: now, as ever, security studies, as a branch of 'policy studies', seeks a transformatory role. That being so, the demands are huge, because the dangers of a vacuum are so great. The choice is not whether there will or will not be an international culture. *De facto* there is, and it populates the different, dialectically tensioned boxes in the figure above. The choice is whether, being alive, it will be conscious or not and, if not, as Gray fears, subordinated to a single, unconscious, cultural model crushing all others.

The lawyer and philosopher, Philip Allott, argues, in one of the first and most profound guides to thinking about global security, that prerequisite is the achievement of a self-conscious culture of society congruent with the scale of its operation and existence.[71] 'An international society, which is not a spiritual totality,' he suggests, 'generates *international hypertrophies* of all kinds, to fill its spiritual emptiness. International society is swept by intermittent and unpredictable paroxysms of wild energy.'[72] These are world-scale events (wars hot and cold, nation-making, alliance-making and the other actions of diplomacy), world-transforming economic phenomena and world-scale phenomena of consciousness itself. With deliberate ugliness of language, Allott calls the phenomenon of an unselfconcious but hugely energised international society 'the juggernaut of mass international unculture'. Unchanged, he argues, it will continue as it already has to alter and destroy countless local cultures, 'enslaving and exploiting and changing human beings as effortlessly and as thoughtlessly as it has cleared forests, moved mountains or polluted the atmosphere, drained the earth of irreplaceable resources'.[73]

Allott, at the global scale, is echoed at the local scale by Keane. Both confront the deepest fear in security studies, evident in Walt's illuminating 'Renaissance' article, which is that only the continued pursuit of general laws stands as a bulwark against both practical and conceptual anarchy. For Allott or for Keane this is a crippling misunderstanding. Intellectual and practical authoritarianism offers no viable solution. 'I want to emphasise that cultivation of *public spheres of controversy*, in which the violent exercise of power is monitored non-violently by citizens, is a basic condition for reducing or eliminating incivility and for minimising the chances of its return...' argues Keane.[74] Allott sees us stuck in a clumsily misconceived international society. It is, he observes ironically, a society fit for governments; and it exists at a moment when the circumstances of the 'power shift', described by Mathews, open for the first time since the late eighteenth century both the question and the opportunity to reconceive governance in ways which engage the primary security concerns of every individual, regardless of national jurisdiction. To do so would be to achieve the good order of a self-ordering society (*Eunomia*): to fail, Allott warns, is to be condemned to live again the experience of national societies, which had to discover painfully how to redeem themselves in the name of democracy and justice.[75]

Allott's advocacy of self-conscious global culture and Keane's of public spheres of controversy at the local scale both exhibit the same relaxed but insistent view of the relationship between cultural diversity and universal principles that is the driving value of cosmopolitanism. Indeed, protection against authoritarianism depends upon the relationship being symbiotic, and being felt to be so between groups that differ on most things, but hold in common the priorities of life and liberty. That active and, by its nature, continually debated settlement cannot live without toleration; so toleration is the essential political quality for the defence of liberty, itself the indispensable prerequisite for peace, and for its constant companion, self-sufficient (hence self-correcting) enlightened understanding.[76] A peace of cultural diversity, defended liberty and toleration is a living, substantial peace, not a passive political residuum when the anger has died or been killed.

The opening sentence of Kant's essay on Perpetual Peace of 1795 explicitly severs all that follows from such a view: ' "The Perpetual Peace": a Dutch innkeeper once put this satirical inscription on his signboard, along with the picture of a graveyard.' What Kant then attempts, and what we are now invited by need and circumstance to try again two centuries later, is to describe the moral intellectual foundation of living peace. That is no academic's whimsy or conceit. It is the very stuff of socially constructed values and threats. Like Buzan and the Copenhagen School, Kant long before them understood the material power of ideas; so, tongue in cheek, he continued his introduction by pre-emptively disarming his Classical Realist critics. 'The practical politician,' he continued, 'tends to look down with great complacency upon the political theorist as a mere academic. The theorist's abstract ideas, the practitioner believes, cannot endanger the state, since the state must be founded upon principles of experience; it thus seems safe to let him fire off his whole broadside, and the worldly-wise politician need not burn a hair.'[77] Except, of course, Kant does not believe that for a moment; and neither do Allott, Buzan or Keane; nor should we.

Taking the pilot on board

Summing up a review of 1,000 years' search for peace, Michael Howard concluded that 'if anyone could be said to have invented peace as more than a pious aspiration, it was Kant. He was almost alone in understanding that the demolition of the military structures built up in Europe over the past millennium would be no more than a preliminary clearing of ground.'[78] The quality in Kant's view of the nature of peace, and of the process by which fallible mankind might reach it, that Sir Michael highlighted, is the one which expresses the essence of cosmopolitanism. Kant is often represented as being rather an austere and bloodless thinker whose thought is too intimidating to be accessible, let alone actively useful. So it is a sort of reassurance that the author of one of the clearest short expositions of his philosophy writes that 'since Kant is one of the most difficult of modern philosophers, I cannot hope that I have made every aspect of his thought intelligible to the general reader. It is not clear that every aspect of his thought has been intelligible to *anyone,* even to Kant.'[79] We may take this as authority to press on, relying on the professionals where we need help with the philosophy, but on ourselves in the main relevant writings, which are his political writings. In these, he is nothing of the sort. His writing is perfectly accessible; his imagery is both amusing and humane; for in fact *Perpetual Peace* turns on a value which is at the same time profound and familiar to all.

Kant believed that the key quality of durable, self-sustaining peace is that of hospitality. Hospitality captures the essence of the intersection between cultural diversity and universal values, and locates it in the one social context where nearly everyone is obliged to negotiate a *modus vivendi* – the family.

Living peace depends upon the general acceptance of each person's 'cosmopolitan right' (the kernel of what is nowadays called a human right, following the formulation of the 1948 Universal Declaration of Human Rights). So that observance of this fundamental right may be universal, Kant confines it to its essential. It arises from necessity. 'All men are entitled to present themselves in the society of others by virtue of their right to communal possession of the earth's surface. Since the earth is a globe, they cannot disperse over an infinite area, but must necessarily tolerate one another's company.' The right which may be claimed is not that of a guest, for that implies that the claimant could become a part of the household upon which the demand is made. Cosmopolitan right is a right of resort only: 'hospitality means the right of a stranger not to be treated with hostility when he arrives on someone else's territory.'[80]

Universal hospitality is a shrewd and pragmatic framing as a prescription for political behaviour of the driving principle of the moral law, stated in the Categorical Imperative. The Categorical Imperative is the nub of Kant's advice on how to order political priorities. It is categorical because it is mandatory, and it is a composite law of reason, with three separate parts. The first tells us 'to act only that maxim which I can at the same time will as a universal law'. And what might this golden rule be? The second formulation: 'So act that you treat humanity, both in your own person and in the person of every other human being, never merely as a *means,* but always at the same time as an *end.*' Do as you would be done by, in short, says Scruton. It is not hard to see how this principle speaks to a time when, again, the individual and the rights of the individual are central. So if the form of the law is universal (first part), then the content derives from treating people as ends, not as means (second part) which informs the adjudication of competing rights as we shall shortly see. We thereby see 'the will of every rational being as a universally legislative will'; and this to the third imperative, in turn: 'every rational being must so act as if he were by his maxims in every case a legislative member of the universal kingdom of ends.' Here, Scruton succinctly explains, 'nothing conflicts with reason, and the rational being is both subject and sovereign of the law which there obtains'.[81]

What this does not help us with are less than perfect circumstances where the Kingdom of Ends cannot be achieved in this way. This is an objection that causes some to question the utility of the whole scheme of thinking and it is discussed at the end of this section. But for the moment, the point to grasp is that Kant's identification of hospitality as the framing requirement for living peace is part of the content of the moral law as defined by the second imperative: 'do as you would be done by.' The hospitality principle also conforms with the Universal Principle of Right ('Every action which by itself or by its maxim enables the freedom of each individual's will to coexist with the freedom of everyone else in accordance with a universal law is *right*') and expresses the universal law of right that follows from it ('let your external actions be such that the free application of your will can coexist with the freedom of everyone in accordance with a universal law').

Then there is the matter of motivation. What sources energise actions? Kant's views on this are among the most pertinent for modern times. He poses the issue by asking what ends are duties also? For Kant, there were two: one's own perfection and the happiness of others. Where they conflict, the Principle of Right gives us resolution; and – completing the circle that takes us back to the needs of the stranger at the door – our satisfaction of the stranger's right to hospitality is also our duty. Kant saw more clearly than anyone at his time how the invitation to satisfy rights in a way that promoted peace and not war required an equal and convergent reply from a sense of duty that was inner-impelled. (This operates essentially between individuals, but scales up, as he argued in *Perpetual Peace*.) The alternative was to rely on the state, or some other over-ruling power; which, of course, presumed a coherent large-scale agent. What makes Kant's way of thinking so useful for our early-twenty-first-century task is that he offers a way of prescribing and guiding practical actions where there is no unitary Leviathan, or where those suffering with unsatisfied or abused human rights – like the poor, hungry and powerless – have no other option than to rely upon the inner sense of duty propelled (in Kant's terms) by the Categorical Imperative within the rich and powerful, to quicken their will to act.[82]

Kant's principle of cosmopolitan right as universal hospitality has already once, but covertly, reappeared at a shaping moment in the creation of modern politics. In 1948, it is squarely present in Article 1 of the Universal Declaration of Human Rights ('All human beings are born free and equal in dignity and rights. They are endowed with reason and conscience and should act towards one another in a spirit of brotherhood'). It is muscular too: for Kantian hospitality extends as far as to underpin the call to arms signalled by the triggering discovery of 'barbarous acts which have outraged the conscience of mankind'. From that outrage have come Nuremberg and the Genocide Convention on the legal side, and acts of humanitarian military intervention, breaching sovereignty, on the other.

In addition to his reputation for being intimidating, there are three other reasons why one might hesitate before accepting that Kant is an appropriate contemporary guide who can save us from reinventing wheels that he already invented for us.

The first lies in the three key requirements (what Kant called 'definitive articles') for a perpetual peace, of which the principle of hospitality is the third. The first states that 'the civil constitution of every state shall be republican', and the second that 'the right of nations shall be based on a federation of free states'. The second follows from the first and the reason is the same: consent. Without consent there can be no living peace. 'Under a constitution where the subject is not a citizen, and which is therefore not republican, it is the simplest thing in the world to go to war', whereas, Kant argued, citizens with much to lose would be risk averse. By extension, states of this nature would form into a pacific federation (*foedus pacificum*), different from a treaty relationship which ends one war only; this would be a covenant of nations united to banish forever the scourge of war.

While the second definitive article is not far from describing the achievement of the UN Charter, the first is manifestly far from the modern state of affairs. So does this reduce Kant's usefulness to us? Michael Doyle asked the right question when he wondered what language Kant would use were he alive now. He concluded that, 'By "republican" Kant means a political society that has, from the formal–legal point of view, solved the problem of combining moral autonomy, individualism and social order.' Our word for this is liberal; and, if it is substituted for 'republican' in the first of Kant's three requirements, we may accept its meaning easily and believe that it does no violence to Kant's argument.[83]

The second ground for hesitation is at face value more difficult to remove, especially since Kant's rejection of the individual's right of rebellion against government appears to be unequivocal, and proceeds from the primary weight which he places upon the individual as the animator of the decisions which make society (the three interlocking parts of the Categorical Imperative seen in the first definitive article of perpetual peace just explained this). It is an approach sharply in contrast to Rousseau's General Will which, in its nature, permits of the possibility of a legitimated alternative basis of power that can challenge an *ancien régime*. For Kant, sovereignty is indivisible, *logically*. But is that a moral position also? Two philosophers (Beck and Axinn) feel that this is less clear-cut, particularly since Kant was known to sympathise with the French Revolution; and another comments on their discussion that 'if, like Kant, you praise on one page what you've condemned on the last, you bloody well better have a double standard'. Professor Dyke goes on to advocate the virtue of having a strategy to achieve a second best result, when circumstance frustrates the ideal Kingdom of Ends, and believes that Kant shared that view.[84]

So that may be one part of an answer to our question, which is Doyle's, reposed. What would Kant say now, looking back on the civil and uncivil wars of the twentieth century, and especially at the pathological governments which pulverised social contracts along with their own subjects? The other part, given by Professor Reiss, his editor, speaks of a posthumous note in which Kant speaks of the right to resist the ruler if the fundamental contract has been violated. It is only a hint, and Reiss is careful to explain that it forms no part of his published work; but combine it with his stated opinion that obedience to the law is not absolute: that passive resistance is acceptable, and we may guess reasonably where his liberal convictions might place him today.

The third ground of hesitation is more bound to appearance than to substance; but appearance matters in the beauty contest of political philosophies that seek to present themselves as practical. Is not Kant's appeal to reason and duty, even his less lofty advocacy of the principle of hospitality, an appeal *against* the grain of nature? A strong emotional ground of appeal in classical realism is that it asks for no allowance to be made: our nature is fallen, selfish.

Yet, when the ethologist, Jane Goodall, studied the manner in which the chimpanzees of the Gombe Reserve in Tanzania treated strangers arriving at a group, she observed both the hostility and often murderous rejection that we might expect, but also – and equally – the way in which chimpanzees were observed in acts of altruism towards strangers known not to be related to them. It may be a selfish altruism, in terms of benefit to the gene pool, or reciprocal altruism, whereby supportive bonds outside the family circle can be expanded through tradition. But, as Goodall writes, the chimpanzees show that 'the old adage "one good turn deserves another" is, without doubt, deeply rooted in our primate heritage'.[85] The profound dualisms which mark us – from our bihemispheric brains, through our bilateral bodies to copious evidence of the pervasiveness of dualism and dialectic in religious systems – can happily accommodate the coexistence of selfish Realism and practical Idealism as equally well-grounded.[86]

In common between Kant and his contemporary successors, such as Allott, Booth and Keane, in the interrupted conversation on the independence, rights and duties of the individual in the face of authority is a steadfast rejection of the proposition that cultural diversity implies practical or intellectual anarchy. They all reject the implication that a refocused security analysis, which springs from the needs of individuals in all their kaleidoscopic diversity, is somehow subversive of the defining purposes of analysis. What might this imply for the practice of security studies as it emerges scorched from the recent bonfire of its certainties?

Culture, identity and consciousness

The 'power stroke' in the four-stroke cycle in security studies has not yet been completed; but it has begun, in some respects. It was only the intervention of history, not the debate among scholars, which caused the collapse of self-confidence in Classical Realist security studies after 1989. We cannot count on other *dei ex machina* turning up. The nature and reception of the Huntington thesis is an example of what can happen in the current vacuum, if we are not careful. What is needed, then, is a choice to exploit uncertainty creatively.

By temperament, security studies is not well-suited to this. The high premium that it has placed upon abstraction and systematisation and positivist assertion, to bridge the gaps in knowledge, means that it has been particularly prone to generalisations about culture. Its treatment of both culture and power as social phenomena is generally of a sort from which historians and anthropologists would recoil. In consequence, its repertoire of discussion about what actually constitutes power has been narrow, viewed from outside, which is curious given the centrality of the issue to the discipline.

In a deeply-fissured, inevitably interconnected and actively violent world, these deficiencies could be costly. There has been until recently too great a distance between the study of security and the study of culture and society, not least because the conversation was not seen to be relevant or necessary. But now it is, in several quarters.

The door through which a concern with culture has most vigorously burst into the academic study of security is arguably that opened by a feminist perspective. The recognition that men and women are differently and unequally incorporated into myths of security, as protectors and protected respectively, argues Ann Tickner, necessarily pushes questions of identity to the fore.[87] That, in turn, helped to trigger a vigorous and sobering auto-critique, bravely voiced by Booth, which made visible the strongly constrained militarised, masculinised assumptions incorporated unconsciously into the discipline. New self-awareness coincided with awareness of the proliferation of non-state actors at the end of the Cold War. Together, they demand a different answer to the basic question of security studies: what needs to be secured? Plainly still the state, but more than the state. Repetition of that basic question is helping to propel new responses within the security studies community, most prominently in the work of the Copenhagen and critical security studies schools.[88] But in voicing this, it is equally important to be clear what is *not* being said. Yes, culture counts, but not as a tyrannical cultural relativism, for that, in Booth's words, gives 'a totalising picture of specific cultures, producing a false view of the world'. He calls it 'black-boxing' the units of analysis, and it makes us prone both to giving up faith in universal rights and duties, and to the consequences of Huntington's clashing cultures replacing the reified state as a new set of billiard-balls on the Classical Realist (now neo-Realist) billiard table. That way of bringing an awareness of culture back into security studies is both empirically falsifying and ethically flawed. Again, Booth has captured it precisely: 'Cultural relativism is flawed as an approach to politics, but cultural sensitivity must inform all we do.'[89] This is exactly the balance of toleration to be struck between university rights and cultural variation which is expressed in Kant's principle of hospitality, and it also tells us which things about culture in global politics we do not know, and would benefit from knowing. So, these are heartening developments, which help to identify, by their relative absence so far, two issues which might profitably be further investigated to realise the power stroke in security studies – a real renaissance in contrast to that proposed by Stephen Walt.

The study of stereotyping and the reinterpretation of power politics

The first is to take a more systematic look at the use and abuses of stereotyping in security studies. The second is to accept the challenge just spelt out to take up in the early-twenty-first century the late-eighteenth-century task of conceiving how, in a world of new agents and new forms of power, security studies can contribute, as it always has sought to, to the creation of a safer world: a new power politics.

Many years ago, Joseph Needham, the most prodigious student of Chinese science, delivering a paper on Chinese pharmacology to an audience of mainly medical undergraduates, explained that the different amounts of active principle in a drug are described as qualities – the soldierly, the magisterial and the princely quality, respectively. Which of these, he asked his audience, describes the drug with the largest quantity of active principle? Overwhelmingly, the undergraduates voted for the princely quality. Wrong, explained Needham. In Chinese thought the highest quality of power is that which obtains the desired effect with the least force, or, in pharmacological terms, the smallest quantity of active principle. The medical students, he wryly observed, were simply revealing a common underlying feature of European civilisation. Its obsession with raw power. More means better, safer.

Perhaps because it has believed itself to be armed with privileged insights deriving from accumulated knowledge about the controlling structures of security, security studies has only weak in-built defences against capture by idiosyncratic cultural norms in a world where pluralism is a significant concern. It is defenceless precisely because pluralism is not thought to be a significant concern.

One consequence was that security studies was ill-prepared to explain the 1989 revolutions. They exemplified a different sort of Realism. This was practical idealism of a late-eighteenth-century sort. The Central Europeans demonstrated what students of colonial and post-colonial societies had long understood, namely that the weapons of the weak involve the manipulation of perceptions; and they are not puny because they are subtle.[90]

Stereotypes are the indispensable shorthand that we use to make it possible to navigate in a complex world of strangers. They are among the most effective weapons of the weak. They offer self-defence to the physically weak, who make masks behind which to hide, both to retain some little freedom of autonomous action, and a sense of self-respect.[91] They are also the cruel bridle that is thrust upon those whom we wish to silence and dehumanise, as a preparation for torture and killing. Academics employ stereotypes to kill also. The Huntington and Kaplan theses mentioned previously are good examples of energetic deployment of stereotypes to ward off the confusions of complexity. The attraction is strongest for those who subscribe to the most systematic, deductive theories, among whom the practitioners of security studies are to be found. Harriet Wong's review of the treatment of stereotyping in academic international relations literature confirms this impression, and thus provides a foundation for the case to open up this topic.[92] Her study ranges across North Atlantic and, to a certain extent, Chinese sources. Similar reviews of other cultural and language areas are now needed.

This chapter has shown that eagerness to make ideas active in policy has been a constant theme in security studies. It is realistic in its recognition of the hermeneutic nature of ideas. Therefore it can also be dangerous. The power stroke in the four-stroke cycle is therefore deliberately a *double entendre*. It is concerned both with the subject of power and with altering the practice of power: with understanding and with doing. That confluence of purpose, Booth observed, was the reason above all why war and peace studies were, in his view, less in antipathy than in potential cooperation.

The study of stereotyping will help to fill one important void in our self-awareness. It stands under the wing of understanding. Among the central concerns of political idealism in the late eighteenth century was continuation of the Renaissance search to define the boundaries of obligation between individual and society,[93] to which was added an optimistic exploration of the potential application of practical reason to the attainment of political virtue. At the end of the 'long twentieth century', Allott has reminded us that those same questions return.[94] This is the substance of power politics, which needs now to be re-examined from a practical idealist rather than a Classical Realist perspective. R.B.J. Walker has pungently stated the requirement: 'Questions about security cannot be separated from the most basic questions of political theory, but they also cannot be left in the care of those who have allowed questions of political theory to curdle into caricature.' Correctly, he located the task at the very root of modern political theory.[95]

Turning to the second aspect, how shall we reconceive global society in ways that will help it to become self-conscious and thereby safer?

A research agenda on power politics for security studies in a world seeking global security has four obvious areas of prime concern. In the first instance, it is naturally to take account of the power shift in political agency, as described by Mathews. The transformation of agency touches everything else. Part of this transformation, I argued, is displayed in the simultaneously explosive and implosive force of globalisation. The very nature of the internal dynamic of globalisation is deeply in dispute. It is expressed through an amplified range of factors and actors. Some of these are ill understood; others are still largely ignored; many are quite new; all of them together compose a unified programme for empirical research by security studies practitioners, because they shape the 'politics' part of power politics. Gray's trenchant critique of shallow optimists for globalisation has galvanised this area of thinking. The *Foreign Policy* 'globalisation index' is a productive line of empirical research to pursue.

The second dimension of the agenda is both predictable and appropriate for security studies, given its history. It re-examines the principles and potentials of force as a consequence of the transformation of war, the proliferation of empowered actors, the embedding of the cosmopolitan priorities and yet the enduring role of state power. These are the concerns of the rest of this book.

Third, the involute of force – reward – also needs to be reconsidered. The return to centre stage of old terrorism (misleadingly called new terrorism by some), described in the previous chapter, makes this case with painful clarity. What are the limits on the power of diplomacy when the scope for either deterrence or bribery is negligible? Sharply constrained, it might seem.

However, fourth, the new power politics must go back to basics, which means to Weber.[96] That, surely, is the lesson of the way in which questions of culture, identity and consciousness have barged their way forward?

Security studies was born into an environment where respect for the hierarchy of forms of power was great. Formal, expert power advanced and ruled. Customary power was the power of the past. The story of progress was, in these terms, of the depersonalisation of politics: the march of civilisation from custom to contract. The fickle power of charisma was more regarded than that of custom, in so far as it formed part of understanding the minds of dictators. Yet at the turn of the millennium, customary power has not withered away. On the contrary, much of humanity lies under its sway, but in a complex, hybrid manner. The power of charisma, harnessed to the eager forces of the information revolution, is made both wider and less easily understood, in consequence. Modernity means the simultaneous action of all three of the Weberian triad in ways that are deeply unclear yet vitally important. To investigate this is the 'power' part of the new agenda of power politics, and in this way, we may both understand the nature of global civil society, and bring it to consciousness. It is an exercise in practical idealism, in the late-eighteenth-century sense.

But the issue is not one of substitution: new lamps for old. The ending of the post-Cold War interregnum has transfused the veins of state power – formal power – with fresh energy. Therefore, aspects of the old power politics revive, notably in battles over the control of international institutions. The image of the ghost of Theodore Roosevelt waxes. Henry Kissinger believed that he was a much under-appreciated President, and an able exponent of the power politics of Classical Realism which he espoused and practised with Richard Nixon. The phantom of President Wilson (who Kissinger believed to be an impractical and vague realist, and a much over-estimated President, but one who unfairly overshadowed Teddy Roosevelt's memory) wanes.[97] Yet plainly the diplomacy of the new era cannot dispense with either.

The prescriptive objective of our new power-politics is to find ways of reconciling right action with political action. 'I can indeed imagine a *moral politician*,' writes Kant, 'i.e. someone who conceives of the principles of political expediency in such a way that they can coexist with morality . . . it should be ensured that . . . political institutions are made to conform to natural right'[98] – right as entitlement and as moral rectitude. And this, indeed, is what I believe we are seeing being attempted in the efforts to reconcile duty, state sovereignty and humanitarian intervention, which is examined in the next section. Both ghosts – Roosevelt's and Wilson's – prowl the corridors of power in the early twenty-first century; but each, in different ways, is diminished. Roosevelt's unconstrained state instrument is tied down.

Wilson's reliance on multilateral institutional agencies is frustrated as much today as when he failed to persuade congressional opponents, lead by the Chairman of the Foreign Relations Committee, Henry Cabot-Lodge, to accept Article X of the Covenant of the League of Nations. Wilson drafted it personally and refused to negotiate the language. It prohibited any unilateral use of force by one member state against another, on pain of collective retribution: 'The members of the League undertake to respect and preserve as against external aggression the territorial integrity and existing political independence of all members of the League. In case of any such aggression, or in case of any threat or danger of such aggression the Council shall advise upon the means by which this obligation shall be fulfilled.' Wilson called this the backbone of the Covenant, and maintained his refusal to accept reservation of it until his death on 25 September 1919. On 19 November, by fifty-five to thirty-nine, the Senate voted not to ratify without reservations and so the treaty died too.[99] As one reads McNamara's and Blight's clear and radical agenda for reducing the risk of major killing in the future, their reiteration of what they call Wilson's multilateral imperative rings like a cracked bell when (as we shall in the next section) we look at the recent record of multilateral initiatives. We need to listen to both ghosts if we seek actions to match hopes.

In these confused and conflicting circumstances of the new era, sovereign military means are frequently called upon, not to preserve our personal peace from aggression, as in 1914 or 1939, but rather to accomplish a different and subtler task. Increasingly, military power is deployed in order to protect the potential for, rather than the reality of living peace. It is asked to provide the practical bulwark holding back the forces of uncivil violence, thereby matching and reinforcing the legal bulwark built from the modern evolution of international law: neither is straightforward or uncontested.

In this pursuit, practical idealism, to give utopian realism – Carr's words – their proper historical resonance, applied to the agenda of the new power politics, does not rebuke the tradition of Realism in security studies. It transcends it: for it aims to achieve a unity of purpose and procedure which Carr had originally suggested should be our common goal: 'there is a stage where realism is the necessary corrective to the exuberance of utopianism, just as in other periods utopianism must be invoked to counteract the barrenness of realism. . . . Mature thought combines purpose with observation and analysis.'[100] Maturity in our thinking is the key. What, exactly, does that mean?

Kant, our clear-thinking and clear-sighted guide, gives us our marching orders in even more rousing terms than Carr. When, in his late fifties, he began to write about politics, in the years immediately before the French Revolution, one of the first questions which he addressed was, quite simply, 'What is Enlightenment?' He replied with words that reverberate [the emphases are added]:

> *Enlightenment is man's emergence from self-incurred immaturity.* *Immaturity* is the inability to use one's own understanding without the guidance of another. This immaturity is *self-incurred* if the cause is not lack of understanding, but lack of resolution and courage to use it without the guidance of another. The motto of enlightenment is therefore: *sapere aude*! [Dare to be wise – Horace] Have courage to use your *own* understanding![101]

Part II

Rights, duty and the uses of force

5 Intervention in contention

In the usual leaden language of diplomatic communiqués, this one opens in expected form. 'Chinese President Jiang Zemin and Russian President Boris Yeltsin held the second informal summit on 9 and 10 December 1999, during which they had an in-depth exchange of views on issues of common interest.' But what were the issues of common interest on which in-depth exchanges of views were had? Three times in the communiqué the Chinese and Russian authorities poke at the raw nerve which evidently ran, exposed and twitching, through the meeting:

> The two leaders maintained that all members of the international community should be treated equally, enjoy the same security, respect each other in their choice of development paths, respect each other's sovereignty, not interfere in each other's internal affairs ....
>
> The two sides also stressed that the equal status of all sovereign states should be guaranteed...
>
> The two sides point out that negative momentum in international relations continues to grow and the following is becoming more obvious: the forcing of the international community to accept a unipolar world pattern and a single model of culture, value concepts and ideology ... and the jeopardising of the sovereignty of independent states using the concepts of 'human rights are superior to sovereignty' and 'humanitarian intervention' ...

This repeated and principal anxiety about the dilution of state sovereign rights has one or two other 'negative momenta' attached to it, of which, interestingly, a purported weakening of the role of the United Nations and the Security Council is prime. 'The seeking of excuses to give irresponsible explanation or amendment to the purposes and principles of the UN Charter' is the precise term. It refers to the manner in which the NATO operations in Kosovo were justified in 1999, but reads oddly in view of the capricious vetoing earlier that same year of the UN Preventive Deployment Force for Macedonia (UNPREDEP) by China, an act precipitated more by Macedonian recognition of Taiwan than anything happening in the Balkans.[1] But the sentiment – and the passion – expressed through the communiqué is not in doubt.

Both the occasion and the construction of the Sino-Russian communiqué underscore the correctness of Professor Peter Jones's assertion that 'the two global norms that are most widely recognised in our world are human rights and the principle of national self-determination'.[2] How the relationship between these two norms is regarded informs entirely one's approach to the question of intervention. Views on that relationship are in contention. The two Presidents were in no doubt in their communiqué that antipathy between the two rising norms was deep-seated, structural and perhaps ineradicable. Jones does not share that dogmatism; nor is it shared in what follows in this chapter, where an approach to sovereignty is encountered, which tends to the other pole of the spectrum, arguing for a principle of structural harmony between the norms.

At the least, Jones observes, there is no useful generalised proposition to be made. It depends whether human rights are interpreted as a lowest common denominator, a highest common factor or as an ideal: as a moral minimum, a basic moral structure or a comprehensive morality in his terms. And it also depends on the nature of the state. Is it pathological, committing genocide and democide? Is it authoritarian and quick to execute those whom it deems to be criminal? Or is it collapsed? Plainly, there is considerable difference between the circumstance of functioning or aspirant authoritarian states that feel themselves threatened to the core by human rights expressed as an axiom of the sort of programme for reconstructing power politics on cosmopolitan principles that was described in the previous chapter – even if they believe it to be a Trojan horse for American hegemony – and the circumstances of comprehensively powerless individuals in the vacuum of a collapsed state faced with the imminent prospect of death, mutilation, torture or ethnic cleansing. In most of the principal humanitarian interventions of the Cold War – on behalf of the Kurds and Marsh Arabs in Iraq after the Gulf

War; in Somalia after the collapse of the state in the civil war, which removed the regime of Siad Barre; in face of the Rwandan genocide (whatever judgement is made of the appropriateness and scale of the actions taken); in the cases of Bosnia and Kosovo, of East Timor and Sierra Leone – it has taken evidence of some grotesque outrage to have occurred to galvanise some form of international response.[3] The definition of human rights is set at the moral minimum and the triggering threshold of outrage is high. Yet these cases do not supply enough of the right sort of evidence to explain the passion in the communiqué, which must therefore be sought elsewhere. Illustration of that explanation is equally contemporary in its relevance, but from an older source.

Thucyidides relates that during the Peloponnesian War, the Athenians arrived at the island of Melos, to incorporate it within their maritime empire. Before any hostilities began, a debate took place between the Athenians and the Melians in which the Athenians set out their view of the options before the Melians and the Melians gave their response. Accept the extinguishing of your sovereignty without fighting, the Athenians suggested, and you will find that the burden of our rule is not heavy: we are civilised people and demand reasonable tribute only. There is no dishonour in giving way to the most powerful of states. Resist us, however, and we will crush your city state. We will then slay all the men and make slaves of the women and children. These are your choices, the Athenians suggested: not palatable, we agree, but practical and unavoidable; and you really should not take it personally. That is because it is in the natural order of things that the powerful seek to impose and enlarge their rule, whereas the weak have to put up with what they have to put up with. The Melians replied bravely, that, whereas they heard what the Athenians had to say, they would take their chances, trusting in their military abilities and in the justice of their cause. The Athenians had no place in their logic for that sort of consideration. They received the Melian response, established a siege, conquered Melos and did to its population exactly as they said that they would.[4]

Plainly, the Chinese and Russian Presidents were feeling Melian; for they had no hesitation in providing a thinly-veiled, but nonetheless agitated description of what they perceived to be the behaviour of the last remaining superpower (or 'hyperpower', as Hubert Védrine has more accurately described the United States). Their assent to the *soit-disant* eternal truth of the cynical realism of the Athenian position in the Melian debate resonates throughout. The powerful are doing what comes naturally to them, and the weak are not enjoying having to put up with what they have to put up with.

Among those burdens, as the quotations from the communiqué given above make plain, the hardest to bear is that pattern of military and diplomatic/military interventions around the world interpreted through the two Presidents' eyes. The 'humanitarian' justification is merely a smokescreen. These interventions are conducted at Washington's behest, and in circumstances where the United Nations is either ignored or misrepresented with clever lawyerly words as having assented to such interventions. For if fear and anger at the erosion of state sovereignty is the principal neuralgia in the communiqué, the other repeated theme is that 'the two sides stress that one diplomatic priority for both China and Russia is safeguarding the authoritative role of the United Nations in international affairs'.

That role, the two Presidents asserted, is straightforward and easy to understand. Articles 2(4) and 2(7) mean what they say: all members shall refrain from the threat or use of force against the territorial integrity or political independence of any state and nothing in the Charter authorises the United Nations to interfere in the domestic jurisdiction of any state. The UN was created in an international system of nation states and it is both creature of and protector of those states, or it is nothing. Therefore, the apparently arbitrary behaviour of the United States and its cat's paws, seen from that summit in Beijing, looks all the more threatening.

Two things are evident as the new century opens. The first is a prominent paradox. Whether for noble or ignoble reasons, state sovereignty has become much more conditional than the Sino-Russian position would wish; and more pervasively so than in response to the *Diktat* of any one state, even if it is a 'hyperpower'. There has been a phase change facilitating this, whose result is the empowerment of individuals in technical, political and cultural ways that were previously impossible. But, at the same time that the agents of power and their fulcra of influence proliferate, the pervasiveness and popularity of national self-determination and sovereign independence as the leading choice for framing and expressing public identity also persists. In fact, with the exception of some of the smaller, richer, most globalised countries of western Europe (those which fit most closely Robert Cooper's 'post-modern' category in his tripartite taxonomy of states), the popularity of sovereign independence increases, however functionally eroded it may be by the circumstances of a globalised world.

It is the flame which burns first and brightest in most uncivil civil wars. The study of Sierra Leone in the next chapter will show in detail in one example how control of the symbols and spoils of formal state apparatus was central to the smooth functioning of patronage in the dominant arena where power is exercised and mediated in modern Africa – the informal political economy. It shows too the consequences of friction induced in the management of the patrimonial state by a drying-up of the flow of patronage: a picture reproduced in varying forms and intensities across the continent, from Sierra Leone and Liberia to the Congo, to Somalia (but not Somaliland), the Ethiopian/Eritrean war and in south/central Africa, in stirring tensions in Kenya, quickening crisis in Zambia and the surfaced crisis in Zimbabwe. However anachronistic the expectations invested in the achievement of self-determination may be, it is the fuel which drives the never-ending ethno-nationalist terror campaigns in the Middle East, in Ireland, in the former Soviet space. So the paradox is that whereas circumscribed state sovereignty, and some of the circumscribing forces, like human rights, both rise in popularity and in mutual tension, the institutional structures of each are more reinforcing of each other than in competition. The practical implications of this are spelt out below.

The second thing evident as the new century begins is that the views expressed with brutal clarity in the Sino-Russian communiqué of December 1999 command considerable sympathy among the political élites of many post-colonial states, which have become autonomous within the General Assembly of the UN in the last fifty years. Seen from the perspective of the G-77 countries within the General Assembly, it must be conceded frankly that there is reason for scepticism about the recent nature of humanitarian intervention. As observed, the site of most interventions has been principally among small, poor states, or collapsed states, in the South where atrocities have been committed. But even so, when G-77 representatives note that sixty-six per cent of the UNHCR requested budget in 1999 was for the Balkans, the contrast between the resources and priority given to Bosnia as against Rwanda in the mid-1990s looks inconsistent at best, racist at worst. Some of the frustration felt in this situation burst out angrily at the UN Conference on Racism held in South Africa in September 2001, leading to an American walk-out.

Plainly, there is risk of an even deeper gulf opening between two camps. The agitated and conspiratorial language of the Sino-Russian account, plus an understandable and continuing hankering for the reconstruction of an anti-western front in the minds of their respective political élites, which came to maturity during the last years of the Cold War, make that all the more likely if left unchecked. In a paradoxical sense, the degree to which (for very different reasons) both China and the economically-active parts of Federal Russia have been drawn into the economic and cultural web of globalised capitalism has served to heighten both the sense of powerlessness and anger at that powerlessness felt by authoritarian leaderships whose power to dictate and to dominate their own populations without hindrance is slipping from their fingers. Therefore, it becomes all the more urgent to distinguish where there is and is not common ground, to be as precise as possible about the sources of authority and legitimacy which are available as the underpinnings of interventions when they occur, to have a clear sense of the main trends in international affairs that circumscribe the nature of humanitarian intervention, and an equally clear sense of the nature and possible interrelationships for good or ill between the five principal forms of intervention that can occur. Presented in this way, the role, potentials and limitations of military power in the enterprise can be more clearly seen, and the outstanding problems about humanitarian intervention can be better isolated and illuminated.

Who conducts interventions, when, where and why? The prime actors are drawn from the North Atlantic community; the interventions have occurred in a boom to bust to boom(let) cycle since the ending of the Cold War world in 1989–91; they have occurred in regions with failed or collapsed states, with three notable exceptions, these being the Gulf War (Operation DESERT SHIELD/DESERT STORM); the breaking of the Bosnian Serbs after the massacres of Srebrenica in the summer of 1995 and the Kosovo enterprise of 1999.

Why did all these interventions occur? Clearly, for mixed motives. It would be disingenuous to pretend that the fact that Kuwait sits on top of the largest remaining puddle of oil proven in the world was irrelevant to the scale of effort which the industrial states mounted under American leadership and under a 'sub-contracting' mandate from the UN. The summer 1995 operations against the Bosnian Serbs by NATO were, as was argued in Chapter 3, a defining point in the politics and practice of intervention since the end of the Cold War. The resolve to act was painfully assembled within the NATO Alliance only when the bankruptcy of the UN mission had become staringly evident, with the humiliation and withdrawal of the Dutch battalion of UNPROFOR and when the evidence of genocidal purpose and practice in Srebrenica shamed civilised opinion also.

By the time that the Kosovo intervention occurred, the community of intervening states was psychologically better prepared and politically more robustly led. But the formal reasoning despite, it was still necessary to bet the shop – to put the entire credibility of NATO in question – to galvanise the speed and scale of action that was required; something which the detailed autobiographical account of the war by the Supreme Allied Commander of the day, General Wesley Clark, on the one side and the equally detailed account of how the British Prime Minister, Tony Blair, drove the Alliance forward, on the other, make transparently plain.[5]

In contrast to the narrow reading of the sanctity of state sovereignty, which the Chinese and Russian Presidents drew from Articles 2.4 and 2.7 of the UN Charter, others, and notably the Secretary-General himself, drew attention to the final Clause of Article 2.7: 'This principle shall not prejudice the application of enforcement measures under Chapter VII.'[6] Therefore, once the range of issues triggering Chapter VII enlarges, so, commensurately, Article 2.7 is constrained. The rising concern with human rights over the 1990s has been accompanied by the emergence, first in ethical and increasingly in customary international legal terms, of what Wheeler calls 'the following solidarist claim: states that massively violate human rights should forfeit their right to be treated as legitimate sovereigns, thereby morally entitling other states to use force to stop the oppression.' Acceptance of the validity of this claim, he shows through his analysis of case studies, is by no means general, even within democratic states and principally of these within the United States. But the trend in legitimation of action is unmistakable. 'The key normative change in the 1990s was that the Security Council, under pressure from western governments – who were themselves responding to the demands of public opinion at home – increasingly interpreted its responsibilities under Chapter VII as including the enforcement of global humanitarian norms.'[7]

In order to legitimate a humanitarian intervention, two sorts of linked criteria must be met. The first group is of practical descriptors which define boundary conditions in any given case. The second group concerns the production of legitimate international legal mandate for action to be taken. The second may only be engaged once a case has been successfully made within the first. (This requirement, and hierarchy, is essential to prevent misuse of the special procedures to produce mandates without the Security Council.)

The first group – the boundary conditions – were discussed and clarified in a conference, which brought together many of the concerned constituencies at the British Foreign Office Conference

Centre of Wilton Park in early 2001.[8] The boundary conditions are close to and derived from just war criteria. By rough analogy, these are the *jus ad bellum* equivalents, which we look for at the act of intervention. The first, employing the language of the Universal Declaration of Human Rights, is that the situation should be such as to be 'a shock to the conscience of mankind'. Wheeler calls this a 'supreme humanitarian emergency' and, as will be explained shortly, he sees the area of its potential competence to legitimate exceeding considerably that in which it has already been used. The second of the boundary conditions is that the act of intervention shall be one of last resort. That implies that the nature of intervention, which is under consideration, is principally military. But, as will be argued, whereas this has been in practice the principal nature of major response to supreme humanitarian emergencies so far, it neither need be nor should be particularly in order to meet in the safest way a requirement of the third criteria. This is a requirement for proportionality. But it is drawn more widely than in a context of conflict. It should be interpreted as a requirement that the entire range of actions of intervention shall, at the end of whatever is done, have produced more good than harm. One criterion of that is simply success of the mission. Acceptance of this boundary condition argues strongly for broader, more integrated and more concrete mobilisation of other than military means of intervention, even if military intervention is part of what must be done.

The fourth criterion attaches most immediately to the military aspect of intervention. It enunciates a *jus in bello* criterion, that of discrimination and the preservation of the immunity of non-combatants. General Clark's history of the Kosovo campaign reveals the extraordinary degree of political and legal control exercised over the choice of targets during the air campaign. While accidents, through misidentification of targets (most notoriously the Chinese Embassy building in Belgrade), occurred, the high proportion of missions flown and aborted, because pilots could not meet the stringent requirements of target identification set within the rules of engagement, and the extent to which military lawyers sat side-by-side with air controllers, exercising judgement, shows how important observance of this boundary condition is deemed to be when conducting Diplomatic Military Operations (DMOs). The fifth boundary condition is the one that it is least possible to demonstrate on conclusive evidence, for it relates to motivation. The humanitarian intervention is legitimate when those conducting it possess right intention. This requirement only really generates convincing evidence in the negative. The inappropriateness of the military means, which France sent to Rwanda, ostensibly for the purpose of saving lives in Operation Turquoise, and the manner in which the French forces deployed to support the rump government and give it a chance to regroup against the RPF rebels seemed to many evidence that the French government's priority was in fact to demonstrate its capacity to project military power in the region.[9]

Meeting these boundary conditions, which are case-specific, is necessary, but insufficient alone. Some form of international legal sanction is required. As the boundary conditions have become both clarified and more widely accepted, the ground of greatest contention has moved into this second arena.

In our world, between the twin rising norms of human rights and of self-determination, the first place to look for legitimation of an intervention is to the state concerned. This was the case with the international intervention into Sierra Leone in 2000. It occurred with the full consent of the government of President Kabbah and, that being so, the presence of international forces was not coercive and so was technically not an intervention. The next step along the spectrum from consent to coercion was the INTERFET force sent to East Timor by UNSC Resolution 1264. A condition of the deployment was that it should be with the consent of the Indonesian government of President Habibi. That consent was obtained, albeit under the pressure of diplomatic coercion, in the form of a request for help, on 2 September 1999, and reference to it was included in the Resolution. So the issue was neither straightforward consent nor coercion, but somewhere in the middle – a new issue. Indonesians were pressured on the grounds of their failure to execute obligations towards the East Timorese, which thereby justified a curtailment of their sovereignty. The episode provided support for Kofi Annan's trenchant assertion in his Ditchley Park lecture of 1998. 'The Charter,' he declared, 'protects the sovereignty of peoples. It was never meant as a licence for governments to trample on human rights and dignity. Sovereignty implies responsibility, not just power.'[10] Sovereignty, perceived not in terms of rights but more in terms of responsibilities, is in conformity with the solidarist claim articulated by Wheeler. The problems arise most acutely at the next step and beyond. What is to be done if neither free nor coerced consent can be obtained from the relevant and legitimate regional actors? The answer, of course, is that the issue then falls within the competence of the UN's mission to protect and restore international peace and security under the enlarged interpretation of Chapter VII.[11]

The best example of the Security Council in action was its creation of the INTERFET mandate for East Timor. Not only was it under the Chapter VII formula of 'all necessary measures' and clear, but it was also produced remarkably quickly. This was a consequence of the conduct of a fact-finding mission by Security Council ambassadors to Indonesia, an innovation which strengthened their resolve to act at once upon their return to New York. The fact of Indonesia's consent relieved both China and Russia of their anxieties that the mandate might threaten the sanctity of state sovereignty. But the norm of customary international law has moved well beyond that point. In the appeals chamber of the Yugoslav tribunal in The Hague in 1995, in the case again Dusan Tadic, the Prosecutor stated that 'It is the "settled practice of the Security Council and the common understanding of the UN membership in general" that internal armed conflict may constitute a "threat to the peace".'[12] This view is commonly located as springing, in April 1991, from Resolution 688 of the Security Council and from the Council's anxiety that the Yugoslavian civil war of 1991 might constitute a threat to the peace (Resolution 713). Resolution 688 also defined the refugee crisis among the Kurds, created by Iraq, as being a threat to the peace. In 1992, when sanctioning Operation Restore Hope (UNITAF), the intervention in Somalia, Resolution 794 likewise cited the need to provide a secure environment in which to alleviate the suffering of Somalis to trigger the clause (although in this case not against the will of the state because the state of Somalia had collapsed).

Undoubtedly, the effect of this broadening of the interpretation of threats to international peace and security has been to make the production of the Security Council resolution difficult, if not impossible, in an increasing number of cases. The stress point on the spectrum was reached in 1999 over the issue of the Kosovo mandate.

The NATO states judged that either Russia or China or both would veto an attempt to obtain a direct mandate from the Security Council and, therefore, chose to offer an argument which sought comfort from the UN by a more circuitous route. Article 1 of the Washington Treaty establishing NATO states that the Organisation operates in conformity with the purposes of the UN: a form of words which is drafted carefully and refers to the spirit of the Organisation rather than the precise letter of any Security Council resolution. But under it, support could be adduced for the NATO action from still extant Security Council Resolutions 1199 and 1203 of 1998 demanding that Slobodan Milosevic cease and desist from his actions against other peoples of the Former Yugoslavia. The British government (which was the only one to set out this type of argument formally and publicly) also sought comfort from Resolution 688, by analogy to the Kurdish refugee crisis. It was to this sort of argument that the Chinese and Russian Presidents objected when they condemned lawyerly interpretations in their December 1999 communiqué. But the British case was careful to limit the possibility for precedent-making, confining itself to previous Chapter VII resolutions only, plus a strong argument that the action to be undertaken should be proportionate.

As Wheeler subsequently observed, this was the most explicit humanitarian case to be made since the end of the Second World War and the nature of the response of the international community to it was muted, but broadly sympathetic. That became plain when a Russian attempt to seek condemnation of the action in the Security Council was struck down by a coalition which included six non-aligned Muslim states, stimulated by the memory of the massacre of the Muslims at Srebrenica. Wheeler suggests that what we may be seeing here is an argument of mitigation being made and accepted in the way that pleas of mitigation are submitted within a national juris-diction. And this may be true.[13] But none of this assists with the really hard cases. These are, in the first instance, when an over-whelming case within the boundary conditions can be made and where the UN Security Council mandate is frustrated by a capricious veto such as the Chinese over Macedonia, or an entrenched veto which clearly does not have widespread support within the Security Council or beyond.

Another important norm shift of recent years has been the emer-gence of a strengthening view, which holds that whereas there is a clear preference to use the Security Council to produce a mandate to execute the international responsibility to protect the human rights of threatened individuals and groups, there is now a willingness to consider what, during the Cold War, would have been inconceivable: namely that a Security Council blocked in the manner described above should not be regarded as the final word. One approach to overcoming a blocked mandate argues that there may be a small category of cases in which action without the approval of the Secur-ity Council could be considered. For such cases, the triggering threshold would have to be both high and narrow: mass killings having occurred or a clear threat of atrocity or ethnic cleansing or terror, leading to immediate and irreparable damage. The demand for action should then be presented formally to the Security Council, in order to smoke out hidden vetoes. If a majority of states veto, then the matter ends on the logic for which the veto was originally installed, namely to prevent actions which did not command widespread consent. But, in the circumstance of the capricious veto, then other routes could be taken, of which the first might be to the General Assembly and another might be to regional organisations. The most difficult cases are when individual states take *ad hoc* unilateral action. One of the strongest and most challenging of Wheeler's arguments is that if the criterion of supreme humanitarian emergency is indeed met but the international community is in some way blocked in acting, then an individual state may properly claim legitimacy, derived from natural justice. He, therefore, argues in *Saving Strangers* that he would judge the Vietnamese intervention into Cambodia, the Tanzanian into Uganda and the Indian into Bangladesh to be proper humanitarian interventions under the higher order criteria. Kofi Annan concurred when observing that 'History has by and large ratified that verdict', but also expressed the anxiety that in circumstances lacking the criterion of supreme emergency, some might, nevertheless, attempt to claim cover from the precedent.[14]

In addition to the problem of claiming legitimation beyond and outside the Security Council, the other core problem, for which there is at present no obvious solution, is how to obtain not merely prompt mandate (on a timetable such as was produced in East Timor) but, more particularly, legitimation for anticipatory actions – forms of intervention in the broad construction of the term, beyond the military sphere – which might pre-emptively prevent atrocity. While assenting to the centrality of this problem, Wheeler is driven to the conclusion that at present no mechanism is in view. The risk of abuse – the principal fear of southern and poor world states – is greatest in anticipatory action; and the argument of sovereignty as responsibility under the solidarist claim can only, by definition, be invoked once mass killing, or unambiguous evidence of its imminence was to be seen by all, has begun. Nor are these signals guarantees of action. In January 1994, General Romeo Dallaire, the Canadian Commander of the UN mission in Rwanda (UNAMIR), received detailed information from a Hutu informant warning of the genocide that was planned. Dallaire was also given the locations of arms caches. He requested authorisation to take preventive action, but was refused by UN headquarters two months running. When the crisis of April 1994 exploded and Dallaire requested a reinforcement, so that he might seek to deter or mitigate the violence, his force was reduced.[15] The subsequent publication of a report of the independent enquiry into the actions of the UN in Rwanda allocated the blame for this refusal to key UN officials and to some Security Council members.[16] Among those officials, one with responsibility was the Under-Secretary for Peacekeeping Affairs who, in his most extensive exploration in his issues, now in his capacity as Secretary-General, stated that 'personally I am haunted by the experience of Rwanda in 1994: a terrible demonstration of what can happen when there is no intervention, or at least none in the crucial early weeks of a crisis. General Dallaire,' he continued, 'the Commander of the United Nations mission, has indicated that with a force of even modest size and means he could have prevented much of the killing. Indeed, he has said that 5,000 peacekeepers could have saved 500,000 lives. How tragic it is that at the crucial moment the opposite course was chosen, and the size of the force reduced.'[17] In his speeches on the question of intervention over the years of the transition from the post-Cold War to the new era (1998–2001), the Secretary-General has consistently, but with added stress on each occasion, argued that:

> unless the Security Council can unite around the aim of confronting massive human rights violations and crimes against humanity on the scale of Kosovo, then we will betray the very ideals that inspired the foundations of the United Nations. This is the core challenge of the Security Council and the United Nations as a whole in the next century: to unite behind the principle that massive and systematic violations of human rights conducted against an entire people cannot be allowed to stand.[18]

At the same time, he has argued that prompt and effective relief must be provided; and in that same speech accepted that, with the Security Council blocked by the implicit threat of Russian and Chinese vetoes, nonetheless action in Kosovo had to be taken because of the rejection of a political settlement by the Yugoslav authorities. 'Indeed,' he observed sadly, 'there "are times when the use of force may be legitimate in the pursuit of peace".' In the interests of bringing relief, Annan has been supportive of military actions taken under several modalities, which are discussed below, while on each occasion reasserting his view that the Security Council ensure that its actions are such as to command continuing confidence among the peoples as well as the states of the United Nations.

Kofi Annan is one of two international statesmen who have sought to grapple directly and in public with the problem of reconciling needs with moral and legal mandates and the timely provision of effective action. The foundation of Annan's approach to a strategy for prompt and effective action was established in his Ditchley Park lecture, when he clung closely to the first sentence of the Preamble to the Charter: the Charter was issued in the name of the 'peoples' not the governments of the United Nations. An association of sovereign states, the UN exists to uphold rights belonging to peoples, not to governments. 'State frontiers, ladies and gentlemen, should no longer be seen as a watertight protection for war criminals or mass murderers.' Indeed, recollecting that in French law there is a crime called *non-assistance à personnes en danger* (failure to assist a person in danger), he argued forcefully that 'our job is to intervene: to prevent conflict where we can, to put a stop to it when it has broken out or – when neither of these things is possible – at least to contain it and prevent it from spreading.' In his view, 'the principle of international concern for human rights took precedence over non-interference in internal affairs' from the very beginning of the organisation's life when, the day before it adopted the Universal Declaration of Human Rights, the General Assembly adopted the Convention on the Prevention and Punishment of the Crime of Genocide. 'Since genocide is almost always committed with the connivance, if not the direct participation, of the state authorities, it is hard to see how the United Nations could prevent it without intervening in a state's internal affairs.'[19]

He took these ideas forward in an audacious manner in his speech to the 54th Session of the General Assembly in September 1999, when the Secretary-General confronted the Sino-Russian view (to be expressed two months later in their joint communiqué) head on. He entitled his speech 'Two concepts of sovereignty' and argued that whereas state sovereignty existed and continued, it was now joined by a new form of sovereignty: 'individual sovereignty – and by this I mean the human rights and fundamental freedoms of each and every individual enshrined in our Charter.'[20] The argument was audacious because it could not be concealed that the claims of the second and co-equal – or even superior – sovereign could not but circumscribe in some way the powers of the other. Indeed, the force of Annan's argument was to reverse the flow of morally and legally legitimating energy in the relationship between individuals and the state as Vattel had spelt it out in the middle of the eighteenth century:

> Nations or states are political bodies, societies of men who have united together and combined their forces, in order to procure their mutual advantage and security. It thus becomes a moral

person (sic) which has understanding and will and is competent to undertake obligations and to hold rights ... By the act of civil or political association, *each citizen submits himself to the authority of the whole body* (emphasis added).[21]

Annan was asserting the limits on the autonomy of the state should citizens not procure mutual advantage and security. His approach therefore embraces a broad construction of sovereignty and, equally, calls for as broad as possible a definition of intervention to include but extend well beyond the military. The *pros* and *cons* of this for the purposes of practical politics are taken up below. As to the question of co-equality, it is plain that Annan basically subscribes to Wheeler's 'solidarist claim' and not to Chesterman's more conventional interpretation of the inviolability of states' rights. In coming to that judgement, as Annan has made clear in words and in actions (such as authorising the independent enquiry into the failures in Rwanda), he feels both personal and institutional responsibilities for failing those victims. A similar combination of intellectual and moral drive informed the thoughts and actions of the other major statesmen to have tackled these questions in public.

Speaking in the House of Commons on the afternoon of Tuesday 23 March 1999, Prime Minister Tony Blair stated, as he sought to explain the reason for NATO's bombing of Serbia that was about to begin, that 'We must act to save thousands of innocent men, women and children from humanitarian catastrophe, from death, barbarism and ethnic cleansing by a brutal dictatorship. We have no alternative to act and act we will.' One month later, when it had become plain that aerial bombardment alone was not going to lead to Mr Milosevic's capitulation, and (as we now know) shortly after the Prime Minister had received a report from Paddy Ashdown (former marine commando and leader of the Liberal Democrat party), which warned him that 'You think you are winning this war. I think you are losing it', Mr Blair began to push Bill Clinton and his other NATO allies to nerve themselves for an invasion of Kosovo if the refugees were to be returned. In his note to the Prime Minister, Ashdown summarised the situation neatly: 'This is the first war in history that is being fought for refugees. And we have set ourselves an unforgiving measure for its success. If they don't go back, we have lost.'

Intellectually persuaded of the need to prepare a land invasion force, on 20 April 1999 at NATO headquarters, Blair stated the underlying reason for the operations in ringing terms:

To see people herded onto trains and taken away from their homes and to hear the stories that those refugees have come back from Kosovo with – and heaven only knows what we will find when we get into Kosovo – to hear those is either to awaken our conscience and make us act or it is to say that we have no conscience and no will to act in the face of something which is appalling and wrong ... a whole people displaced and dispossessed simply because of their ethnic identity. My generation never thought we would see those scenes in Europe again. Our task is very simple. Our will in seeing it through is total.[22]

NATO's fiftieth anniversary Washington summit failed to produce support for Blair's advocacy of a ground invasion. But the Prime Minister was not daunted. He flew on to Chicago, where on 22 April 1999 he delivered a speech, which set out the foundations of his position in the way that Annan's Ditchley Park had done ten months before. Blair, like Annan, returned to the implication of the act of genocide to assert that combating such acts could never be a purely internal matter. We cannot turn our backs on violations of human rights, he said, for the reasons which he had expressed so passionately a couple of days before at the NATO HQ. From this common ground, Blair then moved on to territory which the Secretary-General of the UN, by function of his institution and office, could not explore, although the next month in his speech at The Hague he made plain his reluctant acceptance of the necessity of the NATO action. Blair, as Prime Minister of the country that was principally pushing the alliance, took the opportunity of his Chicago speech to set out the most explicit procedure hitherto described by a senior statesman, to regulate how the terrain beyond an unequivocal and direct Security Council mandate should be entered.

He began by observing that 'If we wanted to right every wrong that we see in the modern world, then we would do little else than intervene in the affairs of other countries...' Therefore, we require a filter which can be generally applicable and which may be used to distinguish systematically between those cases where an agent, whether international coalition or individual state, both could and should act. His speech carefully sought to link pragmatic and ethical criteria. He proposed five elements for his filter.

The first embraced the five boundary conditions and especially that of supreme humanitarian emergency: it asked, 'Are we sure of our case?' The second shared Annan's view that the activity of intervention should be broadly construed. In particular, Blair focused on diplomacy and linked the legitimacy of military intervention to being able to demonstrate that diplomacy had been exhausted. (In the case of the Kosovo conflict, this has remained a matter of live controversy focusing particularly upon the clause inserted by someone in the American government into the terms offered to Milosevic at Rambouillet, which would have allowed NATO forces free access to all the territory of Serbia – a condition which may have made narrow military sense, but which was certain to act as part of the diplomatic spoiler which it became.) Blair's position, then and since, has been that the Rambouillet negotiations did fulfil the criterion of his second element: 'Have we exhausted diplomacy?'

The third element of Blair's filter combined a key pragmatic consideration with elements from Just War doctrine in order to address one of the issues which is politically most inflamed in the whole question of intervention, namely when it occurs in some places and not others. The practical element of Blair's approach was to ask bluntly whether, if intervention occurred, it could be successful, because if there was no hope then it should not be started. To intervene and to fail is to do more harm than good, thus failing the test of the third boundary condition. Under this element, he could offer objective logistical reasons for not engaging in certain parts of the world, although, as will be discussed more fully in the last chapter, those sorts of statements do not answer fully the question which resonated among G-77 states, 'If Kosovo, why not Chechnya?' Blair's third element, he hinted in the Chicago speech, also embraced a central principle of Just War doctrine. If the victory cannot be obtained through proportionate means, then the same overriding third boundary condition that one should do no more good than harm might not be met: so, the issue is not just one of prevailing by all means, but prevailing by means that are proportionate and discriminate. The importance of meeting those requirements is quite central to the chances of prevailing if the objective is to produce a permanent and benign alteration in the geopolitical facts on the ground. Bombing Grozny, the capital of Chechnya, flat did not meet these Just War criteria and, to date, Russia has not prevailed in any permanent way. While quietly sympathising with the Russian case against that of the Chechen rebels, western countries found it impossible to support the means that were used and have, therefore, been drawn into increasingly vocal condemnation of the Russian conduct of this war.

The fourth element returns to the broad construction of the act of intervention. To be sure, all these five elements are mobilised for the purposes of legitimating a military intervention; but, just as the second element demanded evidence of failure in conflict prevention, so the fourth asked, 'Are we prepared for the long haul?' Each of the principal episodes of intervention since the mid-1990s has seen the issue of follow-through raised to higher prominence. In the case of Kosovo, the appointment of Bernard Kouchner as the directing coordinator of international efforts to reconstruct the province at the end of the conflict and once the refugees had returned, was the most overt move yet in this direction. But the discoordination of an expensive international effort, lying on top of a failure to produce any substantial reconciliation between Serbian and Albanian residents, meant that the effort could not be regarded as a success. Nonetheless, recollecting, perhaps, British experience of Northern Ireland, Blair was right to stress the importance of checking that sufficient political will existed to follow through, before entering. The point being made was rather different from the narrowly military way in which this question has tended to be discussed in the United States. It is about more than the virtue or vice of declaring 'exit strategies'.

However, the most challenging and novel aspect of Blair's filter lay in the fifth element. The test to be met was that the action be seen to be 'in the national interest'. Here, Blair became the first powerful statesman of recent times to articulate explicitly a cosmopolitan interpretation of national interest; for he answered his test by observing that the mass expulsions from Kosovo were in the British national interest – thus warranting the expenditure of British money and perhaps of British lives – because 'they demanded the notice of the rest of the world...' He supported this view with two batteries of justification. One argued from enlightened self-interest by pointing to the dangers that uncivil civil wars can spill across borders; that in dealing with dictators, the lesson of history is that it is cheaper and safer to stop them earlier than later; and third – the argument which really helped to maintain the cohesion of the NATO alliance – that a failure to prevail would encourage other dictators and aspirant *genocidaires* to believe that NATO did not have the resolve to stand up to them.

This last point is a familiar one in modern strategic history. One variant, employed by Richard Nixon, was what he once described to Henry Kissinger as the 'crazy man approach' to deterrence: if the Soviets think I am crazy enough to do X then they'll believe that I might be crazy enough to do Y. A closer analogy was the argument made explicitly by Mr Blair's predecessor, Margaret Thatcher, at the time of the Falklands war, when the demonstration effect of success in such a precarious operation at long range, would help the Soviets and other enemies think twice. But Blair went much farther than these predecessors; for, to the realist arguments, he added ethical ones grounded in the same soil as Annan's argument had been.

In the case of the Blair administration, the other practical expression of that same belief that the legitimacy of power was conditional upon the protection of the rights of the individual, and, by extension, that the civility of society depends in part upon its willingness to execute its duties towards others who have no claims upon it other than their suffering, was the incorporation into British national law as 'Convention rights' of the European Convention on Human Rights by the British Human Rights Act of 1998.

Indeed, while the Act does not give judges the formal power to strike down legislation, the provisions of Sections 3 and 4 are startling. Section 3 lays upon judges a responsibility to read and give effect to primary and subordinated legislation in a way which is compatible with Convention rights; and Section 4 gives courts the power to make a 'declaration of incompatibility' if such is found. The expectation is that in the majority of such cases the legislature will wish to revise the legislation. This, an eminent professor of law maintains, is 'unquestionably the most significant formal redistribution of political power in this country since 1911, perhaps since 1688...'[23] It signals a domestic adoption of the principle of conditionality in Wheeler's solidarist claim, as well as giving judges an enlargement of responsibility that is not unproblematic. But while making that point, Professor Gearty, in his inaugural lecture to a chair of Human Rights Law, also captured the implication which the introduction of the Human Rights Act has for lawyers. 'It requires arguments to be framed in terms of principle – it tries to close the gap between our ethical and our professional selves.'[24] Precisely that sentiment describes the consequences for politicians of accepting Blair's description of national interest.

Blair was, in effect, inscribing the requirement of Kant's categorical imperative as a necessary element, in a view of national sovereignty that comes close to Wheeler's solidarist claim. Blair was asserting that, if the previous four elements of his filter had been satisfied, then the case for action was to be made in terms beyond those of enlightened self-interest: it was a moral obligation.

A week after Tony Blair delivered his Chicago speech, the implications of the fifth element in his filter were subjected to their most extensive and rigorous examination to date by one of the tiny group of international statesmen best qualified to address this topic, as a consequence of his life experience. On 29 April, the playwright, dissident leader, former political prisoner and now President of the Czech Republic, Vaclav Havel, addressed the Senate and House of Commons of the Parliament of Canada on the issue of the state and its probable position in the future. Like Blair, the immediate stimulus to his remarks came from the Kosovo war, which he described resoundingly as 'probably the first war ever fought that is not being fought in the name of interest, but in the name of certain principles and values ... because decent people cannot sit back and watch systematic, state-directed massacres of other people. Decent people ... cannot fail to come to the rescue if the rescue action is within their power.' Havel's defence of the Kosovo action was framed in terms of the hierarchy in actions and institutions which he saw emerging from 'the realisation that a human being is more important than a state' (a theme which resonates with Annan's choice to return to the very beginning of the Preface to the Charter of the United Nations to ground his case). But Havel pressed the implications of his views more incisively than either Annan or Blair had done.

His central thesis was that 'the glory of the nation state as a climax of the history of every national community and the highest earthly value ... is already past its culminating point.' Acknowledging that, among the many functions of the state, was the emotional one which fires identity politics and wars of identity, he argued that the unavoidable, functional inter-relationship of a world embraced in the negative and positive arms of globalisation, was that 'the idol of state sovereignty must inevitably dissolve'. He looked to a future when 'most states will begin to transform from cult-like objects, which are charged with emotional contents, into much simpler and more civil administrative units ... merely one of the levels in a complex and stratified planetary societal self-organisation.' While this aspiration might still be some way away, and, he observed wryly, might sound odd coming from a head of state addressing the representative bodies of another state, he was clear that there was already a practical consequence for the way in which national action could and should be justified. He contrasted the category of national interest, which tended to divide rather than to bring us together, with that of principles which, he suggested, unite us rather than divide us. 'Principles must be respected and upheld for their own sake – so to speak, as a matter of principle – and interests should be derived from them.'

Havel did not deny that the NATO action in Kosovo lacked a direct Security Council mandate, and by implication, he did not have difficulty with the oblique appeal to precedent. But he signalled bluntly his willingness to rely upon 'respect for the laws of humanity, as they are articulated by our conscience', if no other source of legitimation be found because, in his view, the priority of human rights over states rights was fixed and so he concluded: *'L'état est l'oeuvre de l'homme et l'homme est l'oeuvre de Dieu.'* For Havel, the implication of his analysis for the practical issue of intervention was both clear and inescapable. The changing nature of the state in international politics and the construction of individual identity 'among other things should gradually antiquate the idea than noninterference that is, the consequence of saying that what happens in another state, or the measure of respect for human rights there, is none of our business'.[25] In like measure, the speech attracted extravagant praise and extravagant condemnation as an act of gross irresponsibility.

All these utterances, and in particular Blair's Chicago speech, caused many, including the Presidents of China and Russia, to conclude that a new regime in international affairs was being swept to power. But was that really so? And has subsequent evidence supported the contention or not? There have been three convergent views, each originating from different points of departure, which support the opinion that the pattern of interventions in support of human rights does not thereby overturn an international system based on the principles of state sovereignty. The first observed, cynically but accurately, that in their detail the cases do not support the contention that sovereignty is under threat. Only in the case of Kosovo was it on the horizon and then only because the issue was one of secession. In East Timor no-one except the Australians had recognised the Indonesian claim over the territory, so it was not at issue there. And, as observed above, in the case of Sierra Leone, the recognised national government invited and welcomed the presence of external troops. Furthermore, *Realpolitik* determines that where interventions do occur they are not against members of the Permanent Five on the Security Council or their allies, nor are they against major regional powers. Interventions cannot occur without a framework leader and the lead country, therefore, needs to see some vital issue in the intervention (as Australia did in the threat of boat people fleeing from East Timor, for example).

The second line of reasoning is Annan's. By casting both state interests and the interests of peoples in the same currency of sovereignty, he seeks to argue for congruence as the natural order of relationship. This line permits the solidarist claim to be slotted in neatly and in a manner which supports the principle of sovereignty by emphasising how a particular regime has forfeited its right to power through breach of those implicit conditions. This is an argument akin to one made many years ago by the anthropologist, Max Gluckman, who pointed out that, whereas rebellion in pre-colonial Africa might appear to be incoherent, violent and disruptive, it was in fact structurally reinforcing of the social order, because it repainted the lines which distinguished legitimate from illegitimate tenure of power: a similar argument is made about the concept of the 'mandate of heaven' in Chinese history. Remove the unworthy incumbent and the legitimacy of the office is thereby strengthened.[26]

The third convergent line is most closely associated with Professor Adam Roberts, who has frequently and trenchantly restated it. The most striking political feature of recent interventions is that they are extremely hard to mount politically, let alone to execute successfully once an operation is under way. The general effect of all this evidence of the difficulty experienced at each step in mounting an intervention is to underscore the very opposite of the Chinese and Russian Presidents' fears. Far from being a new norm of international behaviour, interventions are plainly exceptions and, as such, by application of Gluckman's logic about rebellion, they are structurally reinforcing of the norm of non-intervention in the internal affairs of states, a norm which, in Adam Roberts's memorable phrase, 'makes the world go round'.[27]

But interventions do not occur in a vacuum. In fact, the context has been changing rapidly as international affairs moves from the post-Cold War period to the new era. Five trends in particular are simultaneously noteworthy and perplexing: noteworthy for the degree to which each has gained in the clarity of its definition; perplexing in that three pull in one direction and two in another. Of the three trends militating against the likelihood that the recent pattern of interventions will be maintained, let alone accelerated, the first is evidence of a decreasing appetite for acts of humanitarian intervention among the countries which have hitherto provided the human and material resources for interventions. Episode by episode, the Secretary-General of the UN has found it increasingly difficult to raise contingents of the right type and quality at the right time: one of the Brahimi commission's recommendations was that experience showed that it was better to send no contingent than to send one composed of inadequately trained or equipped personnel. This trend has had implications for the manner in which military forces are both provided and deployed for humanitarian intervention.

Second, the spotlight which in the mid- to late-1990s was trained upon the issue of humanitarian intervention in the period following the failures of Srebrenica and Rwanda has begun to move. Particularly since the arrival of the Bush Jnr administration in the United States, commentators have begun to speculate on the implications of a move to a new era of strategic rivalry, tied in the first instance to a change in the tone of Sino-American relations. But this shift is not propelled most powerfully, or even principally, by a change of administration. The philosophy, training and equipment programmes of the American armed forces since the defeat in Vietnam have all been directed more towards the eventuality of a threat to American security which could demand a major theatre war (being equipped for which might, therefore, deter the same) than for expeditionary raiding. The professional careers of those in high command at the turn of the century tended to have begun in the Vietnam era and were deeply marked by it. The degree to which the Vietnam experience stimulated the US Army in particular to redefine itself in high-tec, high-intensity terms is both illustrated and intelligently discussed in the autobiography of the Supreme Allied Commander at the time of the Kosovo war, General Wesley Clark, to take a prominent example. While this redirection of gaze may have the practical effect of reducing American enthusiasm for participation in humanitarian intervention – especially given the 'Mogadishu effect': the humiliating outwitting of elite American forces by General Aideed – the debate about human rights and intervention both affects and is affected by this trend in ways which are discussed more fully in the final chapter of this book.

The third trend piles on top of the second and is itself composed of three strands. The first of these is the general retreat from multilateral agencies. While frequently represented as principally an American policy, it is plainly more general. Certainly there has been a strong reaction among American politicians to the expulsion of the US from the Human Rights Committee, for example (an act which was to a considerable extent a self-inflicted injury, given that the US did not campaign actively for its re-election and lacked an ambassador at its UN Mission after Mr Holbrook's departure). But in less lurid fashion, many of the richest countries have begun to withdraw their enthusiasm for working through the UN and also their resources. The most telling evidence of this is the trend for countries to contribute less to the aid and developments agencies of the UN and to channel their resources more through national or regional development agencies. Nor is this retreat from multilateral institutions confined to the UN. Most dramatic evidence was the shift away from the European Commission and towards a re-empowering of the Committee of Heads of States within the European Union at the Nice summit of 2000. The obverse of this retreat is a re-empowerment of state agency in areas which remain uncontroversially under state competence. These are especially the military development and diplomatic spheres of activity: precisely those of importance to strategies of humanitarian intervention. However, the third strand in this third trend reveals the tension within it. For the range of regional organisations, which occupy the space between the UN and the individual member state, are greatly various in their nature, their range of competence and their political legitimacy. This last is especially a problem for the African regional organisations where the status of the legitimacy-conferring states may be itself problematic. Thus attempts to promote regional organisations as a category of political actor which may be used to take up tasks which might formerly have been given only to and through the UN Security Council will not be straightforward. The next chapter illustrates how the conferring of a Security Council mandate for action upon ECOWAS, and through it its Nigerian-dominated military arm ECOMOG, resulted in deplorably undisciplined action which compromised the UN for having authorised the operations of which these were part.

These three trends appear to reduce the likelihood of humanitarian intervention. But the other two trends might suggest otherwise. One aspect of the fourth has been explored already, and others follow shortly: all relate to the rapid clarification of the ethical and legal perspectives, which, as we have seen, are opening a much broader view of international responsibility to act on evidence of gross abuse of human rights. Shortly we will review the five forms of intervention broadly construed, of which military intervention is one. Here too there has been rapid and detailed clarification of options and strategies. It is ironic that just at the time when the nature of mandates and means for their execution have become swiftly clearer, the appetite to undertake pre-emptive action appears to have diminished in inverse proportion.

Therefore, in light of the fifth trend, one may conclude that future humanitarian interventions are likely to be as they have been in the recent past, principally in response to undeniable evidence of atrocity: for the fifth trend describes the increasing likelihood of need for action in three regions of the world above others. The first of these is on the continent where most interventions have so far occurred. Both Angola and the Democratic Republic of the Congo are enormous and fractured areas beyond the competence of any of the current contenders for power to govern in an efficient and unified fashion, even if the will for this existed. Instead, both regions contain running civil wars and the prospect of sudden flare-ups of violence at any time. While the situation in Sierra Leone is less violent and arguably with better prospects for resolution than at any time in the decade since civil war began, the potentials for breakdown there, and even more so in neighbouring Guinea and Liberia, remain and so an active threat of reversion to widespread uncivil war remains. In central and eastern Africa, the focus of most immediate threat of political violence appears to have moved from the Great Lakes region southwards to Zimbabwe. A particular destabilising feature of this region is the high prevalence of HIV/AIDS in the political elite (which is preferentially infected). It adds a further unknown variable to the mix of forces which strive to control patronage in the patrimonial post-colonial African state. Nor are these regions of risk in Africa an equal set; for should the Democratic Republic of Congo, for example, become the site of atrocities, even if the growing reluctance of the technically competent states to act could be overcome, action might be blocked by the third element of Blair's filter, because no realistic way of prevailing could be seen.

A similar objection would likely block military intervention should the need for action arise in the Asia–Pacific region. Here the circumstance most discussed by regional experts is the possibility of the break-up of Indonesia with the humanitarian emergencies in Irian Jaya and Aceh provinces. But in this region, where, with the exception of the highly unusual circumstances surrounding the legal status and the referendum result in East Timor, there is no track record of international humanitarian intervention in the way that there is in sub-Saharan Africa and the Balkans. Furthermore, heated rhetoric defending the sanctity of state sovereignty does not only come from the leadership of communist China. Prime Minister Mahathir of Malaysia has been a vocal focus of criticism of the West. He has frequently and mercilessly pilloried the double standards of western behaviour. His objection to intervention is construed as broadly as Kofi Annan sought to do but for other purposes: Mahatir, for example, has used blanket assertions of the rights of sovereignty to deny the right of any other parties to express views, let alone declare interests in the management of globally significant resources, notably the shrinking rainforest that is located on Malaysian territory. Should any of the federal Asia–Pacific states fracture in ways that meet the boundary conditions for humanitarian intervention, the two very different but militarily significant states, which bracket the region North and South – Australia to the South and Japan to the North – would, with their allies, be faced with severe tests.

Tests of a different sort already begin to present themselves in the third region where the risk of humanitarian emergency is high. The geopolitical region, which is marked to the West by the new borders of the Russian Federation and to the East by the People's Republic of China including Tibet, contains many newly independent fragments of the former Soviet space, which, by virtue of their great oil and mineral wealth (and in the former case the entailed matter of the security of long-distance pipelines), have straightforward strategic importance in the contemporary global economy. Any demand to act in the face of a supreme humanitarian emergency in this region invites the international community to contemplate forms of intervention, which are well beyond the narrow construction (military intervention in the context of declared genocide), but not as far as to trigger strategic confrontation in the rapidly renuclearising world of strategic rivalry that is explored in the last chapter. To date, the problem of this 'middle space' has received little applied analysis within the mission of responsibility to protect human rights worldwide.[28] However, the international community has already delivered a view on the management of the 'middle space' and this region through the ambivalence of its reaction to the botched and bloody Russian attempt to suppress the rebellion in Chechnya. The Chechen war has already had an impact on the way that both China and India might frame and deal with their own separatist threats. For if separatist claims are answered with massive and indiscriminate use of force, the likely response, as has happened in Chechnya, is two-pronged: regrouping for guerrilla warfare in the disputed territory and seeking to conduct terror attacks, in this case in Moscow and other parts of Russia. In such a circumstance, the fragmented separatist disputes can rapidly be lumped under the most powerful of condemnatory labels of terrorism and extremism, which will in turn help to embed the conflict by alienating all those who share the ethnic or religious characteristics of the separatists.

The gravest danger, argued Professor Legvold, is of a transregional alienation of Islamic populations, which could at some point lead to what has never previously existed, namely a coherent bloc. Professor Huntington's feared future, in which strategic competition would be between self-aware and coherent cultural blocs might, ironically, be forged by a process similar to that whereby, in Vietnam, the US applied sufficient massive military force to the people and the place to bring into existence in the Viet Cong a crude approximation of the conspiratorial, Chinese-manipulated Vietnamese resistance, which was certainly an inaccurate description of the Viet Minh at the moment of French defeat and withdrawal after the battle of Dien Bien Phu in 1953.[29] Should such a future unfold in this key region, the impact on international peace and security could be quite direct.

A clear implication of even limited speculation about possible risks in the former Soviet space and the Asia–Pacific region is to underline the fairly narrow confines within which military forms of intervention taken in isolation can hope to effect permanent changes on the ground, such that the outcome of the action is more good than harm.

Five linked but different sorts of action can be taken once a responsibility to protect the human rights of an identified group has been accepted. The victims may be individuals not citizens; the principal agents of action nonetheless will be states, coalitions and organisations of states and, in particular, democratic states propelled by public opinion. Each of the five types of action is plainly a form of intervention and for descriptive purposes there is no reason not to call them such, or indeed to see their deployment either sequentially or in combination as aspects of an episode of intervention. That way of viewing these actions would be consistent with the spirit of analysis for which the speeches of Kofi Annan, Tony Blair and Vaclav Havel has been taken as indicative foundation stones. However, for political reasons, it may be wiser not to represent this span of five forms of action in this way. If the aim is to ensure, in moments of acute crisis when all else has failed and atrocity has occurred or is imminently threatening, that action is taken, practitioners prefer to confine the meaning of intervention narrowly to its military aspect alone.

Thus conflict prevention and the imposition of different sorts of sanctions are represented as aspects of pre-intervention preventive diplomacy in order to avoid the muddling which can occur if, for example, World Bank funding or IMF programmes are represented as aspects of intervention, given that the term induces such negative connotations in the minds of many representatives of former colonial states. These different ways of representing the same range of activities are to be found in the analytic and practitioner communities respectively, but with senior statesmen, such as those discussed here, pushing the practitioner community to accept a broad construction as employed here.

It is self-evidently preferable to stop something before it starts and, therefore, Annan's advocacy of a culture of prevention in his

1999 essay, amplified in the way that the millennium General Assembly session was approached, cannot be denied, particularly in the face of a rising incidence of major natural disasters in the 1990s (three times as many as in the 1960s), as well as the rising number of uncivil wars in that same decade.[30] Annan gave prominence to the case for conflict prevention because he saw it not only weakly attempted but with diminishing, rather than increasing effort and resources. The perceived mismatch between needs and means can be narrowly represented in terms of the diversion of state-aid resources away from multilateral into national programmes: a 40 per cent decrease in emergency relief aid reported by the Red Cross for the last half of the 1990s, for example. But a second reason has, with ghastly suddenness, overshadowed the diminishing trend of effort.

When Ariel Sharon took his fateful walk to the Temple Mount, the action marked not only the opening of the second intifada (and most likely the planning for the 11 September 2001 attack), but also the rapid discrediting of the oversold application of industrial relations negotiation techniques to international diplomacy. The collapse of the so-called 'peace process', when it became clear that the Clinton administration's attempts to build up Yasser Arafat into a credible negotiating 'partner' had failed, has been a brutal shock to those who had confidence in these types of preventive diplomacy. The unravelling of the so-called 'Good Friday Agreement', to bring about a resolution of the intercommunal conflict in Northern Ireland, which was brokered with such effort by the Prime Ministers of Ireland and the United Kingdom during the first eighteen months of Mr Blair's premiership, underlines the same point. If, within twenty years or so, the fecund Catholic population will outnumber the less fertile Protestants in a conflict of such systematic cultural difference and antagonism, the demographic *Realpolitik* suggests that the Catholics have little to gain from an early closure when the birthrate will give them their way through the democratic process in the not too distant future.

However, perhaps the most fundamental problem about conflict prevention, which has prevented it from making much headway as a usable tactic, is the absence of a coherent policy-applicable explanation of how abatement of structural violence (by increasing standards of health, education, agricultural productivity, etc.) can or will pre-empt physical violence. In face of such depressing evidence, two related, much more hard-edged approaches to conflict prevention have begun to attract interest. Both look more to the use of sticks than carrots, understanding that the inducements of 'soft' prevention, especially when deployed in a context constructed on faulty assessments of the competences and standing of the parties, is unlikely ever to prevail. Equally, they recoil from Luttwak's advice, which is to stand well back and allow war to burn itself out like a bush fire, since only when one side is victorious and the other defeated will there be a reliable peace.[31]

When Under-Secretary for Peacekeeping Affairs, Kofi Annan had named the idea of 'coercive inducement'; and Professors Daniel, Hayes and de Jonge Oudraat seek to give it form. They see coercive inducement as a particular variant of coercive diplomacy and distinct from the active use of armed force through strategic raiding, in the manner illustrated in the case study in the next chapter. The nub of their case is that military forces should be deployed early, but with a mission more closely akin to that of traditional UN peacekeeping than that of peace enforcement:

> The underlying purpose of all coercive inducement, as with peacekeeping, would not be to unduly favour the victory or defeat of one or another of the competing groups (as might be a nation's purpose when engaging in coercive diplomacy in general), but rather to help contain the crisis, to keep it from getting worse so that peacekeepers and peacemakers can work with the conflicting parties to help make things better.

They see these forces deployed in a reactive mode and employing *cordons sanitaires*, safe havens and other passive, positional defences. However, they recognise that, in practice, the coercive message of such a deployment is only credible if, on the one hand, the force is manifestly capable of looking after itself should things go badly, and, on the other, of moving from a passive to an active role, should circumstance and mandate require it. Given the painful difficulties experienced in Bosnia as the international community fumbled its way across this dividing line from UNPROFOR to S-FOR during 1995–6, the task is easier said than done. The authors recognise this and, recognising it, insist nonetheless that there is virtue in providing a backdrop of coercive implication to all stages of the international community's involvement in a humanitarian emergency, including conflict containment, should it occur, and conflict resolution once violence has been dampened down.[32] Jentilson takes a narrower slice, confining his concept of coercive prevention to the period before hostilities break out, when there is still a chance of stopping it.

Jentilson argues robustly that provision of a military threat, with elements both of deterrence and the threat of compellence associated with diplomacy and 'smart' sanctions perhaps, is the way to rescue Annan's call for a culture of prevention. It gives muscle to the diplomats, rather in the way that the gathering military preparations of the international community may have strengthened the message of the special mission by the ambassadors of the Security Council to Indonesia in the middle of the East Timor crisis. He, like Daniel *et al.*, recognised that a preventive deployment is only likely to be safe and successful if there is self-evidently will and capability to escalate. Jentilson suggested that had there been a substantial preventive deployment in April 1999, when the UN was negotiating with the Indonesian government over the East Timorese independence referendum, a time at which violence was already bursting out in the territory, quite possibly subsequent violence could have been prevented or greatly diminished. He believed the same would have been true had UNPREDEP, the UN preventive deployment force for Macedonia, been similarly boosted.[33]

The difficulty with the case for coercive inducement or coercive prevention is that, in practice, it is hard to separate a credible deployment for these purposes from any deployment of military force. Indeed, the effects being requested from military deployment by the proposers of these concepts are, in fact, the leading edge effects of successful forces deployed with diplomatic/military objectives into hostile environments. Thus one must conclude that coercive inducement and coercive deployment may belong in theory to the realm of conflict prevention but, in practice, are only likely to be successful as aspects of deployments equipped and mandated to use all necessary means to end violence. The reconfiguration, reinforcement and associated logistical build-up supporting General Mike Jackson in Macedonia with the Allied Rapid Reaction Corps of NATO, as the 'ground option' code named 'Bravo Minus' (a ground offensive to expel Yugoslav troops from Kosovo) was prepared, was certainly an example of coercive signalling as part of an ultimately successful preventive diplomacy; but it was indistinguishable from the mission to prevail.

The second form of action open to the international community is the imposition of sanctions under Chapter VI of the UN Charter. Twelve sanction regimes were applied during the 1990s, and some in novel ways. In addition to 'traditional' sanctions against states, targeted sanctions against non-state actors were attempted in the contexts of the conflicts both in Angola and Cambodia, and specifically in aid of democracy building during the Sierra Leone civil war in 1997.[34] But the fundamental reservations about sanctions, as a means of preventing conflict, are three. First, the use of sanctions during the decolonisation decade, against South Africa over its occupation of what later became Namibia and against the white regime in Rhodesia, after its unilateral declaration of independence, was that circumvention was too easy if friendly neighbours and friendly multinational businesses could be persuaded to defy them. However, the historical experience which most swayed opinion in the 1990s was of the sanctions imposed upon Iraq in respect of Saddam Hussein's continued persecution of the Kurds in the North and the Marsh Arabs in the South. These illustrated both the other reasons why broad sanctions did not command enthusiasm: for, second, it was hard to show causal effect and, third, it was hard to make the sanctions discriminate so that they hit the leadership of Iraq rather than the long-suffering people. Two ways of making economic sanctions bite more precisely were studied by the Carnegie Commission on Preventing Deadly Conflict. For this reason, it favoured commodities sanctions, which hit state revenues first. But it warned that, to be effective, such sanctions have to be applied in just the way that they usually cannot be, namely swiftly and comprehensively. Greater consultation with international corporations was advocated, since such bodies often have a better understanding of the economic levers which can influence particular governments than other actors. But the Commission offered no view on how corporations might be induced to play a role which they could regard as potentially compromising of their future interests. The former Foreign Minister of Australia and Co-Chairman of the International Commission on Intervention and State Sovereignty, Gareth Evans, has argued for a refinement to the classical model, suggesting that, rather than maintaining sanctions at full force until compliance, a valuable improvement in options could be achieved by unbundling sanctions and then lifting them by stages in response to compliant behaviour.[35] The attraction of Evans's proposal is that it reinforces good behaviour and cannot be represented as appeasement.

The other approach is an extension of that used against the Khmer Rouge in Cambodia and UNITA in Angola. 'Targeted' sanctions focus even more narrowly, seeking to freeze the personal assets of leaders or to deny them access to hard currency. These are steps which can limit the ability to buy arms and to maintain patronage networks; and the attraction of a sanction regime, which can accord with Article 50 of the UN Charter that endorses the importance of discriminating in impact between the innocent and guilty, is clearly attractive. But the Carnegie Commission recognised that 'targeted sanctions are extremely intrusive and set a stark precedent for dealing with ruthless behaviour'.[36] The Commissioners were therefore attracted to the proposal in one of its Commission's research reports, which advocated a second collective measures committee be mandated by the General Assembly, which could police the application of targeted sanctions and also act as a point of contact with the multinational business community.[37] However, the record of sanctions as an effective way of pre-empting uncivil war has been only slightly less discouraging than that of preventive diplomacy. Neither of these lines of approach can yet demonstrate a decisive achievement to its credit; and the waning enthusiasm and strength of multinational agencies does not encourage great optimism in the future.

The same cannot be said of the third line of action. There have been dramatic innovations and political successes. It is by its nature a highly targeted form of intervention, and it is unaffected in its fundamentals by the changing balance between multilateral and national institutions.

Of all the forms of intervention other than military intervention available to the international community, approach through the law is the one which signals most clearly the limits of tolerated behaviour. So the moving cursor of customary international law traces lines in the sand and, thereby, signals where a transgressor may expect to be confronted. All this has been explored above. In a brief but trenchant paper, the distinguished international jurist, Alain Pellet, confirmed Wheeler's solidarist claim:

> In the case of human rights violations, sovereignty is never a defence; in cases of gross violations of human rights it has no role to play; it does not impede the Security Council from concluding that such violations create a threat to the peace and to draw the appropriate consequences in accordance with Chapter VII of the Charter; and it cannot even protect heads of states from international prosecution.[38]

Pellet's last statement is the most contentious and is still resisted by some; but, as will be seen, even in this area there has been remarkable clarification during the 1990s. During this decade, the role of law, in three varieties, developed greatly, serving simultaneously the function of tracking and marking changes in the consensus of interpretation (for example, of Article 2.7 of the UN Charter) and providing means of punishment and hence deterrence of future transgressors.

Since being in a position to meet the test of proportionality is one of the boundary conditions defining a case for humanitarian intervention, and is incorporated in Mr Blair's five-element filter, it is not surprising that the laws of war and their application, in particular to the definition of rules of engagement, the selection and precision in attacking targets, was thrust to the fore during the Kosovo air campaign. General Clark's memoir described graphically the operational implication of this heightened requirement, while Professor Roberts observed that the category of legitimate target included key aspects of Serbian state power, as well as its military forces, before the campaign ended.[39]

As much discussed in the press was the second development in the realm of international law, with the reanimation of the Nuremberg criteria and procedures through the creation first of the War Crimes Tribunal for Yugoslavia and then that for Rwanda, situated in The Hague and Arusha respectively, and in the making of which the South African jurist, Richard Goldstone, played a central role.[40] Kofi Annan welcomed the actions of the tribunals for the Former Yugoslavia and Rwanda as a 'powerful tool for deterrence ... in their battle against impunity lies a key to deterring crimes against humanity.'[41] However, Justice Goldstone himself observed that *ad hoc* tribunals are of their nature unsatisfactory because each time one is established everything must be built from the ground up. Therefore, he shared the enthusiasm for the Rome Statute of the International Criminal Court, which was adopted by the UN Diplomatic Conference of Plenipotentiaries on the establishment of an International Criminal Court in Rome on 17 July 1998, with the US as the most conspicuous and (from its point of view) surprisingly isolated objector.

The US feared that, despite Part II, Article 5, Section 1, which severely confined the jurisdiction of the Court to 'The most serious crimes of concern to the international community as a whole', attempts would be made to construe that narrow permission broadly; to invoke use of the Court when, in fact, other national jurisdictions might be competent and capable and delivering safe justice. But a tide seemed to be flowing. After a period in the doldrums, The Hague tribunal experienced first the voluntary surrender of Bilijana Plovtic, former President of the Republika Srpska and then the extradition of Slobodan Milosevic himself in 2001. The ending of the civil war in Sierra Leone led to canvassing prospects for a further *ad hoc* war crimes tribunal to bring to justice the perpetrators of atrocity, notably by the Revolutionary United Front. A conviction of former Rwandan Prime Minister, Jean Kambanda, in September 1998, who pleaded guilty to genocide, marked another step forward, for he was the highest ranking political leader to have been convicted by an international court to that point.

A vocal constituency among principally American international lawyers argues that the popular broad construction of international law is not law but 'just distracting rhetoric for those too squeamish to face the essential lawlessness of international affairs'. The proper American position, argued Professor Rabkin, is that there can be no open-ended consent to accept directives or obligations or restrictions on the US government, whatever other countries may choose to do. Each obligation to which consent is given must receive a separate, new consent and such consents cannot ever displace the authority of the constitutional organs of the US nor can they direct the way the US government will treat US citizens inside the territory of the US.[42] It was reservations of this sort which caused the US Senate to refuse to ratify the League of Nations and which also underlie unwillingness to submit itself to the proposed ICC. International law in the traditional and narrow construction really cannot be about matters such as human rights or the environment. In the case of the ICC, Rabkin writes, the US would be in breach of its own constitution were it to deliver Americans up to trial by such a court, and certainly not for actions undertaken in the service of the US government: for it would circumvent all the safeguards of due process guaranteed in the US Bill of Rights. International law is only real law in a narrow construction referring to inter-state relations: so the very fact that crimes against humanity involve no international component makes its claim to standing particular obnoxious in Rabkin's eyes.[43]

Stated in these terms, the issue looks like a tug of war between the rights of states and the rights of individuals in the way that it was presented by President Havel before the Canadian legislature; and looked at in these terms it seems that the interests of the 'state firsters' (the Presidents of China, Russia, Rabkin and those of his views) are in eclipse, as those of the 'universal righters' are in the ascendant. However, this would be to overlook what has been in many ways the most remarkable – and certainly the most effective – set of responses to the rising responsibility to protect human rights. This has occurred within domestic jurisdictions, and within those jurisdictions arguably the most far-reaching developments have been within the United States.

The relationship between the 'black letter' law of a national juris-diction and the rulings, conventions and declarations which compose customary international law has always been iterative: practice and principles expressed in the one, shaping practice and principles in the other. The most direct way in which citizens can benefit from the articulation of rights is when an international declaration, such as the European Convention on Human Rights, is domesticated within a national jurisdiction in the way that the British Human Rights Act of 1998 did for British citizens. The vigorous exploitation of its appear-ance within British domestic law, with cases being pursued, many successfully, in areas as varied as planning law, privacy and the right to voluntary euthanasia, shows how the domestication of general principles can lead to actions with real and far-reaching con-sequences. But more far-reaching still have been the clarifications and extension in both criminal and civil law of the Pinochet extradi-tion in Britain with respect to the former and the Filartiga case in the American jurisdiction in the latter. Both cases involved courts in finding, in the first instance, that cases involving actions by foreigners undertaken elsewhere than within that jurisdiction were nonetheless judiciable. In the Pinochet case, it was established that, from the date that the Torture Convention had been domesticated in British legislation, the actions of Pinochet in Chile became visible. In his opinion at the third hearing before the Law Lords, the Lord Chief Justice, Lord Brown Wilkinson, affirmed that large-scale torture was one of the crimes against humanity which had the char-acter of *jus cogens*, which therefore justified states in taking 'univer-sal jurisdiction over torture wherever committed. International law provides that offences *jus cogens* may be punished by any state because the offenders are "common enemies of mankind" and all nations have an equal interest in their apprehension and prosecution.'[44]

Geoffrey Robertson QC judged the historic importance of the Pinochet case to lie in the fact that 'he was the first to be held poten-tially liable to prosecution for a crime against humanity committed in peace time, notwithstanding a cloak of sovereign immunity which the state he headed was determined not to waive'.[45] The analogues in international law to this domestic procedure are thus, in the first instance, support of *ad hoc* criminal tribunals, which extend the Nuremberg principle for those charged with crimes during times of conflict and, by extension, the ICC to whose statute the United Kingdom was a signatory and the US was not in 1998. But this does not mean, as some have represented it, that the US is not a party to these developments in legal process. It is, but through civil and not criminal law.

Lord Brown-Wilkinson referred to the doctrine of *hostis humani generis* – the enemy of all mankind – whose acts are in violation of the Law of Nations taken as *jus cogens*. Exactly the same approach was taken in the first judiciary act for the US passed in 1789 and now codified in 28 U.S.C. ¶1350. The Alien Tort Claims Act was conceived with pirates in mind as the enemies of mankind. It stated that, 'The district courts shall have original jurisdiction of any civil action by an alien for a tort only, committed in violation of the Law of Nations or a treaty of the United States.' This Act gave non-American citizens the opportunity to pursue damages against another non-citizen of the US in an American court if, for example, pirates stole the cargo of a ship. Judgements rendered became so-called 'transitory torts' meaning that wherever the pirate went the wronged party could pursue him.

Used a couple of times at the beginning of the life of the Republic, the Alien Tort Claims Act slept mostly until it was reawakened in 1980. The plaintiffs were Dr Joel Filartiga and his daughter, Dolly, prominent critics of the Paraguayan regime. They alleged that the defendant, Americo Norberto Peña-Irala, a former police inspector general of Paraguay, had, with state authority, tortured to death their son and brother, Joelito. They sued for the tort of wrongful death, claiming that the act of torture had been 'committed in violation of the Law of Nations'. The defendant had come to the US and overstayed his visa and was in the custody of immigration officials. The district court judge conceded that 'Official torture violates an emerging norm of customary international law', but interpreted 'law of nations' narrowly, excluding a state's treatment of its own nationals. Accordingly, the case was dismissed. The matter was referred to the Second Circuit court, which requested interpretation of the statute and in 1980 the Departments of State and Justice issued a joint *amicus curiae* memorandum, which supported the exercise of the jurisdiction. The Second Circuit court therefore overturned the dismissal and found the Filartiga case to be judiciable. Analysing the importance of the Filartiga decision, Professors Blum and Steinhardt observed 'substantial parallels between the late twentieth century and the period around 1789 when U.S.C. ¶1350 was enacted'. Interpreting the implication of the joint *amicus* submission, they note that, in contrast to Rabkin's narrower construction mentioned above, a newer mode of international law-making emerges based on two main premises. The first is that international conventions, declarations and resolutions are a higher form of state practice; the second that states 'may constitute customary law by expressing in notably formal and consensual ways their shared aspirations for a world order'. Those aspirations may be, and indeed are, reflected in international declarations, which may be, like the Universal Declaration of Human Rights, regarded as authoritative within national jurisdictions, but – and this is the heart of the reason for looking so closely at national legal roots to effective action – they write that 'because the emerging world order continues to be built upon a reality of state sovereignty, nothing can be a core norm which does not command the "general assent of civilised nations"'. Nor is the traffic in one direction only where principles, expressed in customary international law, are transferred across and adopted domestically in the way that the British Human Rights Act did with the European Convention on Human Rights: 'Courts applying U.S.C. ¶1350 after Filartiga,' Blum and Steinhardt concluded, 'will serve a constitutive role in the formation of international law itself.'[46]

The Second Circuit's opinion on Filartiga relied upon declarations, such as that on human rights, as authoritative statements of the international community, in coming to the view, shared later by Lord Brown-Wilkinson, that torturers were enemies of all mankind and that torture was in breach of the Law of Nations. Applying the same logic and criteria, Blum and Steinhardt suggested that, in addition to torture, genocide, summary execution and slavery probably also furnish a basis as four core human rights violations, all of which have been the object of unequivocal condemnation, for successful application of the Alien Tort Claims Act.

Thus, in 1995, Mrs Kadic, on her own behalf and on behalf of her infant sons Benjamin and Ognjen, launched an action against Radovan Karadzic, seeking damages on their own behalf and acting as representatives of victims of various atrocities including brutal acts of rape, forced prostitution, forced impregnation, torture and summary execution, carried out by the Bosnian Serb military forces as part of a genocidal campaign, conducted in the course of the Bosnian civil war. In early 1993, Karadzic was admitted to the US as an invitee of the United Nations and was at that time personally served with a summons and complaint in these actions. Rather as with Filartiga, the district court first found the matter not judiciable, but the Second Circuit overturned this on appeal.

Chief Judge Jon Newman noted in his opinion that he was aware that, by his judgement, the scope of application of the Alien Tort Act was being seen to enlarge. In particular, he wrote that 'we do not agree that the Law of Nations, as understood in the modern era, confines its reach to state action. Instead, we hold that certain forms of conduct violate the Law of Nations whether undertaken by those acting under the auspices or only as private individuals'.[47] The Court of Appeal also rejected Karadzic's claim of immunity from service of legal process, in which he relied on the headquarters' agreement between the UN and the US. So on different fronts, the available hiding place for perpetrators of human rights abuses appears to be being restricted: the perpetration of any of the four core human rights violations in time of war or in time of peace are now available to be pursued within national jurisdictions through the criminal and the civil law equally and the ability of defendants to escape such processes appears to be shrinking quickly. Academic lawyers, impressed by the Filartiga case and its consequences within the American jurisdiction, now argue for its principles to be applied in other jurisdictions to 'take Filartiga on the road'.[48]

Taken together, the mutually reinforcing developments within international law and important national jurisdictions, are, in Justice Goldstone's view, beginning to have important consequences in the areas of enforcement.[49] The finding that an American court may be *forum conveniens* is a particularly important piece of the picture. It both capitalises upon the cosmopolitan principles written into the US constitution at its drafting – principles suddenly central to the global political agenda at the beginning of the twenty-first century – and in a practical and powerful way, it brings the US in, despite all signs that it will continue to stand out from the process of elaborating and using international courts. Henry Kissinger, himself the subject of attention and the recipient of writs while travelling, worried of the dangers residing in the momentum towards universal jurisdiction through international courts. This, he believed, risks substituting the tyranny of judges for that of governments. 'Historically,' he noted darkly, 'the dictatorship of the virtuous has often led to inquisitions and even witch-hunts.'[50] Nor is his argument merely self-interested. Elsewhere in his essay, he argued that too great a reliance on international procedures may sap the will and eventually the capacity of national communities adequately to police themselves in these matters.

In this regard, the extradition of Milosevic to the *ad hoc* tribunal in The Hague delivered mixed messages. Whereas it undoubtedly revived the fortunes of the tribunal, and was actively sought with one part of its mind by the American government, in another part the implication will be unwelcome. For the extradition involved a change in the constitution of Yugoslavia and the possibility of creating a trial within the country that, through international participation and observation, could have been guaranteed to meet required standards of conduct, was never fully explored. Thus, for those Americans who never trusted the promises of the Rome Statute for the ICC to confine itself only to the most serious cases where no other forum was possible, the Milosevic extradition provided disagreeably reinforcing evidence. It would be rash to believe that the elaboration of methods to pursue those who infringe fundamental human rights through national and international channels will always or automatically be harmoniously and mutually reinforcing. At least in the case of the US and criminal law, the indications are to the contrary. But what cannot be denied is that universal principles have been most efficiently expressed through national jurisdictions, most notably through Pinochet and Filartiga in Britain and the US, and that such actions target the message of deterrence more precisely and surely upon those contemplating torture and genocide, and with none of the worrying collateral effects to be seen inescapably when economic sanctions are employed.

In short, the development of the protection of human rights within national jurisdictions shows how, in practice, Kofi Annan's view of two sovereignties – of the state and of the rights of peoples – can be made mutually reinforcing. In this respect, a message from the legal and judicial mode of intervention is not dissimilar from that to be seen in the narrowest and colloquially popular conception of intervention, namely by military means.

When the Cold War ended and with it the presumption that the ideological enmities of the superpowers would always block the fuller exploitation of the powers which the drafters of the UN Charter intended that organisation to have, there was much optimism that for the first time the UN might activate the Military Staff Committee, described in Article 47. Article 47(3) expressed the hope that the MSC 'shall be responsible under the Security Council for the strategic direction of any armed forces placed at the disposal of the Security Council'. And Article 43 described how member states might make armed forces and facilities available. But no state has made an Article 43 agreement and none of the proposals made at that time made any serious headway: neither oblique approaches to giving the UN real military capability nor proposals for volunteer forces.[51] Instead, when the Iraqi invasion of Kuwait produced a real and present danger that demanded a military response, Security Council Resolution 678 of 1990 authorised member states cooperating with the government of Kuwait to use all necessary means to restore international peace and security to the area. It was, in effect, a 'subcontracting' mandate which requested the states concerned to keep the Security Council regularly informed on the progress of the actions undertaken, which was barely done. In the debate, which issued the Gulf War mandate, the Indian representative stated that while the subcontracting to the American-led coalition was necessary and not to be impeded in this case, such arrangements should not be taken as a model for the management of future crises. In fact, a decade later, subcontracting to a framework nation (in this case Australia), which could thus shape and lead a militarily efficient UN intervention under a direct Security Council mandate, was the way in which the operations in East Timor were conducted; and that way of proceeding was endorsed by the Secretary-General when, in his 1998 Ditchley Park lecture, he observed that 'at least for the foreseeable future such operations will have to be undertaken by member states or by regional organisations ... that formula developed in 1990 to deal with the Iraqi aggression against Kuwait has proved its usefulness and will no doubt be used again in future crises.'[52]

The terrorist attacks of 11 September 2001, which shattered the twin towers of the World Trade Center and destroyed a portion of the Pentagon in the US, were followed swiftly by an unprecedented combination of actions. First, on 12 September, the invocation for the first time in its history by NATO of Article V – the very core of the Alliance's being, which deems that an attack on one shall be regarded as an attack on all – and the next day by Resolution 1368 passed by the Security Council unanimously, not by vote but by all members standing. This resolution both condemned the atrocities and expressed the view that all necessary means be used (the Chapter VII formula) to restore international peace and security. The resolution did not immediately mandate a subcontracting arrangement; rather it expressed the Council's preparedness to be informed of proposals. But, as this book goes to press, the expectation must be, in light of the Secretary-General's observations, that the coalition to act against the perpetrators of the 11 September attacks and those harbouring them will take the subcontracting form. The prospect of the UN being given the sort of authority that Chapter VII of the Charter provides is probably more remote now than it was at the end of the Cold War.

Two other models of military intervention have been demonstrated during the period of the interregnum. One might be described as 'deep coalition' action without direct Security Council mandate (although possibly with claim on an indirect mandate as was argued in the case of Kosovo) and employing a constrained spectrum of military means. That constraint, however, derives from the demands of the coalition not for strategic reasons. The Kosovo air campaign is the most visible and dramatic case in point. General Clark's memoirs are revealing not least for the extent to which, amidst a constant barrage of detailed technical instruction, he received no clear, positive strategic guidance on what it was that he was expected to achieve. He records, rather acidly, that the strategic guidance he was given was principally about what not to do. The constraints encountered in the Kosovo campaign, when contrasted to the manner in which the Gulf War coalition was mandated, the INTERFET intervention in East Timor was conducted and the military aspect of the response to the 11 September 2001 terrorist attacks are being approached, underline the attractiveness of the subcontracting model of military interventions.

So too does the experience of technically defective UN mandated forces, which fell into difficulty and whose experiences prompted the recommendations of the Brahimi report. The UNAMSIL force deployed to Sierra Leone was one of the most ambitious operations of recent years and it fell into the deepest dangers of compromise and even of military defeat. The rescue of UNAMSIL was the occasion of a successful example of the third model of intervention. This is when a sovereign state undertakes an intervention, which is independently legitimated by international law, for example, the need to rescue entitled citizens from danger. But the force being present, it then is used to rescue, then help to reconstruct and guide the UN operation first from the outside. The British forces which landed in Sierra Leone in May 2000 remained throughout under national control. But this did not prevent their commander from devising a subtle and ingenious strategy, which simultaneously performed these several tasks.

The story of what happened in Sierra Leone during 2000 is told in the next chapter, which shows how the action of a sovereign state can underpin and reinforce that of the international community in the military sphere rather in the way that, as was just argued above, occurs in the legal and judicial forms of intervention. But the case study also shows rather clearly the underlying principles which guide the use of military force when employed for strategic raiding. As the book goes to press, it is already plain that the general shape of military actions, which may need to be taken as a consequence of the terrorist attacks of 11 September 2001, will also be a form of strategic raiding: in this case for the purposes of capturing Osama bin Laden and the key members of the consultative council and executive committees of his organisation al-Qae'da. By the time that the book appears, the actual shape of those operations may have been demonstrated in detail. If more military operations like those undertaken in Sierra Leone are to be part of the future, another of the lessons of that case study, taken up in Chapter 7, is the importance of permitting devolution of politico-strategic control, as well as tactical and military control, to the commander in the field.

That is what Brigadier Richards was given in Sierra Leone and what General Clark was denied in Kosovo. Nor is that simply a product of two greatly different political contexts: it is also, as General Clark observes, a consequence of the characteristic of the different British and American military cultures and their respective ways of war: ruefully, Clark wrote, 'In the British system, a field commander is supported. Period. That is the rule. A field commander is given mission-type orders, not detailed and continuing guidance. It is a wonderful, traditional approach, one that embodies trust in the commander and confidence in his judgment as the man on the scene. The American military has always aspired to this model, but has seldom seemed to attain it.'[53] Clark's story of Kosovo is such as to cause Michael Ignatieff to wonder whether 'far from consolidating a consensus behind the idea that military force can be used successfully against egregious violations of human rights, the Kosovo war seems in fact to have undermined support for humanitarian intervention...'[54] Finding the right way to use the different strengths and avoid the different weaknesses of the key militarily competent nations – and among them especially the most powerful by orders of magnitude, the United States – poses one of the most important and neuralgic questions for the medium-term future in the use of force.

There is a nice irony, not lost on General Clark, who ends his reflections by observing that the ideas and values which are sweeping the world, of freedom, of human rights and international law, are for the most part American values: the US Constitution is the one best configured for national support of cosmopolitan objectives;[55] yet the American way of war, primarily influenced by the Sherman doctrine, and most comfortably employed within its terms and under its moral arguments, is ill-prepared for expeditionary warfare. The scars of Vietnam were scratched open again in Somalia. In these circumstances, perhaps the most productive and practical way forward will be to make informal divisions of labour, which give diplomatic/

military operations to those countries and those units within the US armed forces (the Marines, some airborne forces, the Rangers), but with the bulk of American forces held in reserve for purposes of deterrence or wide area industrial-type warfare of the classic twentieth-century form. It is too early to say whether the shocks of the terrorist attacks will force a wholesale revision of America's philosophy of warfare as it has been practised at least since the Vietnam war.

The fifth and final dimension of intervention is one which is very likely to be rapidly promoted in visibility by the pursuit of bin Laden and his organisation in their Afghanistan fastnesses. That the Taliban regime, which sheltered bin Laden, presides over a country which has been visited with devastation of biblical proportion from all the horsemen of the Apocalypse, brings the issue of what happens after military interventions much more starkly to the fore. Wheeler's case studies most prominently, but others also, show how the strategic opportunities created by military interventions of whatever sort have frequently been wasted to the point of being squandered, on occasions, because of the failure hitherto to produce a full cycle plan for an intervention, which would include detailed arrangements for the establishment of the administrative, social and economic agencies necessary to provide a safe and reliable context for the reconstruction of civil society in a collapsed state. The need for this was first made apparent by the redoubtable Dame Margaret Anstee as she first conducted and then later described the impossible task which she was given, as Special Representative of the Secretary-General, amid the continuing civil wars of Angola.[56] The need for as well-defined a package of post-conflict administrative services as was provided by the military for initial stabilisation was a lesson of INTERFET in East Timor and the same point was made eloquently by the expensive and ill-coordinated attempts of the different agencies that entered Kosovo under the direction of Bernard Kouchner, who was appointed as a latter-day viceroy to oversee the reconstruction of civil services. The crisis within Afghanistan, created by the combination of twenty years of civil war, three years of unprecedented drought, the predations upon their own people by the Taliban regime and the likely consequences of a strategic raid in order to pursue al-Qae'da, coming on top of the cascade of earlier experiences, has led to open discussion for the first time of the need to reawaken one of the most important of the sleeping chapters of the UN Charter.

Chapter XII describes the international trusteeship system. Article 75 empowers the UN to administer and supervise territories, which may be placed under its authority by individual agreements as trust territories. The purposes of establishing a trusteeship administration are, in Article 76, related back directly to the purposes of the UN as set out in the first article of the Charter. The difficulty in re-animating the device is that Articles 77 and 78 appear to lock the device of trusteeship into the period of the UN's creation: for the categories of territories defined in Article 77 are those former colonial territories then held under mandate, those which may be detached from enemy states as a result of the Second World War, and 'territories voluntary placed under the system by states responsible for their administration'. Article 78 states that no territory already a member of the UN could be administered under the trusteeship system. There is no provision for collapsed states. However, in the aftermath of the September 2001 shock, a renewed will appears to be emerging to find ways to interpret the Charter language constructively in a manner which would bring the UN 'downstream' in the whole process of intervention, giving it enlarged and primary responsibilities for restoration and reconstruction, including the coordination of its specialist agencies and those, in turn, with the aid and non-governmental organisations.

In sum, the pattern at the end of 2001 appears to be one of a diminishing appetite for intervention in tension with a manifestly increased need and future likelihood in face of supreme humanitarian emergencies. Following 11 September, there is a certainty of action against the perpetrators of the terrorist attacks and those harbouring them across a wide spectrum of intervention, including all the means discussed in this chapter.

This being so, it makes it all the more important to gain quickly a sense of which characteristics of military power are likely to be the most important in these new roles and which areas of military activity will need to be the site of most intensive study and possible reconfiguration. These are the subjects, respectively, of the next two chapters.

6   Strategic raiding

Why Clausewitz is becoming operationally relevant, again

'The best strategy,' writes Clausewitz, 'is always *to be very strong*;
first in general and then at the decisive point.'[1] Since being very
strong everywhere all the time is a counsel of perfection, not least
because of the ubiquitous operation of 'friction' upon armed forces
in action, the qualifier in the observation is extremely important.
Since 'everything in war is very simple, but the simplest thing is difficult ... producing a kind of friction that is inconceivable unless one
has experienced war',[2] there is both safety and advantage in designing fairly controlled actions minimising the friction surfaces which,
applied at the decisive point, can have a disproportionate turning
effect on the entire course of events. From this general principle
comes Clausewitz's definition of tactics: 'The use of armed forces in
the engagement.'[3] Scaled up, the same insight defines strategy: 'The
use of the engagement for the purpose of the war.'[4] From this relationship everything else flows. Clausewitz spells out the role of the
strategist in detail and in consequence. His account is worth quoting
at length:

> The strategist must therefore define an aim for the entire opera-
> tional side of the war that would be in accordance with its
> purpose. In other words, he will draft the plan of the war, and
> the aim will determine the series of actions intended to achieve
> it: he will, in fact, shape the individual campaigns and, within
> these, decide on the individual engagements. Since most of these
> matters have to be based on assumptions that may not prove
> correct, while other, more detailed orders cannot be determined
> in advance at all, it follows that the strategist must go on

campaign himself. Detailed orders can then be given on the spot, allowing the general plan to be adjusted to the modifications that are continuously required. The strategist, in short, must maintain control throughout.[5]

A classic example of this from recent history are the orders drafted in the field by General Smith before committing British forces in the Gulf War. The orders are brief and follow exactly the sequence of the paragraph cited above: first, the General conveys to his subordinates his objective for the entire campaign and then explains in broad terms how he intends to order the forces and fight them under several general hypothetical courses of events that could unfold, depending upon the decision of the Iraqi forces. However, since local circumstance will be infinitely various, the order also conveys a general instruction to junior field commanders that when they find themselves in doubt they should always take the initiative, since this will keep them safer: to be active is to set the parameters of the engagement and to control them and, thereby, to impose one's will upon the enemy in giving the terms of battle.[6]

Given the opening premise, the value of force multipliers other than mass is self-evident. Where he describes the significance of the engagement, Clausewitz ranks the priorities strictly. As in Smith's Gulf Orders, Clausewitz also advocates the value, wherever possible, of standing on the offensive. An engagement, he observes, can have the conquest of an object or of a locality as its objective, or the destruction of the enemy's forces; and these can be undertaken in a defensive or in an offensive manner. Being on the defensive, protecting a locality or an object or one's forces, is plainly a less useful contribution to the overall strategic aim than an offensive engagement to the same ends. The offensive both protects and advances. And within the three, the destruction of the enemy's forces by offensive action is the objective which predominates. But, interestingly for modern purposes, Clausewitz goes on to qualify these objectives by observing that there really is a fourth: for, if the enemy can be sufficiently misled about the intentions of the attacker that he can be defeated without being destroyed – by being morally disarmed, for example – then for the purposes of an offensive engagement that is a valuable outcome to achieve.[7] So, therefore, among force multipliers the one to be valued more than almost any other is the ability 'to take the enemy by surprise. This desire is more or less basic to all operations, for without it superiority at the decisive point is hardly conceivable,' writes Clausewitz. 'Surprise therefore becomes the means to gain superiority, but because of its *psychological effect* [emphasis added] it should also be considered as an independent element. Whenever it is achieved on a grand scale, it confuses the enemy and lowers his morale.'[8]

Richard Betts identifies several common features from an historical study of when surprise attacks succeed. The first is the precision in the attacker's understanding of the expectations and behaviour of the victim. That is what enables the surprise attacker to get 'inside the decision loop'. Deception is clearly a great help: it can prevent the victim collecting any sort of efficient intelligence and it can also act as a cover for the third reason for success in surprise attack which is miscalculation of the attacker's intention, due to a combination of psychological factors and political premises. Betts calls this 'the logic of craziness'.[9] These are, in Clausewitz's terms, tactical properties because they inform the design of the particular engagement. Yet the surprise which he prizes most is of a strategic quality: it is the capacity to 'surprise the enemy by our plans and dispositions', not just by launching clever and unpredictable attacks. It is that quality which can lead to an enemy's comprehensive moral disarmament.

Just in the same way that in Chapter 4 we saw how late-eighteenth-century political and philosophical thinking has acquired particular relevance and resonance for the early-twenty-first century, there is a good reason for beginning this case study by returning to that same period; but to Clausewitz, because, in his field, although for different reasons of course, he has acquired more than just a theoretical (some might say totemic) importance. Once again his writing has a practical relevance to thinking about the nature of modern military operations.

During the twentieth-century era of mass warfare, the role of raiding was strictly tactical: contributing to leveraging engagements which might (but, in the context of the Western Front in the First World War, usually didn't) break the immobility of positional trench warfare. Imagine Siegfried Sassoon bravely lobbing bombs into the German trenches on night raids into No Man's Land. Technology did make this sort of warfare a bit more efficient in the attack (gas and then eventually, when it appeared on the Somme, in September 1916, the tank) but none of this could break the superiority of the defence decisively: and so the Great War proved to be a gigantic object lesson demonstrating the truth of Jan Bloch's earlier predictions about its nature.

When, during the second part of the European civil war, technology enabled raiding to take wing, Sir Arthur Harris argued that the means were now to hand, through area bombing, to win wars by *strategic* raiding. On 7 December 1943, Harris wrote to the Air Ministry claiming that 'The Lancaster force alone should be sufficient but only just sufficient to produce in Germany by April 1st 1944 a state of devastation in which surrender is inevitable.'[10] Harris's working assumption was that by smashing Germany indiscriminately he would smash popular morale, which, in turn, would undermine political will. In a memorandum of 1 August 1944, Lord Portal questioned both the belief that there was some magical automatic connection between popular morale and political will, and the action: he agreed that a focused attack on Berlin might influence the German high command at a decisive moment, with a similar blow against one other major city perhaps; but he questioned the rationale of indiscriminate destruction. The value of the Portal memorandum for our purposes is not the debate about targets, however; it is that it firmly pushed the claim of area bombing to have advanced into the strategic category back into Clausewitz's tactical box.[11] Put in different but helpful terms by one of Clausewitz's modern successors, the destructive accomplishment of Bomber Command exceeded the culminating point of efficiency in that its political (and indeed economic) consequence might turn out to be quite counterproductive.[12] The economist, J.K. Galbraith, was a member of the team which assessed the effect of strategic bombing in Germany after the surrender. He reported how the destruction of homes and other places of employment actually increased the supply of labour to protected war industries during the later days of the war, making Luttwak's point.

All this is not to say that the concept of strategic raiding is an impossibility. It may have proved to be so during the era of mass warfare, but it certainly was not in Clausewitz's day. He mentions several examples, including Bonaparte's famous crossing of the Alps in 1800, as cases from 'the higher and highest realms of strategy [which] provide some examples of momentous surprises'.[13] When Napoleon crossed the Alps, the Austrian army surrendered its entire theatre of operations in consequence. That was a strategic raid. And strategic raiding is again not only a possible but arguably a desirable way of employing military force in the new era of the twenty-first century. However, before we can turn to the case of contemporary West Africa, there is a further dimension of the history of strategic raiding to be sketched and this is a tough topic. It is tough not because it is difficult history to describe, simply that it is neuralgically sensitive, even now, to discuss it. The most extensive previous experience of strategic raiding was during the era of colonial conquest in the nineteenth century. That being so, it is best to strike down the demons before they arise by observing that our purposes in this part of the chapter are to understand how the deployment of military force produced the effects which it did, not to pass any moral judgement upon the purposes for which the deployment was undertaken.

Sir Garnet Wolseley's invasion of Asante, 1874

The threat of armed force always lay in the background of imperial rule: that is one of its defining characteristics. But the manner in which its message is conveyed, and hence how its power takes its effect, exists across a spectrum. During the period of 'informal empire', which lasted for nearly three-quarters of the nineteenth century in Africa, the spirit of Victorian expansion was one where, wherever possible, the flag followed trade.[14] The historian of empire, Anthony Low, describes this as a period of impact. In this period, power was exercised as influence or, as it became more marked, by what he calls 'sway'. 'Sway,' wrote Low, 'is exemplified by the Zanzibar proverb "When they pipe in Zanzibar, they dance upon the lakes".' Under 'sway', there is awareness of the existence of military threat although no deployment of military force is yet needed to underline the point. After the scramble for Africa began in earnest and colonial powers vied with each other to control contested areas of the continent, military presence became more visible and direct. This, Low called the period of ascendancy. Power was exercised as predominance ('interfere as little as possible but, if you have to act, settle matters yourself') and, lastly, when direct control was exercised over a colony, then it was simply that: direct control. That might be the consequence of the exercise of naked military power.[15]

Military force was employed within Low's spectrum in three basic ways during the period of the establishment of colonial rule: in fixed form, as forts or garrisons; as presence, with naval patrols: and as concentrated force, in strategic raids. The coastal settlements of European traders along the West African coast were more or less fortified as the threat of local violence or inter-imperial competition demanded. Sierra Leone, a colony the name of whose capital, Freetown, told of its origins in the suppression of the slave trade, was regarded as one of the most successful (which meant, in part, least troublemaking) of the West African colonies. Britain has had an involvement with this part of West Africa for 450 years; first as a source of slaves, then from 1807 as a Crown colony for those freed, not least through the actions of the Royal Navy's long-running anti-slavery patrols. Freetown became a noted centre for mission and educational activity – a tradition of importance in understanding the roots of the current civil war.

Sierra Leone was ruled by Sir Arthur Kennedy as Governor in 1852–4 when, rather than mocking the liberated Africans who had acquired English and become successful traders, clerks, teachers and the like, he encouraged a policy whereby the European trading houses on the coast would be complemented by upcountry traders of indigenous origin. Kennedy's policies in Sierra Leone were followed broadly by his successors, and when Kennedy returned as Governor-in-Chief for the whole region in 1868 he sought to apply his approach to Sierra Leone more widely. One aspect of this was to reduce and eventually withdraw military garrisons from forts, as he sought, by the establishment of patronage networks, to extend power through influence and sway rather than by direct control. His willingness to withdraw the garrisons not only from Bulama and Koya, but also from the large fort of Sherbro and maybe later from the Gambia and elsewhere, substituting native African policemen for imperial forces, was on the one hand welcome to a War Office that was keen to reduce expenditures; but, on the other, such a policy had costs through increased requirements for different sorts of imperial forces.

A round-table discussion in 1869 led to an agreement by the Admiralty to station two cruisers between Lagos and Bathurst 'with instructions to their commanding officers to attend to any requisitions they may receive from the Governor at Sierra Leone for their cooperation and assistance on any necessary service'.

In 1870 Kennedy requested naval assistance in order to punish a chief who had attacked a trading settlement in the Sherbro area. The Navy refused to act, arguing that there was no threat to life or property. Indeed, the warships left the Sierra Leone area and the Admiralty then announced that it would only maintain the unpopular and unhealthy West African station for the six months of each year, outside the wet season. Kennedy was understandably bitter and complained that he would never have agreed to withdraw the Sherbro garrison under such conditions. But this produced no change in the Royal Navy's attitude and, indeed, the garrison was later remanned. Professor Hargreaves writes of the episode that, 'It was a first warning of the fragility of the fashionable hopes that treaties, stipends and moral influence could provide an adequate basis for an expanding "informal empire" of West African trade.'[16] Kennedy knew that a credible backing of force was required if power at the earlier part of the spectrum was to be exercised. In Low's memorable image, the colonial ruler had a choice as to whom he might be: a magician or a gunman: and once the magician lost his magic then the gunman had to pick up his gun and be prepared for the moral dilemmas faced by France in the Battle of Algiers – or get out.

The objective of strategic raiding in the colonial context was to apply concentrated military power in a way which would sufficiently alter the equations of power on the ground that, after the end of the intervention, things would not be able to return to the way they were before. The invasion of Asante by Sir Garnet Wolseley in 1874 provides a clear example. Again, it must be stressed that in rehearsing this history our interest is solely in observing the way in which Wolseley was successful in his aim to control the King of Asante (Asantehene Kofi Kakari), an act which had long-lasting consequences for all aspects of the Asante experience of colonial rule. That story is not our subject here; nor any judgements upon the rightness or wrongness of the actions described.[17]

The Asantehene (King) Kofi Kakari, who had been brought to power by a 'war party' in 1867, succeeded Osei Kwaku Dua I, who is remembered as 'the most peaceable of the dynasty'. He sought to consolidate Asante power through trade. In contrast, at his swearing in, Kofi Kakari is reported to have assured his supporters that 'my trade shall be war'.[18] In fact, Wilks argues, the tightening of British control over Elmina and the western coast was incompatible with the fundamental strategic interests of greater Asante and so war was unavoidably on the cards, and opened in 1873. It carried Asante forces successfully to the outskirts of Cape Coast. But an anti-war sentiment in Kumase (the capital) arose and the army retired, taking European and African prisoners with it.

Responding to public interest and will, parliament granted £800,000 and General Sir Garnet Wolseley assembled his force of over 4,500 (2,500 European regulars and the balance of West Indian, Sierra Leonean and Nigerian soldiers (the Hausa artillery) for what Bernard Porter described as a 'petty little colonial war'.[19] Wolseley's expeditionary force landed at Prasu in the first week of January 1874. The British element came from the Naval Brigade, the Royal Welsh Fusiliers, the Black Watch and the Rifle Brigade, supported by large numbers of African carriers brought from the Cape Coast, as well as sixteen Hausa gunners under Captain Rait. As soon as his HQ was established at Prasu, Wolseley took the initiative. He wrote in blunt terms to the Asantehene, making much of the fact that Imperial troops were now landed and on their way 'for the purpose of invading your territory to enforce compliance with my just demands which I shall presently lay before you'. These were for the release of all prisoners, both European and African, the payment of an indemnity of 50,000 ounces of gold and the conclusion of a new peace treaty to be signed in the capital, Kumase, after the delivery of hostages to ensure compliance.

While this letter was being written, the Asante envoys (six senior counsellors of the King) were shown a newly-completed bridge over the river Pra and a Gatling gun in action. That evening, having seen these things, one of the envoys committed suicide. The others buried him and returned to Kumase. The terms having been delivered, flaunting his power, Wolseley then began a deliberate and public march towards Kumase along one of the Great Roads – the trade and military arteries – of the kingdom, leaving the choice to the Asante of the terms under which he would arrive: as negotiator or as enemy.

The British advance forces, Lord Gifford's scouts, reached the Adanse scarp, below Kwisa, on 16 January, without having met opposition. The Asante border patrol (the *nkwansrafo*) had no permission to give battle which puzzled Gifford, who mistook them for combat troops. But an Arabic charm (*saphi*) was found there which, when translated by one of the Hausa soldiers, proved to be a prayer that the white men would fight among themselves and fall ill and go home. This charm, Wilks argues, was the Asantehene's last attempt to avoid battle. He, in the meantime, was coming to rely increasingly on his Muslim advisers, hoping that their good offices might hold back the invaders.[20] The European captives were released, appearing in Wolseley's camp at Monsi on the 23rd. A letter from Kofi Kakari begged Wolseley to advance no further and promised to pay the indemnity and to release the African (Fante) prisoners.

Wolseley replied demanding immediate release of the Fante, half the indemnity, and hostages as tokens of good faith. He promised to advance slowly to give time for compliance, and then to enter Kumase with an escort of 500 to sign the treaty. The hostages demanded included the Queen Mother (who Wolseley probably did not realise was one of the leaders of the anti-war party), the Crown Prince and heirs to several important chiefdoms. Whether or not Wolseley realised it, this was an impossible demand. The Asante government had ordered remobilisation on the 9th, and by the 10th, preparation of bullets and rations was seen in Kumase. Asamoa Nkwanta, a commander who was highly respected and liked by the troops, and who was not identified with the war party, was appointed field commander under another moderate, Mamponhene Kwabena Dwumo as supreme commander. This shrewd move raised the morale of the Asante forces for the coming battles. The Asante-hene's freedom of decision was, by now, plainly circumscribed by the council.[21]

By the 30th, the entire European force, commanded by Brigadier-General Sir Archibald Alison, was concentrated at Insafu, and scouts had reported a strong Asante force (Asamoa Nkwanta's field force) south of Amoafu. A major engagement took place there, in dense wet forest, on 31 January, where the superiority in range and destructiveness over the muskets used by the Asante of imperial rifles, and especially of the Hausa seven-pounder artillery, resulted in moderate casualties in Wolseley's forces but very heavy casualties among the Asante. The Black Watch carried the burden of the engagement with repeated charges. Alison described the fighting as fiercer than anything he had experienced in India or the Crimea. Wolseley's force marched out of Amoafu on 2 February and, although subjected to some heavy skirmishing at Fomena, Wolseley decided to press on to Kumase, about fifteen miles away.

He began his advance on the capital on 3 February at daybreak and at 11.30 messengers bearing a flag of truce brought a further letter from the Asantehene 'complaining that the General's rapid movements put him into confusion' and seeking some ground for further negotiation of the terms. In particular, Wolseley's demand for the surrender of the Queen Mother and the Crown Prince as hostages was something to which the Asantehene found it impossible to agree. Wolseley was unbending and a further engagement at Odasu occurred the following morning, less intense than the decisive battle of Amoafu but marked by a prolonged charge through all ambushes, by the Black Watch, their way cleared by the Hausa artillery. Upon entering Kumase, following behind the Black Watch, Wolseley found the capital crowded with armed soldiers who offered no further resistance; some shook hands with the imperial troops, and gave them water. Meanwhile, civilians were fleeing into the forest. He wrote to the Asantehene, 'You have deceived me, but I have kept my promise. I am in Kumase...' and modified the hostage demand, agreeing to accept others than the Queen Mother and Crown Prince, and then to sign a peace the next day. No-one came. Overnight the city emptied of people, including the soldiers with their weapons.

He had not achieved his fullest objective. Casualties and sickness meant that Wolseley could not risk another battle, and so he relied even more heavily upon information ops for the final phase. The British inspected the palace and treasure house, and on the 6th, removed as much as could be carried by thirty men as prize (including important ritual objects and royal regalia), laid charges in the stone building, blew it up and burned the city before withdrawing.

This destruction was seen as final evidence of the failure of the war party's policy. The council sent a merchant after the retiring force, to express the Asantehene's desire for peace, and to persuade Wolseley to await negotiators. He agreed, and stopped at Fomena. Asabi Antwi, one of the Asante government's senior diplomats, reached him on the 13th with 1,000 ounces of gold as a token of goodwill. Wolseley presented his full terms, which confirmed Asante loss of control over Elmina and the western Gold Coast, but gave freedom of trade with the British Protected Territory. He demanded 50,000 ounces of gold. The Asante queried the amount, but signed that day. The councils in Kumase agreed and Asabi Antwi ratified the Treaty at Cape Coast on 14 March. Sir Garnet, however, had already left for England on 4 March.

On 12 August, Kofi Kakari swore before a British official that he renounced authority over the region of Dwaben, and from that moment support for him dwindled terminally in the council. Deeply worried that secession, particularly of Dwaben, might now dismember the state, Kofi Kakari was charged before the national assembly (the *Asantemanhyiamu*) and deposed in October 1874. In a compromise, he was allowed to go into exile.[22] Although, within two years, Asante control over Dwaben had been reasserted, and not all the war indemnity was paid, the raid had permanently altered the political geography and the nature of Asante's relations with the wider region and the wider world.

The image of Africa

So powerful and distorting are the lenses through which Africa is seen by the outside world that it is very difficult to read materials such as the description of Wolseley's Asante campaign of 1874 usefully in the way that is being attempted here for the purposes of practical comparison, because both the actions described and the idioms used sensitise some of the oldest rooted and most powerful inter-racial stereotypes.

In his study of the image of Africa, Professor Curtin documented the very long history of a European image of Africans as simultaneously simpletons and supermen: half devil and half child. That they could survive the deadly climate of the West African coast which carried away white men from black water fever and other fatal illnesses made them conspicuously different and somehow superhuman; but, at the same time, the apparent absence and/or fetish-like exoticism of their material culture in the eyes of European traders on the coast, views bolstered later for their own purposes by the evangelical missionary movement of the early nineteenth century, made them seem childlike.[23] Europeans were patronisingly charmed by the adoption of their language, clothes and habits by, for example, the emerging African elite in Freetown by the mid-nineteenth century. To these two lenses two others must be added as well.

The first is the myth of Primitive Africa. It represented the African as a noble savage, whose nobility lay in the degree to which he was untouched by western influence. From this perspective has come a long tradition of writing extolling the martial virtues of the Masai, the Zulu, the Ndebele and indeed the Asante people. Westernised Africans are less 'authentic' than nearly naked warriors. Related to this third distorting lens is a fourth which Professor Hopkins called the myth of Merrie Africa.[24] This holds the view that, before the corrupting influence of alien colonial powers appeared, there had been a jolly tranquillity about pre-colonial Africa. That sort of view was attractive to the myth-makers who supplied the ideologies for the movements of decolonisation and national liberation: it formed a useful analogue to the central case which was to blame all Africa's ills by the middle of the twentieth century upon the consequences of its colonial experience, particularly as expressed in the theory of 'underdevelopment' – which argued that, far from producing a spill-over of wealth and opportunity into the hinterland, the setting of trading posts and colonies started a process akin to a pernicious anaemia in the economy of the affected parts of the continent.[25]

More recently, the four lenses of colonial stereotyping have had added to them a new hypothesis which employs them too, in parts. The anthropologist, Paul Richards, described this as the 'new barbarism' thesis about post-colonial Africa. Its principal triggering source was the article entitled 'The coming anarchy', which Robert Kaplan published in the *Atlantic Monthly* in February 1994 after a visit to Sierra Leone. The war in Sierra Leone, which had begun three years before, is cited by Kaplan as a prime instance of this new barbarism. It is close to Huntington's views on culture in that both hold that cultural identity is an essential and basically unchanging feature of social systems: the complex history of manipulating identity and fighting for advantage through so doing – something at the very centre of the African experience of colonial rule – is entirely missing from this point of view.[26]

Second, the thesis depends upon another very old established stereotype about Africans: that they have an unquenchable biological tendency to populate their countries to bursting. The new twist which Kaplan added was to observe how environmental collapse could well be the consequence of this and thus in turn a stimulus to conflict. Richards calls this part of the argument 'Malthus-with-guns'. The sort of violence which this mixture of culture clash, resource competition and environmental breakdown can provoke is by its nature seen as anarchic and almost apolitical.

All these aspects of Kaplan's new barbarism thesis became extremely influential in the mid-1990s and have remained influential in assessments made by governments of the motivation of irredentist groups, such as the Revolutionary United Front in Sierra Leone. Such organisations are seen as essentially anarchistic and lacking in political agenda, whereas, Richards, the anthropologist with intimate local knowledge, maintains that is far from the truth. He is also convinced that neither demographic pressure nor environmental stress (e.g. deforestation) has played a motivating role. But for the moment the point to be emphasised is that the presence and widespread use of these five distorting lenses of stereotype mean that it is extremely difficult for even the best motivated of observers to obtain a clear and empirically robust view of what is going on in any particular African society, particularly on very short acquaintance.[27]

The heart of Richards's case is the same being made here, namely that one needs to be very careful about which universal statements one generalises. The case here is that in recognising and acting to protect an irreducible core of fundamental human rights regardless of circumstance, time or place, one must at the same time be careful to provide as faithful an account as it is in one's power to do of the people, society and culture at issue, in all their special uniqueness. 'Citizens of weak but modern states in Africa need and deserve room for creative manoeuvre if they are to build islands of security and archipelagos of peace within the limited material resources at their disposal,' wrote Richards. '...Outside commentators owe a duty of care not to weaken, through ill-informed misrepresentation, the cultural mortar with which these fragile structures will be cemented together.'[28]

The acid test for any theory is whether it adequately explains the evidence; and the central problem with the 'new barbarism' interpretation of contemporary Africa is that, were this true, it is hard to see how anything would work at all. Yet manifestly, somehow or another, Africa works. To understand how, it is not necessary to have recourse to special culture-specific theories to explain African peculiarity: that is to look through the twisted optics of stereotypes. What it is important to do is to look at evidence of actual events and to do so in an adequately multi-disciplinary way for the simple reason that the reality of politics in contemporary Africa is exceptionally multi-faceted. The explanation needs to be comparative so that it integrates the experience of contemporary Africa with the rest of the world: barbarism in one place must be a word that describes barbarism anywhere; and the explanation needs to be historical because so much of what happens in contemporary West Africa is a consequence of the deep history of the people and the place – just as is the case anywhere else in the world.

It is within these five dimensions that Professors Chabal and Daloz offer an astringent corrective to any of the inherited and old colonial stereotypes or to the new barbarism. What they explain is that in the first place you will never find the answer to anything if you look in the wrong place and the wrong place to seek the axes of power and power relations in contemporary Africa is in the 'formal' political setting or within the 'formal' economy. They extend the fruitful study of the informal economy – that which is invisible to statistics or to governmental structures, but within which most Africans live – to power structures. For they are aware that power exists in many different forms – customary, charismatic or reciprocal, as well as formal. So the power that matters is the power which flows through informal structures of patronage relationship networks where patrons and clients are involved in complex sets of reciprocal obligation as they compete for the control of resources. Those resources are not only diamonds or a trade route; they are also the political allegiance of groups or regions in towns or shanty towns as well as all the instruments of the post-colonial state. These are also up for grabs.[29] Chabal and Daloz argue that

> all African states share in a generalised system of patrimonialism and an acute degree of apparent disorder, as evidenced by the high level of governmental and administrative inefficiency, a lack of institutionalisation, a general disregard for the rules of the formal political and economic sectors, and a universal resort to personalised and vertical solutions to societal problems.[30]

Once one grasps that the power which really matters is not the ability to command flags, Mercedes Benz, State House and meetings with representatives of the World Bank, but that which flows through the patronage networks invisible to the disinterested or uninformed eye, many things begin to become systematically comprehensible. In these circumstances there is general disorder, but this disorder is not a condition which tends towards the chaos and disintegration described by the new barbarian school of thought. In fact – although it seems paradoxical – disorder is a creative condition, and a productive one too; and this is the essence of the view that Chabal and Daloz propose. The paradigm which they offer for understanding contemporary Africa is what they call 'the political instrumentalisation of disorder'.

Two aspects of this perspective need to be stressed. First, the instrumentalisation of disorder does not stand in contrast to a process of 'modernisation' with its political arm of 'democratisation'. In fact, Chabal and Daloz (like many Africanists) are sceptical about the degree to which models of representative democracy, imported from the former colonial world and adopted in appearance at least at independence by many black African states, could ever work. Their view is supported by simple statistics such as the ones on voter involvement.

In an important West African study entitled *Creating Political Order*, which prefigured much of the Chabal/Daloz case, it was shown how typically the highest levels of voter participation occurred in the elections just before independence and possibly immediately thereafter, but that a steep slide of interest and involvement in formal politics then occurred unless it was coerced (as in many cases it was). The 'mass' political parties of the independence decade were frequently hollow. Zolberg's memorable image is that they were like puffed-up bullfrogs.[31] Not dissimilar views are expressed about active voter abstentions in the democracies today. Rather than seeing conflict between their hypothesis and modernisation, Chabal and Daloz offer us an explanation of how modernity is handled. It is handled rather efficiently. 'It is thus not a question of Africans being more "traditional" (meaning backward) than others. Rather it is the much more pertinent fact that being both traditional and modern is at once justifiable and instrumentally profitable.'[32] In short, the political instrumentalisation of disorder describes a perfectly rational strategy for managing the strange political economy which the twentieth century has created in places like Sierra Leone with very long histories of contact to the outside world (first through the slave trade) and more recently an exotic mixture of extraordinarily well-adapted indigenous agricultural subsistence farming[33] and enclaves specialised on commodities with export value only. Few things are more spectacularly useless for local purposes than diamonds.

The second quality of this explanatory hypothesis, already mentioned but worth restating, is that it does not depend upon culture-specific arguments. Therefore, it does not divorce Africa from the rest of the world, hence this analysis from potential utility in other places. What it explains to us is that the assumed boundaries between the realms of the political, the economic, the cultural and the religious, which Europeans carry in the back of their heads, will not be helpful here any more than in other areas of uncivil wars. Mainly, the importance of patronage as the medium of politics means that the realm of politics is pervasive. That being so, a further and highly significant observation follows. The individual is the central point of reference. While it is true that individual rationality is essentially based on communal logic – the quality of social relationship which makes reciprocity so central to the workings of modern African politics – it also means that there is a clear space for the introduction of the core values of fundamental human rights. That gives the lie to the argument which says that there is no role for the regime of universal human rights which does not affront 'African values'. On the contrary, Africa is no different from the former Yugoslavia, only less immediately responded to in the mid-1990s. The logic in the application of the Blair Chicago speech criteria for intervention discussed in the previous chapter is universal.[34]

Uncivil war in Sierra Leone, 1991–2000

The reason why the civil war broke out in Sierra Leone in March 1991, when the RUF entered eastern Sierra Leone from Liberia, is explained by Professor Richards in terms of a crisis of the patronage networks, which had sustained the Sierra Leone state. The big men who controlled the informal political structures were, by the mid-1990s, experiencing a double crisis. World recession had reduced the prices of many raw materials and countries like Sierra Leone were also exhausting some of their best sources of minerals; while the ending of the Cold War meant that many sources of aid money, which had been a useful lubricant of the informal political economy, were also drying up. This, argued Richards, threw patrimonialism into a crisis of legitimacy, because if it was unable to fund its networks of reciprocal exchange then the loyalty of clients to patrons would begin to erode. In particular, this became an inter-generational issue.

In Sierra Leone, a nation which for 200 years had been built up around western models of schooling, the crisis became acute when the end point of much patrimonial redistribution, namely the payment of school fees, was brought into question. The depth of the crisis in Sierra Leone was evident when President Momoh (Siaka Stevens's chosen successor) admitted in a speech in the eastern town of Kailahun (to become an RUF stronghold) that education was a privilege and not a right. So when the National Provisional Ruling Council (NPRC) overthrew President Momoh in April 1992, the motivation was not just young officers mutinying over pay and conditions at the war front but also it was an indictment of the previous regime's mismanagement of the patrimonial state. Captain Valentine Strasser, appointed the leader of the coup, said as much in his broadcast announcing the coup, when he stated that 'our schools and roads are terrible' and calling for their repair.[35]

The RUF, whose public face and voice on the airwaves was a former itinerant photographer from Kailahun, Foday Sankoh, originally had a political programme not dissimilar to that which the soldiers declared in their coup. A small force in 1991, which Richards estimates to have been no more than 100 or so guerrillas at that time, the RUF sought to overthrow the All People's Congress (APC) one-party regime of President Momoh and to restore multi-party democracy. But the credibility of such demands was quickly tarnished because of the use of terror and looting. The logical target to satisfy the demands for education and welfare lay in Freetown, the city; but the RUF, made introverted by its existence in the deep forests, turned its violence upon its hapless rural neighbours.

The basic tactic of the RUF, like the National Peoples' Front of Liberia run by its strategist, Prince Yormeh Johnson and its spokesman Charles Taylor, was the forcible conscription, and subsequent political co-option to the cause, of children. The use of young people was one of the characteristics of the RUF that the outside world first noticed, along with its use of mutilation. While both are activities which put the RUF beyond the pale under the criteria of universal human rights, neither tactic is without its logic.

> The war in Sierra Leone is best understood as a drama of social exclusion. The rebel leaders are energetic, determined people who feel strongly about being excluded from the networks of patrimonial support ... they appeal to a constituency of young

Sierra Leonians who are the victims of state recession in the mining districts. Their political analysis is that violence is justified to recover the nation for the people, on the grounds that patrimonialism favours only the selected few...[36]

Therefore, if the RUF wishes to halt the rice-harvest, amputation of women's hands conveys that message; of fingers to dissuade people from voting; of feet, that they not try to run away. These are not magic or witch-craft messages; they are terrifyingly rational.

Richards's central argument is congruent with that of Chabal and Daloz. It is that the

> Crisis of the patrimonial state (often invisible to outside agencies – since so much redistribution is *ad hoc*) is one of the main consequences of the ending of the Cold War in Africa. A dangerous vacuum has been created around the edges of many African states into which some of the wilder elements in civil society are drawn to try their hand at alternative forms of political organisation ... the biggest challenge for all citizen action is to enter into a debate about the nature and future of patrimonialism.[37]

The geopolitics of modern Sierra Leone are dominated by stark contrasts. Alluvial diamonds were first discovered in the east of the country in the 1930s, but only began to be worked extensively after the Second World War. The diamond mining sector stands alongside the stagnant semi-subsistence agricultural sector and this forms the employment pattern for many young Sierra Leonians: moving from semi-subsistence rice cultivation to the urban slums or to the mines and then returning to a rural slum when Freetown or the diamond fields fail. The RUF recruited among the youth in the diamond areas, and gave them a chance to live out the life of John Rambo, hero of one of the most popular action films screened in the camps at the workings.[38] The second contrast embraces the first: between the forest and the single dominant city of Freetown on the coast. So Richards argues that the nature of the military campaigns waged by the rebels during the 1990s formed an extended dramatic text of a war between these contrasts. In a local saying, 'the leopard comes to town' (the leopard being a long-established figure of malign and illegitimate power in Sierra Leone), Richards argued that he might equally have named his book 'Fighting *with* the Rainforest' as 'Fighting *for* the Rainforest'. Thus the importance of encircling and terrorising, if not occupying Freetown and its environs, symbolically expressed the reasons for the war in the first place: the crisis of the patrimonial Sierra Leonian state. Since the motives of recruits on all sides – Kamajo, RUF, RSLMF – were essentially similar, the swapping of sides, the making and breaking of alliances, looks less puzzling.

The next five years of the civil war in Sierra Leone consisted of complex and fluid formings and reformings of alliance among the different parties striving to control the spoils of the state. For present purposes it is not necessary to track all the twists and turns of these years, but the broad outline is needed in order to understand how the international community in general and the British in particular came to the aid of President Kabbah and as enemies to Foday Sankoh's RUF in May 2000.

Valentine Strasser was ousted in a bloodless coup in January 1996 and the reformed NPRC, led by Brigadier-General Bio, undertook to permit the elections scheduled for February 1996 to go ahead. The oldest political party in Sierra Leone, the SLPP (Sierra Leone People's Party) won 36.1 per cent of the legislature vote and its presidential candidate, Ahmad Tejan Kabbah, a UN development worker and veteran politician, won 59.49 per cent of the presidential votes in a run-off second round election on 15 March. This election and these figures are important because, along with the evidence of the infringement of fundamental human rights (through torture, mutilation and the recruitment of child soldiers), it composes the underpinning for the international case supporting Kabbah rather than any of the other factions competing for spoils with him.

At the end of 1996 a peace agreement was made between Kabbah and Sankoh, but in the letter only. Kabbah was doubtful of the loyalty of the Republic of Sierra Leone military forces (RSLMF) and therefore used irregular Kamajo 'hunters' and mercenaries from the South African Executive Outcomes to wage bush war against the RUF, in which good progress was made. The Kamajo could match the RUF in knowledge of the forest tracks and so choke off their supply routes. Frustration in the armed forces led in May 1997 to a coup, led by Major Johnny-Paul Koroma. Kabbah was forced to flee to Guinea and the Armed Forces Revolutionary Council (AFRC) led by Koroma entered into a power-sharing arrangement with the RUF. Sankoh gave his approval to this, although he was detained in Nigeria where he had gone, apparently to try to buy weapons, in February.

There was widespread international condemnation of the coup and the SLPP now began to organise the Kamajo to fight a bush war against the AFRC/RUF who were in Freetown: a reversal of position from before. Meanwhile, the United Nations mandated ECOMOG, the military arm of ECOWAS (the Economic Organisation of West African States), to restore Kabbah. The Nigerians, who provided the greatest part of ECOMOG, launched a ferocious war against Freetown, bombarding the city in September, and in October 1997 the AFRC/RUF government conceded. At Conakry a deal was struck which would give immunity to Koroma, a 'role' for Sankoh and a six months' period of transition to restore the Kabbah government. But the Conakry agreement did not hold. ECOMOG continued to fight Koroma's regime until it was overthrown in February 1998. Kabbah was restored in March of that year.

The violence continued. In January 1999 the RUF invaded Freetown again. A fierce war ensued during the year, with ECOMOG, mercenaries and the Kamajo forces pursuing the RUF. There were allegations of atrocities committed on all sides. Britain provided material assistance to the pro-Kabbah forces, who were able to force the RUF to negotiations, ending in the Lomé agreement of 7 July, brokered by officials from Togo, Nigeria, Burkina Faso and Liberia. At Lomé, the RUF dropped their demand for the removal of the ECOMOG forces, which made way for an agreement to permit power-sharing. The terms gave the insurgents four key government posts and effective control over the country's mineral wealth. Also, significantly there was to be a total amnesty for the rebels for their conduct since the outbreak of the civil war in 1991. The death sentence which had been imposed on Sankoh was lifted.

The international community welcomed the agreement, because at least it appeared to have stopped the fighting – an assumption soon proved wrong; but the amnesty was heavily criticised and seen as a major victory for the RUF. On 3 October Sankoh and Koroma returned to Freetown and held a joint press conference with President Kabbah. At it, they apologised for the atrocities carried out during the eight years of the civil war and promised to strive for a speedy implementation of the Lomé agreement. On 22 October the Security Council unanimously adopted Resolution 1270 to establish a 6,000 member peace-keeping force to be known as the UN Mission in Sierra Leone (UNAMSIL) with a six-month mandate to oversee the implementation of Lomé. In December, the IMF approved 15.56 million SDRs (Special Drawing Rights) for post-conflict reconstruction. These were all signs of the international community paying serious attention.

Following the Security Council resolution, the process of putting together the force elements for UNAMSIL began. In February 2000, as it became apparent that there would be a security vacuum with the phasing out of ECOMOG, the Security Council voted to increase the force from 6,000 to 11,000. But it encountered difficulty as soon as it entered Sierra Leone, with reports that Indian and Ghanaian elements were prevented from deploying to the eastern Bendu region later that month. Furthermore, the Commander, an Indian General, Vijay Jetley, interpreted his brief in a traditional UN peace-keeping manner, as one of neutrality between the parties, which impeded development of close relations with the Kabbah government.

Matters did not improve for UNAMSIL and on the very day that ECOMOG officially handed over to it, the RUF attacked Kenyan UNAMSIL soldiers at Makeni and took hostages in Kailahun. On 4 May, 208 Zambians, who had been sent to relieve the Kenyans in Makeni, were taken hostage. Their thirteen armoured personnel carriers were captured. On 6 May, 226 Zambians surrendered to the RUF, bringing the total number of hostages now held by the RUF to over 500. The same day the Secretary-General of the UN requested the United Kingdom and other countries to help shore up the situation; for on 6 May the RUF, using the captured APCs, began to advance on Freetown. Lunsar, on the approach road, fell to them and on 7 May they were at Masiaka and Rogberi junction, sixty-five kms away from the capital.

The UN mandate for UNAMSIL and the Secretary-General's urgent request must be seen in the context of acute and general recollection of the international community's failure to act in Rwanda. The UN report on general failures over the crisis, including by its own organs, was widely praised for its candour. Kofi Annan, in particular, was applauded for ordering the enquiry since his own role at the time was subject to criticism by it. One of the decisions following the Rwandan crisis had been to establish a high-readiness brigade (SHERBRIG), but SHERBRIG was not to be seen. Richard Connaughton cites a letter which he received from the military advisor to the United Nations Department of Peace-keeping Operations, Lieutenant-General Giulio Fraticelli, which explained that SHERBRIG at that time was only available to Chapter VI (embargo and sanction) operations and that the Sierra Leone mandate was under Chapter VII (enforcement).[39]

The British forces that were deployed in Operation PALLISER were not placed under UN control, although, as the narrative will reveal, their presence intimately affected and shaped the UN role. Nor was this the first deep British involvement in the Sierra Leone civil war. Already there had been considerable public criticism in the UK when it became known that large arms shipments had been made to the Kabbah government after the Koroma coup in the murkiest of deals. Kabbah traded arms for mineral concessions through the intermediary of one Rakesh Sakera, whom the Foreign Secretary, Robin Cook, memorably described as 'an Indian business-man, travelling on the passport of a dead Serb, awaiting extradition from Canada for alleged embezzlement from a bank in Thailand'.[40] The British problem was that loose drafting of the UN arms embargo resolution made it applicable both to the Koroma/RUF junta and to the Kabbah forces. It was drafted into British law as a blanket ban, which was therefore the formal policy; whereas the intention of policy was to back the ousted President, which was done in this opaque and convoluted way. Even more contentiously, it emerged that mercenaries, operating under the British company, Sandline, had played an instrumental role in the gun-running. Its proprietor, a former Guards officer called Tim Spicer, maintained, with some documentary evidence, that the Foreign Office was well aware of, and approving of, his actions. In the event, the enquiry into the so-called 'Arms for Africa' affair exonerated ministers and blamed offi-cials, although none named suffered demotion.

The other heavily engaged state was Nigeria, once expelled from the Commonwealth for human rights violations. Its record as prime provider of ECOMOG was tarnished by corruption and allegations of atrocity during the fighting between January and July 1999. It was into this context that Brigadier David Richards first entered, sent to Conakry and Freetown in January 1999 to conduct a recon-naissance based on HMS *Norfolk* and also to bring back the British High Commissioner in exile, Peter Penfold, who had been a strong supporter of Kabbah and thus forced to flee to Conakry at the time of the coup.

Richards and HMS *Norfolk* arrived to find Freetown being shelled; but on landing, nevertheless, he was swiftly taken to meet President Kabbah where he was greeted enthusiastically. He also met the ECOMOG commanders. On the basis of his assessment, he was able to advise on ways to help save the Kabbah regime. British financial aid to beef up ECOMOG was provided which helped to force the RUF to accept the Lomé accord. Richards made several more visits and, therefore, was a known quantity in the local political scene when he arrived in Freetown at the head of a reinforced opera-tional liaison and reconnaissance team (OLRT) in May 2000. As Connaughton observes, the first hours of a rapid reaction deployment are disproportionately important and in the case of Operation PALLISER this was especially so.

Operation PALLISER, 6 May–15 June 2000

In the first week of May 2000, as Commander of the Joint Forces HQ at Northwood, Brigadier Richards was preparing to travel on Friday the 5th to Ghana for an exercise. However, the previous day the crisis in Sierra Leone, which was now in the 'surfaced' category of PJHQ's four broad categories of conflict (quiescent, stirring, quickening and surfaced), became the subject of discussion for deployment and within hours a first concept of conduct to effect a Non-Combat Evacuation Operation (NEO) to evacuate entitled personnel, mainly British passport holders, had been prepared. Given the urgency of the developing crisis, this NEO would have to be conducted by the Spearhead battalion of air-delivered troops, which was at that moment being provided by the First Battalion the Parachute Regiment, with support from HMS *Ocean*, the helicopter carrier with Royal Marines embarked, leading the Amphibious Ready Group (ARG). She was currently in the Mediterranean, a week's steaming away from Freetown. Late that afternoon, news was received that Cabinet had decided on action and the immediate despatch of Richards leading an enlarged OLRT was authorised. He departed at 10.00 a.m. on the Friday. The team reached Lungi airport, across the bay from Freetown, at midday on Saturday 6 May. Having established communications to London at Lungi, they crossed to Freetown by civilian helicopter.

Map 6.1 shows how the road from Lungi airport to Freetown follows a horseshoe course which leads (in order) to the villages of Lungi Lol, Port Loko and Rogberi Junction (where the road to Makeni, in the interior, and where the RUF High Command was located at that moment, is met), thence over the Rokel Bridge to Masiaka, Waterloo and on into Freetown. Control of the horseshoe road is vital to the protection of the city and it was now under threat from the advancing RUF. It was instantly plain to Richards that a NEO could not be conducted without troops to secure both the airhead and the assembly point, and means to cross the bay without relying on the horseshoe road. So he requested PJHQ to release immediately the lead company of the Spearhead battalion, to be followed by the rest of the group, and also to provide heavy helicopters. Accordingly, four Chinook CH47 helicopters were also ordered to Sierra Leone from Britain.

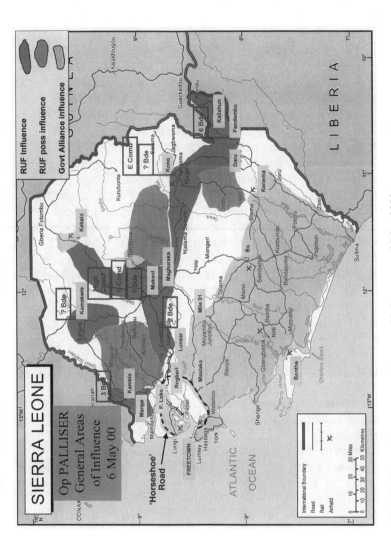

Map 6.1 Sierra Leone: general areas of influence on 6 May 2000.

With active French as well as Senegalese assistance, Dakar became the forward mounting base and the first elements of 1 Para arrived there at 4 o'clock on the morning of Sunday 7 May, leaving the HQ element to set up in a tent city, and then passing on directly to arrive in Freetown that evening. The first pair of Chinooks also arrived in theatre on the Sunday evening, only thirty hours after having been tasked and having flown 3,500 miles from the UK in an astonishing feat of airmanship. The Amphibious Ready Group of HMS *Ocean*, with 42 Commando embarked, also included the Royal Fleet Auxiliary (RFA) *Fort George* and logistics ships *Sir Tristram* and *Sir Bedevere*, as well as the type 22 Frigate HMS *Chatham*. It received orders to sail from Marseilles via the Straits of Gibraltar down the West African coast. The aircraft carrier HMS *Illustrious* with thirteen Harrier aircraft embarked and accompanied by the RFA *Fort Austin* were ordered south from Lisbon.

On the Sunday, the UNAMSIL force commander, General Jetley, with his staff, were in a meeting with Bernard Miyet, the head of the Department of Peacekeeping Operations and his military adviser, General Fraticelli, who were visiting UNAMSIL from the UN in New York. Brigadier Richards entered the discussion unannounced, and was invited to stay. He had already sent soldiers travelling with the OLRT party to conduct a quick reconnaissance of the Waterloo area on the Saturday evening. From their report, it had become plain to Richards that the situation on the horseshoe road was critical and there was a danger that UN forces might withdraw that evening. Freetown was rife with rumours that the RUF had already taken Masiaka and was on the road to Waterloo, with government forces and UNAMSIL falling back rapidly. There was palpable fear in the local population that they were about to be subjected to a repeat performance of the RUF attack of the previous year, which had led to the mutilation and death of many thousands. With the Spearhead lead company in the air and on the way, Richards ordered advance force elements with him to proceed at once to Waterloo to advise and assist the Nigerians and Jordanians to maintain their position there that Sunday night, which they did.

The RUF had meanwhile opened a second axis of attack from Mange towards Port Loko, to threaten Lungi airport, and there were doubts about the ability of joint UNAMSIL and government forces to hold there, as well. Meanwhile, the fortuitous presence of Bernard Miyet during that crucial Sunday meeting meant that it was possible to establish clearly the terms of a working relationship between Brigadier Richards and General Jetley. Brigadier Richards's already established contacts with President Kabbah helped to consolidate an important triangle of communication.

Immediately upon arrival, the lead company of the Spearhead battalion secured the Lungi airfield and the Aberdeen Peninsula, which were the two areas judged to be vital ground for any NEO. At the same time, the OLRT turned itself into a Joint Task Force HQ (Forward) (the Main being at the forward mounting base in Dakar for the moment). Brigadier Richards was appointed joint task force commander, his HQ colocated with the High Commissioner, Mr Alan Jones, at the British High Commission.

On Monday 8 May, 1 Para secured the wider perimeter of Lungi airport to protect against the threat from Mange, and thickened up the security presence on the Aberdeen Peninsula, also. News was then received of violent demonstrations in Freetown. About 10,000 people marched to demonstrate outside Foday Sankoh's house (he was still nominally Vice-President in the transitional government at this time). His bodyguards fired into the crowd, killing twenty-one people. But despite this, a number of demonstrators managed to enter and sack the house, although Sankoh himself escaped and fled the city. At 15.50 the Chinooks were ordered into Freetown to fly low and noisily in a visible demonstration of strength. The Paras on the Aberdeen Peninsula established an evacuation centre for the NEO at the Mammy Yoko Hotel and on 9 May the Chinooks began flying entitled personnel from there across the water to be evacuated by Hercules from Lungi to Dakar. Of the total of 442 people evacuated, 299 left during the first forty-eight hours, leaving an estimated 600 or so entitled people still in Freetown. In fact, after the initial deployment of British forces the demand for evacuation quickly diminished.

Meanwhile, the naval task forces were approaching, *Illustrious* passed Dakar on the 10/11th and the ARG with 42 Commando arrived but was held over the horizon on 12 May. At this point, a secondary mission commenced to facilitate reinforcement and support of UNAMSIL via Lungi. It was also decided that the Paras would be relieved by 42 Commando. During these days there was some discussion as to whether to move the HQ from Senegal to Lungi, or into Freetown, or to base it afloat. In the event, on 13 May it was decided that the main HQ be relocated to Freetown in the British High Commission and Dakar became the rear HQ, these changes to be effected on 18–19 May. A stroke of good luck was that the JTFHQ Signal Squadron was already in Ghana for the planned exercise and so was acclimatised and equipped to support the communications needs of the Main and Forward HQs.

During this period, Richards was accomplishing two further tasks. First, to secure release of the hostages being held by the RUF and, second, to design a plan which would use the British forces to galvanise and hearten both the UNAMSIL forces and the Sierra Leone government forces: indeed to find a way in which to make the government forces a manoeuvre force for the UN. Coordination of policy was accomplished through daily meetings of all the key British personnel at the British High Commission and once the mission mandates had been set by London, effective strategic as well as tactical decision-making was devolved to this fast-reaction loop.

Employing all forms of assets and effects, it was possible to further dishearten the RUF and to help produce a change of heart in Charles Taylor, the President of Liberia and their principal external supporter. In any event, most of the hostages were released on 16 May. In pursuit of his second task, Richards helped to stitch together an unholy alliance of 'government forces' to support Kabbah. It consisted of ex-Sierra Leone army personnel, of Kamajo fighters, of the 'West Side Boys' and others. The British forces galvanised this force logistically and, together with UNAMSIL elements, they succeeded in pushing the RUF back to where they had been before they began their advance on Freetown at the beginning of the month. Although Port Loko had been under regular night attack since 11 May, government forces had recaptured Masiaka and the RUF had pulled back to Rogberi Junction. Sankoh was out of contact with his forces and no-one seemed to have taken his place. Furthermore, there were indications of a split between the eastern (Kailahun) and northern (Makeni) commands of the RUF. In particular, this was true of a fraction led by the Kailahun battalion commander 'Maskita' (Samuel Bockarie), which had been heavily involved in diamond smuggling with Charles Taylor's Liberia, and always thought to have been somewhat publicly distant from Sankoh. (In fact, if the anthropological analysis of the RUF, described below, is broadly correct, this supposition is unlikely to have been of decisive significance.)

Of great importance in building cohesion between the parties was the developing relationship between Brigadier Richards and General Jetley. The latter became persuaded of the former's view that in order to fulfil its mandated mission, UNAMSIL could not, nor should, adopt the traditional UN posture of peace-keeping neutrality, but that in fact all the external forces were present for the same purpose of supporting the government of Sierra Leone against the insurgency. As part of this change of view, he persuaded the General to allow UNAMSIL forces to participate in the active drive against the RUF. Building and maintaining this relationship was one of Richards's most important tasks.

The appearance of British warships looming close to the shore and extensive patrolling by paratroopers which had begun on the Aberdeen peninsula as early as 9 May had a calming effect on public opinion in Freetown, but naturally meant that British forces were the prime target for RUF counter attack. On 17 May the one major incident of the operation occurred at Lungi Lol, just North of Lungi airport. At 4.45 a.m. the Pathfinder Platoon of 1 Para identified about forty RUF moving along the road towards them. The rebels engaged the Para position who responded with full force, killing at least four RUF and recovering weapons including a rocket-propelled grenade launcher. The psychological effect of the engagement was immense in deterring the RUF and in further enhancing the reputation of the British troops in the eyes of the UNAMSIL and Sierra Leonian forces. On the same day, Sankoh was shot in the leg and captured by his erstwhile allies, the AFRC, and taken via Major Koroma's house to the guardroom in Cockerill barracks. An angry crowd gathered and, in response to a request from the Inspector General of Police, the British forces lifted Sankoh and his police escort with a Chinook helicopter to a place of safety and his continued custody.

The next phase of Operation PALLISER began at that same moment with the chopping of HQ and permission being given by the Secretary of State for commando assets to be used ashore. Therefore, heavier artillery was unloaded from the ships slung under the helicopters – itself a further visible signal of strength – and the decision was taken to start training the SLA (the Secretary of State announced publicly a decision to arm the SLA on 25 May). The combined British and other forces began to push more aggressively. HMS *Chatham* came conspicuously up river and Jordanian Special Forces were deployed. On 25 May the RUF released more hostages to Charles Taylor of Liberia and by 28 May government forces were poised to take Lunsar. On 30 May 1 Para handed over formally to 42 Commando and President Taylor announced his support for peace talks involving Sankoh. Harriers flew daily presence flights, but by now the aim was to start to thin out the HQ and to wind down the British presence.

However, the problematic nature of the follow-on was illustrated when the government forces were forced to withdraw from Lunsar back through Rogberi Junction to south of the Rokel bridge. Reacting to this, on 3 June a combat-experienced Indian Grenadier battalion deployed forward and quickly consolidated a strong position.

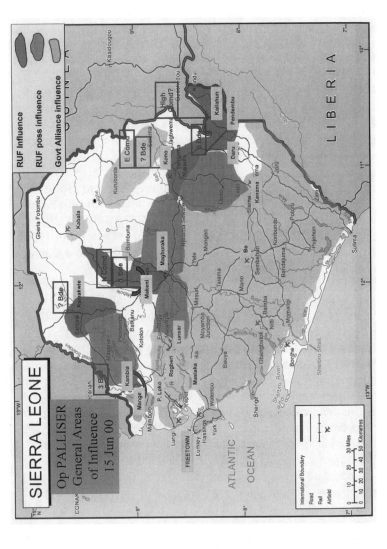

Map 6.2 Sierra Leone: general areas of influence on 15 June 2000.

This first positive move by the UNAMSIL forces had a major effect on the morale of all and coincided with reports that the RUF was possibly pulling out of Makeni (which actually occurred on 12 June).

UNAMSIL now held the horseshoe road and government forces were again advancing on Lunsar with the indispensable support of the Indian battalion. RUF leadership were first fixed, and then eventually fled from Makeni, leaving their forces behind and once the UNAMSIL was fully reinforced to its mandated level of 11,500 (which occurred on 11 June), withdrawal of the main British force by 15 June began to seem feasible. Robin Cook, the Foreign Secretary, visited on 7 and 8 June. A German journalist covered his visit. 'In recent weeks, desperate people once again welcomed their heavily armed and well-trained saviours,' she wrote. 'We love the British soldiers – they are our salvation,' a nineteen-year-old Bobby Kamara told a reporter, to the applause of bystanders. 'They are well-equipped. They are not as fearful as the UN soldiers. They do not steal from us. We want them to stay.' Two weeks ago a young man pleaded with Robin Cook, 'Please don't go.' Cook had been visiting a camp in Freetown where the victims of mass amputation had found refuge.[41]

Yet on 15 June the main force departed. Map 6.2 shows the dispositions of the parties at the end of the operation. A training mission of 200 was left behind, as well as a small force exclusively to extract the captured British Major Andy Harrison. During this drawdown phase, the importance of info ops increased. These types of operation employ the public media, psychological operations and electronic warfare, including deception. They were undertaken directly to protect British forces, but increasingly by the government of Sierra Leone's own info op campaign.

An example of a tactical info op conducted by the Sierra Leone forces, occurred on 13 and 14 June when RUF attempted to flush Sierra Leone government forces out of the critical town of Lunsar using a vehicle-mounted anti-aircraft gun. An ambush was prepared between Lunsar and Rogberi Junction with the aim of killing the escaping SLA. In the event, intelligence permitted the Sierra Leone government's sole Hind helicopter-gunship to intercept and destroy the vehicle-mounted gun; but it became clear from intelligence that those at the ambush were not aware that the gun had been destroyed. It was therefore decided that a spoofing operation be undertaken and the ambush units were deceived into thinking that their main fighting asset was still functional. The bogus call sign gave a summary of the helicopter attack and, having won the confidence of the commander of the ambush (Colonel Komba Gbundema – one of the main RUF field commanders in northern Sierra Leone), the SLA intelligence cell was able to provide personal details about him to the spoofing radio operator. Eventually, Gbundema gave his location. At this point, the deceit was unveiled and the RUF realised that they had been communicating with their enemy. The SLA then informed Gbundema that they knew all about him, including his family details and informed him that the Hind helicopter was en route to attack, with him as the first target. Within two hours of the initial spoofing call the RUF attack on Lunsar ceased.

A major larger-scale success was achieved by the SLA by these means, also using the Sierra Leone government Hind helicopter-gunship. It was used both to drop pamphlets and to conduct precise attacks on RUF HQ in the vicinity of Makeni. The aircraft's targeting was linked to radio broadcasts as well as leaflets and newspapers (*Lion News*). The text of one such leaflet, on which was a photograph of the Hind helicopter, read: 'RUF: this time we've dropped leaflets. Next time it will be: a half-inch Gatling gun or 57-mm rockets, or 23-mm guns or 30-mm grenades or ALL OF THEM, signed Republic of Sierra Leone Armed Forces.' *Lion News* of 29 May 2000, aimed at civilians, showed pictures of amputees and stated sarcastically, 'On behalf of the residents of Makeni, the Editor of *Lion News* wishes to thank the leadership of the RUF for: No medical services; a breakdown of law and order; no more aid workers; no food aid; crumbling buildings; no public services; no education; no future for our children; no normality; no safety ... RUF: NO Future: No Life.' The RUF could see, hear and feel that the net was closing; that the SLA could strike at will. This pattern of psychological and information operations continued over a period of nine days and was so successful that not only did the RUF High Command move to its eastern stronghold of Kailahun, but also a major evacuation occurred of over 60,000 civilians, many going south to Mile 91, where they were seen and described on the BBC World Service by a correspondent, Mark Doyle.

The media survey reported by Paul Richards ascertained that 83 per cent of the sample listened to the radio regularly and that the BBC World Service/Africa Service was by far the most important international station. Of the sample, 48 per cent were regular listeners (56 per cent in Bo, 41 per cent in Freetown, 37 per cent in Kambia). Eighty-five per cent of men said that their main reason for listening to the radio was as a source of news. This compared to the lower, but still remarkably high figure of 65 per cent of women. The BBC audience, however, was more sharply gendered: 73 per cent men, 27 per cent women, possibly because of the level of English required.[42] Therefore, reports by correspondents on the World Service can be seen to have had high rates of penetration in the zone of conflict, and may thus have also contributed to the information operational effect. However, UNAMSIL and the SLA were unable to exploit this vacuum at that moment, which left it open for the RUF to return, which makes the point that taking ground by using virtual threats is only effective if it is followed up by real physical presence.[43]

In the case of Wolseley's Asante campaign and of Operation PALLISER, the result was a sufficient transformation of the strategic context to warrant the term 'strategic raiding'. But in each case the strategic advantage was not exploited to the full. In the PALLISER context, this was because the process of rebuilding the Sierra Leone army to a point where it would be effective relative to the RUF and capable of dictating terms to it, although probably not defeating it in detail, could not be done overnight.

Matters were complicated when, in late August, soldiers of the British training mission were captured by a group of 'West Side Boys', including child soldiers, who had once been part of the unholy alliance supporting Kabbah, but had now split. Their rescue necessitated a massive and swift combined intelligence operation, leading to a surgical strike (Operation BARRAS) on 9 September. The seven hostages were rescued in twenty minutes, but fighting continued until the late afternoon in order to secure the area prior to the extraction of the force.

Then, on 20 August, with his approval from captivity, Sankoh was replaced as RUF leader by the field commander, Issay Sessay. Employing Mary Douglas's analysis of the anthropology of 'enclave' sectarian movements, it can be seen that this replacement of the externally-visible figurehead may be less disruptive of the movement than hierarchically-minded observers might think. The RUF is like other cult-like and millenarian movements detailed in Chapter 3 (American survivalists or the Branch Davidian cult immolated at Waco, Texas, or Melanesian 'cargo' cults or medieval followers of Joachim of Fiore). The world-view of such an encapsulated movement is entirely consistent, and encased in a hard, but brittle shell that separates it from the views of the rest of the world. Movement members go to great lengths to maintain this, both by their shared beliefs and indoctrination, which is reinforced in response to external condemnation. Leaders of egalitarian 'enclaves' gain authority from prestige, not structure; they are a product and sign of the general world-view inside the enclave; so through the ages, opponents have regularly failed to extinguish millenarian movements by focusing too closely upon their leaders.[44]

General Jetley's health had been undermined by malaria. He left Sierra Leone in September, before the end of his tour, handing command to his Nigerian deputy, Brigadier-General Garba. The RUF began to press forward.

Faced with a resurgence of violence, which might vitiate the new situation created by PALLISER, the British government moved swiftly to reinforce, by info and psyops means above all, the message of its continuing engagement and preparedness to return to Sierra Leone. Operation SILKMAN brought Brigadier Richards and his Joint Force HQ back to Freetown and, a little later, the ARG to the waters close off-shore. The six-ship group conducted amphibious exercises, firepower demonstrations, helicopter overflights and a march of 42 Commando through the city. In London, a Defence Minister, Baroness Symons, announced in Parliament that British forces might return in strength to Sierra Leone should UNAMSIL's position come under threat. This was Professor Low's 'sway' category of force, with teeth. On 1 November the Kenyan General, Daniel Opande, replaced Brigadier-General Garba and, without incident, over the period coincident with the presence of the ARG, two Bangladeshi battalions deployed to replace the Jordanians and Indians, who were finally withdrawn some time later.

Brigadier Richards and the JFHQ were, in effect, conducting a further strategic raid, to shore up the gains of PALLISER. But this time, Operation SILKMAN was focused on training the SLA and persuading the RUF that their mission was not likely to succeed. The message was not lost on the local media, which published headlines such as 'RUF beware! British give 30 day notice! (*Salone*) or 'Britain shows big stick!' (*Awoko*). In late November, as a parting message (SILKMAN ended on 8 December), prominent notice was given to the visit of an RAF team which, it was announced, was conducting a survey for possible future deployment of fast jet fighter-bombers. A publicity hand-out showed an RAF Tornado at speed.

However, what was visible on the ground to the RUF were the appearance of a fast-growing and increasingly combat-capable SLA; the success of President Conteh and the forces of Guinea in rebuffing the RUF operations against that country (thereby opening the prospect of possible envelopment of the RUF from north, west and south); the continuing cohesion of the 'Unholy Alliance' supporting Kabbah – a coalition now including Sankoh's former ally Johnny-

Paul Koroma – and the simultaneous announcement of a further large increase in the size of UNAMSIL.

UNAMSIL was now under new command. General Opande was supported by a British Chief of Staff. Brigadier Alastair Duncan came with a reputation as a battle-seasoned officer. He had commanded the second tour of BRITBAT in Bosnia, at which time his robust and successful approach to any opposition, Serb or Croat, to his mission to escort convoys earned the British battalion the nickname SHOOTBAT. This infusion into UNAMSIL was tangible evidence of the continuing unanimity of purpose of the international community. The success of Op SILKMAN depended upon the close and successful coordination of operational actions with diplomatic statements from the FCO and the MoD in London and the UN in New York.

In face of this Information Operations-led sequel, the RUF signed a cease-fire at Abuja on 10 November, within a month of the start of SILKMAN on 14 October. Brigadier Richards and the JFHQ left West Africa for a second and final time, after a stay of six weeks. They left General Opande's UNAMSIL, the SLA and associated allies in a stabilised situation within which it was possible to resume the plan to confine and marginalise the RUF.

Arguably the most important strategic change achieved by UK action in Sierra Leone was to cause President Charles Taylor of Liberia to reconsider his close support of the RUF and, at a distance, Colonel Gaddafi, likewise. The origins of the RUF's war lay in an extension of the conflict in Liberia, and this was the exit route for smuggled diamonds. Recapturing control of the diamond areas is necessary if the financial and human recruitment to the RUF is to be choked off, coupled to a vigorous programme of reconstruction, especially in the educational sector. General Opande, UNAMSIL and the new model Sierra Leone army continue to pursue the British-provided strategic plan to drive the RUF steadily backwards and to regain government control of the diamond-producing area. Both the objective and the means of reaching it were being established from the moment of Brigadier Richards's first arrival.

As well as devising a master plan for future operations, handed on for others to use, his had been a strategy of cementing the UN–Sierra Leone government coalition together to become the means to achieve it. The main actuator for this coalition was, in the first place, to keep the food supply provided by the UN going to government forces. To this the Secretary-General's Special Representative, Mr Sadré, had agreed, thus providing the necessary adjunct to the technical training and the resupply of ammunition to the Sierra Leone government and other logistic coordination facilitated by the British presence.

But the lesson, in short, is that while it is very difficult to plan for the follow-through, strategic advantage is gained if there is at least a model available for adaption, in the same way that the speed of the initial deployment would have been impossible unless PJHQ already possessed working HQ arrangements, for example, which could be instantly transported half-way across the world.

Lessons

What characteristics of these operations appear to have been most essential to ensure success? Both Sir Garnet Wolseley and Brigadier David Richards plainly subscribed to Clausewitz's evaluation of the importance of surprise and the maintenance of tempo, as expressed in the order and demonstrated in action by General Sir Rupert Smith and the British Division during the Gulf War. Interviewed by the *Berliner Zeitung*, Brigadier Richards described the concept of operations thus: 'It is a matter of deploying a well-trained and adequate military force so quickly that the problem is paralysed.'

Wolseley commenced his march to Kumase with a speed which he maintained, which bewildered and disoriented the Asantehene. He demonstrated his intent with such brutal clarity that it was part of the manner in which he conducted psychological operations from the outset of his campaign. He sought to overawe his enemy and to appear (although not actually to be) contemptuous of his power. That is to be seen in the nature of the letters which he wrote; in his peremptory refusals to treat with the King and with his demand for the surrender of many of the most important people close to the King. Wolseley may have done this last thing in the mistaken belief that he was demonstrating the breadth of British power; whereas had he understood from the outset the impossibility of what he was demanding he might perhaps have been able to avoid some of the fighting on the road to Kumase.

The deliberate showing to the envoys of the bridge and the fire-power demonstration by the Gatling gun were both intended to impress the Asante with the pointlessness of resistance to such potent force and this message was backed up by the fact that, as Wolseley moved into the interior, he was always in the position to support movement with disciplined firepower from the Black Watch and support from the seven pounders of the Hausa artillery – which were his equivalent asset to the Sierra Leone Government's Hind helicopter. The decisive engagement in the rainforest ravine of Amoafu had a similar effect on Asante morale to the Lungi Lol encounter with the Paras on 17 May 2000 on the RUF.

Wolseley's entire operation, like Richards's, employed the psychological effects of the force as the main effort. It was conducted as a massive act of political theatre. He moved defiantly up one of the great highways of the Asante kingdom and, on reaching Kumase, his actions were all calculated to belittle the King's power in the eyes of his subjects, actions culminating in the looting and blowing up of the treasure house, the removal of ritual objects and the firing of the city. Just as in the last days of PALLISER, and throughout SILKMAN, the tempo of psychological operations increased during the period of Wolseley's withdrawal to the coast. He left them something to think about, which precipitated a power struggle in the Asante council that lead to the overthrow of the war party and the eventual unseating of Kofi Kakari as Asantehene. But, in the short term, Wolseley's tactics led to the signing of the Treaty of Fomena and its subsequent ratification after his departure for Britain.

Throughout, Wolseley held both strategic and operational command of the campaign in his hands alone. This was by force of circumstance: there was no chance of referring for instruction elsewhere; but this was clearly important in permitting him to devise his campaign and to maintain tempo such that he was, in modern parlance, 'inside the decision loop' of the Asantehene and the Asante council.

The functional similarities of context between 1874 and 2000 are evident. Like Wolseley, Richards was a military officer conducting a military campaign with an intensely political role. Unlike him, one requirement which the modern commander had was to produce the political result desired with the minimum use of force and in full view of the world's media, hence by exploiting all the other force multipliers latent in his force, which included the media, of course. It is evident that from the outset Brigadier Richards was intensely aware of the importance of information operation and psychological warfare effects that his force could produce. He also could build upon his own reputation as a known actor in the events of 1999 and, as already quoted from his newspaper interview, he was aware that speed and the maintenance of tempo was one of his greatest potential strengths. By the same token, the political leverage achieved in Operation SILKMAN exploited the favourable fulcrum provided by PALLISER and BARRAS.

The 1874 and 2000 operations were undertaken with similar overall size of forces. But, whereas Wolseley's people were all with him in the field, PALLISER involved the deployment of 4,500 personnel (of whom 1,500 were ashore), including an aircraft carrier, a helicopter carrier with escorts, a Spearhead land battalion, advanced forces, Hercules transport aircraft and Chinook heavy-lift helicopters, all conveyed over 3,500 miles from a standing start to being in full operation within one week and the whole supported by the established and exercised relationships between PJHQ and the Joint Force HQ elements in the field. This capability meant that Richards was able to begin to act to get 'inside the decision loops' of all other parties from the moment that his OLRT set foot at Lungi airport on the Saturday lunchtime.

The narrative demonstrates how it was possible for him to elaborate the dual strategy of conducting the NEO while at the same time preventing the visible collapse of UNAMSIL and sustaining and rebuilding the Sierra Leone Forces. Fortunately, the mixture of forces required for the NEO was appropriate for the secondary mission, which was being engaged within a week although not publicly announced until a little later. The good fortune of the relative positions of the ARG and the *Illustrious* meant that the benefits of naval presence and the much wider range of military effects which they provided could be quickly deployed. As important was the fact that stocks could be held afloat, particularly in the RFA *Fort George*. Thus, from the overflights of Freetown by the Chinook helicopters immediately after the killings outside Sankoh's house on the afternoon of 8 May and the commencement of patrols of the Aberdeen Peninsula by Paratroopers from 9 May, Richards deliberately and continually used the theatrical potentials of his force to rebuild morale and to dishearten the RUF and, one may guess, at a distance, but of crucial importance to the course of events, President Charles Taylor of Liberia.

The information operation campaign which was mounted as soon as the main force arrived was very extensive and involved the full spectrum of media activities, including vernacular radio programmes and the printing of newspapers, as well as posters and leaflets. To these were added electronic warfare and radio intercept capabilities. Once fixed-wing aircraft arrived, their principal use was to provide 'presence flights', again as adjunct to the fact that information operations and psychological warfare were, in many ways, the main axis along which the force achieved its objectives. The British forces imparted momentum, and provided the plan; the SLA and

UNAMSIL increasingly provided the 'filling in' behind needed to consolidate gains on the ground.

However, the Info Ops axis could not have been exploited so successfully without another unusual characteristic of Operation PALLISER, namely the fact that an adequate spectrum of necessary forces was deployed from the very outset, so that the commander had a choice of instruments to hand which would not have been available in the more typical, dribbled deployment. If he had to hit hard, he could, and it was known that he could; so, by and large, he did not have to. It was the same lesson demonstrated when NATO provided, and General Smith used, artillery and air-strikes to halt and drive back the Bosnian Serb forces of General Ratko Mladic with UNPROFOR in Bosnia in the summer of 1995, thereby contributing to the pressures that led to the Dayton Accord.

But all this was contingent upon establishing the right relationships with all other parties – allies, as well as enemies – at the start. Arguably, the success of PALLISER was decided on the first Sunday when Richards joined the UN meeting, obtained Bernard Miyet's authorisation for UNAMSIL to coordinate with him and then sent his soldiers to ensure that UNAMSIL stood at Waterloo through the Sunday night and did not retreat in the face of the advancing RUF. None of this would have been possible unless the commander had the imagination and flexibility to size up and seize opportunities such as that of the UN meeting and possessed the operational (*de facto* strategic) authority to translate his intent instantaneously into action.

A distinctive feature of Richards's management of the relationship between intelligence, information and command was the institution of the daily meetings of all the elements of British presence in Sierra Leone which took place at the British High Commission. This reinstituted Field Marshal Lord Templar's approach to anti-guerrilla operations in Malaya. It enabled Richards both to maintain tempo and to drive the operation forward. Each element of the British presence could undertake its daily tasks with a clear and current understanding of the commander's objective, of achievement relative to that objective, therefore of the distance still to go, and the efforts required.

In this respect, it was thoroughly unusual for modern times that Brigadier Richards's position was so closely akin to that of Sir Garnet Wolseley: both field commanders had received strategic intent from London; both were then able to work out its implication and application in the theatre in detail, unimpeded, devising and coordinating diplomatic, military and political strategies. In this way, the control of PALLISER was 'inside the loop' not only of enemies but also of interdepartmental consultation and decision in London. It is much to the credit of the authorising ministers that they were prepared to trust the JTF commander in this old-fashioned way.

The experience stands in stark contrast to the impossible situation in which, he reports, General Wesley Clark found himself during the Kosovo campaign in 1999. Like US commanders in Vietnam before him he was 'spun' and micro-managed and bombarded with tactical advice from the Pentagon, but given no positive strategic guidance, least of all from the Commander-in-Chief, President Clinton. He was only told what not to do, which included preparation of a credible military threat to the Milosevic regime. Richard Betts describes his command as 'compromised by more conflicting pressures – political, diplomatic, military and legal – than any other in history'. The picture painted by the former SACEUR is such as to persuade Michael Ignatieff, reviewing his book, to the view that 'far from proving that the American military can stop human rights violations with military power, there is a dangerous lack of effective tactics, strategy and doctrine that will accomplish that aim'.[45] This account being even only partly true, to an even greater extent it shows how much more unlikely it would be to expect the degree of deft handling of the diplomatic/military sword that was done in Sierra Leone, in almost any coalition context other than one dominated by a 'framework' nation with unified command. That was the case in the Gulf War – an American war, not only led, but fitting into the philosophy of the American way of war – with others helping. And Sierra Leone was a British operation – not only British guided, but fitting the philosophy of the British way of war.[46]

Therefore, the careful and ultimately highly successful relationship that was established between British forces, UNAMSIL and the government forces in Sierra Leone repays study as a guide for the best management of future emergencies.

The clear-sighted Brahimi report into the conduct of recent peace-support operations by the UN came, amid a range of practical suggestions for improvements in performance, to an underlying political judgement.[47] This was a frank recognition that the UN structures are not likely soon to be trusted with the direct command of complex diplomatic/military operations by the key force contributor nations. One lesson of Sierra Leone is to regard this not as a condemnation but as an opportunity. By the skin of its teeth, UNAMSIL was saved from calamity by the arrival of the British. The political repercussion of the collapse of one of the largest UN forces mandated would have been considerable and unpredictable.

What was developed in practice on the ground was a way of using an independently-commanded national force first to rescue, then to help to reconstruct and reanimate (providing essential comms and logistic support, for example), finally to deploy the UN forces within a strategic plan, devised by the British, and in coalition with the equally reconstructed and reanimated SLA. Having done this, it was possible to scale back the independent presence and to infuse the UN structure by provision of key officers and associated services.

All this was only possible because, in the threat to entitled persons, the British possessed a legitimate ground to act independently; but, as the Gulf War showed, it is possible to give a so-called 'framework' nation the necessary latitude to conduct complex offensive operations under a sub-contracting type of UNSC mandate. That was criticised a decade ago. But perhaps it has more to recommend it than was then thought? Certainly – as Brahimi concluded (¶102–69) – there must be vigorous evaluation of the quality and capacities of troops offered for service, and those not reaching the required standards must not be deployed.

But the issue can, and should, be pressed further. The logical extension of Brahimi, in light of the deficiencies in the follow-on in Kosovo as much as in Timor and Sierra Leone, is to formalise the conclusion straightforwardly. Faced with a responsibility to protect people at risk of human rights abuse, the UN should focus upon the timely production of a well-drafted mandate. That was what happened over the East Timor crisis, following the path-breaking fact-finding mission of the UNSC ambassadors to Indonesia. Well-drafted means that it gives devolved authority to the 'framework' nation or nations so that if they have the will to act, but no national mandate of the sort the British had in Sierra Leone, they will have confidence to move without fear of interference. But at the same time – and this is what has been lacking hitherto – the UN should be equally engaged in defining requirements for the follow-on phase, as part of full cycle planning. Recollecting General Fraticelli's observation to Mr Connaughton, a virtue can be made of what else seems to be a criticism.

By specifying that UN directly controlled roles will be *only* within the follow-on phase, the mix of resources required will be quite different: not combat troops but gendarmerie and customs officers; not generals but judges and administrators; not combat engineers but mine-clearers, highway, railway, power-generating and sanitary engineers. Thus, Chapter VII can be the more efficiently executed so that the larger and longer tasks of post-conflict reconstruction may be better taken in hand. These will live not under Chapters VI or VII, the minatory chapters, but within Chapter XII – the sleeping clauses of the Charter which describe the responsibilities of Trusteeship, where the international community steps in to splint the broken bones of an injured civil society by providing the full range of services to assist its rehabilitation and return to civilised and peaceful life.

A German journalist, commenting a week after withdrawal of the main forces, wrote of the British troops:

> intervention in the fate of Sierra Leone has also awakened suspicion of recolonisation. That may be. But this kind of intervention does have a certain charm – especially as the locals have given the Whites such a hearty reception whilst they fear their own soldiers and regard the Blue Helmets as useless. The withdrawal of the main British contingent has allayed any suspicion of over-presumptuousness – and makes the operation appear all the more justified.

Coda: what happened next

The Sierra Leone Army became increasingly active, independently, during 2001 after extensive British training, and the UN force was deployed increasingly widely and successfully in constabulary roles across the country. Then, in May 2002, Sierra Leoneans voted in the first general election since the civil war was ended in the manner related in this chapter. Kabbah campaigned on the slogan, 'De war dun dun' (i.e. the civil war is really over). Mark Doyle, the BBC's long-serving West Africa correspondent, reported that turn-out was remarkably high for a country that is now materially one of the poorest in the world, and whose broken infrastructure is still in disarray only two years after the end of hostilities. As remarkably, all the principal personalities and parties wished to take part and were also permitted to do so. President Siaka Stevens's All People's Congress, the party of the one-party state of the later 1970s and 1980s, led now by Ernest Koroma, polled well in second place. By an error in electoral procedure, it became known that the army had voted heavily for Johnny-Paul Koroma; but Kabbah won a decisive popular mandate without the need to hold a second round of voting, and that was not contested by the army. Sankoh remains in gaol where, reportedly, he has suffered a nervous breakdown; but the RUF made peace (again) in January 2002 and, led by Pallo Bangura, one of Sankoh's aides, the RUF (which actually stood, and was permitted to stand) obtained about 2 per cent.

7 Command in the new era

Four clear lessons emerge from the analysis of strategic raiding in West Africa. All of them rotate around the role of the force commander. The first is that, if one hopes for success, then the force commander must succeed in getting within the decision loops both of the enemy and any parts of his own higher command structure which might constrain his freedom of action. Given this devolution of both strategic and operational command into his hands, it becomes possible for him to shape strategies which follow the Clausewitzian sequence: tactically, in that he shapes engagements for the purposes of the battle; strategically, in that he shapes battles for the purposes of the war. In this way, the case studies showed successful commanders controlling the four domains of time, space, perception and knowledge in ways which increased their area for strategic manoeuvre: it was true of Wolseley; it was true of Richards; it was, in contrast, not the case for General Wesley Clark.

Second, for such a nature of command to be exercised, it was essential that the political authorities did not deliver detailed orders, but only mission-type orders. A latitude, which was granted to Brigadier Richards in Sierra Leone, and which he exploited to the full, was quite exceptional when contrasted with the degree of constraint that has come to be typically applied to operational commanders, not merely by choice but (as ¶21(d) below, p.233, discusses) because the technologies of communication permit this degree of interference. Therefore, the granting of command latitude in circumstances where alternatives are easily possible is both the more remarkable and commendable in respect of the judgement of the higher political authority.

Third, the case studies reveal that the success of the entire operation is hostage to the commander's flair. That is the very thing which is feared. It strengthens the bureaucratic instinct to exploit the technical possibility to constrain the commander's freedom of action. Yet only if the commander is both able and permitted to do so can he contribute drive and direction at the point where it can meaningfully exploit the possibility of getting inside the relevant decision loops of others.

The final lesson, which the case studies underscore, is that only through fulfilment of the previous three can a subtle and interacting deployment of all the potential effects of the force be marshalled, sequenced and applied. In the strategic raids of Wolseley and of Richards, it is plain that the leading vectors of the force effect were psychological and information operations. The choice for higher political authorities, illustrated by these cases, is therefore plain: the chance of gaining success in the safest and least costly way, judged both in terms of lives and money, is in inverse proportion to willingness to permit the circumstances described in the first three lessons to flourish.

These lessons are drawn from cases of strategic raiding in the conduct of diplomatic/military operations (DMOs). Strategic raiding is only one of the several main forms in which military force can be deployed. However, before 11 September 2001, it was already plain that, for the purposes of executing the responsibility to protect human rights, the strategic raid would likely be the primary vehicle for that purpose. After the atrocities of 11 September 2001, the reasons to study strategic raiding have become all the more compelling: for the military segment of a total strategy to combat terrorists is most likely also to be cast within this form. Given that the US has announced the suppression of terrorism as a prime mission, and given the sources of terrorism, as described in Chapter 3, which show the nature of linkage between circumstances of structural violence and the emergence of terrorist threats, one may, with slightly greater confidence than in the previous month – and for the worst of reasons – advance the case for the importance of the strategic raid.

The manner in which the Clausewitz principles were translated into modern action was demonstrated by General Smith in the Gulf War. His orders were cited as illustration of this point in the previous chapter. A decade later, General Smith reflected upon the likely effect of new circumstances for the nature of warfare.[1] He described five characteristics of warfare in the new era, all of which are facilitating requirements for successful strategic raiding in support of either of the two emerging principal missions of DMOs and counter-terrorist operations.

First, he observed that, where force is employed, there is a general expectation that destructive effects will be minimal and localised and that, wherever possible, political outcomes will be achieved directly without the prior passage through a major action that has produced technical military defeat in detail. In such circumstances, all ranks acquire, consciously or not, a potential to be strategic decision-makers. Consequently, the General advocated the importance of training to ensure that the 'strategic corporal' is fully conscious of his power. In the British Army, this vertical 'indoctrination' of all ranks with a clear understanding of the Commander's intent, is called 'mission command'.[2] Mission command is what Brigadier Richards exercised in Sierra Leone. Adaptation of the mission command approach is an important component of the way in which command arrangements will need to be adapted to the new circumstances of twenty-first century operations. What will be required is both 'modularity of organisation' and – equally vital – 'modularity of thought'. (The formulation of this insight is owed to Brigadier Mungo Melvin.) What that means is that to focus upon institutions and structures overwhelmingly is a dangerous illusion. An illusion because the structures will only work if Commander's Intent animates people at all levels; dangerous because 'modularity of thought' will not occur without effort in training and explanation, so that on campaign people will know *why* they are asked to switch and add to their roles and duties.

Returning to General Smith's argument, his second proposition underpins the case for adapted and deepened mission command. Actions for either principal purpose will not take place in classical or military engagement. Wars will be fought among people and this, Smith observed, told him, among other things, that his equipment must be capable of operating in that environment. Ideally, he said, the equipment should not exceed one of the three standard sizes: a sea container, the back of a Land Rover and the size of a standard house door frame. But, far more challenging than the demands on weapons designers, are the demands on how weapons might be used to achieve the objective of the mission. Weapons are means of projecting destructive energy: but the effects principally required from them, in new era warfare, must target not so much the inventories of the opponents' hardware as the intentions of the opposition's commanders.

The third characteristic, a consequence of both the first two, but in tension in particular with the second, is that one should fight so as not to endanger or lose the Force. That is particularly so in wars of choice, which, by definition, DMOs are. It may be less so the case in counter-terrorist raids responding to traumatic shock such as the US experienced on 11 September 2001.

The fourth characteristic is that, as the British Army discovered in Northern Ireland, one must anticipate time-less operations. To talk of 'exit strategies' or to set departure dates is to cede main advantage to the opposition. Timeless operations are a necessary aspect of targeting intentions above all: for the aim must be to produce embedded, changed trends of behaviour – one of the defining criteria of success in a strategic raid.

Finally, Smith stated as a general principle that one should expect to use technical systems in unexpected ways. This, he observed, would be more than the usual improvisation of battle where one weapon system is adapted for use in a different role (anti-aircraft guns as anti-tank weapons, for example). Here the point is both broader and more challenging, for it is the self-conscious configuration and deployment of the force, in ways to maximise other than its kinetic energy effects: in particular, the psychological and information operation effects used with such striking results by Richards in Operation PALLISER.

Smith's five characteristics, combined with the four lessons from the case studies of strategic raiding, already point towards the critical importance of command in the new era. The case becomes decisive when one adds a further dimension, namely a template which helps us recognise both the manner in which the commander uses the different characteristics of the resources to hand, and, in so doing, exploits quite different ways of thinking as he executes his political and military roles simultaneously.

In truth, Clausewitz's most often quoted dictum – that war is the continuation of politics by other means – has never existed without its shadow involute. That much is clear when the proposition is placed within the context of his other major arguments, and, in particular, his identification of the third, the psychological, mode of operation.

The degree to which the DMO strategic raids just described illuminate the involute – that politics may be the continuation of war by other means (*may*, note, not *always must be*: for there is a necessary degree of asymmetry between the twin statements in any society that is not totalitarian) – the reader may judge. Attention turns sharply towards the other arena within which strategic raiding will most likely occur – when Clausewitz's preferred among his six options of offensive or defensive actions, namely to carry the fight offensively to the enemy's forces, will be chosen.

Where combat, whether between Napoleonic armies or at the Battle of Kursk in the greatest tank battle of all time, could be seen and thought of as a discrete activity, it was both possible and proper for a clear division of labour between political and military authorities to be maintained. That sequencing is still reflected in the commonly held view that the military moment stands waiting upon the failure of all other means of conflict prevention or resolution: that, in so far as it plays a role in that first period, it is passive, through signalling a set of deterrent threats; but that once diplomacy has demonstrably failed and the activation order has been passed, the soldier moves into the same contested geopolitical space that had previously been under negotiating or diplomatic contest, but does so on his own terms. This sequencing, built upon a Shermanite view of war and a way of war derived from it, may be observed as the post-Cold War military forces, whose equipments and philosophies were fashioned for an earlier age now gone, go through the command post exercise of the transition from peace to war.

Yet, manifestly, for the reasons rehearsed by Smith in June 2001 and listed above, this will no longer do. It will not do for the successful conduct of strategic raids in protection of fundamental rights; it certainly will not do as military forces are integrated into a broad spectrum approach to the prevention and suppression of terrorism. A better model, one which tracks more accurately the contours of the world in the new era, is required if military force is to play a productive and not obstructive role in combating this range of security threats.

Both the obverse and the reverse of Clausewitz's proposition linking politics to warfare are well captured by Nigel Howard in his work on confrontation analysis.[3] Howard reached his insights from a close study of the theatrical or dramatic interactions between negotiating parties. In this, his approach has much in common with that of Roger Fisher and the Harvard Negotiation project. Whilst both approaches recognise the potential for negotiation breakdown or for transition to conflict in antagonistic confrontations, they also both recognise the opportunity to channel the energy of antagonism into a positive solution. The essence of this, in Fisher's approach, is successful disentanglement of problem from antagonist and, ultimately, harnessing one of the most powerful among social attractors: the deeply rooted human tendency to bond in adversity against a common enemy.[4]

Howard's confrontation analysis is more specifically directed towards contexts in which military forces are deployed under constrained rules of engagement (RoE), such as in support of the civil arm, as in Northern Ireland, or in DMO contexts. He represents the options by analogy to a game of cards and shows how, using this analogy, it is possible for the commander to play combinations of cards, or sequences of cards, which blend his diplomatic and his military effects in ways which simply cannot be captured in the received view of the transition from the circumstance of peace to the circumstance of war. This aspect of his approach is reminiscent of game theorists like Steven Brams, who early recognised that, in the interests of a successful outcome, it was often beneficial to threaten or inflict a little pain at the same time as one displayed the rewards of cooperation.[5] Another rather racier way of making Brams's point was Theodore Roosevelt's dictum that one should talk softly but carry a big stick.

Close reading of the narrative history of operations in Sierra Leone during 2000 shows how the role, which Richards designed for himself and then carried through as force commander, is far more accurately represented by Howard's card-playing analogy. Finding the analysis congenial for retrospective explanation of his own decisions as force commander, first in the Gulf then in Bosnia, Smith suggested that a different verb would help. 'Shuttling' better captured the continuous process of switching between the diplomatic–political mode of confrontation and the politico-military mode of conflict. Figure 7.1 illustrates this point.[6]

The top of the figure shows the spectrum between perceived threats to the homeland and DMOs. By and large, and for perfectly

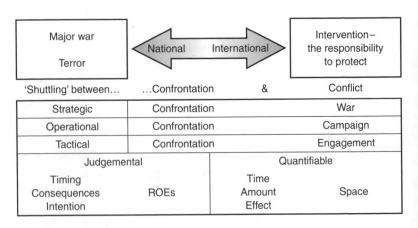

Figure 7.1 'Shuttling' between confrontation and conflict.

obvious reasons, the response to terror or to major war will likely be independent and national in its root and in its driving force, even if it acquires coalition or alliance dimensions. The responsibility to protect those at risk of supreme humanitarian emergency starts off as an international responsibility and is usually first signalled in international *fora* such as the United Nations even if, at the end of the day, effective action also has to arise from independent national will. The range of possible modalities was discussed in Chapter 5. The latitude of choice is greater on the right-hand side of the figure.

If, as now seems certain to be the case, the two prime military missions of the foreseeable future will be countering of terrorism and a continuation of humanitarian intervention, then the bottom part of the figure represents the context within which the commander of a strategic raid has the chance to work. Smith's point about the need for a more vigorous verb may be represented in a hypothetical example. In a given circumstance of entrenched ethno-nationalist competition (the Balkans, the Congo, Afghanistan, the former Soviet space...) there will be a strategic confrontation between the parties. At a certain moment it may quite suddenly lose its seeming stability and, passing over a catastrophe cusp, descend into another form and level: perhaps the campaign level of armed conflict. The outcome of battle or exhaustion or starvation of munitions may return the situation to one of operational confrontation, which may again break down into a series of incoherent tactical engagements. At this point, an external actor may intervene and succeed in suppressing the engagement level of conflict by simultaneously acting at the tactical and strategic level of confrontation.

This point was earliest grasped in the British Army's Field Manual entitled 'Wider Peacekeeping'[7] which first drew attention to the difference between strategic and tactical consent in a hostile environment. The author of that manual, Colonel Charles Dobbie, argued there and later under his own name, that a force commander had an overriding intelligence requirement to judge the quality of consent which bounded his operational environment. If he possessed strategic consent for his presence but was faced with local opposition, then he might, with some confidence, act robustly to suppress local opposition. This was done by the same Alastair Duncan who became Chief of Staff to UNAMSIL, when, as Colonel, he took responsibility for convoying supplies to Vitez through regions where he faced local opposition but had strategic consent. However, if strategic consent is absent then the appearance of progress on the ground can be both deceptive and dangerous. Accordingly, it is vital for the commander's judgement of the permissiveness of his operational environment to be translated into his intent and for that intent to be successfully conveyed to all ranks, down to that of the strategic corporal. That, in the previous chapter, is what was illustrated from Smith's Gulf War orders.

Adding to Howard's confrontation analysis, Smith named the principal qualities and activities which, in his experience, preoccupied the commander as he simultaneously worked the two sides of confrontation and conflict in a DMO. Confrontation calls for judgemental qualities and is principally driven by the commander's judgements of timing and the consequences of action and their interaction with other circumstances on his judgement of the intentions of others and of himself. All of this is expressed in the manner in which the rules of engagement of his force are shaped and graded for different circumstances. In contrast, in conflict he is much more preoccupied with quantifiable entities: how much? How quickly? How widely? In what form?

In previous generations, soldiers saw the right-hand side of the diagram as their terrain and believed that an ability to command within its terms was sufficient. Now, it is apparent that that capacity is necessary only: sufficiency lays on the commander a requirement to be able to shuttle successfully between the modes of confrontation and conflict and to exercise all necessary skills, as appropriate, for each combination or phase as – in Howard's analogy – he plays his 'hand' with mixtures of colours and powers of card.

A practical conclusion emerges from all of this. Of all the aspects of an armed force, the one which is most intensively and centrally exposed by the demands of strategic raiding is the exercise of command. Whereas the single most important constituent element for success in command in the new era cannot be produced by any structural reforms of the organs of command, for it is the genius of the commander – as ever it has been – plainly those structures do need to be re-examined, understood and tested to ensure that they are broadly supportive of the commander in his function and not a drag upon his heels. There is considerable anecdotal evidence to suggest that many command functions in HQ suffer from cultural lag and do indeed drag upon the commander's heels. To escape from them, some (and this was Smith's approach in the Gulf War) simply remove themselves physically from the main HQ and conducted strategic analysis in a mobile tactical HQ with only close associates, in the form of component commanders, present. A similar device was employed in Sierra Leone through the daily coordinating briefing meeting chaired by the British High Commissioner.

For excellent reasons, there is stronger resistance to changing the organs and functions of command than most others within modern military forces. That is because mistakes in this would be potentially fatal to all other aspects of the force; so a strong resistance to the reformation of command practices is no thoughtless reflex conservatism. It is soundly based. But there comes a moment when everything, including command and HQ functions, must be re-examined. This was already a strong case from the evidence of DMOs since 1995. With the arrival of the anti-terrorist mission, that case is strongly reinforced.

The remainder of this chapter consists of a lightly edited version of a scoping paper, written first in 1999, which sought to explain to the military community the different convergent dimensions of the case for commencing such work. It was prompted in part from the discovery that certain types of information, which are essential in order to understand the present functioning of command arrangements, have simply never been collected. Prominent among these data are an understanding from practical observation of how information flows within an HQ and, in particular, how, structurally, the HQ arranges the 'merit order', which gives relative priority to different categories of information. One implication of the advent of strategic raiding in the new era is that the information flows and merit orders may need to become both broader in their scope and more agile in the reordering of what is presented to the commander and his close staff to support them in a 'shuttling' between confrontation and conflict.

The case is made in twenty-three numbered paragraphs, as follows:

1. The act of command in a social organisation, for example a military or diplomatic agency, is simultaneously an *electro-chemical*, a *mechanical* and a *psycho-social* phenomenon. It is the actuator of all that follows – whether intended or unanticipated. If its likely requirements can be guessed, then the means can be roughly prepared, but probably never more than that. This is an uncomfortable but unavoidable process of opportunity/cost allocation, since no-one can (or should, maybe) seek to cover all eventualities. Therefore, it follows that, in any reconsideration of strategy for the new age, a focus upon the issue of command assumes a logical priority both in force planning and in the identification of capabilities, which

supports it. It also, incidentally, places a premium upon clear thinking, because it suffers from muddled or cloudy political instruction disproportionately more than logically consequent areas.

2. Capabilities, for the purposes of this chapter, are taken to mean more than equipment, or even equipment *plus* personnel (while recognising that the new concept of 'equipment capability' is a positive advance over previous practice). These together provide the *means* of action. But means are ineffective without an efficient plan for their employment (the *way*), which is a product of thought exercised at three levels (see next paragraph). Yet prevailing requires more than good means and an efficient plan: it requires *will*. Capability, therefore, equals *means* $\times$ *way*^{2} $\times$ *will*^{3}.[8] Thus defined, the centrality of command issues to force planning becomes plain.

3. Command is exercised at three levels – strategic, operational and tactical – that have, in the past, frequently been confused and conflated. Therefore, there is a potential for confusion in the future. First, this is because the terms within which command is analysed are *the same for each level*, but the requirements for each level are *different*. Second, the levels of command are most commonly interpreted in an *institutional* sense, whereas to consider future requirements we need to be able to think of them in *systemic* terms of 'top down' command, 'bottom up' command and their interaction which corresponds to the operational level. The operational level is the one where the other two views fuse: outwards and upwards (strategic); inwards and downwards (tactical). Viewed systemically, the function of the operational level is thus pivotal: when it fails to form a secure link between intention and action, it leads to polarised behaviour with dangerous consequences for both strategic and tactical judgement and action (see ¶21(b)).

4. In contrast, viewed *institutionally and historically*, the operational level first arose within the German armed forces of the First World War, responding to the new requirements of massed manoeuvre. It was greatly developed further in Soviet military art, and became centrally important to the type of warfare that broke the backbone of the Third Reich in the East. The nature of command in massed warfare of attrition has been extensively studied since then. One might add that the militarisation of politics thereby confused tactical with strategic aims, and was one of the most specific and arguably dangerous features of framing the Cold War confrontation in nuclear terms. It has served to embed this type of category error – confusing

systemic with institutional interpretations of the levels of command – deep in the dominant contemporary cultures of military force.

5. A premise of this chapter is that the principal challenges in the new era most probably do not lie in this area, and therefore it is not discussed further. It focuses upon the new era issues of diplomatic/ military operations (DMOs) and, latterly, of anti-terrorism operations. Here, one might suggest, the key requirement is for *depth in structure*. What that means was well illustrated by the spring 2000 events in Sierra Leone. The UN force lacked systemic coherence, and therefore failed when faced with high-intensity operations (where high intensity is defined not by the volume of firepower, mass or speed of operations, but by the low degree of control which the force had over the main risk variables affecting it[9]). The British force under Brigadier Richards, in contrast, displayed depth in structure and did not: it converted a higher to a lower intensity situation, illustrated in the previous chapter.

6. The executor of an operation (the Force) is described and bounded by three interlaced triangles – one each for the strategic, operational and tactical levels – the sides of which are the *end*, *means* and *way* of the activity. The command activity within that Force is also governed by a nest of three *end/way/means* triangle of its own: separate but embedded. In all cases, the mechanics of interaction are the same. Problems on either side – hand or brain – can obstruct the other.

7. In the case of the command activity that is the present focus, the *end* that the thought wills is facilitated by the *means*, which may be taken to bundle together both the *channels of communication* and the *messages*. The *way* in which *means* turn intentions into actions depends on the culture within which the organism lives. It conditions its manner of behaviour. Culture sets in-built limits and (of special importance to the exercise of command) as one aspect of that, it programmes patterns of recognition and response: intuition.[10] Contemporary research on cognition suggests that these 'soft-wired' capacities to recognise patterns are probably enhancements of 'hard-wired' pathways in the human brain: so the pattern-recognition mode of problem analysis and response may touch deep structures in our psycho-social conformation.

8. Historically and institutionally, the strategic level of command used to be embedded within an international system of self-conscious, self-constituting states – entities described and treated as

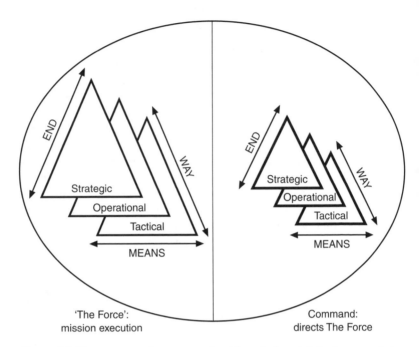

Figure 7.2 How command processes should track those of the force, and vice versa.

moral beings since the mid-eighteenth century. These Leviathans operated through the dynamic balancing of powers within an anarchic global society of states. This system was clearly described by modern students of international relations and the realism of that description was generally accepted.[11] The discrete territory of military power was sharply etched: it was the continuation of politics by other means.[12] It was also the final arbiter – the gladiators' arena – within which contested claims to power were adjudicated fatally, and therefore decisively.[13]

9. Strategic command is now conducted under strongly contrasting conditions. When the twentieth century ended functionally, in 1989, we entered a new era, the first decade of which has failed to demonstrate yet any decisive defining characteristic, despite a good deal of premature trumpeting suggesting otherwise.[14] Therefore, it is still to be neutrally named, simply as new. The successful mass casualty terrorist attacks of September 2001 in the US do not, in themselves, represent a qualitative Rubicon that has been crossed, for reasons explained in

Chapter 3. However, the nature of the competition for power is plainly changed from the classical mode described in the previous paragraph, by the arrival of competing non-state actors (see ¶13).

10. In this new era, in the realms of social behaviour inhabited by military agencies, each of the three simultaneously defining and circumscribing dimensions of the triangle of strategic command, is in question: the *ends* are no longer self-evident or clear (e.g. 'mission creep' in Bosnia); the *means* are currently configured for war-fighting and assumed to be sufficient for DMOs, which may not be the case;[15] the *way* is no longer unselfconsciously consensual: in fact, there are stark and systematic divergences between apparently closely allied nations, and between state and non-state actors. Furthermore, there are frequently divergences between civilian and military interpretations of all three dimensions.

11. This is a very unusual circumstance. The last time that this circumstance pertained was at the time of the Renaissance. At the beginning of the modern era, which the Tofflers described as the 'Second Wave', city states – new agents of power that expressed in embryonic form the nation state which became the dominant form of social power for the rest of the millennium – adopted the new instruments of power arising from the revolution in military affairs to new and more cruelly ambitious ends than raids and skirmishes to seize plunder.[16] The return of circumstances, marked by similar characteristics, dictates the need to reconsider the nature of command.

12. The *ends* towards which military power can be employed have always submitted, at the tactical level, to the paradoxical logic of strategy as Clausewitz explained it: the worst weather is the best; the roughest terrain is the safest, etc. It is subject to the same paradoxical logic at the strategic level also. Reviewing the outcome of many campaigns, Edward Luttwak concluded that – entirely in conformity with the paradoxical logic – the most reliable way in which to frustrate one's strategic political objective was to achieve decisive and humiliating military defeat of the enemy, *vide* the crushing success of the Six Day War in 1967, sowing the seeds for the *intifada* twenty years later.[17] Such outcomes, he suggested, arose from the persistent tendency to confuse the tactical with the strategic levels of analysis, which are separated here. The result of elision is commission of gross errors in the nature of response and signalling.

13. A defining characteristic of the New Era is transformation in the nature of political agency. Just as in the Renaissance, the dominant

form is challenged and becomes diluted. Non-state actors, and not only, but also terrorists, barge onto the stage, and within the taxonomy of states, we find a growing category of failed or collapsed states: the 'post-imperial, pre-state chaos' described by Robert Cooper as the characteristic of the first of his tri-partite categories of states (pre-modern, modern and post-modern).[18] They join the grim, existing twentieth-century regiment of authoritarian, totalitarian and communist states whose special feature was to devour their own citizens: 160 million in contrast to the thirty-five million lost to 'conventional' hostilities of war, described in Chapter 1. Together these compose the terrain into which democracies, that base their identity in the defence of human rights, find themselves drawn by circumstance and pushed by their own beliefs and public for the twin functions of acting upon the responsibility to protect the powerless and the desire to protect ourselves against terrorist attacks.

14. Such are the circumstances for DMOs or for counter-terrorist operations. The most likely form for either is the strategic raid, so the demands of either are probably not dissimilar: they are the terrain for the exercise of strategic command. The essence of such operations is the intimate intertwining of strategic political objectives with the display and use of force.[19] It therefore follows that renovation of the procedures for strategic command involve as thoroughgoing a reform of civilian as of military procedures.

15. The *way* in which the strategic level of command is exercised in the new era DMOs is further complicated by two conflicting circumstances. The first is that the *way* of execution is increasingly confounded both by limitations of circumstance, and by differences in culture. This necessarily affects the manner in which the command function can be framed and conducted. (See diagram on p. 228.) Today, the only militarily competent context within which international operations can be safely placed are either NATO or 'virtual' NATO – and more so likely the latter than the former.[20] The geo-political alliance has evident constraints; but its military procedures are the 'operating system' for any forms of competent coalition military operations nowadays, as the 1999 East Timor UN operation showed. Yet, within this alliance, both actual and virtual, there coexist two distinct ways of war: the American way is reluctant to engage, but, once committed, is massive in scale and in intensity: the reasons for this arise from quite central defining characteristics of the identity of the Republic. In contrast, the European way remains

closer to its nineteenth-century colonial origins. The Sierra Leone case study illustrated and then discussed that.

16. The *way* is thus doubly confounded as we enter the new century: from one direction, the systematic cultural differences between the American and European ways coincide with the arrival of unimpeded American freedom of action. Seen by fearful onlookers as a new bout of isolationism, but by most Americans as a more – or less – justified form of unilateralism in the general good, it composes one of the central questions of the moment.[21]

17. From the other direction, the manner in which NATO was enlarged collided with the structural inadequacy and the absence of common purpose within the European institutions to leave a remarkably fragile foundation upon which to seek to ground an autonomous European alternative.[22]

18. At the tactical level, the *ends* towards which command is exercised are made less easy to frame in terms of military objectives as discussed at ¶7.[23]

19. The conclusion is puzzling and frustrating to commanders, especially American commanders. What are we supposed to do? Win, but with avoidable casualties, to salve the pride of the enemy? Take unnecessary risks once combat is joined? It is the polar extreme of the Chinese view of the role of force within the spectrum of instruments of power, expressed by Sun Tzu, which argues that victory by inscrutable immobility and the inculcation of paralysing fear in the enemy is the most elegant and most desirable.

20. The background of the modern British Army in colonial, expeditionary war since the Boer War, and especially in light of its operations in Northern Ireland, has made it unusually sensitive to the constraints that exist near the boundary with constabulary action in support of the civil arm.[24] But it is not clear that the command structures which it possesses are well matched. To enter an army HQ configured for armoured warfare in 2000 is to enter a microcosm which, in physical appearance, in procedures and in protocols (for example, the linear structuring of 'J' [Joint] functions) has been essentially the same for fifty years. Most importantly, the *end* to which such an HQ is intended is only with difficulty bent to the political signalling requirements of DMOs. In practice, it has only been under the influence of exceptionally focused and decisive leadership, combined with long experience of the practice by the officer corps, that such organs

have been successfully rendered fit for the new purpose. The history of the evolving, contrasting episodes in the Bosnian intervention provide a rich ground of evidence for this. A minor premise of this chapter is that inspired improvisation is too large a risk.

21. Quite apart from the unresolved matter of what the right message is to send in order to achieve the desired *end*, the *means* for their transmission are under pressures, leading towards fracture. Two general sources of pressure have been indicated already: problems in the Force obstructing the exercise of command (¶6) and problems in the *way* of command frustrating the creation of fully efficient capability. These coalesce into five specific pressures deserving of note:

a   First, there is a case to answer of maladaption to purpose of command structures and procedures within its own terms (terms which are oriented towards overwhelming technical defeat in detail over a period of days or weeks): the *way* obstructing the *means*. Jim Storr suggested that, in fact, the time horizon of a division commander should be hours rather than days; and therefore the modern field HQs accumulate too much information that is irrelevant to the command decision process. He suspected that much effective operational practice at present is actually the avoidance of ineffective and distracting procedures.[25] He grounded his views on decision-making in Klein's work.

b   A second direction from which pressure comes is recognition that decision-making under stress may demonstrate at different times great decisiveness and speed or sudden lassitude and indecision. The *means* is the man, and the man changes under pressure: Napoleon famously had such a spell in the middle of the battle of Waterloo. Dodd made the case that, by analogy with the different speeds and functions of the human neural and endocrine systems, there are possibly good reasons and functions for this phenomenon; but that pre-supposed an HQ structure fit for the purposes dictated by the new *ends*, which we may not have.[26] Absent the structure to contain and channel these forces fruitfully, she suggested that we would be prudent to assess their potential for akinesia and discontinuity.

c   That warning intersected with a third that is related, but broader and more systematic. Dodd employed the expository potentials of catastrophe theory to illustrate her case. Catastrophe theory is an elegant and powerful piece of topological mathematics, which was discredited in some eyes by over-enthusiastic application in social contexts in the 1980s. It deserves to be rescued from those doldrums. In particular, the link between Bayesian decision processes and Catastrophe theory is seen as the vital next step in validation of the Catastrophe Model.[27] It is argued that they may be an underrated resource as we seek to explain the manner in which an abrupt 'change of phase' can occur in an operation, corresponding to the interaction of dynamics operating at different rates.

d   Fourth, new technology plays a role also, but not a prescriptive one: technology is neutral in itself. If the possession of technical means stimulates unwarranted over-confidence about the degree of physical or psychological control of a situation, then the effect may be to make matters go badly, but much more quickly. The dogged refusal to delegate in the American army in Vietnam was made hugely more paralysing and damaging by the arrival of liberal supplies of radios and helicopters. Martin van Creveld gives a memorable description of the way in which the layers of command above a platoon in the jungle pile up – literally – over the soldier's head: his Major in a tree-top Huey; his Brigadier in a Chinook above that; his General in a circling B-707 and his President choosing targets for him in the White House.[28] The *means* were savagely undermined by the *way* in which the Force was directed and handled, and the technological improvements in the command processes turned out, in these broader circumstances, to be no gain at all, but rather the opposite. Conversely, the lesson of this is not Luddite: it is to reiterate Montgomery's first principle of war: selection and maintenance of aim. The lesson underscores the importance of reconsidering future command processes from first principles, and thus it echoes at the tactical level the earlier message of this chapter at the strategic level.

e   Finally, the yet further provision of instantaneous, processed intelligence to the battlefield commander through the digitisation revolution has an evident potential to clear the fog of war, at least to some extent.[29] Whether the effect is positive or negative will depend upon the command context within which it is used. Indeed, especially if there is great reliance on one – any – major single approach, either by choice or by circumstance, then through Clausewitzian irony, a whole new set of potentially lucrative targets (the nodes of the information space) has been created. The opportunities for fatal counter-measures make the spiking of such data systems especially lucrative.[30]

22. The *way* in which tactical command is exercised is thus also seen to be stressed by the five pressures within the *means* of command. There are three primary expressions of this. The first has already been mentioned: it is the creative tension between 'top down' 'rational choice' command and 'bottom up' RPD modes (see Note 3). The second reflects the first, and is its structural analogue: it is the extent to which decision is centralised or devolved (the Vietnam example). The third describes the consequence of the first two sets of choices made: will the command decision be made with consent or by consensus?

23. If the commander's way of reasoning and communicating intention are not understood by and congruent with subordinates' ways of reasoning, trust may be eroded and wary consent arising from duty rather than consensus may be accompanied by stress that is both unintentional and preventable. Such instances have been studied in analysis of the Gulf War.[31] Plainly, the tactical third dimension mirrors the tensions present in the problems about the *way* of command at the strategic level. Indeed, Professor Glynis Breakwell has suggested that within the functioning of the three levels of command, viewed systemically, an insufficiently understood aspect is the nature and potentially discordant interaction of micro-cultures of command in coalition operations. This issue has obvious salience for DMOs and for anti-terrorist operations, as examples of complex and delicate 'shuttling' actions where perfect internal communication within the Force, and full understanding and internalisation of Commander's Intent, is especially important.

Part III

The nuclear issue in the new era

8 Some pointers towards thinking about the nuclear issue in the new century

If the radiance of a thousand suns
were to burst into the sky
that would be like
the splendour of the Mighty One...
I am become Death, the shatterer of worlds.

Lines from the *Bhagavad Gita* which passed through
Robert Oppenheimer's mind on 16 July 1945
at Alamogordo, New Mexico, while witnessing the
first atomic test

Things that change

During the intervening years, since the collapse of Soviet Commun-ism pronounced the functional end of the twentieth century, the international community has enjoyed the luxury of thinking less about the nuclear issue than it did during the preceding five decades of the Cold War. Now the 'interregnum' is ending – the new era beginning in the minds of many on 11 September 2001, although this book has suggested that the qualitative changes predate the terrorist attack in America – and with it, that luxury. The interregnum is coming – sadly but not unexpectedly – to be seen as a period of lost opportunities. Survey the surface level of conventional politics only that have appeared earlier in this book. The golden moment with Russia was wasted; the European project may be in jeopardy, haemorrhaging from wounds self-inflicted over the Balkans; deluded by the false promise of 'conflict resolution', the Middle East is back at the brink; the Indian sub-continent is firmly, visibly, nuclearised; the crises in west, north-eastern, central and southern Africa do not cease to deepen; Japan stumbles into twilight; Indonesia may fall apart and China may become both politically and culturally more alienated by the manner in which it is being approached by a more truculently unilateralist United States foreign policy. The discovery of a theoretical common cause in opposition to Islamic terrorism may moderate that Chinese alienation, although that is yet to be seen; but the assumption of a new world role by the USA in the fight against terrorism has no effect upon the unilateralist tendency.

It has never been easy to think clearly about nuclear weapons at any time during the history of their existence. No more so now than then. The purpose of this chapter is not to launch substantive arguments about the *pros* and *cons* of the ethical, legal, military and political cases that might be made around the nuclear question in 2002, but to engage principally the logically prior task. The objective is to describe the terrain within which the most important substantive questions in the contemporary hierarchy might stand. This hierarchy is a product of evolution in contemplation of the nuclear issue during the preceding decades. The chapter is therefore mainly about *meta* questions and a necessary precursor to describing the scope of these *meta* questions is to set out the characteristics of thinking in each of the three phases of the nuclear age to date.

The cloud laced with fire which seared the pre-dawn New Mexico sky and all its successors – the two in Japan and then the series of atmospheric tests of the 1950s, their terrible beauty celebrated in the closing sequence of Stanley Kubrik's *Dr Strangelove* – have become emblematic of the dark ambivalence which has enveloped the Enlightenment project of applied science ever since: on the one hand, the 'technological sweetness' of the Manhattan project as a challenge to the intellect; on the other, the words from the *Bhagavad Gita*: and both sets of thoughts flowing through the mind of the same Robert Oppenheimer.

This ambivalence – of creating huge power which seemed somehow to transcend the proper limits of human enterprise – was foremost in many minds that morning. General Farrell famously wrote in his diary 'we puny things are blasphemous to dare tamper with the forces heretofore reserved to the Almighty'. Atomic, and later nuclear weapons, form and inhabit a space of the most stark contrasts. Not only the moral ambivalence, therefore, but also the deep secrecy and invisibility of nuclear weapons and their world had always made the task of thinking about these devices metaphysical – pervasively present, yet functionally invisible. Such unconditionally absolute power as vaporised the two Japanese cities plainly did not fit easily into traditional ways of thinking about military instruments; and so in western thinking the track laid out by Bernard Brodie towards a commensurately unconditional and absolute strategic logic opened up. The perfection of destructiveness could become the surest foundation of perfect peace in a peculiar but inviting paradox which, if accepted, could anaesthetise the moral qualms. Winston Churchill described it: 'a curious paradox has emerged. Let me put it simply. After a certain point has been passed it may be said that "the worse things get the better".... Safety will be the sturdy child of terror, and survival the twin brother of annihilation.'[1]

But the first polarisation about atomic weapons occurred within the Manhattan project before Alamogordo. On the one side, Leo Szilard and those who subscribed to his Memorandum: on the other General Grove and eventually the agreement of the Interim Committee to reject the strategy of a demonstration shot, but instead to recommend use without warning on a Japanese city. From the Szilard Memorandum and the different but associated stand taken by Professor Rotblat through his refusal to continue in the Manhattan project after the German surrender, came views symmetrical in scope to that embodied in the Great Deterrent logic, which Einstein and Russell described in their Declaration as a logic tending towards insanity and likely to be eventually fatal to humanity. To what extent does the representation of the nuclear problem embodied in those counterpoised views still serve, especially after 11 September 2001?

Nuclear weapons exist in the world of 2002 in many ways that are quite different from the world of the early 1950s – the classical 'nuclear moment' of the newly successfully tested thermonuclear device and of Stalin's Soviet Union. Nuclear technology is no longer the acme of the Enlightenment scientific project. In many ways it is old science. The leading edge cursor has moved into tracing the human genome and into the study of global systems dynamics, to take but two contemporary examples. Atomic and nuclear weapons can now be manufactured with relative ease in many shapes and varieties, with tailored yields, such that they can be easily incorporated into the military strategies of certain countries, as usable parts of the arsenal if so wished, although not (yet) by sub-state actors, as the experiences of the Aum Shinrikyo cult showed. So overt and covert proliferation are uncontroversial *faits accomplis*. Their unexpected histories are especially revealing for us now, and are examined shortly.

Second, with the ending of the central superpower confrontation, the nuclear powder trail which led from any regional conflict of importance to the possibility of a central strategic nuclear exchange has been cut (except in the increasingly irrelevant European theatre, where the previous play was staged). The possibility of the use of a nuclear weapon being reflexively and almost unstoppably world-destroying has now been greatly reduced. Or, put the other way round, the possibility that a nuclear next use might occur has probably risen in consequence.

Third, the world-destroying capacity of atomic energy that first blinded and then oppressed the minds of the watchers at Alamogordo in 1945 is no longer unique. Since 1945, humanity has taken steps which may indeed have contributed to the building of a 'doomsday machine'; but it is not Dr Strangelove's. Over the last two decades our discovery of the global systems stresses that result from anthropogenic action is ironic as well as alarming. Alarming because the indicators suggest increasingly that there are fewer negative feedbacks, more positive feedbacks and an earlier likelihood of significant onset from global climate change than was thought even when the Intergovernmental Panel for Climate Change first convened a little over a decade ago. Ironic because the manner in which humanity appears to be producing a serious threat to global security is through unanticipated and unintended synergies between otherwise benign and pacifically-intended actions of self-enrichment. Nuclear weapons fit within this way of framing world threat but incidentally to their formal purpose. Their importance resides principally in the consequences of their manufacture and deployment, of which the most extreme threat lies in the nuclear waste legacy of the Soviet nuclear project of which the outlines were sketched in Chapter 2.

The final dimension of the world in 2002 which is different and important in shaping the way we may think about nuclear weapons now is the consequence of another – indeed, in retrospect, *the* other great legacy of the world war: the modern formulation of human rights. It was inscribed in the preamble to the great institutional hope for the abolition of the scourge of war, namely the United Nations Charter. But as most of this book has been concerned to explain and investigate, it has only really been since the ending of the Cold War that human rights has returned with power to occupy a central position in the global agenda.

Coincident with the impact of the forces of globalisation that have undermined the technical capacity of authoritarian regimes to isolate their people from the rest of the world, the last decade has seen a steady and continuing refocusing away from state's rights and onto individual rights as the index referent. 'Civil society' has blossomed from being a stunted sociological term. It now describes what growing constituencies of politically-active people regard as the primary source of legitimation in public affairs. Civil society is in tension – and often competition – with governments; and, when in collision with them, then possessed of a trumping power. The rising importance attached to individual rights has been a component, along with judgements in international courts, in framing a line of argument whereby an individual can seek to delegitimate a state's possession of nuclear weapons. Two recent cases in the Scottish jurisdiction have seen first a sheriff and then a jury (acting against the judge's instructions) support such an argument to the obvious discomfort of the British government. Both verdicts are currently subject to challenge by the Crown. This is far from the New Mexico desert and the stark clarities evident to the watchers of half a century ago. Yet it is only half the story: for the relationship between the rising consensus on the duty to protect human rights and nuclear weapons in today's world is, as in most issues touched by the atom, deeply and perversely paradoxical.

Phase One

The first phase opened when three ingredients were present. The perfect explosive was one, of course. It became available in July 1945. The second was a perfect enemy. That took longer, but not much; for it was in active preparation, but not revealed, by August 1945. Gar Alparovitz has persuasively shown how deeply the desire to forestall Soviet entry into the Asian war influenced the decision to use the Bomb twice in Japan. Truman's psychological need to have 'a hammer on those boys' was why the Potsdam conference of the Big Three was delayed until Alamogordo had confirmed the Bomb. Nagasaki followed Hiroshima remorselessly to pre-empt the deadline for Soviet entry into the war, which was set to occur on 15 August and was forestalled by the Japanese surrender on 14 August.[2]

The status of the Soviet Union was formalised by George Kennan in the Long Telegram of February 1946, and publicly in the 'Mr X' article ('The sources of Soviet conduct') in *Foreign Affairs* of July 1947. A state that was no state, but a hijack by ideological terrorists; an illegitimate and aggressively expansionist project of world domination, unamenable to normal diplomacy ('there can be no compromise with rival power and the constructive work can only begin when Communist power is dominant...') and susceptible only to containment was, indeed, a perfect enemy in a world of pitchy black and shining light. Pioneering work with the new dark art of opinion polling tracked the speed with which enemy image shifted from

Germans to Russians during 1945–8. The blending together of containment of the perfect enemy with the formal rationale for possession of the perfect explosive was therefore present from the creation; but the third ingredient – product of this cookery – took a little time in the baking. It was perfect mutual misunderstanding of the one atomic 'super' power by the other.

That was no regrettable accident; rather it was a requirement of the circumstance. From the western side, it was a logical necessity, for the Great Deterrent threat to be believable, that one assumed an enemy capable of being deterred: able to understand the threat, to be frightened by it and then to adapt behaviour functionally in direct consequence. These assumptions underlay the celebrated Chiefs of Staff paper of 1952, composed by the great men themselves during a retreat to Greenwich, which underpinned the British strategy to acquire the Bomb. The convolutions of formal western nuclear 'doctrine' (the word itself revealing of the basis in faith of such opinions) were not simply responses to technological possibility, although that played a significant part. Importantly, they were responses to a perceived failure of the perfect enemy to be deterred. In the moves from the Great Deterrent to Mutually Assured Destruction to Flexible Response, to the 'counter-force' targeting strategy of PD-59 in the 1980s, a grasping for credibility that always slipped away, like a will-o'-the-wisp, was to be seen in the spiralling action/reaction of the nuclear arms race (see Figure 8.1).[3]

The meaning of this enterprise has been stated by many analysts, but is in a particularly neat formulation from the pen of Avner Cohen. He explains that the dynamic on the 'justification/escalation' side of Figure 8.1 lies in the tension between what he calls the 'usability problem: the more deterrent-like we make nuclear deterrence, that is, the more "usable" we make the weapons for the sake of the threat's credibility, the more likely it is that the weapons will be used', contrasted to the 'credibility problem: the more we treat nuclear weapons as *sui generis*, that is, as "unusable", the more incredible the threat to use them becomes, and the more likely the threat will fail'.

On the Soviet side, in contrast, the special status accorded to nuclear weapons by western formal strategic doctrine was not present. The figure does not apply and so that sort of dilemma may have been avoided. Stalin and his military saw atomic weapons as bigger, better artillery, and, as such, part of military strategies of astonishing reach and ruthlessness which contained, in the Soviet view, both positive pre-emption and the engendering of the only

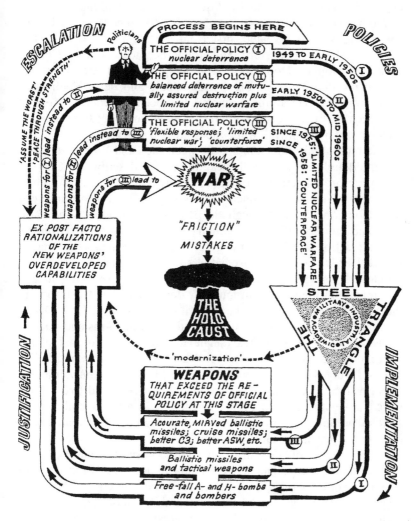

Figure 8.1 The forces involved in the spiralling dynamic of the nuclear arms race on the western side during the Cold War.

effective deterrence – self-deterrence – as a consequence of the speed with which Soviet shock attacks would overrun western territory. Peter Vigor and Christopher Donnelly of the Soviet Studies Centre at the Royal Military Academy, Sandhurst, gave detailed accounts of Soviet *Blitzkrieg* in the 1980s.[4] The concept of regional land and maritime theatres of regional operations (TVD – *teatr voennykh deystvii*) and their exploitation, contained and expressed these objectives. This systematically different way of thinking about the Bomb has been confirmed in detail since 1991, once the actual plans and missions were revealed, first from East German sources. The earlier analyses of western Sovietologists, most notably Charles Dick, Christopher Donnelly, Jacob Kipp, Michael MccGwire (in particular), Phil Petersen, Stephen Shenfield and Peter Vigor were thus vindicated. Yet all these scholars had been regarded as more or less eccentric by the western military establishments at the time; and their cases did not prevail while the Cold War was alive.

The mutual misunderstanding between the Cold War adversaries had the double effect (paradoxical, of course) described in Chapter 2. Misinterpreted actions stoked the enemy images one of the other, and thereby fuelled their nuclear arms efforts. They also reinforced the ideological divide through the *Realpolitik* of military prepara-tions and military alliance. Symmetry in diplomacy was fixed in the action–reaction development of NATO and the Warsaw Pact and of the nuclear weapons and associated strategies, which the two sides developed. As already indicated, these processes were systematically different from the outset but mutually dependent. The frustration in the West that was felt with the passivity inherent in a Great Deter-rent threat coupled with technological drive in the arms and nuclear industries to develop SIOPs (single integrated operational plans) with more and more precise targets: the Implementation and Policy side of Figure 8.1. The trajectory imparted from this contribution to the arms race spiral was such that, as Paul Bracken and Bruce Blair were among the first to argue, fragility in command and control systems became the principal threat that might lead to inadvertent nuclear use during the later Cold War.[5]

An awareness of the dangers of mutual misunderstanding broke in from time to time. The active attempt by Kennedy's ExComm to design a golden bridge over which General Secretary Khruschev might retreat without loss of face, detailed in Chapter 2, was instru-mental in defusing the first of the two great shocks of this phase of the nuclear history. The manner in which a mixture of mutual mis-understanding with quite different philosophies of the military man-agement of nuclear weapons could easily become fatal, was demonstrated during the second shock, the 'Able Archer' incident of November 1983.

The Cuba crisis generated political will to put arms control on the rails and the Partial Test Ban treaty became the progenitor of many children of similar type. In the nuclear area, these have included not only its extension, the Comprehensive Test Ban, but also a raft of more oblique nuclear arms control proposals and measures, such as a Freeze, SALT I and, latterly, behavioural modification that depends on efficient verification.[6] The ingenious programme of seismic verification of the test site at Semipalatinsk, conceived by Tom Cochran of the Natural Resources Defense Council, and others, laid the foundation for currently active arms control measures of similar type, in particular the proposal for de-alerting and for fissile material cut-off. A second line of descent in this genealogy included the Non-Proliferation Treaty, of which more in a moment. But, at this point, it is sufficient to observe that its existence depended upon the inscription of a discriminating principle that protected the declared nuclear status of France and Britain in particular. Neither of the old imperial/new nuclear powers of Europe would have accepted a formula that did not preserve their position; and the implicit hierarchy between mature and responsible and less mature and less responsible societies has rankled from that day to this, most particularly in India.

This abbreviated account of the history of formal nuclear doctrine and actual consequent actions during Phase I illustrates well the duality woven into thinking and possessing nuclear weapons at this time. For the most reliable real effect of their presence was none of the above. Within the superpower confrontation, what may we reasonably believe the role of nuclear weapons to have been? As the late McGeorge Bundy eloquently put it, it was surely to have made already cautious states somewhat more cautious, by virtue of their 'existential' power.[7] In addition to their contribution to the spiral of mutual misunderstanding, nuclear weapons at that time may be thought to have also had a countervailing power: to have conditioned the context within which the politics of confrontation were pursued. Where more was attempted, at Cuba or with 'Able Archer' – and in different ways with each – the world stood in peril. Nor is it clear that the control efforts attempted during this first phase through arms control were ever more than palliative and, as such, may have been worse than useless in that the impression could be gained that an attempt to cap the nuclear problem was being seriously undertaken. That certainly was the view of Alva Myrdal in her angry and accusatory book, *The Game of Disarmament*. In any dialectical contest of strength with the powers of scientific and industrial innovation on both sides and embedded in an ideological dispute that was religious and fundamental in its nature, one could expect little more.[8]

Phase Two

The very first issue to be considered by the newly-convened United Nations in the first meeting of the General Assembly in Church House, London, was that of the internationalisation of nuclear energy. The Baruch Plan scuppered this and, from that moment, anxiety about the proliferation of nuclear weapons into other hands than those of Britain and the United States (who together originally developed them) and then shortly after Kurchatov's work, the Soviet Union, was a continuing worry.

The reasonable expectation was that all those who could acquire atomic and nuclear weapons would. Albert Wohlstetter published famous extrapolating graphs which showed an inexorable upward rise in the number of nuclear weapons-capable and nuclear weapons-possessing states: and Tom Lehrer provided suitably laconic musical accompaniment with his celebrated 'proliferation tango', reaching its logical conclusion ('Let's all stay serene and calm/When Alabama gets the Bomb!'). In fact, France and China were the only overt pro-liferators during the Cold War period and there were far fewer covert proliferators than Wohlstetter's chart predicted.[9]

Some who could proliferate decided fairly publicly that they wouldn't (Canada, Japan – of course – and Sweden). Some who could, did so covertly and then had second thoughts on grounds of marginal cost and utility to their perceived local and regional pur-poses (Argentina and Brazil); another developed a full capacity and then decided voluntarily and still covertly to destroy it when the apartheid regime saw the writing on the wall. It was not prepared to hand over nuclear weapons to the successor South African regime. Accidental nuclear states created by the splintering of the Soviet Union chose to denuclearise. This leaves two other categories of covert proliferators: the regional competitors in the Indian sub-continent and a changing menu of pariah states with Israel as the constant.

Thanks to the magisterial work of George Perkovich, the history of the Indian project is now, for the first time, accessible across its long duration. Perkovich documents how with Nehru's support, Pro-fessor Homi Bhabha set the effort in place only a very little while after the beginning of the nuclear age. He argues that the move from covert to overt status was as much a consequence of a generation of Indian nuclear engineers reaching retirement and therefore pressing for the culmination of their lives' work, as it was of any cerebral or strategic decision.[10] The India–Pakistan story is an especially important source of evidence for the purposes of assessing future trends, and will be returned to for that purpose below; but it is the Israeli project which provides us with the most detailed insight into the strange dynamics of the rise and fall of proliferation during the Cold War. Within a literature that has now become quite extensive, particularly important has been the publication of Avner Cohen's history of the Israeli project (which, in approach and scope has now been paralleled by Perkovich's India study) and the illuminating essays in Louis René Beres' collection entitled *After Armageddon*.[11]

Among nuclear weapons states, Israel has consistently been unique, in that it alone can make a credible threat of nuclear use as part of a military strategy and expect to be believed. Even before the revelations of Mordecai Vanunu kicked in the door to the basement where Israel kept its bomb and allowed everybody to see what was there, the deployment of Hawk missiles during the 1973 war had conveyed a Soviet type of message about what Israel might do in an extreme military reversal. All that the post-Vanunu revelations have added in this regard has been some detail to confirm the existence of an appropriate size and composition of atomic arsenal, including in particular mini-nukes and enhanced radiation devices. But the Israeli example of the seamless integration of nuclear and non-nuclear capabilities into a comprehensive and flexible war plan may have a much wider and deeper significance than for the fifth Arab–Israeli war only. The 2001/2 American Nuclear Posture Review, and associated war plan, show striking conceptual similarities to the Israeli model, as is further explained below.

But in the Middle Eastern neighbourhood arguably, the policy of what Cohen calls 'opaque proliferation' was optimal from Israel's national point of view. It gave the country both existential and counterforce threats, while at the same time preserving a degree of diplomatic manoeuvre, which would be lost once the nuclear capacity was officially declared.

In the context before Vanunu's revelations forced Israel's hand, both Gerald Steinberg and Alan Dowty, writing essays in the Beres book of essays debating Israel's options, conclude that (in Steinberg's words) 'It would appear that on balance and in the current circumstances the costs associated with the abandonment of deliberate ambiguity would not be balanced by the benefits of an overt nuclear posture.'[12] But that option has now been removed and Israel's position is, therefore, much more closely aligned to that of India or Pakistan.

There is, however, one important difference in that Israel's pariah state status means that it has in the past been able to use its nuclear capacity to coerce successfully: to coerce, not its enemies but its friends. There is persistent authoritative assertion that in the tense days after the successful surprise Egyptian crossing of the Suez Canal at the outbreak of the 1973 Yom Kippur war, when Israel's consumption of munitions was at a very high rate and the United States appeared to be dithering about resupply, an Israeli indication of the existence of a 'red line' for the Arab armies played a part in hastening the American decision to strip the arsenals of US forces in Germany of the categories of munition required in order to resupply Israel.

The observation is of more than parochial interest because it underscores (but from a quite different direction of approach) one of the central difficulties about the formal logic of nuclear deterrence, namely the cultural requirement that the party to be deterred should be either in receipt of a message of threat that is entirely understood and accepted within the cultural references of that party, or that the party to be deterred should share sufficiently closely the cultural norms of the party sending the message. The difference between nuclear and non-nuclear deterrence or compellence is straightforward in this regard. The latter can present a credible threat of use that is much less dependent upon the fine-tuning in signalling that must be associated with an instrument that was so much less obviously usable during the Cold War era when it was, by policy and circumstance, locked into a 'ladder of escalation'.

During the Cold War nuclear weapons were called upon to serve a purpose within the principle of deterrence in a classical inter-state system, and to become the principal regulatory mechanism for war prevention within that system. The incoherence which arose in consequence is therefore simply stated. Borrowing Cohen's words again: 'in essence the principle of nuclear deterrence is incoherent for attempting to preserve *both* our pre-nuclear intuitions about politics and war and our post-nuclear understanding.'[13]

Running consistently through the Cold War era of thinking about nuclear weapons, therefore, has been one track of anxiety about efficiency, linked to credibility and another rather different one that was uneasy about the moral implication of threatening indiscriminate destruction even in a good cause. As mentioned above (pp.238–9), such anxieties could be quietened by one of two devices: either by elaboration of a commensurately comprehensive enemy image or by employment of a modified form of General Sherman's logic expressed in his exchange of letters with General Hood, quoted in Chapter 1. This form of moral justification has been important in the western logic of nuclear deterrence during the Cold War.

The uncomfortable juxtaposition of these two types of proposition bumped along in unfriendly companionship from the late 1940s until 8 p.m. Eastern time on 23 March 1983. Ronald Reagan had become increasingly, personally, uncomfortable with the internal contradictions just sketched. Therefore, he delivered the so-called Star Wars speech. In his diary entry for that evening, the President wrote:

> We had a group in for dinner at the White House ... I did the speech from the Oval Office at 8 and then joined the party for coffee. I guess it was OK ... I did the bulk of the speech on why the arms build-up was necessary and then finished with a call to the scientific community to join me in research starting now to develop defensive weapons that would render nuclear weapons obsolete. I made no optimistic forecasts – said it might take 20 years or more but we had to do it. I felt good.

Not everyone felt that way.

In her biography of the President, Frances Fitzgerald describes how several among the dinner guests that evening, who included the Secretary of State, the Joint Chiefs of Staff and Edward Teller, the father of the H-bomb, were pretty much appalled.[14] The reason was not hard to seek because by touching together the two wires between the argument for expediency and the argument from morality, Reagan opened a circuit which, when energised, might lead to the delegitimation of the possession of nuclear weapons in the eyes of democratic public opinion. The shocks continued, with the closest call occurring during the unscheduled afternoon session on Sunday 12 October 1984 at the Reykjavik summit, during which Reagan proposed the abolition of all strategic nuclear weapons.

It is now fairly well-established that the meeting foundered towards 6.30 p.m. over irreconcilable differences about the Strategic Defense Initiative. But it was the manner in which the two Presidents had allowed their fingers to loosen the very roots of formal nuclear deterrence which appalled believers in the status quo. Henry Kissinger had warned in the Press just before the meeting of the danger of letting a President wander into negotiation without a suitable straitjacket. And so it was like an avenging angel that Prime Minister Margaret Thatcher descended upon Washington on Friday 14 November to rail against the proposal to eliminate ballistic missiles and thereby to dismantle extended nuclear deterrence over Europe and, incidentally (for it was logically impossible that it should be otherwise), to abolish the independent British nuclear deterrent without prior consultation.[15]

The Reykjavik summit (described later by Strobe Talbot as 'one of the strangest episodes in the annals of nuclear diplomacy') was intended as a brief and relatively informal meeting to prepare for a forthcoming Washington summit. It capitalised upon the first and most congenial meeting between Reagan and Gorbachev which had taken place during the 'fireside summit' in Geneva. While the Americans went to Iceland with that relaxed aim in mind, the Soviet position, in contrast, was extensively prepared, with defensive briefings of all likely American responses to positions, beforehand. Frances Fitzgerald quotes the President as having said, 'Hell. He [Gorbachev] doesn't want to set up a summit. He wants to have a summit. Right here,' which was quite right.[16]

Yet while most of the western political community took Mrs Thatcher's view and sought in time to regard Reykjavik as a lost weekend, in fact the loosened soil around the roots of formal nuclear deterrence was not reconsolidated during the remaining six years of the Cold War era. Therefore, the importance of Reagan's utterances at face value (and there is no need to engage in the entertaining sport of seeking to deconstruct his real motives) was to advance a 'psychological disarmament' which gained its most forceful expression in the astonishing CFE (Conventional Forces in Europe) Treaty which, in its mutual inspection, monitoring and verifying regimes confirmed in clearest detail the draining of any remaining energy from the Long Telegram's view of the Soviet Union by the time that that enterprise went quietly into oblivion. In so far as nuclear strategy was much discussed (which was little) or defended in the West during those last years of the Soviet Union, it was increasingly through McGeorge Bundy's argument for the existential effect of the existence of the knowledge which could make a nuclear weapon. On the Soviet/Russian side there has been a twist in the tail.

With the abolition of the Soviet Union and its dramatic and terrifying plans for massive military occupation by all means, including nuclear means, at the earliest stage, of the TVDs surrounding its borders, a fundamental change occurred in Russian nuclear thinking. The military establishment of Russia, accepting the gigantic reductions in number and commensurate loss in efficiency of Russia's conventional armed forces, has embraced increasingly a western Cold War view of how nuclear weapons should be viewed. The emphasis on constructing a small but survivable submarine-mounted strategic force is formally justified in contemporary Russian doctrine in terms which are perfectly congruent with western explanations from the earlier era. Risks associated with this force, from accidental launch, can and, one hopes, will be sufficiently addressed by proposals such as Bruce Blair's initiative for mutual de-alerting; and, once these highly practical and more or less immediate steps are taken, the issue of a nuclear threat arising by formal means from the Russian capacity will be even more sharply demoted in the ladder of nuclear-associated risks to global security. The principal risks attached to Russian military nuclear enterprises comes from other parts of the nuclear cycle and are so-called 'legacy' issues, which will return for discussion in the next section.

Phase Three

The third phase in thinking about nuclear weapons – the one in which we now live – opened during 1999. It was precipitated by the NATO intervention into Kosovo and by two aspects especially of this confused and confusing episode. The first was (paradoxically) the clarity with which Prime Minister Tony Blair set out the framework within which he rationalised and justified the operation, in his Chicago speech of 22 April 1999 (more fully discussed in Chapter 5). In particular, within the five criteria which he proposed, it was the third that awakened the nuclear question: 'Do we have a viable military option?' This was quickly translated around the world into the question, 'Why Kosovo? Why not Chechnya?', an issue of selectivity which throbs painfully within the continuing debate about the grounds of intervention to fulfil the responsibility to protect human rights against the actions of pathological governments.

The second aspect of Kosovo delineates the third from the second phase. It was the public assertion in India of the lesson of Kosovo, viewed from the point of view of other countries which might have reason to fear the attention of those prosecuting 'humanitarian intervention'. Plainly, if one wishes to avoid such attentions, the prudent course of action is as quickly as possible to gain overt nuclear status. Therefore, the news late in 2000 that the Russian government might be about to supply the military government of Burma (the SLORC) with a 'research reactor' simply underscores the point being advanced here. It also should warn those western leaders who have become over-enthusiastic about Mr Putin to have a care. A subtext in similar vein which was not articulated by Indian voices, but is certainly heard described as a hypothetical possibility, is that the same results can be achieved by threatening other forms of mass destruction (notably with biological agents), the delivery of which would most likely be by oblique or so-called 'asymmetric' means; although, as discussed in Chapter 3, this is much easier said than done. Giving life to a specific new argument for nuclear status was not an expected outcome of concern for human rights.

Thus we see that at the beginning of the new millennium, the nuclear issue is closely and somewhat surprisingly engaged as one of four points of interaction. They are, respectively, the protection of human rights; the principle of the responsibility to protect citizens' human rights lying upon the international community; conditionality of sovereignty: the degree to which the democratic or undemocratic nature of a regime now qualifies its legitimacy within the international inter-state system; and fourth the possession of covert or overt nuclear capability.

Examining this quadrilateral, six framing observations may be extracted which together project the hierarchy within which substantive questions about the nuclear issue in 2001 may be placed.

When fitted into the kaleidoscope of other anthropogenic threats to global security, the status of nuclear energy as an uniquely potent threat to human survival continues to blur. Indeed, looking only a short distance into the future, it is possible that, despite the generally failed promise of huge investment over decades in fast breeder and fusion routes to electricity generation, we may nevertheless be on the verge of a renaissance in nuclear electricity generation.

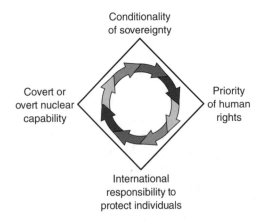

Figure 8.2 The new nuclear points of intersection.

Early in the UK Ministry of Defence's February 2001 description of the strategic context of British security, it is noted that Britain will soon face a severe problem of oil and gas supply (90 per cent dependent on imports within fifteen years), given the rapid dwindling of North Sea reserves.[17] Add to this the approaching block obsolescence of France's first generation reactors, the increasingly strong evidence for the positive feedback of the carbon cycle in accelerated global warming and the absence of other near-term base load electricity generating technologies (in no small part a consequence of opportunity/cost starvation of research in renewables), and one can hypothesise another development, namely a blunting of the sharply anti-nuclear sentiment that has percolated much of western public opinion for the last twenty-five years. Already more or less uncontroversially embedded in the post-Soviet space, the threat of global climate change may yet force western societies to love the atom, reluctantly.

The Brahimi report, arising from the crisis in UN peacekeeping operations during the later 1990s, recommended that in future the role of the UN should be the production of mandate and not the technical control of military forces required for peace enforcement and other types of diplomatic/military operation. The virtue, or otherwise, of the recommendation was discussed earlier: what is important for this chapter is the way in which the drift of analysis in the Brahimi report sustains a view which may be drawn from other evidence also: we enter the twenty-first century with a generalised retreat from multilateral executive agency in international affairs. An interesting precursor illustration of this point came with the manner in which European states chose to address the threat of mad cow disease (bovine spongiform encephalopathy). To the evident dismay of EU officials, states reverted to the national level as the source of primary action. Simultaneously, the same group of the richest and most powerful states is the same which has felt the need to sanction interventions other than through a direct mandate of the UN Security Council. The Kosovo episode was the most recent and still contentious example of this.

Third, and led by the United States, there is a clear public intention to bear down upon non-democratic states possessing or threatening to possess nuclear technology, other technologies of mass destruction and associated ballistic and other delivery systems. The rather odd history of engagement with North Korea during the last two years of the second Clinton Administration and the associated and continuing story of National Missile Defense come most particularly to mind.[18] But it was part of the continuing process of non-negotiated unproliferation which had seen the abandonment of nuclear weapons capabilities by South Africa, South Korea, Taiwan, Byelorus, Kazakhstan and Ukraine, all following the precedent set in Latin America by Argentina and Brazil.

But the crux of the world's nuclear future at the opening of the twenty-first century is to be found in the nuclear plans and strategic ambitions of only one country, of course: the United States. These plans are expressed in three forms: the Single Integrated Operational Plan (SIOP), which is a deeply-guarded secret, but whose broad characteristics have been deduced by non-governmental experts;[19] the Nuclear Posture Review (NPR) of January 2002, details of which have been released more extensively, and the declared weapons and infrastructure to support these.[20]

The NRDC study suggests that the most current presidential guidance for the 2001 SIOP was President Clinton's Presidential Decision Directive 60 (PDD-60) of November 1997. While removing all reference to an ability to wage protracted war successfully (which had been a theme of President Reagan's National Security Decision Directive 13 of 1981), PDD-60 nonetheless 'calls for the U.S. warplanners to retain long-standing options for nuclear strikes against military and civilian leadership and nuclear forces . . .'[21]

President George W. Bush's directions, as related in the Pentagon briefing of 9 January, amplify that theme and deserve to be quoted fully:

> we are trying to encourage a positive relationship with Russia. And we believe that we can do that by establishing a new framework of relations that sets aside the sort of Cold War hostilities, in particular the idea of ending the relationship with Russia that is based on mutual assured destruction. This seems to be a very inappropriate relationship given the kinds of co-operation, for example, that have been evinced in the last few months in the campaign against global terrorism.
>
> We also underscored the fact that the Cold War approach to deterrence, which was highly dependent upon offensive nuclear weapons, is no longer appropriate, which is not to say that we think that nuclear weapons don't continue to play a role in that. We think they play an important role, a fundamental role. But we also believe that other kinds of capabilities will be needed in the future.
>
> The other thing the President gave us, obviously, was to try

to develop a framework in which we were able to reduce to the lowest number of operationally deployed nuclear weapons ... And additionally, we are trying to achieve these reductions without having to wait for Cold War arms-control treaties, and placing greater emphasis both on missile defense capabilities and also on the development of advanced conventional capabilities.[22]

Three features of this reported new presidential direction are noteworthy and helpful in seeking to understand what is actually going on, and what may be planned: the reliance on new high technology, both nuclear and non-nuclear, to provide new 'options'; the restatement that nuclear weapons remain 'fundamental' and the expressed desire and willingness to effect this transition from present to future force posture without negotiation with, or possibly even reference to, other states' parties. Later in the briefing, this is represented as a

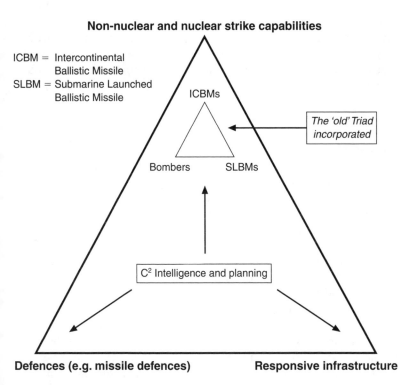

Non-nuclear and nuclear strike capabilities

ICBM = Intercontinental
Ballistic Missile
SLBM = Submarine Launched
Ballistic Missile

ICBMs

Bombers   SLBMs

The 'old' Triad incorporated

C² Intelligence and planning

Defences (e.g. missile defences)   **Responsive infrastructure**

Figure 8.3 The new triad.

'journey' from the old 'strategic triad' (of land, sea and air-based strategic nuclear weapons) to a 'new triad', which, as the figure reproduced from the briefing shows, absorbs the old. How should we interpret this? Both culturally and materially.

There are four vital cultural messages in the briefing on the NPR. The first is confirmation of the abiding American faith in the ability of high technological innovation to offer an escape from difficult moral and political dilemmas. President Reagan's discomfort, which he resolved in his speech and his diary on 23 March 1983, reverberates through the commitment to missile defence technology development. However, at the same time, the commitment to the 'fundamental' role of nuclear weapons is reaffirmed, but now in the context of a drive towards usability, not deterrence. Third, this reflects that eagerness to preserve and to extend 'options' that was most recently affirmed in the Quadrennial Defense Review of September 2001, which stated that a spectrum of capability was required to 'assure allies and friends', to 'dissuade competitors', to 'deter aggressors' and to 'defeat enemies'. Finally, the NPR is predicated upon a quiet but firm rejection of constraint of action by any entangling alliances or treaties. This includes, most particularly, a refusal to be limited by the Cold War era nuclear arms control treaties (while, at the same time, asserting that limits would be *voluntarily* observed) and, likewise, the Comprehensive Test Ban.

Wariness about agreeing to any constraint upon independent American action permeates the doctrine. It is the analogue of its political purpose which is – in the precise descriptive sense of the word – imperial in intention. For this strategy is intended to deter or to destroy the nuclear, biological or chemical warfare capacities of others by all necessary means, including nuclear attack: to force less nuclear and biological threat to the USA by provision of new types, and scarcely any fewer numbers, of US nuclear means to threaten or to attack others.

This is not immediately apparent, since both the publicly stated presidential directions and the figures given of operationally deployed nuclear weapons suggest a planned and gradual reduction from the 6000 weapons of 2002 under the START I terms (which are being voluntarily observed) to 1700–2200 operationally deployed strategic nuclear weapons by 2012. To achieve this, four ballistic missile-carrying Trident submarines (USSs *Ohio, Michigan, Florida* and *Georgia*) will be converted to carry 154 conventionally-armed Cruise missiles each; the MX/Peacekeeper ICBM will be deactivated and the requirement that the B-1B heavy bomber have a nuclear role will be removed.

The picture is clouded by adoption of a new terminology. First, a distinction is made between *active* and *inactive* warheads. The former have limited life components, such as tritium, installed; the latter do not.[23] The NRDC estimates that there are 8000 active and 2700 inactive warheads in the stockpile in 2002. The active inventory is now further sub-divided into *operationally-deployed* warheads, so called 'responsive force' warheads and spares. Responsive force warheads are active warheads, not fitted to delivery vehicles, but held in secure storage from which they can be returned to service in days, weeks, months or longer, depending upon the particular system. Spare active warheads are thought to compose 5 to 10 per cent of the total of operational warheads. Under the SALT/START counting rules, only *operationally deployed strategic* warheads are counted. Dr Stan Norris, the NRDC's nuclear weapons expert, calculates that the actual total stockpile consisted of 10,656 intact warheads in all categories in January 2002, that it will be 10,590 in 2006 and 9908 in 2012.[24] Whereas the numbers in the 'operational' category may fall, those in the 'responsive force' and 'spare' categories may grow. The end result is little change.

Nor is that all. The NPR briefing announces a requirement for new *types* of nuclear weapon, especially those capable of penetrating deep underground before detonating, to destroy 'hardened and deeply buried targets'. To do this, the entire American nuclear weapons infrastructure is to be reanimated. Advanced warhead design teams are to be re-established at the Los Alamos, Sandia and Lawrence Livermore National Laboratories; the capacity of the Pantex weapons assembly/disassembly plant at Amarillo, Texas, is to be doubled, and new nuclear component manufacturing capacity is to be built; new tritium and enriched uranium production capacity is to be constructed (the former to be active by 2003), and the Nevada test site is to be refurbished by 'replacing underground test-unique components' in case a decision is made to recommence testing.

In congressional testimony on Thursday 14 February 2002, John A. Gordon, Head of the Department of Energy's National Nuclear Security Administration, confirmed all this in more detail. In particular, he stated that the bunker-busting warhead designs would proceed to component and sub-assembly tests. The full NPR report, seen and quoted in the *New York Times* by Michael R. Gordon, apparently underscored this: 'While the United States will make every effort to maintain the nuclear stockpile without additional nuclear testing, this may not be possible in the indefinite future.'[25] At the same time, the pace of development of anti-ballistic missile defences will be maintained.

The thrust of the policy is to build both strategies and a nuclear arsenal that are seamlessly integrated into war-fighting plans that may include (in the NPR's words quoted by Michael Gordon) 'an Iraqi attack on Israel or its neighbours, or a North Korean attack on South Korea, or a military confrontation over the status of Taiwan.' Nuclear attack on terrorist facilities where weapons of mass destruction may be being fabricated is to be contemplated. This all looks very much like what is known of Israeli nuclear strategies and stockpiles.

Yet, while one can understand how the Israeli example might appeal to American weapons designers and tactical war planners, the fundamental difference in their effect upon global security of Israel developing an integrated nuclear and non-nuclear warfighting capacity for its tough neighbourhood and the United States doing so, should be evident to those with strategic and grand strategic responsibilities in the White House and President Bush's close circle. Yet the evidence of the Nuclear Posture Review, as it dribbles into public view, suggests that this is not so. So the Kosovo selectivity question, discussed on page 251, returns with redoubled force; and potentially – ironically – American options for shaping global politics are prematurely foreclosed.

The success up to now of unproliferation with non-democratic or quasi-democratic states thus stands in increasingly clear contrast to the situation with seven of the eight recognised and threshold nuclear weapons states which are democracies: the United States, the United Kingdom, France, Russia, India, Israel and Pakistan.

In all of these, the case for nuclear possession is known to, and by and large approved by, the public. Perkovich judges that, in the Indian case, 'To constrain or abandon these capabilities would be to give up something of perceived value. Democracy means that decisions to do so must be popularly supported.' In none of these states can one see the likely emergence of prevailing majority constituencies for that action. Indeed, as Perkovich further observes, among this group of states, the problem may be *more* likely to be ventilated in India than in any of the others. The reason for this is that the twin objectives of Indian foreign policy since independence have been, on the one hand, attainment and general acceptance of

India's global role and, on the other, the assertion of Indian moral superiority to its colonial past and previous masters. In the case of the longstanding nuclear powers, Perkovich observes that they, 'See their nuclear arsenals as measures and guarantees of their global status. Indeed, the UK, France and Russia now cling to nuclear weapons as arguably the last vestiges of this status. These states may require greater adjustments to prepare themselves to undertake their non-proliferation commitments to roll back their own nuclear arsenals.'[26] The fact that suspension of the sanctions imposed on Pakistan following the nuclear tests was one of the rewards that General Musharraf received for his support of the hunt for Osama bin Laden served only to underline the normalisation of nuclear possession, which both India and Pakistan desired. This comment frames importantly the third of the principal questions attaching to the nuclear issue in the new era, exposed in the final section below (pp. 000–000).

The Nuclear Posture Review provides the conceptual matrix and describes the material infrastructure that will support future American military responses to a world that includes Osama bin Laden and his like; and, as has been documented, it is less of a break with the past thinking and practice than has been represented superficially. Therefore, it is not surprising to see considerable carry-over from nuclear phases One and Two. Again, one sees the spiralling dynamics of Figure 8.1, with different new warheads and weapons designs about to emerge from the Steel Triangle. And, especially, we see the beginning of a transfer of Cold War nuclear deterrence by Mutually Assured Destruction, from Russia to China.

In a speech given in Arlington, Virginia, on her birthday (16 November 2000), Dr Condoleezza Rice set out important parts of her vision for the incoming Bush Administration's approach to global politics. In particular, she distinguished between the problem of dealing with what she called rising and falling powers. America's approach to China, as a rising power, composes the fifth observation, and to Russia, as a falling power, the sixth.

Within the strategic studies community, it is fairly widely accepted that there are three most likely contexts within which nuclear next use might occur. The Middle East and Indo-Pakistan confrontations are two, but the third is the one in which the United States is most intimately involved. This is the dispute with mainland China over the future status of Taiwan as an island state whose people have expressed their views about their future through some form of democratic process. The Chinese missile test over the island; the forward deployment of US aircraft carriers in the proximate area; the development of a suite of ballistic missile interception technologies, notably in this respect the Aegis cruiser-based Naval Theatre Missile (NTM) system; the associated rising rhetoric on both the Chinese and American sides with regard to the Taiwan situation are all ingredients which seem to be composing a new context for formal strategic nuclear deterrence in the twenty-first century. The appointment of Mr Andy Marshall, long known for his suspicion of Communist China, to the fundamental review of American strategic priorities may have particular importance in this connection and that review lead to a further crystallisation of the China scenario as a primary planning criterion for US force sizing and shaping in the near future. Whether the adoption of the anti-terrorism mission will disturb this is not evident as this book goes to press; but given the structural momentum of force structures, it is not to be assumed that it will.

In contrast, the management of Russia, as a declining power in Dr Rice's account of the contemporary strategic world, comes to focus increasingly on the threat of nuclear theft and of radioactive contamination latent in the vast and ill-maintained nuclear infrastructure inherited from the Soviet military nuclear project. There is engagement from outside powers, notably the American construction of the Mayak waste fuel repository. Other countries with advanced nuclear technological expertise, notably Finland (her next-door-neighbour), the other Scandinavian countries, France and the United Kingdom, are seeking to find ways to help Russia mitigate and eventually neutralise these latest threats. France has taken on the task of managing the most dangerous of the Soviet navy's nuclear fuel tenders, the *Lepse*. The United Kingdom has announced an £84 million programme, but, at the time of writing, awaits assurances that British engineers will be permitted to work side-by-side with Russian engineers on all these projects. This is because, on past evidence, it is unwise to fund projects in Russia unless personnel from the donor country are actively involved in the execution of the work. If they are not, the likelihood is that the work will not be done and the money will disappear unaccountably, as has happened with both Norwegian national and European Union funding in this vital area.

However, Mr Putin's brilliantly adroit exploitation of the situation after 11 September 2001 to Russia's advantage may well reanimate this quiescent relationship. Putin had four clear goals to secure by collaboration with the anti-terrorism coalition: deflection of western criticism of his handling of the Chechen rebels was obviously one. So too the opportunity to settle scores in Afghanistan, a second. But a third could be discerned: the chance after a successful collaboration with real forces and real intelligence against a real and unpleasant enemy to return with politeness and warmth to the suggestion that a heavy investment in missile defence might not be cost effective – and in any case it would carry problems for the newly found amity. Fourth, the opportunity to make a strategic partnership of some substance with NATO instead of the thin and sour thing which was the NATO–Russia Permanent Joint Committee would give Putin some unexpected and welcome latitude in managing his most important bilateral relationship, that with Germany.

A new hierarchy of questions about the nuclear issue

This review of the way in which thinking about the nuclear issue has developed through the three phases of the nuclear age has shown that one conclusion at least may be drawn with confidence. The analysis and resultant hierarchy of issues at the beginning of the atomic age no longer serve efficiently.

What then are the questions which seem to press themselves to the top of the hierarchy today? From the foregoing account, five stand forward:

1 The erosion of the morally-exceptional case, both by the emergence of other anthropogenic threats of mass destruction and by the delegitimation of deterrent or compellent threats of mass destruction, as a consequence of the advance of human rights in international and national jurisdictions, has a double-edged effect. Important struts are knocked out from under both the Great Deterrent defence of nuclear possession (as advanced most eloquently by Sir Michael Quinlan), and from the abolition case which rests upon the impossibility of meeting the Just War criterion of proportionality.[27] Therefore, what *type* of ethical arguments and what *specific* ethical arguments, both for possession and for abolition of nuclear weapons, may now be made? This is both an ethical and, by extension, eventually legal question.

2 With the retreat of international institutions, the return to the state in many areas of global international intercourse and the abolition of the Cold War contexts within which the mechanisms of summitry and superpower arms control were formed, the forum of 'classical' arms control between blocs, negotiated in sequences of 'summits', has become dilapidated. Therefore, what

agents and what *process of engagement* should be privileged? Will we see a return to lonely states caught in a web of sequential power political confrontations and concessions, for example? This is a utilitarian question.

3   Within the quadrilateral between the nuclear issue; the legitimation of sovereignty by democratic mandate; the rise of human rights in the international system and the growing willingness to contemplate intervention in execution of the responsibility to protect human rights, how is the problem of unproliferation by democracies to be tackled, given that democracies, and especially the United States, as the 2002 Nuclear Posture Review reveals are demonstrably more recalcitrant than authoritarian regimes in this regard? One hastens to add Perkovich's rider that 'these observations and propositions regarding democracy and unproliferation are not meant to disparage democracy or recommend authoritarianism. Rather, they are to suggest further research into the ways in which democracy affects nuclear policy-making.' This is a question about the fundamentals of democratic practice and the role of the philosopher-kings for which a starting point is to be found in Book X of Plato's *Republic.*

4   If the Sino-American disagreement over Taiwan is, as appears, coming to be expressed in terms of military and nuclear confrontation, *in what practical ways* does this new strategic nuclear confrontation differ from the previous Soviet–American one, and *in what conceptual ways* is it to be interpreted – ways analogous to the manner in which Phase I of the Soviet–American confrontation was expressed and explained above (p.241)? This is a new question.

5   In light of the previous questions, is it possible to disentangle the nuclear issue from the other three points of the quadrilateral?

Conclusion

Threads and bearings

Threads

What pattern and what strength of fabric can be woven from the threads that have been spun in this book?

At first glance, the dominant impression is of the fragility of the fabric of civil society as we enter the twenty-first century. The contrast between regions of sanctuary and regions of strife is brutally and often bloodily delineated. Once again, the *Limitanie* – the border guards of the Roman Empire – stand at their ancient posts on the Danube bend. Nor is the analogy unintended or inapposite. For ours, too, is an imperial era and will be for the foreseeable future. One historical thread of this work has been to document those aspects of the recent past from which the United States has emerged as modern hegemon.

In discussing this central aspect of modern international politics, the book has had little patience for *marxisante* reflex protests of much of the European Left. One of the most instructive aspects of the response to the terrorist attacks of 11 September was to observe the swift, almost instinctive turning westwards of both the British political class and people. The emblematic moment of this was when the Queen ordered that the Band of the Household Division play the American national anthem on the forecourt of Buckingham Palace during the Changing of the Guard – a gesture which produced huge resonance in the United States and cemented further the cultural as well as political unity of the Anglo-American relationship. In contrast, whereas peoples in Europe undertook spontaneous street demonstrations, notably in Berlin, the immediate reaction of much of the political class and the media, expressed in European newspapers, was a barely concealed *Schadenfreude*: the Americans were overbearing and they had this coming.

The reason for my impatience with such views is not that the United States is innocent now of all wrongdoing any more than it has been in the past. The greatest mistake in the strategy of the response to the terrorist attacks of September 2001 was President Bush's announcement of the establishment of military tribunals to try (and possibly execute) captured al-Qae'da suspects.[1] The dreadful mistake of the Vietnam war has been paid for with damaged lives and anguished consciences of a generation of young Americans. It is well-established that the degree of psychological breakdown which soldiers experience in and after warfare (afterwards in the form of post-traumatic stress) is directly correlated to the degree to which they believe themselves to be supported by the society for which they fight and the degree to which they can believe wholeheartedly in the justice of their cause.[2] What seems to have been lost on many critics is that the grim, double-edged history of the Americans in Vietnam – what they did to the Vietnamese and what the experience did to themselves – reflects to the credit of the society. For when the chips are down, the United States is not and never has been an imperial hegemon, which engages in democidal or genocidal slaughter of its own people. Its imperial record from the time of Teddy Roosevelt and the Rough Riders through the support of a train of unsavoury South American dictatorships, including the infamous involvement in the overthrow of the Allende regime in Chile and the installation of the military junta of General Pinochet, still does not compose, in the scales of history, the very worst of crimes. And in the other scale is to be found a bundle of American values and American products, which the later twentieth century demonstrated to decisive effect was irresistible to most other peoples, who aspired to have them.

That second bundle includes what is now one of the oldest operating constitutions, whose remarkable drafting, skilful and continuous reinterpretation in the courts, has put the United States in an unusually congenial position to embark upon its era of imperial rule. For, as has been remarked several times in the foregoing pages, the United States alone operates a pre-French Revolutionary constitution, which therefore embodies those elements which we are now striving to accommodate afresh in the recasting of the social contract in most other societies. But this is to run ahead of ourselves.

The American half-century so far, since the end of the World War, has pitched the world's economy decisively into a mode of globalised liberal capitalism. This much was understood by Abel

Aganbenyan and others in the close circle advising Mikhael Gorbachev from the early 1980s. It was understood by the gerontocracy in the Chinese politburo who, looking with horrified eyes upon the failure of Gorbachev to hand power down from the apex to the people, decided resolutely upon the reverse course of action: to liberalise the economy and later (perhaps much later) to contemplate reforms in democracy and the personal liberties of the citizen. It has been argued that the source of many, perhaps most, of the jagged shards of fractured identities, which are the cutting edge of indiscriminate violence in the re-animated medieval forms of war to which we have returned after closing down the genuinely new industrial wars of the late nineteenth and twentieth centuries, have been a product in dialectical reaction to the forces of American-driven globalisation.

What does this tell us? Surely that the United States has, for its imperial era, a moral imperative to answer? The moral case for high-minded British imperialists of the late nineteenth century was one of advancing the heathen and uncivilised masses of brown and black peoples: what Kipling called the 'white man's burden'. The American responsibility at the threshold of the twenty-first century is not to shirk its obligation to play a role, which it alone has the financial, economic and military power fully to execute, in sustaining the international community as it comes to terms with shouldering the responsibility of virtuous intervention in protection of human rights.

All trends and themes have been seen to be the products of the influence of 'deep history'. Even in times and circumstances where people have forgotten (or appeared to forget) the times and experiences which shaped their social identities, those influences have nonetheless shaped them. So a strong thread in this work has been to insist upon the responsibility to uncover and to trace the pathways of those historical roots. In the terms made famous by Fernand Braudel, and stated in the Introduction, the rapid oscillations of event history can rarely be satisfactorily explained in their own terms. Only when we have demonstrated that, at the very least, we have checked for the influence of trends (*histoire de la conjoncture*) and of the long term may we responsibly invite the reader to take our opinions on short-term events seriously. Throughout this book an attempt has been made always to follow that advice. The most overt demonstration of the technique was made in the case study on strategic raiding in Chapter 6.

The story of virtuous intervention in West Africa in 2000 was also used to strengthen another thread that has run throughout this work. The preoccupation with 'deep history' applies not only to the world of the Other. Sun Tzu's advice had two parts. Looking at ourselves as children of the Enlightenment, the inheritance is somewhat mixed. With John Gray, this book shares a sense of sadness at the extent to which the mismanagement of the forces of globalisation has, in many and insidious ways, undercut the potential for a robust and exportable universal liberal political economy. That has been the ironic consequence of the success of the American global economic project. What has amplified such negativity of consequence has been the manner in which those forces of globalisation have interacted with a political world of nation states. The relentless erosion of sovereignty in fact and the more recent and courageous decision to begin to negotiate the consequences of that erosion in political theory and international constitutional practice, compose another of the strong and more colourful threads in the piece.

Much of that colour is owed to the good fortune that in our own past we can recover and renovate important, relevant and subtle sources of thought.

Two eighteenth-century thinkers in particular have visited these pages (as a quick scan of the index will reveal). The study of operations in West Africa began by advancing the case for a full re-examination of all aspects of the thinking of Karl von Clausewitz. In particular, it was argued that, until recently, analysts and practitioners had focused upon only two of the three modes of warfare, which Clausewitz described. The evidence of the recent past is that the leading edge of effect in the use of military force is more often psychological than directly physical. And so Clausewitz's return to relevance is another of the threads.

So too – most extensively in the later part of Chapter 4 – is the case for the reinterpretation of the political writings of Immanuel Kant. The value of his concept of hospitality as the pivot of cosmopolitanism was embraced and it was shown how well this unostentatious approach to the exercise of obligation in the twenty-first century might work. For linked to the thread of transformation in the status and potentials of state power has been the need to renovate and then promote an understanding of how, in practical terms, one can give meaning and effect to the exercise of duty towards distant strangers who have either no rights, which they could claim, nor standing, which we might recognise as relevant in the language of rights. The strength of Kant for the twenty-first century is that his approach to political power and moral responsibility is designed to operate in a far less loosely-structured world than that of the 'long twentieth century', which began in 1789 and ended in 1989.

The third strand of eighteenth-century experience, which has also been a thread running through this work, has been a belief that we are now in a position to give a less tentative answer than Chou en Lai gave to the question, 'What do you think of the French Revolution?' We can now see that the revolutionary route to the righting of wrongs has been, on all major attempts, a failure. Revolutions have voraciously eaten their own children. The key histories of the last 200 years for our purposes have not been how revolutions came about but how, with more or less civility, peoples have escaped from their revolutionary experiences. The most successful have been those whose revolutions did not, at the outset, interfere with patterns of property. The bloodiest have been those which sought to impose collective ownership and behaviour on *kulak* or peasant populations. Barrington Moore Jnr's general thesis seems to be well-confirmed.[3]

Our intimate relationships with war led humanity close to the brink of catastrophe several times during the last century. Therefore, a further thread in our account has been to stress that, amazingly, on the threshold of the new millennium, humanity has received a reprieve and been given another chance. And just in time too. For another thread in the work has been to identify a range of new threats to humanity as a whole, which seem to be approaching swiftly.

Framing most of these is the growing precision of our understanding of the systemic changes to the global climate. Whilst no direct causal read-off is safe as a basis for security planning – water shortage does not automatically imply water wars – nonetheless, the evidence of what contributes to anthropogenic climate change is both instructive and alarming. For the common feature is precisely the *absence* of direct causal effect. Mostly we are confronted with an analytic task of great complexity, which is characterised by unexpected and often bizarre synergistic effects. Sensitisation to such interactions was the principal contribution of James Lovelock and his immensely influential 'Gaia' hypothesis.

What the global climate modelling, led by the Hadley Centre of the UK Meteorological Office, shows is how a sequence of apparently innocuous trends can build into a 'risk cascade'. The avoidance of risk cascades which can lead to irretrievable breakdown of natural processes is a theme not confined to the natural world alone. It is a further thread running through this work. The history of our near escapes, particularly in the nuclear era of the superpowers, provides lurid confirmation of the way in which a chain of small miscalculations or misperceptions can escalate into a cascade, the result of which is a danger far greater than the sum of the component parts of the process which brought us there. In the case of the Cuban crisis, we were saved from the precipice by self-conscious psychological management of the crisis by President Kennedy and the Ex-Comm. In the Able Archer episode twenty years later, the danger was arguably greater because there was no self-conscious awareness of the risks being run; so luck played a greater part.

The aftermath of 11 September 2001 provides an excellent laboratory in which we can assess the relative strengths and weaknesses of crisis management; but that is merely the most recent example of an increasing vulnerability in the conduct of modern international affairs.

So what should we make of the fabric of our many threads? Some of the threads are vibrant and strong. Some of them are very old. Some placed in contact with others do not produce strength but weakness. So the fabric of our future contains areas of fragility as well as an underlying structure of historical depth and robustness. Some things change, to be sure: but for an historian, it is those things which do not change that are far more interesting and often difficult to explain: for changelessness in human affairs is not to be equated with the motionlessness of a stone in the bottom of a pond. Passive, inert, it lies there until some energy is imparted to it from an external source to make it do otherwise. Not so in human affairs where changelessness is the product of constant social reproduction. It is motionless in the way that a ball, balanced on the top of a jet of water from a garden hose, is motionless in space, yet only remains there because of the constant infusion of energy from the water jet. Such 'dynamic stillness' is, as the analogy suggests, particularly prone to sudden collapse – switch off the water or flick the ball. This is the picture of the world of war that is woven into our fabric.

Bearings

What of the pattern in the fabric? Like the knotted star-maps of Polynesian oceanic navigators in the Pacific, the threads in our story can be used as a guide from which we may take bearings with which to navigate into an uncertain and inadequately charted future.

This book has emphasised the importance of five objectives upon which we would be wise to take bearings. The first two chart a channel in safe waters; the other three give us warning of shipwreck-ing obstacles ahead.

The first bearing upon which we shall steer, upon which indeed we already are set, is defined by transformation in the pattern of politi-cal and social agency. The rise and rise of human rights; the reorien-tation of political priorities upon individual in contrast to state rights; the withdrawal of public participation from the exercise of mass democracy in the formal electoral sense; the privatisation of hope and the associated atrophy in the nineteenth-century political lan-guage of optimism about the beneficial exercise of state power in the public good all contribute on the negative side. But, simultaneously with that disintegration of the old way of expressing social responsi-bility, comes the tightening of others.

Two noteworthy trends are the successful application of consumer pressure and the leverage power of interest groups to the dominant agents in the international political economy of a globalised world, namely transnational and multinational commercial companies. The political analogue, seen since the ending of the Soviet Union, has been the way in which states have sought to amplify their political effect in international affairs through coalitions and alliances bro-kered by and authorised through the United Nations. It is only a seeming paradox that the reinvigoration of the United Nations in its originally intended role as arbiter of international security has, during the tenure of Secretary-General Kofi Annan, depended upon the willingness simultaneously, but for widely various reasons, of the dominant states to work actively through these channels. For several years, the most significant recidivist was the United States. But its record in the manufacture of mandate and the conduct of operations of humanitarian intervention has been no less dishonourable than that of other Permanent Members of the Security Council. So this is a direction which is open for further exploration.

So too is the second. This book has attempted to plant a flag for the practical value of Immanuel Kant's approach to the problem of obligation in a loosely-structured world. Whereas the principle of hospitality provides a beginning, and can be seen already well-entrenched in the philosophy of the Universal Declaration of Human Rights, it is not an end. In pursuit of that end, we must prepare for times when we have to accept second-best solutions. What those may be and how we may ensure that temporary acceptance of a second-best solution does not distort our perspective of what the kingdom of ends is, or curtail our quest, is a difficult and important task for prac-tical political philosophy early in the new millennium.

Both these bearings on the deep-water channel must be maintained while ensuring that we avoid three types of peril.

The first resides in one of the most important paradoxes about the transformation of state power in late modernity. Whereas it is hollowed out in the social sphere (which therefore becomes continuously more vexing and intractable for politicians), through the rise of the human rights agenda, the associated conditionality of sovereignty and the indispensability of the state as prime provider of military and associated financial means, the power of the state grows stronger in the brokerage of international affairs. Therefore, the insights of classical 'Realism' are perfectly adequate when we map the very slow and buffered dynamics of change at the deepest levels of inter-state and interregional confrontation and interests. The book observes that in the next generation or so there is a lively possibility that a return to energy conflicts may sharpen those traditional conflicts of interest, even within such regions as western Europe. The tectonic plates of an international system, in which principally the United States and China are candidates for long-term confrontation, push up jagged underwater rocks upon which we must keep our eye. So too, and part of the same brief, the possibility that such confrontations become even more dangerous under the influence of gross stereotyping. The possibility that Professor Samuel Huntingdon's views of the Islamic world could become a self-fulfilling prophesy is one of the most potentially calamitous consequences that could flow from the activities of al-Qae'da, giving it and its leader most probably posthumous satisfaction of success.

A further shallowly submerged reef which threatens us, and upon which we must keep a close watch, is the rise of unconditional terror. The danger here, this book has suggested, is not necessarily the one that common sense might immediately suggest. Statistically, the ability of sub-state terror to inflict substantial physical destruction is probably fairly limited. It is certainly limited when compared to the destructive potentials of states, especially pathological states committing democide. The danger lies in becoming too narrowly focused with this type of threat to the exclusion of others. This could produce a skewing of analytic effort and that can result in the presence of dangerous blind spots. Furthermore, if associated to this is a disproportionate skewing of resources in the security field, the danger may be compounded. That is especially because it could be the cause of distraction from addressing the roots of structural violence in the poor world. This observation is not to be equated with the commonplace, which sees unconditional terrorism as being in some way a sort of lineal and almost automatic consequence of the existence of structural violence. That is not to rule out the possibility that it may be, but it is also to recollect that the most frequent victim of the violence produced by poverty and injustice are created when violence turns in upon the poor themselves.

The fifth shoal which threatens shipwreck is the one discussed in the last chapter. The return of nuclear weapons to contention is occurring in a context that is substantially different from that into which they were first introduced. The possibility of next use is arguably closer than it has been at any time in the sixty years of the nuclear age so far. The point has been underscored for the public in the context of the most recent crisis between India and Pakistan over Kashmir and in the approach of the fifth Arab–Israeli war. Yet among the threats to human security, which may be anticipated for the twenty-first century, it is also possible that the nuclear threat arising from deliberate use will pose one of the lesser order dangers when taken in isolation, although made all the more powerful when part of the risk cascade.

When all is said and done (and in this book it now is), the charts we have are little more accurate than first approximations; perhaps not even as accurate as the knotted constellation maps of the Polynesians. Therefore, the final admonition must be a warning against placing too much faith in any one navigator. Of all Immanuel Kant's words of advice, those which above all must be our guide are the ones which he borrows from Horace: *sapere aude!* Dare to be wise! Have courage to use your *own* understanding!

Notes

Introduction

1 E. de Vattel, *Le Droit des Gens ou Principes de la Loi naturelle appliqués à la Conduite et aux Affaires des Nations et des Souverains*, facsimile of original reproduced in Vol. I, Carnegie Institution of Washington, 1916, author's translation, pp. 232–3.
2 A. Giddens, *Modernity and Self Identity*, Cambridge, Polity Press, 1991.
3 B. Burrough, 'Manifest courage; the story of flight 93', *Vanity Fair* 496, December 2001, 133–7, 198–202.
4 F. Braudel, *La Méditerranée et le monde Méditerranéen à l'Epoque de Philippe II*, Paris, Librairie Armand Colin, 2ème edn, 1966.

1 War, peace and the future of history

1 For further detail, see Chapter 2, pp. x–y.
2 For an excellent *tour d'horizon* of contemporary historiography, see U.P. Burke (ed.), *New Perspectives in Historical Writing* (2nd edn), Cambridge, Polity Press, 2000.
3 A. Vaughan, *I.K. Brunel: Engineering Knight-Errant*, London, John Murray, 1991.
4 R.T.C. Rolt, *Victorian Engineering*, Harmondsworth, Penguin, 1970.
5 H. Maine, *Ancient Law*, London, Dent Everyman's Library, 1917.
6 'Just as Darwin discovered the law of nature in organic nature, so Marx discovered the law of evolution in human history...', 'Speech at the graveside of Karl Marx, delivered at Highgate Cemetery, London, 17 March 1883', *Karl Marx, Selected Works Volume 1*, London, Lawrence & Wishart, 1942, pp. 16–18.
7 I.S. Bloch, *Is War Now Impossible? Being an Abridgement of 'The War of the Future in its Technical, Economic and Political Relations'*, London, Grant Richards, 1899, pp. 1–8, 147–52.
8 Ibid., pp. 157–9 ('The care of the wounded').
9 Ibid., pp. 347–59 ('The nemesis of militarism').
10 Cit. M. Walzer, *Just and Unjust Wars: a Moral Argument with Historical Illustrations*, 1977, London, Pelican edition, 1980, p. 32.
11 J. Keegan, 'A brief history of warfare – past, present, future', in G. Prins and H. Tromp (eds), *The Future of War*, Amsterdam, Kluwer, 2000, pp. 171–81. See also J. Keegan, *War and our World: the Reith Lectures 1998*,

London, Hutchinson, 1998, and J. Mueller, *Retreat from Doomsday: the Obsolescence of Major War*, London, HarperCollins/Basic, 1990.

12 G. Steiner, *Language and Silence*, Harmondsworth, Pelican, 1969, 'Postscript', pp. 191–5.

13 R.J. Rummel, *Death by Government*, New Brunswick, Transaction Publishers, 1994.

14 Illuminated in the recently-published confidential papers of the Chinese communist leadership, see 'The Tienanmen Papers', *Foreign Affairs*, 2000, 80(1), 2–49.

15 E. Hobsbawm, *Age of Extremes: the Short Twentieth Century, 1914–1991*, London, Michael Joseph, 1994.

16 M. Wight, *Power Politics*, RIIA/Leicester University Press, 1978 (eds H. Bull and C. Holbroad).

17 H.J. Morgenthau, *Politics Among Nations: the Struggle for Power and Peace*, New York, McGraw Hill, 1993.

18 F. Fukuyama, *The End of History and the Last Man*, London, Hamish Hamilton, 1992.

19 S.J. Huntington, *The Clash of Civilizations*, New York, Simon & Schuster, 1996.

20 P. Kennedy, *The Rise and Fall of the Great Powers: Economic Change and Military Conflict from 1500 to 2000*, London, Fontana, 1988.

21 M. Cox, K. Booth and T. Dunne, 'Introduction: the interregnum: controversies in world politics 1989–99', *Review of International Studies*, 25 (Special Issue), December 1999, 3–19.

22 *Global Trends 2015: A Dialogue About the Future With Nongovernment Experts*, Washington, National Intelligence Council, 2000.

23 J. Gray, *False Dawn: the Delusions of Global Capitalism*, London, Granta, 1998, pp. 196, 208; J. Black, *War in the New Century*, London, Continuum, 2001.

24 'The Globalisation Index', *Foreign Policy*, January/February, 2001.

25 E. Burke, *Reflections on the Revolution in France* (1790) (edited and with an introduction by C.C. O'Brien), Harmondsworth, Penguin, 1968; T. Paine, *The Rights of Man* (1791) is magnificently interpreted in J. Keane, *Tom Paine: A Political Life*, London, Bloomsbury, 1995.

26 Judgement of the International Military Tribunal, 22 *Trial of the Major War Criminals before the International Military Tribunal, Proceedings*, 411 (1948), pp. 465–6.

27 G. Robertson, *Crimes against Humanity. The Struggle for Global Justice*, Harmondsworth, Allen Lane, The Penguin Press, 1999.

28 A. Djilas, 'Poor old Slobo', *Prospect*, August/September 2001, 66, p. 11.

29 M.A. Glendon, *A World Made New: Eleanor Roosevelt and the Universal Declaration of Human Rights*, New York, Random House, 2001, quotation at p. 42.

30 House of Lords judgement – *Regina v Bartle and the Commissioner of Police for the Metropolis and Others, ex parte* Pinochet, 25 November 1998, opinion of Lord Justice Steyn.

31 *Climate Change: an Update of Recent Research from The Hadley Centre*, Hadley Centre for Climate Prediction and Research, Bracknell, UK Meteorological Office, November 2000.

32 R.N. Cooper, 'Towards a real global warming treaty', *Foreign Affairs*

1998, 77(2), 66–80; D. Victor, *The Collapse of the Kyoto Protocol and the Struggle to Slow Global Warming*, New York, Council on Foreign Relations, 2001. Frantic efforts to prevent the collapse were made. The note circulated on his own authority by Jan Pronk, President of COP6, showed why the effort was by then beyond retrieval, even without the added help of a spat between the British and French ministers (Prescott and Voynet). J. Pronk, 'Note by the President of COP6', 23 November 2000, 7.04 pm, mss, 14 pp.

33 Paper by B. Buzan at conference on 'The Environment and Security: what are the policy implications?', Centre for the Study of Democracy, University of Westminster, 15 March 2001.

34 For a more extended discussion, see G. Prins, 'Environment and Security', paper for the Green Globe Task Force seminar on environmental diplomacy, London, 11 May 2001, mss.

35 Discussion of the political effects of globalisation composes the agenda of the so-called 'Third Way'. It is best encountered through the academic rather than the polemical literature. Therefore, see D. Held, *Democracy and the Global Order: from the Modern State to Cosmopolitan Governance*, Cambridge, Polity Press, 1995, and D. Archibugi *et al.* (eds), *Reimagining Political Community: Studies in Cosmopolitan Democracy*, Cambridge, Polity Press, 1998.

36 This issue is more extensively explored in Chapter 4.

37 I.S. Bloch, *Is War Now Impossible?*, pp. xxx–xxxi.

2 Cold Wars: The phantom menace: Part I?

1 J.R.R. Tolkien, *The Lord of the Rings*, London, Unwin, many editions.

2 C. Donnelly, 'The future of Russian national security policy and military strategy', Appendix 1, 'The warranty system', in G.A.S.C. Wilson (ed.), *British Security 2010: Proceedings of a Conference at Church House, Westminster*, privately published, 1995, pp. 153–4.

3 M. Kidron and D. Smith, *The War Atlas: Armed Conflict – Armed Peace*, London, Pan Books, 1983; PIOOM, 'World Conflict and Human Rights Map 1998' (www.fsw.leidenuniv.nl/w3_liswo/pioom.htm). Comparison between these maps is a depressing experience.

4 The nub of The Long Telegram's message was: 'We have here a political force committed fanatically to the belief that with the US there can be no permanent *modus vivendi*, that it is desirable and necessary that the internal harmony of our society be disrupted, our traditional way of life destroyed, the international authority of our state be broken if Soviet power is to be secure'; George Kennan ('X'), 'The sources of Soviet conduct', *Foreign Affairs*, July 1947.

5 R. Nixon, *Six Crises*, London, W.H. Allen, 1962; J. Kirkpatrick, *Dictatorship and Double Standards: Rationalism and Reason in Politics*, New York, Simon & Schuster, 1983.

6 These arguments were expertly dissected at the time in A. Kenny, *The Ivory Tower: Essays in Philosophy and Public Policy*, Oxford, Blackwell, 1985, pp. 100–3.

7 McG. Bundy and J. Blight, 'October 27, 1962: transcripts of the meetings of the EXCOMM', *International Security*, Winter 1987–8, 12(3), pp. 32–92.

See also J.L. Gaddis, 'The Cuban Missile Crisis', in *We Now Know: Rethinking Cold War History*, Oxford, Clarendon Press, 1997, pp. 260–80.

8 R. McNamara, speaking at the launch of R. McNamara and J. Blight, *Wilson's Ghost: Reducing the Risk of Conflict, Killing and Catastrophe in the 21st Century*, New York, Public Affairs, 2001; at the Woodrow Wilson Center, Washington, DC, 7 June 2001.

9 See R. Gates, *From the Shadows*, New York, Simon & Schuster, 1996, pp. 270–7; C. Andrew and O. Gordievsky, *KGB: the Inside Story of its Foreign Operations from Lenin to Gorbachev*, London, Hodder & Stoughton, 1990, pp. 499–501; C. Andrew, *For the President's Eyes Only: Secret Intelligence and the American Presidency from Washington to Bush*, London, HarperCollins, 1995, pp. 475–7.

10 The accident occurred at Kyshtym in the southern Ural mountains in 1956. It first became known in the West in 1976 through the writing of an emigré scientist, Zhores Medvedev and, while first denied, was confirmed by the CIA in 1977. For fuller details and a bibliography, see R.D. Lipschutz, *Radioactive Waste: Politics, Technology and Risk*, Cambridge, MA, Ballinger, 1980, pp. 200, 238–9.

11 T. Nilsen, I. Kudrik and A. Nikitin, 'The Russian Northern Fleet: sources of radioactive contamination', 1996, Oslo, Norway (to be found at www.bellona.no); R. Bergman and A. Baklanov, *Radioactive Sources of Main Radiological Concern in the Kola–Barents Region*, Swedish Council for Planning & Coordination of Research (FRN)/Defence Research Establishment (FOA), 1998; A. Diakov *et al.*, 'Nuclear powered submarine inactivation and disposal in the US and Russia: a comparative analysis', *Problems of Material Science*, 1997, 2(8), 37–44; A. Yemelyanenkov and A. Zolotkov, 'Sailing directions classified: a review of radioactive wastes the former USSR dumped in Arctic and Far Eastern seas', *Atom Declassified: Half a Century with the Bomb*, Moscow, IIPPNW, 1996. Further discussion of the local and international political context of these physical problems is to be found in G. Prins, 'Nuclear disaster may still be averted', *Bulletin of the American Academy of Arts & Sciences*, Cambridge, MA, 2001, VIL(2), 23–7.

12 D. Held, *Democracy and the Global Order: From the Modern State to Cosmopolitan Governance*, Cambridge, Polity Press, 1995.

13 S. Strange, 'The Westfailure System', *Review of International Studies*, 25(3), 1999, 345–54.

14 E.P. Thompson, *Writing by Candlelight*, London, Merlin, 1980; H. Tromp, *In staat van oorlog*, Amsterdam, Contact, 1986; *At the End of the Cold War*, Groningen, Origin, 1992.

15 L. Martin, *The Two-Edged Sword: Armed Force in the Modern World*, London, Weidenfeld & Nicolson, 1982.

16 R. Scruton, *England: An Elegy*, London, Chatto & Windus, 2000, pp. 157–61.

17 On meeting the speaker again fifteen years later, he recollected the episode sharply, and stood by his judgement.

18 As observed in Chapter 1, there is still much that is not known about how the Internet is used; and where good empirical evidence can be found, the results are sometimes surprising. Thus, in pioneering work in Russia and Ukraine, the degree to which the Internet is used to facilitate *internal*

communication rather than to open bridges to the outside, is striking. R. Rohozinski, 'How the Internet did not transform Russia', *Current History*, 99(639), 334–48. In contrast, extreme racist groups have taken to the Internet with enthusiasm, with globally-linked protected Internet sites (M. Joyce-Hasham, 'Web Offence', *The World Today*, March 2000, 11–13). However, the pattern is neither automatic nor predictable. When criminologists have studied the manner in which cyber-criminals organise themselves, it appears that their systems are little different from those of Sicilian mafia (D. Mann and M. Sutton, 'Net crime: more change in the organisation of thieving', *British Journal of Criminology*, Spring 1998, 38(2), 201–29.

19 J. Vavrousek, 'Institutions for environmental security', in G. Prins (ed.), *Threats Without Enemies: Facing Environmental Insecurity*, London, Earthscan, 1993, pp. 87–9.

20 P. Jehlicka, 'A comparative investigation into the dynamics of environmental policies in Western and Eastern Europe 1988–93, with special reference to the Czech Republic', PhD thesis, Cambridge University, 1999. The triggering role of environmental protest is clearly seen in S. Humphrey, 'A comparative chronology of revolution, 1988–1990', in G. Prins (ed.), *Spring in Winter*, Manchester, Manchester University Press, 1990, pp. 211–41.

21 T. Homer-Dixon, *Environment, Scarcity and Violence*, Princeton, Princeton University Press, 1999, Fig. 7.1; G.D. Dabelko and D.D. Dabelko, 'Environmental security: Issues of conflict and redefinition', in *Woodrow Wilson Environmental Change and Security Report* 1, Spring 1995, pp. 3–13.

22 N. Wachtel, *La vision des vaincus: les Indiens de Pérou devant la conquête espagnole, 1530–1570*, Paris, Gallimard, 1971.

23 M. Midgley, 'Deterrence, provocation and the Martian temperament', in N. Blake and K. Pole (eds), *Dangers of Deterrence; Philosophers and Nuclear Strategy*, London, Routledge & Kegan Paul, 1983, pp. 19–40.

24 A. Chernyaev, *My Six Years with Gorbachev*, Pennsylvania, Penn State University Press, 2000, p. 399.

25 G. Kennan, 'Memorandum for the Minister', *New York Review of Books*, 26 April 2001, p. 23.

3 The outside and inside of civil and uncivil war

1 On the Thiepval memorial, see J.M. Winter, *Sites of Memory, Sites of Mourning*, Cambridge University Press, 1995, pp. 105–7; G. Dyer, *The Missing of the Somme*, London, Hamish Hamilton, 1994.

2 P. Barker, *Regeneration, The Eye in the Door, The Ghost Road*; S. Faulks, *Birdsong* (several editions of each).

3 G. Barraclough, *An Introduction to Contemporary History*, Harmondsworth, Pelican, 1967.

4 R.G. Collingwood, *An Autobiography*, Oxford, Oxford University Press, 1939, 1970 edn, pp. 79, 81.

5 R.G. Collingwood, *The Idea of History*, Oxford, Oxford University Press, 1946, p. 213.

6 I am grateful to Christopher Donnelly for this information, and for

walking the ground with me. For the context of the Mons campaign, see
J. Keegan, *The First World War*, London, Hutchinson, 1998, pp. 107–10.

7 M. van Creveld, 'Postmodern war', in C. Townsend (ed.), *Oxford Illustrated History of Warfare*, Oxford, Oxford University Press, 1997.

8 J. Keegan, *The Face of Battle*, London, Jonathan Cape, 1976.

9 P. van den Dungen, 'From St Petersburg to The Hague: the significance of Ivan Bloch for the First Hague Peace Conference', in G. Prins and H. Tromp (eds), *The Future of War*, Amsterdam, Kluwer, 2000, pp. 69–83.

10 L. Davidowicz, *The War Against the Jews 1933–45*, Harmondsworth, Penguin, 1975.

11 J. Keane, *Reflections on Violence*, London, Verso, 1966, p. 141.

12 For powerful reflections upon this theme, see E. Vulliamy, 'Bosnia: the secret war', reports, *The Guardian*, 1996; M. Ignatieff, *The Warrior's Honour: Ethnic War and the Modern Conscience*, London, Vintage, 1997.

13 C.W. Previté-Orton, *The Shorter Cambridge Medieval History*, Vol. II, Cambridge, Cambridge University Press, 1952, pp. 660–5.

14 A. Minc, *Le Nouveau Moyen Age*, Paris, Gallimard, 1993; M. Kaldor, *New and Old Wars: Organized Violence in a Global Era*, Cambridge, Polity Press, 1999, pp. 69–89, 114–16.

15 H. Tromp, 'A clash of paradigms: the fall of Srebrenica and its aftermath', mss. I am grateful to Professor Tromp for bringing Mladic's quoted remarks to my attention.

16 J.W. Honig and N. Both, *Srebrenica: Record of a War Crime*, Harmondsworth, Penguin, 1996; D.A. Leurdijk, 'NATO as a sub-contractor to the UN: the cases of Bosnia and Kosovo', in R. de Wijk, B. Boxhoorn and N. Hoekstra (eds), *NATO after Kosovo*, Breda, Royal Netherlands Military Academy, 2000, pp. 121–39.

17 UNA–USA International Task Force on the Enforcement of U.N. Security Council Resolutions (Chairman, Lord Carrington), *Words to Deeds: Strengthening the U.N.'s Enforcement Capabilities*, Final Report, New York, December 1997; E. Greco, *Delegating Peace Operations: Improvisation and Innovation in Georgia and Albania*, UNA–USA Dialogue on the Enforcement of Security Council Resolutions, No. 7, New York, March 1998.

18 C.W. Maynes, 'Squandered triumph: the West botched the Post-Cold War World', *Foreign Affairs*, 1999, 78(1), 21.

19 A. Gearty, *Terror*, London, Faber & Faber, 1991, p. 7.

20 'Reflections on global terrorism: Lockerbie ten years later', Syracuse University, June–July 1998; G. Prins, 'Thinking about terrorism', 17 June 1998.

21 P. Wilkinson, *Terrorism and the Liberal State* (2nd edn), New York, New York University Press, 1986, pp. 156–77.

22 D.E. Kaplan and A. Marshall, *The Cult at the End of the World: the Incredible Story of Aum*, London, Hutchinson, 1996, pp. 235–6.

23 A. Hoffman, *Inside Terrorism*, London, Victor Gollancz, 1998, p. 205.

24 L. Garrett, 'The nightmare of bioterrorism', *Foreign Affairs*, Jan–Feb 2001, 76–89.

25 T.J. Volgy, L.E. Imwalle and J.J. Corntassel, 'Structural determinants of international terrorism: the effect of hegemony and polarity on terrorist activity', *International Interactions*, 23 February 1997, pp. 207–31. *Cit.*

B. Lia and K.H.-W. Skjølberg, 'Why terrorism occurs – a survey of theories and hypotheses on the causes of terrorism', Norwegian Defence Research Establishment (*Forsvarets Forskningsinstitutt*, FFI 2000/02769), May 2000, p. 27: figures from the US State Department's global patterns of terrorism publications *cit.* B. Hoffman, 'New and continuing forms of terrorism' in B. Lia and R.-I.V. Andresen (eds), *Terrorism, Political Violence and Organised Crime – Security Policy Challenges of Non-State Actors' Use of Violence*, Forsvarets Forskningsinstitutt, FFI Report 2000/06444, February 2001, pp. 25–6.

26 Ibid. cit., p. 32.

27 P. Wilkinson, *Terrorism and the Liberal State*, p. 51.

28 A. Gearty, *Terror*, p. 1.

29 Ibid., p. 12.

30 Ibid., p. 21.

31 Ibid., p. 151.

32 Ibid., p. 9.

33 O.M. Sayle, 'Terror and television', *Prospect*, October 2001, 44–5.

34 Ibid., pp. 52–5.

35 *Keesings Record of World Events*, pp. 43971–2.

36 *Keesings Record of World Events*, p. 43885.

37 *Keesings Record of World Events*, p. 43770.

38 P. Hirschkorn, R. Gunaratna, E. Blanche and S. Leader, 'Blowback: special report: Al-Qae'da', *Jane's Intelligence Review*, August 2001, 42–5.

39 G. Chaliand, 'Ce n'est pas une guerre, c'est le stade ultime du terrorisme classique', *Le Monde*, 13 September 2001, p. 13.

40 Hoffman, *Inside Terrorism*, pp. 105–20. Examples of these claims can be viewed at www.creator.org and www.kingsidentity.com.

41 M. Joyce-Hasham, 'Conspiracies on the Internet', mss., March 2000, London, RIIA, p. 19 and Appendix II.

42 P. Fites, P. Johnston and M. Kratz, *The Computer Virus Crisis* (2nd edn), New York, Van Nostrand Reinhold, 1992, p. 63.

43 Kaplan and Marshall, *The Cult at the End of the World*, pp. 96–7.

44 L. Garrett, 'The nightmare of bioterrorism', *Foreign Affairs*, 77.

45 B. Lia and R.-I.V. Andresen, *Terrorism, Political Violence and Organised Crime – Security Policy Challenges of Non-State Actors' Use of Violence*, Forsvarets Forskningsinstitutt, FFI 2000/06444, February 2001, quotations between pp. 35–40.

46 B. Hoffman, 'New and continuing forms of terrorism', in Lia and Andresen (eds), *Terrorism, Political Violence and Organised Crime – Security Policy Challenges of Non-State Actors' Use of Violence*, February 2001, p. 25.

47 Ibid., p. 31.

48 N. Gurr and B. Cole, *The New Face of Terrorism. Threats from Weapons of Mass Destruction*, London, I.B. Tauris, 2000, pp. 34–7, 260.

49 Ibid,, pp. 28–9.

50 B. Lia and A.S. Hansen, *Globalisation and the Future of Terrorism: Patterns and Predictions*, FFI Report 2000/01704, July 2000, p. 101; B. Lia, 'The impact of globalisation on future patterns of terrorism', in Lia and Andresen (eds), p. 35.

51 Some of the ideas expressed through this figure were first discussed in the

Chatham House seminar on asymmetric warfare, which I chaired in 1999–2000. RIIA was under contract to the Defence Evaluation & Research Agency for this work, which was conducted at an unclassified level. I am grateful to Dr Stephen Ashford for drawing an earlier version of this diagram from which the present has been adapted.

52 I am greatly indebted to Colonel Paul Fox (Army Intelligence Corps) for first drawing this diagram for me.

53 Gearty, *Terror*, p. 130.

54 R. Fellows, L. Dodd and J. Moffat, *Catastrophe Theory: A Review of its History and Current Status*, DERA/KIS/ISR/WP000216, June 2000.

4 A brief (and critical) encounter with academic security studies

1 I. Kant, 'The metaphysics of morals' (1797), in H. Reiss (ed.), *Kant: Political Writings*, Cambridge, Cambridge University Press, 1991, p. 174.

2 Obviously, one must guard against a perverse misreading leading to claimed relevance (Kant on the microwave revolution); but equally we may agree with Michael Doyle that 'neglecting the classics can be equally perilous ... we may have toiled to reinvent the wheels they invented.'

3 Derivative because in practice the principal framework of explanation is historical (I am not persuaded that Fred Halliday's distinguishing criteria, which contrast factual and specific history with comparative and theoretical IR, are real (F. Halliday, *Rethinking International Relations*, Basingstoke, Macmillan, 1994, p. 25); uncomfortable both because IR aspires to a more scientific status than history, yet has no distinct methodology and no generally agreed subject matter. It remains (still) fundamentally in debate how much more IR is than the study of war and peace. In Halliday's suggested research programme for IR, it is No. 4 of 5; but that is not the subject of this chapter. Halliday, *Rethinking International Relations*, pp. 242–3 and S. Guzzini, *Realism in International Relations and International Political Economy: the Continuing Story of a Death Foretold*, London, Routledge, 1998, pp. 7–12.

4 'The central questions are concerned with international violence ... A subject that is only remotely related to central political problems of threat perception and management among sovereign states would be regarded as peripheral' is the briefest shorthand, given by J.S. Nye and S. Lynn-Jones, 'International Security Studies: a report of a conference on the state of the field', *International Security*, 1988, 12, 6–7. It is endorsed and glossed in a spirited defence of the narrow reading, thus: '[Security studies] ... explores the conditions that make the use of force more likely, the ways that the use of force affects individuals, states, and societies, and the specific policies that states adopt in order to prepare for, prevent or engage in war', S.M. Walt, 'The renaissance of Security Studies', *International Studies Quarterly*, 1991, 35, 212. In fact, as will become clear, the reference to individuals is egregious; but the rest of the definition is illuminating.

5 This framework may be usefully contrasted with Ken Booth's more precisely chronological account, with which it does not coincide. (He proposes early [1945–55], high [1956–85], late [1985–91] and post-Cold

War phases.) K. Booth, 'Strategy', in A.J.R. Groom and M. Light (eds), *Contemporary International Relations: A Guide to Theory*, London, Pinter, 1994, pp. 109–27.

6 Among the most poignant witnesses to have forced this question forward was Primo Levi (especially in *The Drowned and the Saved*, New York, Little, Brown, 1993). The single most eloquent and continuing voice has been George Steiner ('The Hollow Miracle' [1959], 'A note on Günther Grass' [1964], in *Language and Silence* [Harmondsworth, Penguin, abridged edition, 1970]).

7 Made movingly apparent by Michael Howard in an anecdotal, autobiographical interview, interspersed with music, broadcast on BBC Radio 3, July 1998.

8 E.H. Carr, *The Twenty Years Crisis*, London, Macmillan, 1939, 2nd edn, 1946, reprinted 1961), pp. 62, 53. It should be stressed that what Carr *actually* wrote about utopianism and realism was a lot less stark than the manner in which he has often been portrayed: 'Utopia and reality are thus the two facets of political science. Sound political thought and sound political life will be found only where both have their place' (p. 10). See further K. Booth, 'Security in anarchy: utopian realism in theory and practice,' *International Affairs*, 3 July 1991, 63, 527–45. The most thoughtful and sensitive historical exploration of these questions are Michael Howard's 1977 Trevelyan Lectures, *War and the Liberal Conscience*, London, Temple Smith, 1978.

9 A.J.P. Taylor, *The Origins of the Second World War*, Harmondsworth, Penguin, 1963 edn, containing 'Foreword: second thoughts'.

10 M. Wight, *Power Politics*, 'Looking Forward' Pamphlet No. 8, London, RIIA Chatham House, 1946. The essay was the kernel to Wight's posthumously published *Power Politics*, H. Bull and C. Holbraad (eds), Leicester, RIIA/Leicester University Press, 1978; H. Morgenthau, *Politics Among Nations*, New York, Knopf, 1948.

11 J.D. Frank, *Sanity and Survival: Psychological Aspects of War and Peace*, London, The Cresset Press, 1967, pp. 115–36; D. Yergin, *Shattered Peace: The Origins of the Cold War and the National Security State*, Harmondsworth, Penguin, 1980, pp. 171–4, 283–6.

12 Yergin, *Shattered Peace*, is prominent in making this case.

13 His essay, written in 1945, was published as two chapters of B. Brodie (ed.), *The Absolute Weapon*, New York, Harcourt Brace, 1946, pp. 21–110. Brodie reviewed the later career of nuclear strategy in 'The development of nuclear strategy', Working Paper 11, Los Angeles, Center for Arms Control and International Security, UCLA, 1978 (mss). A compendious narrative of these matters is L. Freedman, *The Evolution of Nuclear Strategy*, London, Macmillan, 1981.

14 F.H. Hinsley, *Power and the Pursuit of Peace: Theory and Practice in the History of Relations between States*, Cambridge, Cambridge University Press, 1963.

15 M. Bundy, *Danger & Survival: Choices About the Bomb in the First Fifty Years*, New York, Random House, 1988.

16 Indeed, for Nye and Lynn-Jones, it was deterrence theory that was the principal, perhaps sole, intellectual achievement of international security studies (Nye and Lynn-Jones, 'A Report of a Conference on the

State of the Field', pp. 6–7); on that view, see also M. Bundy, 'The unimpressive record of atomic diplomacy', in G. Prins (ed.), *The Choice: Nuclear Weapons versus Security*, London, Chatto & Windus, 1984, pp. 42–54; M. Howard, 'The forgotten dimensions of strategy', *Foreign Affairs*, Summer 1979, 975–86.

17 D. Ball, *Politics & Force Levels: the Strategic Missile Programme & the Kennedy Administration*, Berkeley, University of California Press, 1980; S. Shenfield, *The Nuclear Predicament: Explorations in Soviet Ideology*, London, Chatham House Paper 37, RIIA/RKP, 1987; M. MccGwire, *Military Objectives in Soviet Foreign Policy*, Washington, Brookings Institution, 1987; C. Donnelly, *Red Banner: the Soviet Military System in Peace and War*, London, Jane's Information Group, 1988.

18 R. Keohane (ed.), *Neo-Realism and its Critics*, New York, Columbia University Press, 1986, pp. 164–5. Doubtless practitioners will protest that this is too harsh a judgement, and that exceptions abound. But they do not; and the exceptions – critical theory, for example – prove the rule. A revealing insight into the tenacity and reasonableness of Realism, as it became the norm in security studies, is to be found in an unusual autobiographical report from inside that world-view, K. Booth, 'Security and self: reflections of *Cases*, London, a fallen Realist' in K. Krause and M.C. Williams (eds), *Critical Security Studies: Concepts and*, UCL Press Ltd, 1997, pp. 92–3.

19 The 'security dilemma' (that maximum security for A means minimum security for B, which therefore reacts in a way that makes A feel insecure, which therefore acts … etc.) is inescapable if the nature and amount of power is a 'zero-sum' game; but this, as Wheeler and Booth observe, is a questionable view. N. Wheeler and K. Booth, 'The security dilemma', in J. Baylis and N. Rengger (eds), *Dilemmas of World Politics: International Issues in a Changing World*, Oxford, Clarendon Press, 1992, pp. 57–8. See further K. Booth, 'The interregnum: world politics in transition', in K. Booth (ed.), *New Thinking about Strategy and International Security*, London, Unwin Hyman, 1991, pp. 1–28.

20 K. Booth, 'The interregnum: world politics in transition', p. 21.

21 Whereas other accounts have employed judgements on fertility in thinking to discriminate between phases of security studies, I suggest that the presence or absence of challenge is a more useful cursor.

22 For example, R. McNamara, *Blundering into Disaster. Surviving the First Century of the Nuclear Age*, London, Bloomsbury, 1987 and, with J. Blight, *Wilson's Ghost: Reducing the Risk of Conflict, Killing and Catastrophe in the 21st Century*, New York, Public Affairs LCC, 2001; the author of The Long Telegram also changed his views in light of experience. G. Kennan, *The Nuclear Delusion: Soviet–American Relations in the Atomic Age*, New York, Pantheon, 1982, Pt II, 'The Nuclear Age in Crisis'.

23 *Common Crisis. North–South: Co-operation for World Recovery*, London, The Brandt Commission, Pan, 1983; A.G. Frank, *Capitalism and Underdevelopment in Latin America*, New York, Monthly Review Press, 1987; R. Rhodes (ed.), *Imperialism and Underdevelopment: a Reader*, New York, Monthly Review Press, 1970.

24   R. Ullman, 'Redefining Security', *International Security*, 8, 1, 129–53.
25   The most articulate statement of western deterrence theory at that time was given in an essay in the 1981 United Kingdom Defence White Paper, bearing signs of the thinking of the then Permanent Secretary, Sir Michael Quinlan. The main analogy used was that of chess-playing. Since retirement, Sir Michael has set out his views fully in *Thinking about Nuclear Weapons*, London, RUSI, 1997.
26   P. Rogers, M. Dando and P. van den Dungen, *As Lambs to the Slaughter: The Facts about Nuclear War*, London, Arrow, 1981; R. Neild, *How to Make up your Mind about the Bomb*, London, Deutsch, 1981; *The Church and the Bomb: Nuclear Weapons and Christian Conscience* (Report of a working party chaired by the Bishop of Salisbury), London, Hodder & Stoughton, 1982; M. Dando and P. Rogers, *The Death of Deterrence*, London: CND Publications, 1983; N. Blake and K. Pole (eds), *Dangers of Deterrence: Philosophers on Nuclear Strategy*, London, Routledge & Kegan Paul, 1983; G. Prins (ed.), *Defended to Death: A Study of the Nuclear Arms Race*, Harmondsworth, Penguin, 1983. The episode is examined in D. Dunn, 'Peace research versus strategic studies', in K. Booth (ed.), *New Thinking about Strategy and International Security*, London, Unwin Hyman, 1991, pp. 56–72.
27   E.P. Thompson and D. Smith (eds), *Protest & Survive*, Harmondsworth, Penguin, 1980; M. Kaldor and D. Smith (eds), *Disarming Europe*, London: Merlin, 1982; E.P. Thompson, *The Heavy Dancers*, London, Merlin, 1985.
28   D. Ball, 'Can nuclear war be controlled?', *Adelphi Papers* 169, London, IISS, 1981; P. Bracken, *The Command and Control of Nuclear Forces*, Princeton, Yale University Press, 1983; B. Blair, *Strategic Command and Control: Redefining the Nuclear Threat*, Washington, Brookings Institution, 1985; P. Bracken, *The Command and Control of Nuclear Forces*, New Haven, Yale University Press, 1983. Variations on the theme are explored in A. Carter, J. Steinbrunner and C. Zraket (eds), *Managing Nuclear Operations*, Washington, DC, The Brookings Institution, 1987.
29   D. Ball, *Controlling Theater Nuclear War*, Strategic and Defence Studies Centre Working Paper No. 138, Australian National University, October 1987, pp. 25–6, records the incidents of known penetrations of US communications security by the USSR during the Yom Kippur War of 1973.
30   'Three main fallacies in discussions of nuclear weapons', in Blake and Pole (eds), *Dangers of Deterrence*; 'The military and political background of the nuclear age', in G. Prins (ed.), *The Choice: Nuclear Weapons versus Security*, London, Chatto & Windus, 1984, pp. 172–96; W.B. Gallie, *Understanding War*, London, Routledge, 1991.
31   W.B. Gallie, 'The military and political background of the nuclear age', in G. Prins (ed.), *The Choice*, pp. 190–1; for a further, spirited discussion of this theme, see M. Midgley, *Science as Salvation: A Modern Myth and its Meaning*, London, Routledge, 1990.
32   J. Keegan, *The Face of Battle: A Study of Agincourt, Waterloo and the Somme*, London, Jonathan Cape, 1976.
33   M. van Creveld, *Supplying War: Logistics from Wallenstein to Patton*,

Cambridge, Cambridge University Press, 1977; van Creveld, *Command in War*, Cambridge, MA, Harvard University Press, 1985; van Creveld, *The Transformation of War*, New York, The Free Press, 1991.

34 E. Luttwak, *Strategy: The Logic of War and Peace*, Cambridge, MA, Belknap/Harvard, 1987.

35 J. Keegan, *War and our World: the Reith Lectures 1998*, London, Hutchinson, 1998. For an exploration of some of the implications of the transformation of war in the British context, see G. Prins, *Strategy, Force Planning and Diplomatic/Military Operations (DMOs)*, London, RIIA Chatham House, 1998; *The Strategic Defence Review*, London, HMSO, 1998, pp. 1–12.

36 J. Mueller, *Retreat from Doomsday: The Obsolescence of Major War*, New York, Basic Books, 1989.

37 D. Meadows, D. Meadows, J. Randers and W. Behrens, *The Limits to Growth*, London, Earth Island, 1972. The authors replied to their critics by modelling the learning response to crisis, which they called 'overshoot', in Meadows, Meadows and Randers, *Beyond the Limits: Global Collapse or a Sustainable Future*, London, Earthscan, 1992.

38 Information from V. Gelovani and A. Piontkowski, who did this work. The importance of Gorbachev's ability to imagine alternative Soviet futures in strengthening his conviction about the need to act decisively is most fully revealed in the most valuable of the memoirs of his close associates yet to appear, A. Chernyaev, *My Six Years with Gorbachev*, Pennsylvania, Penn State University Press, 2000.

39 T. Homer-Dixon, 'On the threshold. Environmental changes as causes of acute conflict', *International Security*, Fall 1991, 16, 2, 76–116; T. Homer-Dixon, J. Boutwell and G. Rathjens, 'Environmental change and violent conflict', *Scientific American*, 1993, 268, 2, 38–45.

40 S.M. Walt, 'The renaissance of security studies', *International Studies Quarterly*, June 1991, 35(2), 213.

41 In addition to Walt's, another fighting defence comes from Sean Lynn-Jones, 'The future of international security studies', in D. Ball and D. Horner (eds), *Strategic Studies in a Changing World: Global, Regional and Australian Perspectives*, Canberra Papers on Strategy & Defence 89, Strategic & Defence Studies Centre, Australian National University, 1992, pp. 71–107; see also in similar, more recent vein, N.P. Gleditsch, 'Armed conflict and the environment: a critique of literature', *Environmental Change and International Security, Proceedings of International Workshop, Royal Dutch Academy of Sciences*, Groningen, University of Groningen, 1997, pp. 65–80.

42 D. Deudney, 'The case against linking environmental degradation and national security', *Millennium*, 1990, 19, 3, 461–76.

43 G. Prins, 'Politics and the environment', *International Affairs*, 1990, 166; G. Prins, 'A new focus for security studies', in D. Ball and D. Horner (eds), *Strategic Studies in a Changing World: Global, Regional & Australian Perspectives*, Canberra Papers on Strategy & Defence 89, Strategic & Defence Studies Centre, Australian National University, 1992, pp. 178–222, offers a point-by-point discussion of, and disagreement with, S. Lynn-Jones, 'The future of international security studies', in the same volume.

44 J. Oswald, 'Defence and environmental security', in G. Prins (ed.), *Threats Without Enemies*, London, Earthscan, 1993, pp. 113–34.
45 J.T. Mathews, 'Redefining security', *Foreign Affairs*, Spring 1989.
46 J. Urban, 'Czechoslovakia: the power and politics of humiliation', in G. Prins (ed.), *Spring in Winter: The 1989 Revolutions*, Manchester, Manchester University Press, 1990.
47 The triggering role of the environment is clearly seen in S. Humphrey, 'A comparative chronology of revolution, 1988–1990', in G. Prins (ed.), *Spring in Winter*, pp. 211–41.
48 J. Thompson, *The Media and Modernity*, Cambridge, Polity Press, 1995; A.D. Smith, 'Towards a global culture?', *Theory, Culture and Society*, 1990, 7.
49 F. Fukuyama, 'The end of history', *The National Interest*, Summer 1989. Cf. C. Brown, *Understanding International Relations*, London, Macmillan, 1997, pp. 222–4.
50 K. Waltz, *Theory of International Politics*, Reading, MA, Waltz, 1979; B. Buzan, *People, States and Fear*, 2nd edn, Hemel Hempstead, Harvester Wheatsheaf, 1991.
51 N. Rengger, 'Culture, society and order in world politics', in Baylis and Rengger (eds), *Dilemmas of World Politics*, p. 85.
52 G. Prins, 'Bonfire of the certainties', in R. Huber (ed.), *Military Stability: Prerequisites and Analysis Requirements for Conventional Stability in Europe*, Baden-Baden, Nomos Verlag, 1990.
53 E. Hobsbawm, *Age of Extremes: the Short Twentieth Century, 1914–1991*, London, Michael Joseph, 1994.
54 Security studies and the Realist international relations, from which it sprang, were unquestioning children of that settlement; Max Weber, *Theory of Social and Economic Organisation*, New York, The Free Press, 1947, pp. 329–41.
55 J. Garnett, 'States, state-centric perspectives and interdependence theory', in Baylis and Rengger (eds), *Dilemmas of World Politics*, p. 80. Michael Banks gives a captivating account of the snooker match in 'The Inter-Paradigm Debate', in M. Light and A.J.R. Groom (eds), *International Relations: A Handbook of Current Theory*, London, Pinter, 1985, pp. 7–26.
56 J. Gray, *False Dawn: the Illusions of Global Capitalism*, London, Granta, 1998. This awareness has since carried Professor Gray into an equally stark critique of the buoyant Enlightenment interpretation of liberalism whose danger lies, in his opinion, in too easy an equation of the cultural extensions of globalisation with the American Model. J. Gray, *Two Faces of Liberalism*, New York, New Press, 2001. An incisive discussion of Gray's thesis, from a sceptical perspective, is A. Ryan, 'Live and let live', *New York Review of Books*, 17 May 2001, XLVIII, 8, 54–6.
57 B. Barber, *Jihad vs McWorld: How Globalisation and Tribalism are Reshaping the World*, New York, Time Books, 1995.
58 J. Keane, *Reflections on Violence*, London, Verso, 1996; M. Ignatieff, *Blood and Belonging: Journeys into the New Nationalism*, London, Vintage, 1994.
59 A. Giddens, *Consequences of Modernity*, Cambridge, Polity Press,

1990; A. Giddens, *Modernity and Self-Identity: Self and Society in the Late Modern Age*, Cambridge, Polity Press, 1991.

60 J.T. Mathews, 'Power shift', *Foreign Affairs*, January/February 1997.

61 S. Huntington, 'The clash of civilizations', *Foreign Affairs*, 1993, 72, 3.

62 M. Wight, *Power Politics*, Harmondsworth, Penguin, 1979, pp. 168–9, 189–9; 107 ff.

63 Ibid., p. 105.

64 H. Bull, *The Anarchical Society: A Study of Order in World Politics*, London, Macmillan, 1977. An illuminating reflection on the tensions within Bull's *problematique* is to be found in H.R. Alker, 'The presumption of anarchy in world politics: on recovering the historicity of world society', in *Rediscoveries and Reformulations: Humanistic Methodologies for International Studies*, Cambridge, Cambridge University Press, 1996, pp. 355–93.

65 R. Kaplan, 'The coming anarchy', *Atlantic Quarterly*, February 1994, 273(2).

66 J. Keane, *Reflections on Violence*, p. 126.

67 R.J. Vincent, *Human Rights & International Relations*, Cambridge, Cambridge University Press, 1986; M.A. Glendon, *A World Made New*.

68 See S. Sewell and C. Kaysen (eds), *The United States and the International Criminal Court: National Security and International Law*, New York, Rowman & Littlefield, 2000.

69 It is found in the essays in the *Spring in Winter* collection of 1990, notably those by Jens Reich, of Neues Forum in the former DDR and Jan Urban of Civic Forum in the former Czechoslovakia; it is a constant theme in the writing of one of the most engaged and perceptive of witnesses, T. Garton-Ash, *History of the Present. Essays, Sketches and Despatches from Europe in the 1990s*, Harmondsworth, Penguin, 2000.

70 A. Buzan, O. Waever and J. de Wilde, *Security: a New Framework for Analysis*, London & Boulder, CO, Lynne Rienner, 1998.

71 'The culture of a society is the reality of society's reality – for – itself. It is the totality of all the processing of society's total self-process, the imagination of its imagining, the reason of its reasoning. The culture of a society is the society as *spirit*.' P. Allott, *Eunomia: New Order for a New World*, Oxford, Oxford University Press, 1990, 18.1, p. 376.

72 Ibid., 18.24, pp. 384–5.

73 Ibid., 18.25, p. 385.

74 Keane, *Reflections on Violence*, pp. 65–6.

75 Allott, *Eunomia*, 13.109, p. 250.

76 M. Walzer, *On Toleration*, New Haven, Yale University Press, 1997, pp. 90–2. Thus: 'radical freedom is thin stuff unless it exists within a world that offers it significant resistance'. Kant saw it so clearly and simply: 'all that is needed is freedom ... freedom to make public use of one's reason in all matters.' 'An answer to the question: What is Enlightenment?' (1784) in Reiss (ed.), p. 55.

77 I. Kant, 'Perpetual peace. A philosophical sketch' (1795), in Reiss (ed.), p. 93.

78 M. Howard, *The Invention of Peace*, London, Profile, 2000, p. 31.

79 R. Scruton, *Kant*, Oxford University Press, 1982, p. v.

80 I. Kant, *Perpetual Peace*, Reiss (ed.), pp. 105–6.

81 R. Scruton, *Kant*, p. 71. This explanation of the Categorical Imperative is indebted to his at pp. 69–71.

82 A hugely influential essay, which explained that those who died of famine more often did so for lack of moral and legal entitlement to food than from a physical absence of food, was A. Sen, *Poverty & Famines: an Essay on Entitlement and Deprivation*, Oxford, Oxford University Press, 1981. The place where Kant has been most clearly and persuasively brought to bear on the issue of world inequality and poverty is O. O'Neill, *Faces of Hunger: an Essay on Poverty, Justice and Development*, London, Allen & Unwin, 1992. A path-finding exploration of aspects of the issue described here is M. Ignatieff, *The Needs of Strangers*, London, Chatto & Windus, 1984.

83 M. Doyle, *Ways of War and Peace: Idealism, Liberalism and Socialism*, New York, Norton, 1997, p. 257.

84 L.W. Beck, 'Kant and the right of revolution'; S. Axinn, 'Kant, authority and the French Revolution'; C. Dyke, 'Comments' in Symposium: Kant on Revolution, *Journal of the History of Ideas*, July/September 1971, XXXII, 3.

85 J. Goodall, *The Chimpanzees of Gombe: Patterns of Behaviour*, Cambridge, MA, Belknap Press, 1986, pp. 376–81.

86 I am grateful to Lionel Tiger for conversations surrounding these paragraphs.

87 J. Ann Tickner, 'Identity in international relations theory: a feminist perspective', in Y. Lapid and F. Kratochwil (eds), *The Return of Culture and Identity in IR Theory*, London, Lynne Rienner, 1996, pp. 55–6. However, as often has been the case, Ken Booth was among the first to register disquiet, arising from a different cause, the caricaturing of Soviet society and motives, in *Strategy and Ethnocentrism*, London, Croom Helm, 1979.

88 K. Krause and M.C. Williams (eds), *Critical Security Studies: Concepts & Cases*, London, UCL Press Ltd, 1997. The editors' preface provides an acute statement of this challenge, p. ix.

89 K. Booth, 'Three tyrannies', in T. Dunne and N.J. Wheeler (eds), *Human Rights in Global Politics*, Cambridge, Cambridge University Press, 1999, pp. 37, 51. Contrast the approach in L.E. Harrison and S. Huntington, *Culture Matters: How Values Shape Human Progress*, New York, Basic Books, 2001.

90 V.G. Kiernan, *The Lords of Humankind*, Harmondsworth, Penguin, 1972; G. Prins, *The Hidden Hippopotamus. Reappraisal in African History: The Early Colonial Experience in Western Zambia*, Cambridge, Cambridge University Press, 1980; J.C. Scott, *Weapons of the Weak: Everyday Forms of Peasant Resistance*, New Haven, Yale University Press, 1985.

91 This is the device of the prisoner, too, displayed for Europeans in A. Solzynitsyn, *One Day in the Life of Ivan Denisovich*, translated by R. Parker, Harmondsworth, Penguin, 1968.

92 H. Wong, *A Strained and Twisted Eye: Stereotypes and Cultural Misperceptions in the New Era: Implications for Security*, mss, 2000.

93 Q. Skinner, *The Foundations of Modern Political Thought, Volume One: The Renaissance*, Cambridge, Cambridge University Press, 1978, pp. 69–100.

94 Not he alone. See also, O. O'Neill, *Towards Justice and Virtue: A Constructive Account of Practical Reasoning*, Cambridge, Cambridge University Press, 1996.
95 R.B.J. Walker, 'The subject of security', in Krause and Williams (eds), *Critical Security Studies*, p. 63. But do not hope for much help from theorists; it is not prudent to trust them not to curdle also. For example, compare the first and last paragraphs of J. Dunn, 'Reconceiving the content and character of modern political community', *Interpreting Political Responsibility*, Cambridge, Polity Press, 1990, pp. 193–215.
96 M. Weber, *The Theory of Social and Economic Organization (Wirtschaft und Gesellschaft)* (edited and introduced by Talcott Parsons), New York, The Free Press, 1947, p. 328.
97 H. Kissinger, *Diplomacy*, Simon & Schuster, New York, 1994, pp. 29–55.
98 Kant, *Perpetual Peace*, Appendix I, Reiss (ed.), p. 118.
99 R.S. McNamara and J.G. Blight, *Wilson's Ghost*, pp. 6–8.
100 E.H. Carr, *The Twenty Years' Crisis*, p. 10.
101 I. Kant, 'An answer to the question "What is Enlightenment?"' (1784), in Reiss (ed.), p. 54.

5 Intervention in contention

1 S. Chesterman, *Just War or Just Peace? Humanitarian Intervention and International Law*, Oxford, Oxford University Press, 2001, pp. 193–4.
2 P. Jones, 'Individuals, communities and human rights', *Review of International Studies*, Dec. 2000, 26, Special Issue, p. 199.
3 An outstanding analysis of humanitarian intervention through several of the case studies, giving rise to the best account of change in the grounds legitimating humanitarian intervention to date, is in N.J. Wheeler, *Saving Strangers: Humanitarian Intervention in International Society*, Oxford, Oxford University Press, 2000.
4 Thucydides, *The Peloponnesian War* (translated by Rex Warner), Penguin, 1972 edn, pp. 400–8.
5 W. Clark, *Waging Modern War: Bosnia, Kosovo and the Future of Combat*, New York, Public Affairs, 2001; A. Rawnsley, *Servants of the People: the Inside Story of New Labour*, Harmondsworth, Penguin, 2nd edn, 2001, pp. 257–90.
6 Cited by Annan in 'Reflections on intervention', 35th Ditchley Foundation Lecture, 26 June 1998, in K. Annan, *The Question of Intervention*, New York, UNDPI, 1999, p. 6.
7 Wheeler, pp. 12–13, 289.
8 For a fuller account of these discussions, see G. Prins, 'Thinking about intervention: an essay reviewing the international policy debate in early 2001', *RUSI Journal*, August 2001, 12–17.
9 Wheeler, pp. 231–41. An even more stringent indictment is given in L. Melvern, *A People Betrayed: the Role of the West in Rwanda's Genocide*, London, Zed Books, 2001.
10 Annan, ibid.
11 Whereas Wheeler asserts this strongly, and his view is shared here, others take the view that, in so far as this broadening has occurred, it has been

narrow, shakily legitimate and unfriendly to the emergence of an inter-national rule of law. S. Chesterman, ibid., pp. 87–6, 236.

12 Proceedings of the Yugoslav Tribunal, *Prosecutor v D. Tadic* IT-94-1-AR72, October 1995, para. 30.

13 I am indebted for several of these insights to a paper given by Dr Wheeler to a joint seminar of the International Commission on Inter-vention and State Sovereignty and the Pugwash Conferences Workshop on Intervention and State Sovereignty at Pugwash, Nova Scotia, July 2001, which I gratefully acknowledge.

14 Annan, ibid., p. 10.

15 A. Suhrke and B. Jones, 'Preventive diplomacy in Rwanda: failure to act or failure of actions?', in B. Jentilson (ed.), *Opportunities Missed, Opportunities Seized: Preventive Diplomacy in the Post-Cold War World*, study for the Carnegie Commission on Preventing Deadly Conflict, Lanham, MD, Roman & Littlefield, 1999, pp. 257–8.

16 *Report of the Independent Enquiry into the Actions of the UN during the 1994 Genocide in Rwanda*, New York, UN, December 1999.

17 Annan, ibid., p. 12.

18 K. Annan, 'Unifying the Security Council in defence of human rights', 18 May 1999, The Hague, in Annan, *The Question of Intervention*, p. 31.

19 All quotations from the Ditchley Park Lecture of 26 June 1998 in Annan, pp. 3–16.

20 K. Annan, 'Two concepts of sovereignty', address to the 54th Session of the United Nations General Assembly, New York, 20 September 1999, in Annan, p. 37.

21 E. de Vattel, *Le Droit des Gens ou Principes de la Loi naturelle appliqués à la Conduite et aux Affaires des Nations et des Souverains*, facsimile of original reproduced in Vol. I, Carnegie Institution of Washington, 1916, author's translation.

22 Quotations from Hansard, *The Observer* and NATO Information Service cit. Rawnsley, pp. 266–8.

23 *Human Rights Act 1998*, Chapter 42, 9 November 1998, HMSO; K.D. Ewing, 'The Human Rights Act and Parliamentary Democracy', *Modern Law Review*, January 1999, 62(1), 79.

24 A. Gearty, 'What are judges for?', inaugural lecture, King's College, London, 11 December 2000, p. 13, mss.

25 President Vaclav Havel, address to the Senate and the House of Commons of the Parliament of Canada, Parliament Hill, Ottawa, 29 April 1999, text available at www.hrad.cz/president/havel/speeches/1999/2904.

26 M. Gluckman, *Custom and Conflict in Africa*, Blackwell, Oxford, 1955.

27 A. Roberts, 'Postscript on the Kosovo Crisis 1999', in (ed.) *War, Crime and War Crimes: the Röling Legacy*, Groningen, University of Gronin-gen, 2000, pp. 37–43.

28 I owe both this observation and the way of framing the problem of the 'middle space' to Professor Robert Legvold.

29 J. Chesneaux, 'Stages in the development of the Vietnamese national movement, 1862–1940', *Past & Present*, 1955, 7; D. Marr, 'Nationalism and revolution in Vietnam', *Pacific Affairs*, 1977; F. Fitzgerald, *Fire in the Lake: The Americans and the Vietnamese*, London, Macmillan, 1972.

30 K. Annan, 'Facing the Humanitarian Challenge: towards a Culture of Prevention', UNDPI, 1999, p. 2.
31 E. Luttwak, 'The peace-bringing powers of war', in G. Prins and H. Tromp (eds), *The Future of War*, The Hague, Kluwer Law International, 2000, pp. 181–8.
32 D.C.F. Daniel, B.C. Hayes and C. de Jonge Oudraat, *Coercive Inducement and the Containment of International Crises*, Washington, DC, United States Institute of Peace Press, 1999, pp. 22–3.
33 A. Jentilson, *Coercive Prevention: Normative Political and Policy Dilemmas*, Washington, DC, US Institute for Peace, Peaceworks Paper 35, October 2000, p. 33.
34 The Angola sanction regime was specifically targeted against one faction, UNITA, under Security Council Resolution 864 of September 1993. The precedent had been a General Assembly Resolution to target the Khmer Rouge in Cambodia.
35 G. Evans, *Cooperating for Peace*, St Leonards, Australia, Allen & Unwin, 1993.
36 Carnegie Commission on Preventing Deadly Conflict, *Preventing Deadly Conflict*, Final Report, Carnegie Corporation of New York, 1997, p. 55.
37 J. Stremlau, *Sharpening International Sanctions: Towards a Stronger Role for the United Nations*, Carnegie Corporation of New York, November 1996, pp. 62–7.
38 A. Pellet, 'State sovereignty and the protection of fundamental human rights: an international law perspective', in J. Boutwell (ed.), *Pugwash Occasional Papers*, February 2000, I, 1, p. 43.
39 W.K. Clark, *Waging War*: A. Roberts, 'NATO's humanitarian war over Kosovo', *Survival*, 1999, 41(3), pp. 102–23; N. Wheeler, *Saving Strangers*, pp. 271–3.
40 Justice Goldstone has published his experience of these pathbreaking developments in R.J. Goldstone, *For Humanity: Reflections of a War Crimes Investigator*, New Haven, Yale University Press, 2000.
41 Annan, *A Question of Intervention*, p. 41.
42 J. Rabkin, 'When can America be bound by international law?' in G. Prins (ed.), *Understanding Unilateralism in American Foreign Policy*, London, RIIA, 2000, pp. 111–13.
43 Ibid., p. 118.
44 *Ex parte* Pinochet (No. 3) 1999, 2 All ER 97, pp. 108–9, cit. G. Robertson, *Crimes against Humanity: the Struggles for Global Justice*, London, Penguin Press/Allen Lane, 1999, pp. 215–16.
45 Robertson, p. 371.
46 J.M. Blum and R.G Steinhardt, 'Federal jurisdiction over international human rights claims: the Alien Tort Claims Act after Filartiga v Peña-Irala, *Harvard International Law Journal*, winter 1981, 22, 1, 53–113. Quotations at p. 56, pp. 73–4, p. 89, p. 113. I am also indebted to a lecture delivered by Professor Steinhardt in the Global Dimensions Seminar of the LSE Centre for the Study of Global Governance at the UN on 1 June 2001. I am much indebted to Professor Steinhardt both for his remarks during the seminar and his guidance thereafter in the significance of this aspect of American law. I also acknowledge with gratitude prompt and

extensive help in tracking down cases from Alfred Day of the Cornell Law School.

47 *S. Kadic and others v Radovan Karadzic*, Dockets 94–9035, 94–9069, US Court of Appeals for the Second Circuit 70 F 3d 232: 1995 U.S. App.LEXIS 28826, p. 4.

48 J. Terry, 'Taking Filartiga on the road: why courts outside the United States should accept jurisdiction over actions involving torture committed abroad', in C. Scott (ed.), *Torture as Tort*, Oxford, Hart, 2001, pp. 109–33.

49 Goldstone, *For Humanity*, p. 136. See also M. Weller, 'On the hazards of foreign travel for dictators and other international criminals', *International Affairs*, July 1999, 75, 3, 599–617.

50 H.A. Kissinger, 'The pitfalls of universal jurisdiction', *Foreign Affairs*, July/August 2001, 80, 4, 86.

51 G. Prins, 'The United Nations and peacekeeping in the post-Cold-War world: the case of naval power', *Journal of Peace Proposals*, 20 June 1991, 22, 135–55; B. Urquhart, 'For a United Nations volunteer force', *New York Review of Books*, 10 June 1993, 3–5.

52 Annan, p. 12.

53 W.K. Clark, *Waging Modern War*, p. 396.

54 M. Ignatieff, 'Chains of command', *New York Review of Books*, 19 July 2001, XLVIII, 12, 19.

55 Clark, p. 461.

56 M. Anstee, *Orphan of the Cold War: the Inside Story of the Collapse of the Angolan Peace Process, 1992–93*, Basingstoke, Macmillan, 1996.

6 Strategic raiding

1 K. von Clausewitz, *On War*, Princeton, Princeton University Press, 1984 edn, p. 204.

2 Ibid., p. 119.

3 Ibid., p. 128.

4 Ibid., p. 177.

5 Ibid.

6 R.A. Smith, *Directive 2 – Planning*, HQ 1 (UK) Armd Div., 28 January 1991, p. 6.

7 Clausewitz, pp. 236–7.

8 Ibid., p. 198.

9 R.K. Betts, *Surprise Attack: Lessons for Defense Planning*, Washington, DC, The Brookings Institution, 1982, Chapters 4 and 5, pp. 87–152.

10 Cit. B. Paskins and M. Dockrill, *The Ethics of War*, London, Duckworth, 1979, p. 31.

11 Ibid., pp. 35–6.

12 E.N. Luttwak, *Strategy: the Logic of War and Peace*, Cambridge, MA, Belknap Press, 1987.

13 Clausewitz, *On War*, p. 200.

14 R. Robinson and J. Gallagher with A. Denny, *Africa and the Victorians: the Official Mind of Imperialism*, London, Macmillan, 1961.

15 D.A. Low, *Lion Rampant*, London, Cass, 1973, pp. 31–2.

16 J.D. Hargreaves, *Prelude to the Partition of West Africa*, London, Macmillan, 1963, pp. 145–51.

17 The effects of the invasion of Asante upon Asante society are described in one of the seminal books of modern African history, I. Wilks, *Asante in the Nineteenth Century: the Structure and Evolution of a Political Order*, Cambridge, Cambridge University Press, 1975.

18 Wilks, p. 478.

19 B. Porter, *The Lion's Share: A Short History of British Imperialism, 1850–1970*, London, Longmans, 1975, p. 63; Wilks, pp. 235–42.

20 Wilks, pp. 49–50, 240–1.

21 Ibid., pp. 508–9.

22 Ibid., pp. 509–16; the narrative is amplified with some detail from W.W. Claridge, *A History of the Gold Coast and Ashanti from the Earliest Times to the Commencement of the 20th Century*, London, John Murray, 1915, Vol. 2, pp. 100–69.

23 P. Curtin, *The Image of Africa. British Ideas and Action, 1780–1850*, Vol. I, Wisconsin, University of Wisconsin Press, 1964, pp. 58–87.

24 A.G. Hopkins, *An Economic History of West Africa*, London, Longman, 1973, p. 10.

25 W. Rodney, *How Europe Underdeveloped Africa*, London, Bogle-L'Ouverture, 1972.

26 For case studies, see D.C. Dorward, 'Ethnography and administration, a study of Anglo-Tiv "working misunderstanding"', *Journal of African History*, 1974, XV, 3, 457–77; G. Prins, *The Hidden Hippopotamus. Reappraisal in African History: the Early Colonial Experience in Western Zambia*, Cambridge, Cambridge University Press, 1980.

27 P. Richards, *Fighting for the Rainforest: War, Youth and Resources in Sierra Leone*, London, International African Institute in association with James Currey, 2nd edn, 1998, pp. xiii–xvi.

28 Ibid., p. 163.

29 F.G. Bailey, *Stratagems and Spoils. A Social Anthropology of Politics*, Oxford, Basil Blackwell, 1980.

30 P. Chabal and J.-P. Daloz, *Africa Works: Disorder as Political Instrument*, London, International African Institute in association with James Currey, 1999, p. xix.

31 A. Zolberg, *Creating Political Order: the Party States of West Africa*, Chicago, University of Chicago Press, 1985.

32 Chabal and Daloz, p. 147.

33 Described in P. Richards, *Indigenous Agricultural Revolution: Ecology and Food Production in West Africa*, London, Hutchinson, 1985.

34 Chabal and Daloz, pp. 141–63.

35 Richards, pp. 9, 36.

36 Ibid., p. 161.

37 Ibid., pp. 36–7, 161.

38 Ibid., pp. 105–11, reports the fascinating result of preference and viewing surveys among diamond workers.

39 R. Connaughton, 'Military influence and peace-keeping: the reality', *Joint Force Quarterly Review*, July 2001, 26, Washington, DC.

40 Cit. A. Rawnsley, *Servants of the People: the Inside Story of New Labour*, Harmondsworth, Penguin, 2000, p. 177.

41 M. Tkalec, 'Neocolonialism with a human face', *Berliner Zeitung*, 21 June 2000.
42 Richards, pp. 111–12.
43 L. Dodd, 'Notes on tactical and operational level examples taken from information operations in Sierra Leone', mss, April 2001.
44 Richards, pp. 180–1; N. Cohn, *Pursuit of the Millennium; Revolutionary Millenarians and Mystical Anarchists of the Middle Ages*, London, Secker & Warburg, 1970; P. Worsley, *The Trumpet Shall Sound: A Study of 'Cargo' Cults in Melanesia*, London, McGibbon & Kee, 1957.
45 W.K. Clark, *Waging Modern War: Bosnia, Kosovo and the Future of Conflict*, Public Affairs, New York, 2001, p. 396; R.K. Betts, 'Compromised command: inside NATO's First War', *Foreign Affairs*, July/August 2001, 80(4), 126–32; M. Ignatieff, 'Chains of command', *New York Review of Books*, 19 July 2001, XLVIII, 12, 19.
46 This matter is further analysed in G. Prins, *Strategy, Force Planning and Diplomatic/Military Operations*, RIIA, 1998.
47 Panel on United Nations Peace Operations (Chairman Lakhdar Brahimi), UN Document A/55/305-S/2000/809, 21 August 2000.

7 Command in the new era

1 Lecture by General Sir Rupert Smith (Deputy Supreme Allied Commander Europe) to staff of the UK Ministry of Defence, Defence Science & Technology Laboratory, Farnborough, 9 July 2001 (unclassified).
2 Army Doctrine Publication Vol. 2, *Command*, DGD&D/18/34/51, April 1995, Chapters 2–4, 'Mission Command'.
3 N. Howard, *Confrontation Analysis: How to Win Operations Other Than War*, Vienna, VA, CCRP, 1999.
4 R. Fisher and Y. Ury, *Getting to Yes: Negotiating Agreement Without Giving In*, Boston, Houghton Mifflin, 1981: S. Brown and R. Fisher, 'Building a US–Soviet working relationship: ideas on process', in R. Avenhaus, R.K. Huber and J.D. Kettelle, *Modelling and Analysis in Arms Control*, NATO ASI series, Berlin, Springer Verlag, 1986, pp. 319–28.
5 S.J. Brams, *Superpower Games: on Applying Game Theory to Superpower Conflict*, New Haven, Yale University Press, 1985; S.J. Brams and D.L. Kilgour, 'Notes on arms control verification: a game theoretic analysis', in R. Avenhaus *et al.* (eds), *Modelling and Analysis in Arms Control*, pp. 409–19.
6 This figure is an elaboration of an initial sketch by General Smith, which is gladly acknowledged.
7 Army Field Manual Volume 5, Operations Other Than War, Part 2: *Wider Peacekeeping*, London, HMSO, 1994.
8 This way of representing capability, and the formula, is attributed to General Sir Rupert Smith.
9 This important formulation was originally made by the Commandant of the Intelligence Corps (Brigadier C. Holtom). The whole problem of high and low intensity and the manner in which it continues to bedevil debate, is discussed further in G. Prins, *Strategy, Force Planning and DMOs*, London, RIIA, 1998, 'The high–low intensity fallacy' pp. 9–11.

10 Klein studies a wide range of case studies of decisions made under pressure, and describes the Recognition–Primed Decision (RPD) Model. His examples are very largely tactical and instrumental, but the observations appear equally applicable to strategic as to tactical levels. G. Klein, *Sources of Power: How People Make Decisions*, Cambridge, MA, MIT Press, 1998.

11 For example, in M. Wight, *Power Politics*, Pamphlet No. 8, RIIA, 1946; H. Bull, *The Anarchical Society: a Study of Order in World Politics*, London, Macmillan, 1977; F. Hinsley, *Power and the Pursuit of Peace: Theory and Practice in the History of Relations between States*, Cambridge, Cambridge University Press, 1963.

12 But the relationship is one of circular causation: Montesquieu was first to note that political violence only became 'war' when states came into being, and that war made states as states made war: the 'state of war' in his nicely-turned pun.

13 C. von Clausewitz, *On War*, Book I, Ch. 1, Parts 23/4, 1832.

14 The ending of communism was followed quickly by the End of History (Fukuyama) and Clash of Civilisations (Huntington): grand theories, which illuminated the skies for a time, and then burned out (although Osama bin Laden is doing his best to rekindle the 'clash of civilisations' stereotype for his own ends). The makers of the 1989 revolutions had been less flamboyant or confident about the meaning of what they had done, at the time; and that has proven to be the prudent position to have taken over the last decade. See G. Prins (ed.), *Spring in Winter: the 1989 Revolutions*, Manchester, Manchester University Press, 1990.

15 G. Prins, *Strategy, Force Planning and DMOs*, London, RIIA, 1998.

16 W.H. McNeill, *The Pursuit of Power: Technology, Armed Force and Society since AD 1000*, Oxford, Blackwell, 1983, pp. 65–102; A. and H. Toffler, *War and Anti-war: Survival at the Dawn of the 21st Century*, London, Warner, 1993.

17 E. Luttwak, *Strategy: the Logic of Peace and War*, Cambridge, MA, Belknap/Harvard, 1987.

18 R. Cooper, *The Post-Modern State and the World Order*, London, Demos, 1996.

19 G. Prins, *Strategy, Force Planning and DMOs*, London, RIIA, 1998.

20 Further discussed in G. Prins and E. Sellwood, *Preparing for Combined and Joint Operations to Maintain International Security: reflections on a seminar at NATO Headquarters*, UNA–USA International Dialogue on the Enforcement of Security Council Resolutions, No. 4, New York, UNA–USA, 1997.

21 Explored in G. Prins (ed.), *Understanding Unilateralism in America's Foreign Relations*, London, RIIA, 2000.

22 This statement is explained in G. Prins, *European Horizons of Diplomatic/Military Operations*, London, RIIA, 1999.

23 Clausewitz, *On War*, Book I, Chapter 2, famously argues that the enemy's will is the prime and essential target. The point is rendered operational in *Army Doctrine Publication*, Vol. 2, 'Command' (No. 71564), HMSO, April 1995.

24 F. Kitson, *Low Intensity Operations*, London, 1970; *The Army Field Manual*, Vol. 5, Pt 2, 'Wider Peacekeeping', HMSO, first edition, 1994.

25 J. Storr, 'Real people, real decisions: designing HQs to win wars', *The British Army Review*, 1999, 123.

26 L. Dodd, 'An analogy between the human brain and military Command Information System', DRA/CIS/CSS1/N4SBS/TR94033/1.0, Farnborough, DERA, 1995.

27 R. Fellows, L. Dodd and J. Moffat, *Catastrophe Theory: A Review of its History and Current Status*, DERA/KIS/ISR/WP000216, June 2000; J. Moffat and S. Witty, *Changes of Phase in the Command of a Military Unit*, DERA/CDA/HLS/TR000056/1.0, June 2000.

28 M. van Creveld, *Command in War*, Cambridge, MA, Harvard, 1985 ('The helicopter and the computer', pp. 232–60).

29 D. Alberts, *Network Centric warfare: Developing and Leveraging Information Superiority*, Washington, DC, CCRP Publications Series, 1999.

30 J. Moffat and G. Prins, 'A revolution in military thinking? Potential futures for the military art', *Journal of Defence Science*, Spring 2000 [restricted].

31 G.M. Breakwell and K. Spacie, 'Sleep, stress and decision-making', DS(L) 10/94, October 1994.

8 Some pointers towards thinking about the nuclear issue in the new century

1 Cit. L. Freedman, *The Evolution of Nuclear Strategy*, London, Macmillan, 1981, p. 83.

2 G. Alperowitz, *The Decision to Use the Atomic Bomb and the Architecture of an American Myth*, London, HarperCollins, 1995.

3 G. Prins (ed.), *Defended to Death: A Study of the Nuclear Arms Race*, Harmondsworth, Penguin, 1983, p. 135.

4 P.H. Vigor, *Soviet Blitzkrieg Theory*, London, Macmillan, 1983; C. Donnelly, *Red Banner: The Soviet Military System in Peace and War*, London, Janes, 1988.

5 P.J. Bracken, *The Command and Control of Nuclear Forces*, New Haven, Yale University Press, 1983; B.G. Blair, *Strategic Command and Control: Redefining the Nuclear Threat*, Washington, DC, Brookings, 1985.

6 For a pocket account of nuclear arms control, which provides more detail of the categories of arms control agreements, see G. Prins, 'Arms control: lessons learned and the future', in R. Avenhaus, R.K. Huber and J.D. Kettelle (eds), *Modelling and Analysis in Arms Control*, NATO ASI Series, Berlin, Springer Verlag, 1986, pp. 56–69.

7 M. Bundy, 'The unimpressive record of atomic diplomacy', in G. Prins (ed.), *The Choice: Nuclear Weapons Versus Security*, London, Chatto & Windus, 1984, pp. 42–55.

8 A. Myrdal, *The Game of Disarmament: How the US and Russia run the Arms Race*, New York, Random House, 1976.

9 A. Wohlstetter, *Swords from Ploughshares: the Military Potential of Civil Nuclear Energy*, Chicago, University of Chicago Press, 1977.

10 G. Perkovich, *India's Nuclear Bomb: the Impact on Global Proliferation*, Berkeley, University of California Press, 1999.

11 L.-R. Beres (ed.), *Security or Armageddon: Israel's Nuclear Strategy*, New York, Lexington Books, 1986; A. Cohen, *Israel and the Bomb*, New York, Columbia University Press, 1998.

12 G. Steinberg, 'Going public with the Bomb: the Israeli calculus', in Beres (ed.), p. 42.

13 A. Cohen, 'Deterrence, Holocaust, and nuclear weapons: a nonparochial outlook', in Beres (ed.), p. 185.

14 F. Fitzgerald, *Way Out There in the Blue: Reagan, Star Wars and the End of the Cold War*, New York, Simon & Schuster, 2000, pp. 207–8.

15 G. Prins, 'The role of superpower summitry: Recessional', *Political Quarterly*, July–September 1990, 61(3), 263–77.

16 Fitzgerald, p. 363.

17 Ministry of Defence, *The Future Strategic Context for Defence*, February 2001, ¶14, p. 4.

18 J. Newhouse, 'The missile defence debate', *Foreign Affairs*, July/August 2001, 80(4), 97–109.

19 M.G. McKinzie, T.B. Cochran, R.S. Norris and W.M. Arkin, *The U.S. Nuclear War Plan: A Time for Change*, Washington DC, NRDC, June 2001.

20 *Findings of the Nuclear Posture Review*, 9 January 2002, briefing by J.D. Crouch, Assistant Secretary of Defense for International Security Policy, US DoD, slides from briefing are at www.defenselink.mil/news/Jan2002/g020109-D-6570C.html and articles cited in footnote 24.

21 R.G. Bell, then Senior Director for Defense Policy at the National Security Council, *cit.*, McKinzie *et al.* pp. 9–10.

22 J.D. Crouch briefing, 9 January 2002, pp. 3–4.

23 A hydrogen bomb uses a limited fission explosion of U 235 (a 'Nagasaki' type bomb) to trigger a fusion explosion in 'heavy hydrogen' (usually a mixture of the more common isotope with atomic weight 2 (deuterium) with the rarer hydrogen 3 (tritium) injected into the device as a gas). This is a 'limited life component.' The essential feature of a fusion reaction is that, as the nuclei are fused, a small decrease in total mass occurs, which appears as an enormous quantity of energy. But to bring this about, the deuterium and tritium must be heated to extremely high temperatures, which is achieved by the small fission explosion. The two-stage fission-to-fusion explosion is therefore often called 'thermonuclear'. (Even bigger yields can be obtained by wrapping the thermonuclear device in a blanket of uranium: this the Soviets did to achieve the world's biggest ever bang (above 50 Megatons) in September 1961.) A series of diagrams which show how an H-Bomb works is to be found in H. Morland, *The Secret that Exploded*, New York, Random House, 1979, pp. 277–78.

24 'Faking nuclear restraint: the Bush Administration's secret plan for strengthening U.S. nuclear forces', *NRDC Report*, 13 February 2002, p. 6 and Tables 1–3. Nor should one forget the stockpile of disassembled components. Norris calculates that there are yet more weapons: about 5000 plutonium 'pits' and the same number of canned sub-assemblies (thermonuclear secondaries) in storage at Pantex and at Oak Ridge as a 'strategic reserve'. Another 7000 'pits' extracted from weapons dismantled during the Bush Snr and Clinton administrations and declared as excess, are kept at Pantex.

25 Crouch briefing, pp. 7, 12; *NRDC Report*, pp. 4–5; M.R. Gordon, 'US nuclear plan sees new weapons and new targets', *New York Times*,

10 March 2002; W. Pincus, 'Nuclear plans go beyond cuts', *Washington Post*, 16 February 2002.
26 Perkovich, pp. 448, 463.
27 M. Quinlan, *Thinking about Nuclear Weapons*, Whitehall Paper No. 41, Royal United Services Institute, London, 1997; compare J. Schell, 'The folly of arms control', *Foreign Affairs*, September/October 2000, 79(5), 22–46.

Conclusions

1 W. Safire, 'Kangaroo Courts', *The New York Times*, Section A, November 26, 2001, p. 17; A. Lewis, 'Wake Up, America', *The New York Times*, Section A, November 30, 2001, p. 27; A. Neier, 'The Military Tribunals on Trial', *New York Review of Books*, XLIX, 2, 11–15.
2 On this scale, of twentieth-century armies the lowest degrees of mental breakdown in and after combat were experienced by Allied soldiers in the Second World War and by the Israeli armed forces from 1948 to 1982 (but not thereafter). The highest degree of mental breakdown in combat and afterwards occurred in the American armed forces in Vietnam. There, by the time of the American withdrawal, incidences of 'fragging' – men throwing grenades at their officers from behind in order to kill them and thus not to have to follow orders – of pervasive drug-taking and the virtual breakdown of internal discipline were widespread. See N. Sheehan, *A Bright Shining Lie: John Paul Vann and America in Vietnam*, New York, Random House, 1988.
3 Barrington Moore Jnr, *The Social Origins of Dictatorship and Democracy*, New York, Penguin, 1966.

Index

References to figures are shown in **bold**, and those to tables in *italic*.